Bible Secrets Series
Book 3

END TIME
DECODED

M. M. TAUSON
Author of: *Angels & Men*
and *The Deep Things of God*

END-TIME Decoded

Copyright @2018 by Maximiano Maximo Tuason, Jr.

All rights reserved. Use of the literature contained herein is encouraged. However, to protect the integrity of its contents, this book, whether as a whole or in part, except for brief excerpts in reviews, may not be reproduced in any form without the written permission of the publisher.

ISBN 978-971-95293-2-3

Unless otherwise specified, Scripture quotations are from the Authorized King James Version (KJV) of the Bible.

The Minister of Bayith Ha-Shem
Messianic Ministries, Inc., Publisher
P.O. Box 3272, Makati City, 1200 Philippines
e-mail: bayithashem@yahoo.com

Contents

Preface

1. Are These the Last Days? 1
2. The Beginning of Sorrows 19
3. End-Time Kings and Beasts 43
4. Two Women and Their Daughters 65
5. The Beasts of the Apocalypse 91
6. Adversaries and Antichrists 121
7. The Road to Armageddon 143
8. The Day of the LORD 173
9. The Time of the End 205

   Appendices 237

   Endnotes 277

To the Father,

For my Brethren

Preface

I thought this book would never be printed at all. I was under the impression that the fast unfolding world events would have pre-empted its publication. I was wrong. So, as the days and months and years went by, and with increasing understanding, I started work on this third book of the Bible Secrets Series in August 2015.

From childhood, I have always believed the world would come to an end. I was strongly influenced by my mother, who told me that the *diluvio* or cataclysmic end of the world would take place at the close of the twentieth century. That was back in the early 1950s, but her words had always been in the back of my head ever since.

Expectedly, when one is preoccupied with the end-times, by the very nature of the subject, he or she cannot help speculating about when that day would come, which I did. But, later, as I immersed myself in the Bible and grew more spiritually mature, I realized that my conclusions had been based on insufficient or fallacious premises.

Other end-time watchers have fallen into the same trap of date-setting. Many are sincere people who deeply love God and eagerly await the Second Coming of Christ. Let us look back on a number of the more credible predictions. They were few and far between in past ages, but their number has greatly increased in recent times.

1000 A.D.: Millennium End. Many Church leaders believed that the close of the first millennium of the Christian era would see the Second Coming of Christ and the end of the world. In anticipation of the Messiah's return, believers disposed of their belongings and abandoned their homes. When the 11th century began without any apocalypse, doomsayers said they should have started counting from the Crucifixion, not from the Nativity, and the world would actually end in 1033 A.D. This turned out be another miscalculation.

1524: Piscean planetary alignment. London astrologers caused widespread anxiety when they interpreted the coming alignment of planets in the constellation of Pisces (fish, symbol of early Christians) to mean that the world would perish in a massive flood. Before the dreaded date arrived on February 1, 1524, tens of thousands of people sought refuge on higher ground and some even built arks in imitation of Noah. The repetition of the Flood did not come.

1780: "Dark Day." On May 19, 1780, a heavy gloom fell over New England, prompting a religious group known as the Shakers to announce Judgment Day had come. Though the unusually darkened sky, later called the "Dark Day," was most likely caused by a rare combination of smoke from forest fires and heavy fog, it spurred the religious sect to embark on a mission of spreading their message of celibacy as the path to spiritual salvation.

1843-1844: William Miller. A Baptist farmer-minister in New York, Miller announced in 1831 that the Second Coming would be between March 21, 1843, and March 21, 1844. Many of his followers, called "Millerites," sold their properties, dressed up in white, and climbed mountain peaks to meet the Messiah. When nothing happened on either date, the day was moved to Oct. 22, 1844. When Christ still did not appear (known as the "Great Disappointment"), the Millerites disbanded. Some formed what became the Seventh Day Adventist Church.

1910: Halley's Comet. In 1881, it was discovered that the tails comets leave behind contain a deadly gas called cyanogen. In 1910, the *New York Times* and other newspapers reported that the Earth would pass through the debris left by Halley's Comet on May 19 that year. Fearful people bought "comet pills" and bottled air for survival. However, as scientists had said, the cyanogen gas was too dispersed to cause any harm.

1914: Charles Taze Russell. In 1876, Russell, the founder of Jehovah's Witnesses, predicted that Christ would return in 1914. Although World War I broke out in 1914, the Second Coming did not take place. The society predicted at least seven other dates for the occurrence of the event. To date, however, the world still has not ended, and the group is now best known for distributing religious pamphlets door-to-door and refusing blood transfusions.

1936, 1943, 1972, 1975: Herbert W. Armstrong. Founder of the Worldwide Church of God, Armstrong, told members of his church that the "Rapture" (the catching up of the spiritually saved by Christ) would take place in 1936 and that only they would be saved. After his prophecy failed, he changed the date three more times – to 1943, 1972, and 1975 – without any success.

1982: The Jupiter Effect. In 1974, astrophysicists John Gribbin and Stephen Plagemann warned in their best-selling book, *The Jupiter*

Effect, of the coming planetary alignment on March 10, 1982 – seven of the planets, including giant Jupiter, would align on the same side of the sun, creating gravitational effects that would lead to catastrophic earthquakes. After the alignment caused nothing, their book was followed by a sequel, *The Jupiter Effect Reconsidered*.

1982: Pat Robertson. The televangelist proclaimed in a 1980 TV broadcast: "I guarantee you, by the end of 1982 there is going to be a judgment on the world." He expected the "Rapture" of the righteous just before the Gog-Magog (Russian) invasion of Israel which would bring on the Great Tribulation. None of the predicted events came to pass, and he ran for U.S. president six years later.

1988: Edgar Whisenant. A former NASA engineer and Bible student, he believed that the "Rapture" would occur on *Rosh Ha-Shana* (Jewish new year) in 1988. His book, *88 Reasons Why the Rapture Will Be in 1988*, sold 4.5 million copies. TBN interrupted its programs for three days on *Rosh Ha-Shana* to cover the predicted event, complete with tips for people who would be left behind. When nothing happened, Whisenant found a flaw in his calculations and issued a new date. He did so every year for several more years.

1992: Bang-Ik Ha. The South Korean boy-prophet predicted the "Rapture" would take place in October 1992 – before the European Economic Community (EEC), believed to be the "revived Roman Empire" and the prophesied "beast" in Revelation, became a reality as the ruler of the world and declared war on the saints. The foretold date elapsed uneventfully.

1994: Harold Camping. President of the Family Radio Network, Camping predicted that Christ would return at the end of the annual eight-day Jewish festival of *Sukkot* (Feast of Tabernacles), which was to begin on September 27, 1994. The prediction was a total failure.

1997: Comet Hale-Bopp. An amateur astronomer claimed to have photographed an alien spaceship following Comet Hale-Bopp. Although the report was rejected by other astronomers, the Coast to Coast A.M. Show with Art Bell promoted the rumor by offering more evidence from an anonymous astrophysicist. Members of the cult Heaven's Gate took it as a sign that the earth was doomed to end in "apocalyptic flames" and committed group suicide when the comet was closest to earth in order to hitch a ride on the spaceship.

1999: Nostradamus. The seer wrote in *Centuries*, quatrain X.72: "In the year 1999, and seven months, from the sky will come the great King of Terror. He will bring back to life the great king '*Angolmois*'. Before and after Mars reigns happily." It was interpreted as: "In September 1999,

Christ will return from heaven to resurrect the dead (including kings) in the midst of Armageddon." Moreover, in June 27, 1558, Nostradamus wrote to King Henry of France about "a solar eclipse more obscure and gloomy than any ever seen" and "a great removal that we would think the gravity of the earth had lost its natural movement, plunged into the abyss of perpetual gloom, in the month of October 1999." No such things happened.

2000: Y2K. In the early 1970s, some experts saw that computers might read dates in the year 2000 as 1900 dates, because the first programs used only the last two digits for years (e.g., 70 for 1970). The brewing problem was called the Millennium Bug or "Y2K Bug." Many predicted serious problems, such as power grid failure or even accidental nuclear war. In the late 1990s, sales of guns and ammo, survival food and bottled water, batteries, gold and silver, soared. Pastors suggested that Y2K could be the precursor of the Second Coming and Armageddon. January 1, 2000, came with only minor disruptions. People argued if it was because billions were spent worldwide to fix the problem or if the problem was overestimated.

2000: *"Menorah"* Planetary Alignment. Astronomers charted a cosmic alignment of the sun, moon and five planets on May 5, 2000. It was dubbed *"Menorah* Alignment", as the Jewish Temple *menorah* (lamp stand) had seven lights. A book by Richard Noone ("5/5/2000 Ice: the Ultimate Disaster") predicted the Antarctic ice mass would be three miles thick by then and the weight would cause the poles to shift to the equator. Previous pole shifts were said to have brought about ice ages. The predicted disaster did not take place.

2000: Bible Code. In his book *Bible Code* (1995), Michael Drosnin showed how secret words and messages can be found in the Bible using the Equidistant Letter Sequencing (ELS) technique (taking letters from the Hebrew text at regular intervals). He found two Jewish years linked to the phrases "world war" and "atomic holocaust" – 5760 and 5766. In the Western calendar, they stood for the years 2000 and 2006. World War III did not break out in 2000.

2000: J.R. Church. In his book *Hidden Prophecies in the Psalms* (1986), J.R. Church wrote that Psalms 1-100 were year-by-year prophecies for the 20th century. He cited Rabbi Hirsch, who said that Psalm 100 (denoting year 2000)) was the "finale to the previous psalms concerning the approach of the Messianic Era." Indeed, Psalm 100 sounded like the "Rapture" – "Serve the LORD with gladness: come before his presence with singing... Enter into his gates with thanksgiving, and into his courts with praise: be thankful unto him, and bless his name." No "Rapture" took place in 2000.

2000: Great Pyramid. Two books, *The Great Pyramid Decoded* (Peter Lemesurier) and *Great Pyramid Passages* (John and Morton Edgar), revealed studies that the configurations and dimensions of the passages in the Great Pyramid of Egypt were prophetic – with every inch corresponding to a year. The Ascending Passage, which ended in the King's Chamber, suggested "Rapture" in 2000; while the Descending Passage, which terminated in an underground "Pit of Destruction," pointed to the end of the world, also in 2000. Needless to say, the world did not end in the year 2000.

2003: Planet X. Nancy Lieder of "Zetatalk" claimed to have been channeling aliens who told her that Planet X would pass by the Earth on May 15, 2003, bringing about great disasters. Happily, the date went by just like any ordinary day. Other dates for the encounter had been set by the Planet X Community since then, such as 2012.

2006: Bible Code. The other Hebrew year Bible Code author Michael Drosnin found associated with "world war" and "atomic holocaust" was 5766 (2006). As we now know, there should have been no cause for alarm. Like the Jewish Bible Code experts had said, the ELS technique cannot be used to predict the future.

2008: Ron Weinland. The pastor of the Church of God-PKG, self-proclaimed prophet and one of the Two Witnesses of God, announced in his book *2008: God's Final Witness* that "by the fall of 2008, the United States will have collapsed as a world power." As we can see, it looks like the U.S. is still a world power to this day.

2011: Harold Camping. In a far-reaching media campaign, the 90-year-old preacher predicted "Judgment Day" and the "Rapture" on May 21, 2011, marked by a series of "rolling earthquakes." When that forecast failed, he next pointed to October 21, 2011, as the day for the "destruction of the world." That date, however, also went by with nary a ripple, and Camping finally decided to stop making predictions and resigned from his post.

2012: Mayan Calendar. The ancient Mayas of Central America invented the zero, though their math used only three symbols – a dot for 1, a bar for 5, and a shell shape for 0. They could calculate the planetary movements and eclipses with accuracy unmatched until the 20th century. Their calendar started on Aug. 11, 3114 B.C., and had for its end Dec. 21, 2012 A.D., leading to speculations that the world would end in 2012. Many books were written and disaster movies filmed around the Mayan calendar and the end of the world in 2012. The furor ended when the world remained undisturbed that year.

2013: Comet ISON. The comet was spotted in September 2012 by the Russia-based International Scientific Optical Network (ISON). The *Daily Mail* described it as "the Comet of the Century" – about "15 times brighter than the Moon." Some people warned it could be a sign of the Second Coming (ISON: "I, Son"). By January 2013, the comet was ejecting over 112,000 lbs. of dust per minute. There were fears the Earth would pass through the dust cloud left behind. However, ISON broke up on November 28, 2013, as it grazed the Sun. The fears were unfounded.

2017: Jubilee Year. Some prophecy watchmen said 2017 was a Jubilee Year – "year of release" observed every 50 years (the original dates have been lost). It might also be the Grand Jubilee: the 70th and last Jubilee after the cycle began 3,500 years ago about 1500 B.C. in Canaan, the Promised Land. The idea stemmed from the fact that in 1917 Jerusalem was liberated from the Ottoman Empire and in 1967 the West Bank was regained from Jordan. So 2017, another 50 years later, could see the final return of Temple Mount to Israel (together with the appearance of the Messiah).

And now...

Does this book have anything better to offer? In what way do the prophetic expositions in this work differ? In all modesty, as will soon become apparent to the reader, this book has the advantage of comprehensiveness. While the failed end-of-the-world predictions in the past had little or no Biblical bases, the end-time chronology and events presented in this study have been deciphered mostly with interpretations found in the Bible. Yes, the Bible interprets itself!

This writer believes that the Bible, made up of the Old and New Testaments, is complete. Everything and anything we need to know, the Author has placed in the Holy Scriptures. The Bible has all the answers to our questions! All we have to do is prayerfully look.

I hope this book will help you make best use of the precious time remaining to prepare yourself and your loved ones for the soon return of our Lord and Savior. Maranatha!

M.M. Tauson

1

Are These the Last Days?

This know also, that in the last days perilous times shall come.

- 2 Timothy 3:1

Are we truly living in the "last days" prophesied in the Holy Scriptures? In view of the many Biblical prophecies that have already been fulfilled in the past, as well as those yet unfolding in our time, end-time prophecy watchmen and eschatologists aver that we have truly reached the "time of the end."

Old Testament prophets through whom God spoke seemed to know since earliest times that the world would come to an end. For one, Isaiah, who lived around 2,800 years ago, declared, with God speaking through him, that the end of the world had been determined from its very beginning. *"Remember the former things of old: for I am God, and there is none else; I am God, and there is none like me, Declaring the end from the beginning, and from ancient times the things that are not yet done, saying, My counsel shall stand, and I will do all my pleasure"* (Isa 46:9-10).

Modern-day scientists, such as cosmologists and astrophysicists, corroborate a coming end. They postulate that, based on the second law or principle of thermodynamics (entropy), all systems proceed from an orderly state to one of disorder. In short, all things break down and deteriorate. Thus, if the universe had a beginning (generally thought as "The Big Bang"), then it will inevitably come to an end.

Prophecies of the end

Around two hundred years after Isaiah, the angel Gabriel cryptically told the prophet Daniel about the "time of the end": *"And some of them of understanding shall fall, to try them, and to purge, and to make them white, even to the time of the end: because it is yet for a time appointed"* (Dan 11:35).

The time of the end is also referred to as the "end of the days" as we can see in Gabriel's words, *"And he said, Go thy way, Daniel: for the words are closed up and sealed till the time of the end... But go thou thy way till the end be: for thou shalt rest, and stand in thy lot at the end of the days"* (Dan 12:9,13).

Isaiah foretold a Savior who will come at the end of the world. *"Behold, the LORD hath proclaimed unto the end of the world, Say ye to the daughter of Zion, Behold, thy salvation cometh; behold, his reward is with him, and his work before him"* (Isa 62:11).

Christ's teachings

When Christ first came around 2,000 years ago, He gave His disciples inklings as to when the end will come. *"And this gospel of the kingdom shall be preached in all the world for a witness unto all nations; and then shall the end come"* (Matt 24:14). He told them in His parables about some events that will take place at the end of days. *"The field is the world; the good seed are the children of the kingdom; but the tares are the children of the wicked one; The enemy that sowed them is the devil; the harvest is the end of the world; and the reapers are the angels. As therefore the tares are gathered and burned in the fire; so shall it be in the end of this world... the angels shall come forth, and sever the wicked from among the just..."* (Matt 13:38-40,49b).

However, Christ also hinted that the end was still some way off. *"And ye shall be hated of all men for my name's sake: but he that endureth to the end shall be saved"* (Matt 10:22). Nevertheless, He consoled His followers by saying He would keep them company until the end came. *"Teaching them to observe all things whatsoever I have commanded you: and, lo, I am with you alway, even unto the end of the world"* (Matt 28:20).

Incidentally, the word used for "world" in the original Greek text was *aionos*, from the noun *aion*, which properly means "an age" (in the Jewish sense, a Messianic period), as well as by implication "the world". The second meaning was chosen by the KJV translators and may actually be the best English translation.

Christ comforted His disciples with the promise that He would physically return to take them to the Almighty Father's kingdom. *"In my Father's house are many mansions: if it were not so, I would have told* you. I go to prepare a place for you. And if I go and prepare a place for you, I will come again, and receive you unto myself; that where I am, there ye may be also" (John 14:2-3).

Angels confirmed His promise to return as He ascended to heaven forty days after His resurrection from the dead. *"And when he had spoken these things, while they beheld, he was taken up; and a cloud received him out of their sight. And while they looked stedfastly toward heaven as he went up, behold, two men stood by them in white apparel; Which also said, Ye men of Galilee, why stand ye gazing up into heaven? this same Jesus, which is taken up from you into heaven, shall so come in like manner as ye have seen him go into heaven"* (Acts 1:9-11).

Apostolic preachings

The apostles and other disciples faithfully passed on to new believers Christ's teachings about the end of the world after His ascension to heaven. They preached that the end was coming soon. Peter said in 4:7 of his first epistle – *"But the end of all things is at hand: be ye therefore sober, and watch unto prayer."*

Converts to Christianity during apostolic times believed the period they were living in were "the last days." Paul wrote: *"God, who at sundry times and in divers manners spake in time past unto the fathers by the prophets, Hath in these last days spoken unto us by his Son, whom he hath appointed heir of all things, by whom also he made the worlds"* (Heb 1:1-2).

Others used the term "last time." John, the beloved apostle, remarked: *"Little children, it is the last time: and as ye have heard that antichrist shall come, even now are there many antichrists; whereby we know that it is the last time"* (1 John 2:18).

End-time mockers

The apostle Paul, who wrote about half of the books of the New Testament, described the signs of the end-times in his epistles. *"This know also, that in the last days perilous times shall come. For men shall be lovers of their own selves, covetous, boasters, proud, blasphemers, disobedient to parents, unthankful, unholy, Without natural affection, trucebreakers, false accusers, incontinent, fierce, despisers of those that are good, Traitors, heady, highminded, lovers of pleasures more than lovers of God; Having a form of godliness, but denying the power thereof: from such turn away"* (2 Tim 3:1-5). The passage accurately describes our modern times!

If these are truly the last days, then the world will not probably end the way scientists predict – that the earth will be scorched to a cinder when the dying sun flares up into a supernova billions of years from now.

Still, many people today find it hard to believe that the world will really come to a divinely ordained end, because nearly 2,000 years after Christ, the world remains the same! This has led skeptics and unbelievers to question the very existence of God. The apostles, though, knew this well in advance and had warned of unbelievers in the last days. Peter said: *"Knowing this first, that there shall come in the last days scoffers, walking after their own lusts, And saying, Where is the promise of his coming? for since the fathers fell asleep, all things continue as they were from the beginning of the creation"* (2 Peter 3:3-4).

End delayed

There are two usually overlooked reasons why Christ has not yet returned. The first is God's great love for men, whom He has created in His image (specially the elect, His chosen ones). Peter explained, *"The Lord is not slack concerning his promise, as some men count slackness; but is longsuffering to us-ward, not willing that any should perish, but that all should come to repentance"* (2 Peter 3:9).

The second is a principle in prophecy that is little known to many, even Bible-believing Christians. Peter said, *"But, beloved, be not ignorant of this one thing, that one day is with the Lord as a thousand years, and a thousand years as one day"* (2 Peter 3:8). Moses earlier expressed the idea in a psalm some 3,500 years ago. *"For a thousand years in thy sight are but as yesterday when it is past, and as a watch in the night"* (Ps 90:4).

So! In the eyes of the Creator, a thousand years is just one day. Hence, from that divine viewpoint, since the time of the Messiah's first advent, the two thousand years that have elapsed are just two days! Based on this reckoning, we are truly in the last days.

Now, you are probably wondering – if only two "days" have passed since Christ and the apostolic times, how many more "days" of a thousand years each might still be left before the end finally comes?

Scheduled by God

The end of the world appears to have been pre-scheduled by the Creator. The angel Gabriel told Daniel: *"And he said, Behold, I will make thee know what shall be in the last end of the indignation: for at the time appointed the end shall be"* (Dan 8:19). The angel said *"at the time appointed"*, meaning a predetermined point of time in the future.

For those who believe in Bible prophecy, and even those who are just plain curious, the next questions are quite predictable. Can we know when? Will the end come within our lifetime? Or, as many others will quickly say to dismiss the subject, is it a divine secret that the Creator keeps only to Himself?

It does not seem so. A number of prophecies concerning the nation of Israel and the Messiah, several of which contain timeframes, have already been fulfilled. If that is the case, there is strong reason to believe that prophecies containing clues to God's timetable about the advent and return of the Messiah, as well as the end of the world, are in the Bible. Some prophecy analysts today reckon that the Bible consists of about 75% prophecy (up from 25%-33% and 50%-66% estimates in past decades).

That brings to mind another question. If the prophecies have been in the Bible all along, why are they being brought to light only now – after over 4,000 years? (The first book about Job was written about 2100 B.C. and the last by John around 95 A.D.)

Concealed by God

We get a puzzling answer to the foregoing question in Isaiah 29:10-11,14 – *"For the LORD hath poured out upon you the spirit of deep sleep, and hath closed your eyes: the prophets and your rulers, the seers hath he covered. And the vision of all is become unto you as the words of a book that is sealed, which men deliver to one that is learned, saying, Read this, I pray thee: and he saith, I cannot; for it is sealed... Therefore, behold, I will proceed to do a marvellous work among this people, even a marvellous work and a wonder: for the wisdom of their wise men shall perish, and the understanding of their prudent men shall be hid."*

It looks like the Creator concealed those prophecies by blurring the minds of prophets and sages. But... why? Gabriel explained to Daniel: *"But thou, O Daniel, shut up the words, and seal the book, even to the time of the end... And he said, Go thy way, Daniel: for the words are closed up and sealed till the time of the end"* (Dan 12:4,9). So, it becomes crystal clear why – it was not yet time. The prophecies are for the time of the end. They are meant to be opened and known again only at the time of the end.

And, finally, it appears that the time has come. Most people will consider it bad news. But, for those eagerly awaiting the Second Coming of the Messiah, it is music to the ears – much like the sound of choirs of angels singing hymns in the heavenly realms.

God reveals secrets

According to Christ, all secrets will be revealed. *"Fear them not therefore: for there is nothing covered, that shall not be revealed; and hid, that shall not be known"* (Matt 10:26). Moreover, *"It is the glory of God to conceal a thing: but the honour of kings is to search out a matter"* (Prov 25:2). It follows, therefore, that the Creator is not offended when mere men attempt to discover His secrets. On the contrary, He considers it a kingly endeavor.

In fact, the Almighty Father reveals His secrets in order for men to do His will. *"The secret things belong unto the LORD our God: but those things which are revealed belong unto us and to our children for ever, that we may do all the words of this law"* (Deut 29:29).

Furthermore, before God does anything, He tells the prophets so that they, in turn, can warn the people and give them the chance to prepare. *"Surely the Lord GOD will do nothing, but he revealeth his secret unto his servants the prophets"* (Amos 3:7). Below are some of the best known instances when God revealed His plans to the people through His prophets and messengers:

God warned Noah about the flood that would destroy the earth 120 years before it happened (Gen 6:3-18). He told Abraham and his nephew, Lot, about the impending destruction of Sodom and Gomorrah (Gen 18:16-19:28). Through Moses, God instructed the Israelites on how to protect their families with the blood of the Passover lamb before He caused the death of all the firstborn in Egypt (Gen 11:4-7, 12:3-13). God sent Jonah to warn the people of Nineveh that their city would be destroyed in 40 days if they did not change their ways (Jon 3:4-5). Gabriel foretold the destruction of Jerusalem and the Holy Temple (Dan 9:26). Christ told His followers to flee from Judea when they see Jerusalem surrounded by enemies (Luke 21:20-21).

The revealer of secrets

During Old Testament times, the Creator conveyed His messages to His people personally or through the angels and the prophets. Then, it was through Christ during His Son's earthly ministry. Afterward, it is now the Holy Spirit Who is actively communicating with believers. *"Unto whom it was revealed, that not unto themselves, but unto us they did minister the things, which are now reported unto you by them that have preached the gospel unto you with the Holy Ghost sent down from heaven; which things the angels desire to look into"* (1 Pet 1:12). According to Peter, the Holy Spirit reveals secrets directly to believers, thus bypassing the angels who are very anxious to know what those secrets are!

Peter also clarified that the prophecies from the Holy Spirit could not have been made up by any mortal on his own. *"Above all, you must understand that no prophecy of Scripture came about by the prophet's own interpretation. For prophecy never had its origin in the will of man, but men spoke from God as they were carried along by the Holy Spirit"* (2 Peter 1:20-21, NIV).

Besides, only the Holy Spirit, through Whom we received the prophecies in the first place, can correctly interpret them for us. *"But we speak the wisdom of God in a mystery, even the hidden wisdom, which God ordained before the world unto our glory... But God hath revealed them unto us by his Spirit: for the Spirit searcheth all things, yea, the deep things of God"* (1 Cor 2:7,10).

The Holy Spirit has been revealing and will continue to reveal the secrets of the coming end-time events to us. *"I have yet many things to say unto you, but ye cannot bear them now. Howbeit when he, the Spirit of truth, is come, he will guide you into all truth: for he shall not speak of himself; but whatsoever he shall hear, that shall he speak: and he will shew you things to come"* (John 16:12-13).

It seems that the disciples were not yet emotionally prepared for the nerve-wracking scenarios of the Second Coming and the end of the world, so much so that Christ did not share these with them at that time. The Holy Spirit will reveal those secrets to faithful believers at the opportune times.

Signs of the end

A prophecy the angel Gabriel gave Daniel provides us with some solid leads concerning the time of the end. *"But thou, O Daniel, shut up the words, and seal the book, even to the time of the end: many shall run to and fro, and knowledge shall be increased... And he said, Go thy way, Daniel: for the words are closed up and sealed till the time of the end"* (Dan 12:4,9).

The heavenly messenger mentioned two signs that would let us know with some degree of certainty when we shall have reached the time of the end: First, *"many shall run to and fro"* and, second, *"knowledge shall be increased."*

Truly, people today *"run to and fro"*, using various conveyances man has invented: bicycles, motorcycles, cars, buses, trains, ships, airplanes, even space shuttles for tourists are in the works.

And, indeed, knowledge has increased. From the dawn of history through the Dark and Middle Ages, technological advances were far and few between – until the last 200 years or so, when the world began to witness an unprecedented explosion of knowledge, with astounding advances in literally all fields of human activity.

In the mid-20th century, some scholars said that knowledge was doubling every fifty years. About twenty-five years later, they said knowledge doubled every twenty years. In the 1990s, they changed the estimate to every five years. And, in the early years of the twenty-first century, no scholar would any longer venture a guesstimate. Various devices, gadgets, and equipment become obsolescent just a few months after their introduction in the market.

Let us verify this against what archeology, history, and recent events show. For lack of space, below are only some of the most notable discoveries, inventions, and other achievements of mankind from the time Adam was created (4004 B.C.):

4000-1 B.C. (4,000 years)*

Wheel, c. 3800 B.C.
Plow, before 3000 B.C.
Loom, c. 2500 B.C.
Iron Age, from c. 1500 B.C.
Magnetic compass, c. 300 B.C.
Crossbow, c. 300 B.C.
Archimedian screw, 200s B.C

Writing, c. 3500 B.C.
Bronze Age, from c. 3000 B.C.
Glass, c. 2200 B.C.
Gunpowder, c. 700 B.C.
Geometry, c. 300 B.C.
Steel, c. 300 B.C.
Roller bearing, c. 100 B.C.

*(About one major discovery/achievement every 285 years.)

A.D. 1-1500 (1,500 years)*

Paper, c. 100
Windmill, c. 600
Printing, c. 700
Cannon, 1350
Movable type printing, c. 1445

Spinning wheel, Middle Ages
Zero, c. 600
Glass lens, 13th century
Mechanical clock, 14th century
Rifle, 1475

*(About one major discovery/achievement every 150 years.)

1501-1750 (250 years)*

Human anatomy, 1543
Compound microscope, 1590
Telescope, 1608
Steam engine, 1639
Clock pendulum, 1656
Spectrum, 1665
Microorganisms, 1675
Light wave theory, 1678
Calculus, 1684
Laws of motion, 1687

Heliocentric model, 1543
Magnetic field, 1600
Calculating machine, 1614
Barometer, 1643
Saturn's rings, 1659
Cell, 1665
Speed of light, 1675
Spermatozoa, 1683
Gravitation, 1687
Halley's Comet, 1705

*(About one major discovery/achievement every 12½ years.)

1751-1900 (150 years)*

Electricity, 1751
Spinning jenny, 1764
Photosynthesis, 1779
Hot air balloon, 1783
Steamship, 1783
Cotton gin, 1793
Vaccination, 1796
Electric light, 1801
Match, 1816
Bicycle, 1817
Stethoscope, 1819
Portland cement, 1824
Braille, 1829
Reaper, 1834
Revolver, 1835
Telegraph, 1837
Rubber vulcanization, 1839
Doppler effect, 1842
Conservation of energy, 1843
Nitroglycerin, 1846
Safety pin, 1849
Refrigeration, 1850
Foucault pendulum, 1851
Gyroscope, 1852
Bessemer steel, 1855
Continental drift theory, 1858
Int. combustion engine, 1860
Germ theory, 1861
Genetics, 1865
Heredity, 1866
Typewriter, 1867
Periodic table, 1869
Telephone, 1876
Incandescent light, 1879
Electric appliances, 1882
Fountain pen, 1884
Transformer, 1885
Radio, 1886
Electrocardiography, 1887

Concrete, 1759
Oxygen, 1773
Uranus, 1781
Parachute, 1783
Metric system, 1790
Food canning, 1795
Gas lighting, 1798
Steam locomotive, 1804
Photography, 1816
Iron ship, 1818
Electromagnetism, 1820
Microphone, 1827
Dynamo, 1832
Gas refrigeration, 1834
Screw propeller, 1836
Ozone, 1839
Anaesthesia, 1842
Thermodynamics, 1842
Neptune, 1846
Sewing machine, 1846
Bullet, 1849
Cylinder lock, 1851
Airship, 1852
Hypodermic syringe, 1853
Plastics, 1855
Oil well, 1859
Solar energy, 1860s
Machinegun, 1862
Aluminium manufacture, 1866
Dynamite, 1867
Antiseptic, 1867
Electric motor, 1873
Phonograph, 1877
Seismograph, 1880
Manmade fibers, 1883
Motorcycle, 1884
Automobile, 1885
Antibiotics, 1887
Zipper, 1891

10 | END TIME DECODED

Motion pictures, 1893
Radioactivity, 1895
Radium, polonium; 1898
Aspirin, 1899

X-ray, 1895
Electron, 1897
Tape recorder, 1899
Quantum theory, 1900

*(About one major discovery/achievement every 1½ years.)

1901-present (~120 years)*

Safety razor, 1901
Airplane, 1903
Psychoanalysis, 1904
Special relativity theory, 1905
Helicopter, 1907
Battle tank, 1910
Superconductivity, 1911
Isotopes, 1912
Roentgen ray diffraction, 1912
Refrigerator, 1914
Black holes, 1915
Radio broadcast, 1920
Galaxies, 1924
Liquid fuel rocket, 1926
Penicillin, 1928
Expanding universe, 1929
Electron microscope, 1931
Positron, 1932
Fluorescent light, 1935
Mammal parthenogenesis, 1936
Nuclear fission, 1938
Plutonium synthesis, 1941
DNA, 1943
Teflon, 1943
Atomic bomb, 1945
Holograph, 1947
Polaroid Land camera, 1947
Oral contraceptive, 1951
Cloning, 1952
Amino acid creation, 1953
Fiber optics, 1955
Artificial heart, 1957

Air conditioning, 1902
Radar, 1904
Intelligence testing, 1905
$E = mc^2$, 1907
Sulfa drugs, 1908
Atomic nucleus, 1911
Vitamins, 1912
Plate tectonics, 1912
Assembly line, 1913
General relativity theory, 1915
Proton, 1919
Television, 1923
Quantum mechanics, 1925
Big Bang theory, 1927
Scotch tape, 1929
Deuterium/heavy water, 1931
Cyclotron/atom smasher, 1931
Neutron, 1932
Richter scale, 1935
Jet propulsion, 1936
Xerography, 1938
Nuclear reactor, 1942
Aqualung/Scuba, 1943
Electronic computer, 1945
Transistor, 1947
Microwave oven, 1947
Radiocarbon dating, 1950
Polio vaccine, 1952
Integrated circuit, 1952
DNA structure, 1953
Superconductivity, 1957
Earth satellite, 1957

Laser, 1958
First man in space, 1961
Quarks, 1964
Pulsars, 1967
Internet, late 1960s
Bar code, 1970
Compact disc, 1972
Electronic mail, 1972
Genetic engineering, 1970s
MRI human scanning, 1977
Scanning tunnelling electron microscope, 1981
Magnetic propulsion, 1992
3D bioprinting, late 1990s
"God particle"/Higgs boson, 2012

Computer chip, 1958
Quasars, 1963
Heart transplant, 1967
First man on the moon, 1969
Liquid crystal display, 1970
Microprocessor, 1971
CAT scanner, 1972
Video disc, 1972
String theory, 1976
Test-tube baby, 1978
3D printing, early 1980s
World Wide Web, 1989
Dark energy, 1998
Stem cell, 2006
Traces of water on Mars, 2015

*(About one major discovery/achievement every year.)

The Doomsday Clock

In modern times, a recently devised geopolitical prognosticator of the end of the world is the alarming "Doomsday Clock". Let us examine what it is and how it came about.

The Doomsday Clock is a symbolic clock face representing a countdown to possible global catastrophe. It was conceived by an international group of researchers called the Chicago Atomic Scientists, who took part in the Manhattan Project that developed the atomic bomb. After the bombing of Hiroshima and Nagasaki, they began to publish a newsletter and, later, a bulletin.

Since 1947, the Clock's setting has been decided by the Science and Security Board of the *Bulletin of the Atomic Scientists,* advised by the Governing Board and the Board of Sponsors, which includes 17 Nobel Laureates. The closer they set the Clock to midnight, the closer the scientists believe the world is to global disaster.

Nearing midnight. The nearest the Clock came to midnight was in 1953, just eight years after the end of World War II, when it was moved to 2 minutes from the apocalyptic midnight (11:58 p.m.), following hydrogen bomb tests by the U.S. and Russia within nine months of each other.

The Clock is not reset in real time as events occur. Rather than respond to each and every crisis as it happens, the Science and Security Board meets only two times a year to discuss global events. In the closest nuclear war threat, that of the Cuban Missile Crisis in 1962, the problem reached crisis stage, climax, and resolution before the Clock could be reset.

The Doomsday Clock, which hangs on a wall in the *Bulletin's* office at the University of Chicago, originally represented an analogy for the threat of global nuclear war only. However, since 2007, it has also reflected climate change and new developments in the life sciences and technologies that could inflict irrevocable harm to humanity.

In early 2015, the scientists moved the hands of the Doomsday Clock from 5-minutes-to-midnight (11:55 p.m.) to 3-minutes-to-midnight (11:57 p.m.), noting the growing threat of climate change, the modernization of nuclear weapons in the United States and Russia, as well as the problem of nuclear waste.

In the latest Clock setting (January 2018), the *Bulletin of the Atomic Scientists* pushed the hands forward to 2 minutes before midnight (11:58 p.m.) in the wake of recent strident worldwide nationalism, cyber threats, an upswing in terrorist attacks, and US President Trump's comments that global warming was a hoax and that he would like to expand America's nuclear capability.

Blood moon tetrads

The heavenly bodies did not just appear in the skies through random astrophysical processes. According to Scriptures, they have been deliberately set in place for certain reasons. *"And God said, Let there be lights in the firmament of the heaven to divide the day from the night; and let them be for signs..."* (Gen 1:14a).

Through the celestial lights, the Creator conveys visual messages to men on earth. *"And there shall be signs in the sun, and in the moon, and in the stars..."* (Luke 21:25a). As might be expected, some of the most important messages are about the end-times. *"The sun shall be turned into darkness, and the moon into blood, before the great and the terrible day of the LORD come"* (Joel 2:31).

Blood moons.

Several of the most significant heavenly signs of the end-times come in the form of "blood moons." Just what is a "blood moon"?

A full lunar eclipse that occurs at the same time as a Biblical holiday is called a "blood moon." The term does not mean that the moon actually turns blood-red in color, although lunar eclipses often get a reddish tint. The *World Book* explains: "In many cases, it becomes reddish. The earth's atmosphere bends part of the sun's light around the earth and toward the moon. This light is red because the atmosphere scatters the other colors present in sunlight in greater amounts than it does red."[1] In other words, according to the *Encarta Encyclopedia*, a lunar eclipse is frequently, but not always, "faintly illuminated with a red light refracted by the earth's atmosphere, which filters out the blue rays."[2] Moreover, the intensity of the reddish color, when present, varies depending on the amount of dust in the atmosphere.

Lunar eclipses occur infrequently and irregularly. "In most calendar years there are two lunar eclipses; in some years one or three or none occur."[3] Hence, a "blood moon" or full lunar eclipse that coincides with a Biblical holiday is very rare.

Eight blood moon tetrads.

Through the centuries, prophecy watchmen have observed something even rarer: four blood moons in two successive years. They call these extraordinary sets "blood moon tetrads."

A blood moon tetrad is extremely rare. Only eight such tetrads have occurred since the time of Christ. These can be verified through modern astronomical computer programs. Let us review the eight blood moon tetrads and the events associated with them.

1st Blood Moon Tetrad (A.D. 162-163).

1st blood moon: Passover (April 17, 162)
2nd blood moon: Feast of Tabernacles (October 11, 162)
3rd blood moon: Passover (April 6, 163)
4th blood moon: Feast of Tabernacles (September 30, 163)
Significant events:
- Marcus Aurelius became Roman Emperor in 161 A.D. (1 year before tetrad) and intensified the persecution of Christians and Jews, who were martyred at the Colosseum in Rome until the succeeding years of the 2nd century.
- In 165-180 A.D. the Antonine Plague killed 8 million people, one-third of the empire's population (2 years after tetrad).

2nd Blood Moon Tetrad (795-796).

1st blood moon: Passover (April 9, 795)
2nd blood moon: Day of Atonement (October 3, 795)
3rd blood moon: Passover (March 28, 796)
4th blood moon: Day of Atonement (September 21, 796)
Significant events:
- In 796, Charlemagne, king of the Franks, crushed the Avars, eastern European Muslims menacing the Byzantine Empire.
- Earlier, he established a buffer zone between France and Spain, ending centuries of Arab incursions into Western Europe.
- In 809, a famine ravaged the Frankish empire (13 years after tetrad).

3rd Blood Moon Tetrad (842-843).
1st blood moon: Passover (March 30, 842)
2nd blood moon: Day of Atonement (September 23, 842)
3rd blood moon: Passover (March 19, 843)
4th blood moon: Day of Atonement (September 12, 843)
Significant event:
- In 846, Muslim raiders from North Africa attacked and looted the Vatican (3 years after tetrad).

4th Blood Moon Tetrad (860-861).
1st blood moon: Passover (April 9, 860)
2nd blood moon: Day of Atonement (October 3, 860)
3rd blood moon: Passover (March 30, 861)
4th blood moon: Day of Atonement (September 22, 861)
Significant events:
- From 851 to 859, the ruling Moors martyred Christians in Cordoba, southern Spain.
- In 863, the Byzantine Empire defeated Arab armies at the Battle of Lalakaon, Turkey, permanently stopping the Islamic invasion of eastern Europe (2 years after tetrad).

5th Blood Moon Tetrad (1493-1494).
1st blood moon: Passover (April 2, 1493)
2nd blood moon: Feast of Trumpets (September 25, 1493)
3rd blood moon: Passover (March 22, 1494)
4th blood moon: Feast of Trumpets (September 15, 1494)
Significant events:
- On July 30, 1492, King Ferdinand and Queen Isabella ordered all Jews (about 200,000) to leave Spain. Thousands died trying to reach safe havens (1 year before tetrad).
- In 1495, Lithuania expelled the Jews (1 year after tetrad).
- In 1504, a deadly famine struck Spain (10 years after tetrad).

6th Blood Moon Tetrad (1949-1950).
1st blood moon: Passover (April 13, 1949)
2nd blood moon: Feast of Tabernacles (October 7, 1949)
3rd blood moon: Passover (April 2, 1950)
4th blood moon: Feast of Tabernacles (September 26, 1950)
Significant events:
- On May 14, 1948, Israel proclaimed its independence, becoming a nation again after nearly 2,000 years.

- Within 24 hours, Egypt, Jordan, Syria, Lebanon, and Iraq attacked in what became known as Israel's War of Independence. The newly formed, poorly equipped Israel Defense Forces (IDF) repulsed the invaders after some 15 months, with a loss of over 6,000 Israeli lives (nearly 1% of the Jewish population at the time), (1 year before tetrad).

7th Blood Moon Tetrad (1967-1968).
1st blood moon: Passover (April 24, 1967)
2nd blood moon: Feast of Tabernacles (October 18, 1967)
3rd blood moon: Passover (April 13, 1968)
4th blood moon: Feast of Tabernacles (October 6, 1968)
Significant events:
- On June 5, 1967, as its Arab neighbors prepared to attack Israel, the Jewish state launched a pre-emptive strike against Egypt in the south, Jordan in the east, and Syria in the north.
- After the so-called Six-Day War, Judea, Samaria, Gaza, the Sinai Peninsula, and Golan Heights were under Israeli control.
- Jerusalem, which had been divided under Israel and Jordan since 1949, was reunified under Israel's authority.

8th Blood Moon Tetrad (2014-2015).
1st blood moon: Passover (April 15, 2014)
2nd blood moon: Feast of Tabernacles (October 8, 2014)
Total solar eclipse: Biblical New Year (March 20, 2015)
3rd blood moon: Passover (April 4, 2015)
Partial solar eclipse: Feast of Trumpets (September 13, 2015)
4th blood moon: Feast of Tabernacles (September 28, 2015)
Significant events:
- In early 2014, jihadist group ISIS (Islamic State of Iraq and Syria) drove out Iraqi government forces from key cities in western Iraq and seized vast tracts of northern Syria.
- On June 29, 2014, first day of Ramadan, ISIS shortened its name to Islamic State (IS) and declared the establishment of a caliphate, a new global transnational Muslim state.
- The IS claims religious, political and military authority over all Muslims worldwide. In March 2015, it controlled over 10 million people in Iraq and Syria, as well as parts of Libya. Terrorist groups in other countries have announced their affiliation with IS, such as Boko Haram in Nigeria, and the Abu Sayyaf and Maute Groups in southern Philippines.

Two solar eclipses. The 8th Blood Moon Tetrad appears to be specially significant. It coincided with TWO solar eclipses! Lunar eclipses, particularly blood moons, are said to be signs to Israel, while solar eclipses are signs to the world.

Moreover, "eight" (8) is the number of new beginnings (8 people in Noah's Ark repopulated the earth; male Hebrew infants are circumcised on the 8th day; Christ resurrected on the 8th day – first day of the following week; the 8th note begins a new octave; etc.). Is there a new beginning in store for mankind?

Historical milestones?

World-changing events happened shortly before, during, or after each blood moon tetrad. They seem to serve as heavenly markers or milestones in world history, specially in the chronicles of the Jews and Christians. The most notable historical event that took place during the 2014-2015 blood moon tetrad was the establishment of the Islamic State caliphate. Are there still more globally transforming events lying ahead of us? We must bear in mind that some of those historical milestones came as late as 10-13 years after the blood moon tetrads.

Prophecy of the Popes

Another end-time indicator is said to be the "Prophecy of the Popes,"[4] which dates back to the 12th century. In 2013, the resignation of Pope Benedict XVI and subsequent election of Pope Francis (accordingly the last pope) brought about a renewed interest in the "prophecy" in the Christian world.

112 future popes. The story began when Archbishop Malachy O'Morgair (later St. Malachy) went to Rome in 1139 to secure from Pope Innocent II the pallium (episcopal vestment) for his successor as archbishop of Armagh, Ireland. In Rome, Malachy reportedly fell into a trance and had a vision of future popes – 112 in all – who would reign until the end of the world. He listed them down as a sequence of cryptic Latin phrases and showed them to the pope, who had the manuscript deposited in the Vatican's Secret Archives. It was forgotten until rediscovered in 1590, more than 450 years later.

The 112 short mottos in the so-called Prophecy of the Popes purport to predict the line of Roman Catholic popes (along with a few antipopes) beginning with Pope Celestine II in the mid-12th century to Urban VII (pope for 13 days in 1590, after whose reign the prophecies were published), continuing until the supposed 112th and last pope at the time of the end. For brevity, let us initially examine the 1st and 74th mottos.

Celestine II (1143-44). The first motto, *Ex castro Tiberis* ("From a castle on the Tiber"), seemed to have foretold Pope Celestine II, who was born in Citta di Castello along the Tiber River.

Urban VII (1590) had the 74th motto, *De rore cœli* ("From the dew of the sky"); he had been Archbishop of Rossano in Calabria, where a sap called "dew of heaven" was gathered from trees.

Fabricated? Historians noticed a very accurate description of popes up to 1590, but a lack of accuracy thereafter, so they suspect that the first 74 mottos were fabrications written after 1590. Yet, the rest are deemed genuine; mottos 75-112, in contrast to the more literal mottos for earlier popes, use a symbolic language related to the character of each pope and his papacy. The appropriateness of some titles ascribed to popes in the latter prophecies is simply amazing. Here are some of the more striking examples.

Urban VIII (1623-44) was *Lilium et rosa* ("The lily and the rose"); he was a native of Florence, whose coat of arms was a *fleur-de-lis* (lily flower); he also had three bees gathering honey from lilies and roses emblazoned on his escutcheon.

Clement XIII (1758-69) had been prefigured as *Rosa Umbriae* ("Rose of Umbria"); he had been pontifical governor of Rieti at the time it was still part of Umbria.

Pius VI (1775-99) was *Peregrinus apostolicus* ("Pilgrim pope"), confirmed by his papal journey into Germany, his long career as pope, and his expatriation from Rome at the end of his pontificate.

Pius IX (1846-78) fulfilled *Crux de cruce* ("Cross from a cross"), in view of his difficulties and afflictions ("cross") in his relationship with the House of Savoy, whose emblem was a cross.

Leo XIII (1878-1903) corresponded to *Lumen in cælo* ("Light in the sky") when he depicted a comet on his papal coat of arms and became a veritable luminary of the papacy.

Pius X (1903-14), whose reign came under the motto *Ignis ardens* ("Burning fire"), was said to have had a truly burning zeal for the restoration of all things to Christ.

Benedict XV (1914–22). His motto, *Religio depopulate* ("Religion depopulated") was a good match: his papacy spanned World War I and the atheistic Bolshevik Revolution in Russia.

Pius XI (1922–39). *Fides intrepida* ("Intrepid faith") was said to be a suitable epithet – in reference to his faith and actions during the regime of Benito Mussolini, dictator of Italy.

Pius XII (1939–58). *Pastor angelicus* ("Angelic shepherd") was considered appropriate for his role during the Holocaust.

Malachy's prophecies are taken very seriously. It was reported that, in 1958, before the conclave that would elect the successor to Pius XII, Cardinal Spellman of New York hired a boat, filled it with sheep, and sailed up and down the Tiber River, to show that he was *Pastor et nauta* ("Shepherd and sailor"), the motto attributed to the next pope in the prophecies.

John XXIII (1958–63) was instead elected and filled the role described in the motto (*Pastor et nauta*/"Shepherd and sailor"), through his title of Patriarch of Venice, a maritime city.

Paul VI (1963–78), who had a *fleur-de-lis* portrayed in his coat of arms, was said to have precisely corresponded to the motto *Flos florum* ("Flower of flowers").

John Paul I (Aug. 26-Sept. 28, 1978) appeared to have fulfilled *De medietate lunae* ("Of the half moon"); he was born on October 17, 1912, during a half-moon, and was elected Pope on August 26, 1978, the date of a half-moon.

John Paul II (1978-2005) had for his epithet *De labore solis* ("Labor of the sun" or "eclipse"), which was regarded perfect for him; he was born May 18, 1920, during a solar eclipse; and was also entombed on the day of a solar eclipse.

Pope Benedict XVI (2005-2013), the supposed second to the last pope with the 111th motto, *Gloria olivae* ("Glory of the olive"), belongs to the Order of Saint Benedict, whose members are known as the "Olivetans."

Pope Francis (2013-), the supposed last pope, comes under the 112th motto simply as *Petrus Romanus* (Peter the Roman). Advocates of the prophecy find a connection between him and St. Francis of Assisi, whose father was an Italian merchant named Pietro (Peter).

The End. The prophecy adds: "In the final persecution of the Holy Roman Church, there will reign. Peter the Roman will feed his flock amid many tribulations, after which the seven-hilled city will be destroyed and the dreadful Judge will judge the people. The End."

Missing popes? The line "In the final persecution of the Holy Roman Church, there will reign." (*In persecutione extrema S.R.E. sedebit.*) "forms a separate sentence and paragraph of its own. While often read as part of the 'Peter the Roman' prophecy, other interpreters view it as a separate, incomplete sentence explicitly referring to additional popes between 'the glory of the olive' and 'Peter the Roman'."[5] In other words, it leaves open the possibility of unlisted popes coming between the 111th and the supposedly final 112th motto.

2

The Beginning of Sorrows

All these are the beginning of sorrows.

- Matthew 24:8

The disciples asked Christ about the time and sign of His return and of the end of the world. *"And as he sat upon the mount of Olives, the disciples came unto him privately, saying, Tell us, when shall these things be? and what shall be the sign of thy coming, and of the end of the world?"* (Matt 24:3-8). The question was both startling and telling. The disciples were in the dark about the time and circumstances of the Master's Second Coming, but they knew that these would coincide with the "end of the world"!

Signs of the end

His response: *"And Jesus answered and said unto them, Take heed that no man deceive you. For many shall come in my name, saying, I am Christ; and shall deceive many. And ye shall hear of wars and rumours of wars: see that ye be not troubled: for all these things must come to pass, but the end is not yet. For nation shall rise against nation, and kingdom against kingdom: and there shall be famines, and pestilences, and earthquakes, in divers places. All these are the beginning of sorrows"* (Matt 24:3-8).

Christ's response was actually an outline of the prophecies that the apostle John would record in the book of Revelation some sixty-five years later. John survived being boiled in oil and was exiled by Emperor Domitian to the mining island of Patmos in the Aegean Sea, where he received the prophetic visions around 95 A.D. from an angel Christ sent from heaven. The beloved apostle faithfully wrote down everything he saw in the book also known as the "Apocalypse" (from the Greek *apokalyptein*, "to uncover").

Book with seven seals

In his vision, John saw God holding a securely closed book. *"And I saw in the right hand of him that sat on the throne a book written within and on the backside, sealed with seven seals... And no man in heaven, nor in earth, neither under the earth, was able to open the book, neither to look thereon... And I beheld, and, lo, in the midst of the throne and of the four beasts, and in the midst of the elders, stood a Lamb as it had been slain, having seven horns and seven eyes, which are the seven Spirits of God sent forth into all the earth. And he came and took the book out of the right hand of him that sat upon the throne"* (Rev 5:1,3,6-7).

No man in heaven or earth was found worthy to open the book. No less than Christ, the Son of God Himself, would open the book, breaking the seven seals one after another.

Four Horsemen of the Apocalypse

Strangely, a horse appears each time one of the first four seals is broken. The four horses are obviously symbolic. And though some symbolisms are quite obscure, the parallel prophecies that Christ told the disciples, as recorded in the gospel of Matthew, give us a clear idea of what the horses represent.

First seal – white horse.

A white horse appears after the first seal is broken. *"And I saw when the Lamb opened one of the seals, and I heard, as it were the noise of thunder, one of the four beasts saying, Come and see. And I saw, and behold a white horse: and he that sat on him had a bow; and a crown was given unto him: and he went forth conquering, and to conquer"* (Rev 6:1-2).

Some Bible teachers think that the rider on the white horse is Christ and the horse represents the growth and spread of Christianity, because the horseman has a crown, as well as a bow, but no arrows, presumably signifying peacefulness. But, in the parallelism between Matthew 24 and Revelation 6, the white horse and its rider appear to be the symbols of the rise of false Christs and prophets.

"For many shall come in my name, saying, I am Christ; and shall deceive many... And many false prophets shall rise, and shall deceive many... For there shall arise false Christs, and false prophets, and shall

shew great signs and wonders; insomuch that, if it were possible, they shall deceive the very elect" (Matt 24:5,11,24).

False Christs and prophets. Many fake messiahs and seers have arisen since Christ ascended to heaven. From the mid-1st century after the Crucifixion to the end of the 19th century, a period of nearly 1,900 years, some 25 false Christs and prophets became known. But, as we near the time of the end, their number has greatly increased. From the beginning of the 20th century to date, a period of just a little over 100 years, we have seen the rise of many more – no less than 31. Due to space constraint, we will print below only the false Christs and prophets who lived in the 20th– early 21st centuries.[1] (The list for the 1st-19th centuries is in Appendix "A".)

William W. Davies (1833-1906): a Mormon or Latter-Day Saint schismatic leader; claimed his infant son Arthur (born 1868) was the reincarnated Jesus Christ.

Mirza Ghulam Ahmad (1835-1908) of Qadian, India; claimed to be the awaited Mahdi and the likeness of Jesus in character; the only person in Islamic history who claimed to be both.

Cyrus Reed Teed (Cyrus Tweed, 1839-1908): a U.S. physician and alchemist-turned-religious leader and Messiah; claimed divine inspiration in 1869 and, taking the name Koresh, proposed a new set of scientific and religious ideas he called "Koreshanity."

Andre Matsoua (1899-1942): Congolese founder of Amicale; acknowledged by adherents as Messiah in the late 1920s.

Father Divine (George Baker; 1880-1965): African-American spiritual leader; claimed to be God from about 1907 until his death.

Haile Selassie (1892-1975): Emperor of Ethiopia and Messiah of the Rastafari movement; never claimed to be the Messiah, but was proclaimed as such by Leonard Howell and others.

Samael Aun Weor (Víctor Manuel Gomez Rodriguez, 1917-1977): a Colombian (later Mexican citizen) author, lecturer and founder of the Universal Christian Gnostic Movement, which he said was "the most powerful movement ever founded"; predicted in 1972 that his death and resurrection would occur before 1978.

Ahn Sahng-hong (1918-1985): founder of the World Mission Society Church of God; worshiped by members as the Messiah.

David Koresh (Vernon Wayne Howell, 1959-1993): self-proclaimed prophet and leader of the cult Branch Davidians, which figured in a 51-day confrontation with federal authorities near Waco, Texas, ending with the apparent mass suicide of over 80 cult members, including himself.

Menachem Mendel Schneerson (1902-1994): seventh Chabad Rabbi; tried to "prepare the way" for the Messiah; a number of his followers believed he was the Messiah, although he never said this and actually scoffed at such claims made during his lifetime.

Yahweh ben Yahweh (Hulon Mitchell, Jr.; 1935-2007): a black nationalist and separatist who founded the Nation of Yahweh; allegedly orchestrated the murder of dozens of persons.

Nirmala Srivastava (1923-2011): guru and goddess of Sahaja Yoga who proclaimed herself to be the "Comforter" (the incarnation of the Holy Ghost or *Adi Shakti*) promised by Christ while still on earth.

Sun Myung Moon (1920-2012): founder-leader of the Unification Church of Seoul, South Korea; considered himself the Second Coming of Christ, but not Jesus himself. Church members (called "Moonies") generally believed he was the Messiah anointed to fulfill Christ's unfinished mission.

Laszlo Toth (1938-2012): Hungarian-born Australian geologist; claimed he was Jesus Christ as he battered Michelangelo's *Pieta* with a geologist's hammer.

Jose Luis de Jesus Miranda (1946-2013): Puerto Rican founder of *Creciendo en Gracia* (Growing In Grace) International Ministry in Miami, Florida; claimed to be both Christ and the Antichrist; had the number of the name of the beast (666) tattooed on his forearm and referred to himself as *Jesucristo Hombre* ("Jesus Christ, Man").

Wayne Bent (Michael Travesser, b. 1941): member of the Lord Our Righteousness Church (also known as the "Strong City Cult"); convicted in 2008 of one count of criminal sexual contact of a minor and two counts of contributing to the delinquency of a minor.

Riaz Ahmed Gohar Shahi (b. 1941): spiritual leader and founder of the movements Messiah Foundation International (MFI) and *Anjuman Serfaroshan-e-Islam*; declared by the members of the MFI as the Mehdi, Messiah, and Kalki Avatar.

Iesu Matayoshi (b. 1944): established the World Economic Community Party in 1997 on his conviction that he is God and the Christ.

Jung Myung Seok (b. 1945): a member of the Unification Church in the 1970s; broke off in 1980 to found a group now known as Providence Church; considers himself the Second Coming of Christ, but not Jesus himself, and believes he has come to finish the incomplete message and mission of Christ; claims that the Christian doctrine of resurrection is false, but people can be saved through him.

Rael (Claude Vorilhon, b. 1946): "Messenger of the Elohim," a French professional test driver and former automobile journalist; founded the UFO religion Rael Movement in 1972; teaches that life on Earth was created by extraterrestrials called Elohim; claims meeting one in 1973, after which he became the Messiah; devotes himself to the task he said was given by his "biological father," an extraterrestrial named Yahweh.

Inri Cristo (b. 1948) of Indaial, Brazil: claims to be the second Jesus Christ.

Apollo Quiboloy (b. 1950): founder of the Kingdom of Jesus Christ religious group; claims Jesus Christ is the "Almighty Father" and, with salvation now complete, proclaimed himself "Appointed Son of the God" in 1985.

Goel Ratzon (b. 1951) of Tel Aviv: claims supernatural healing powers; reportedly lived with 32 women who believed he was the Messiah; fathered 89 children, all given names that were variants of his own; arrested in 2010 on suspicions that he was abusing his "wives" and children.

David Icke (b. 1952) of Great Britain: described himself as "the son of God" and a "channel for the Christ spirit".

Brian David Mitchell (b. 1953): a fundamentalist Latter-Day Saint (Mormon) in Salt Lake City, Utah; believes he is the foreordained angel born on earth to be the Davidic "servant" prepared by God as a type of Messiah to restore the divinely led kingdom of Israel in preparation for Christ's Second Coming .

Ryuho Okawa (b. 1956): founder of Happy Science in Japan; claims to channel the spirits of Muhammad, Christ, Buddha and Confucius; also claims to be the incarnation of the supreme spiritual being called El Cantare.

Maria Devi Christos (b. 1960): founder of the Great White Brotherhood.

Sergey Torop (b. 1961): calls himself "Vissarion"; founder of the Church of the Last Testament and Ecopolis Tiberkul, a spiritual community in Southern Siberia.

Alan John Miller (b. 1962): formerly an elder in the Jehovah's Witnesses; founder of Divine Truth religious movement in Australia; claims to be the reincarnation of Jesus of Nazareth.

David Shayler (b. 1965): a former M-I5 agent and whistle-blower; declared himself the Messiah on 7 July 2007.

World Teacher (manifested 1977): said to be the theosophical Maitreya, the Messiah of all religions; said to have descended from the higher planes and manifested in a physical body in early 1977 in the Himalayas; on 19 July 1977, reportedly took a commercial flight from Pakistan to England; now living in secret in London; promoted by New Age activist Benjamin Creme of Share International.

Second seal – red horse.

The symbolism of the second horse and its rider is more obvious. The animal's color, and the rider's implement and mission are dead giveaways. *"And when he had opened the second seal, I heard the second beast say, Come and see. And there went out another horse that was red: and power was given to him that sat thereon to take peace from the earth, and that they should kill one another: and there was given unto him a great sword"* (Rev 6:3-4).

The color red is indicative of blood, denoting bloodshed; the sword is an instrument of violence, thus conflict and fighting are suggested; and the phrases *"take peace from the earth, and that they should kill one another"* are quite literal, pointing to warfare.

The parallel prophecy in the book of Matthew thoroughly confirms their identity. *"And ye shall hear of wars and rumours of wars: see that ye be not troubled: for all these things must come to pass, but the end is not yet. For nation shall rise against nation, and kingdom against kingdom"* (Matt 24:6-7a).

Wars. Renowned historians Will and Ariel Durant noted in one of their books (*The Lessons of History*, 1968, p. 81) that "in the last 3,421 years of recorded history, only 268 have seen no war."[2] That translates to less than 8% of peace time throughout almost three-and-a-half millennia. Let us view some of these armed conflicts in history by revisiting the ten deadliest wars on record in terms of casualties.

Mongol Conquests, 1206-1368 (60 million+ deaths). Their forays began in the early 13th century, marking the birth of the nascent, expanding Mongol Empire. They soon controlled much of Asia and Eastern Europe by the mid-1300s. The Mongol raids and invasions witnessed some of the deadliest wars in human history up to that period. The terror gripped Europe on a scale not seen again until the 20th century. More than 60 million lives were lost in the Mongol rampage.

Thirty Years War, 1618-1648 (5 million+ deaths). In 1618, King Ferdinand II of Bohemia tried to enforce Catholicism in his lands, but the Protestant nobles of Bohemia and Austria rebelled and named their own king. German and Spanish forces fought for Ferdinand, who was elected Holy Roman Emperor in 1619. Denmark, England and Holland sent an army to oppose him in 1625. Sweden joined the Protestants in 1630, then France in 1634. The war turned into a rivalry between the royal Bourbon family of France and the Austrian Habsburgs. In 1648, a new Holy Roman emperor signed a peace treaty ending the war; but, by then, it had already taken over 5 million lives.

Napoleonic Wars, 1803-1815 (6½ million+ deaths). These were a series of wars declared against Napoleon's French Empire by rival coalitions. It all began with the French Revolution of 1789, playing out on an unprecedented scale through the mass conscriptions of soldiers. Napoleon's armies conquered much of Europe, but were defeated after his disastrous invasion of Russia in 1812. The end of the wars restored the Bourbon monarchy in France and saw the creation of the Concert of Europe. Over 6½ million people had died.

American Civil War, 1861-1865 (800,000+ deaths). A local war fought within the fledgling United States between the "North" (the "Union") and the "South" (the "Confederacy" formed by several slave-owning southern states), it was also called the War between the States. The conflict had its roots on issues of slavery and its extension into the developing western territories of America. Over 800,000 people were killed during the war.

Empire of Japan Conquests, 1894-1945 (20 million+ deaths). Japan became a world power after defeating China (1894-95) and taking over Taiwan. They also won the Russo-Japanese War (1904-05). Japan next occupied Korea (1910) and Manchuria (1931), and moved into Southeast Asia (1936). By 1942, during World War II, the Japanese empire stretched from the eastern edge of India through Indonesia, and from the Aleutian Islands near Alaska to the Solomon Islands in the South Pacific. Japanese imperialism ended with the two atomic bombs dropped on Hiroshima and Nagasaki in 1945. By then, however, the overall cost had reached over 20 million lives.

World War I, 1914-1918 (50 million+ deaths). The First World War began in Europe in 1914 when Archduke Franz Ferdinand of Austria-Hungary was assassinated in Sarajevo, capital of Austria-Hungary's province of Bosnia-Herzegovina. It was called the "Great War" and the "War to End All Wars," because it was the most widespread fighting the world had ever seen up to that time. More than 65 million men were mobilized for the armies and navies of the combatant countries, grouped in two opposing alliances – the Central Powers and the Allies. At war's end, the total death toll was estimated at a staggering 50 million plus.

Russian Civil War, 1917-1922 (7 million+ deaths). Near the end of World War I, most Russians wanted out of the bloodbath. Bolsheviks, members of Russia's dominant Social Democratic Party, signed a treaty giving up territory to Germany. Many did not agree, and fighting broke out between the Bolshevik Red Army and the White Army, with many foreign fighters participating, such as the Allied Forces and pro-German groups against the Red Army. The war lasted only 5 years, but claimed over 7 million lives.

World War II, 1939-1945 (70 million+ deaths). The second global conflict was fought by most of the world's nations, including all the great powers. It began with the expansionist ambitions of Adolph Hitler, the Fuhrer of Nazi Germany. Just like in the First World War, the protagonists formed two opposing military camps: the Axis and the Allies. As the greatest of all wars in history, the Second World War was marked by the mass deaths of civilians, including the Nazi Holocaust genocide, and the only use of nuclear weapons in warfare. The war resulted in over 70 million fatalities.

Vietnam War, 1955-1975 (1 million+ deaths). After World War II, Vietnam was occupied by two of Japan's adversaries, Great Britain and China. The British helped restore French rule in the south, while the Chinese backed the Viet Minh in the north who were fighting for the independence of all Vietnam. This led to the 7½-year French Indochina War. In 1954, a treaty divided the country into North and South. U.S. military advisers began helping the South Vietnamese army. North Vietnam supported the communist National Liberation Front or Viet Cong. This soon flared into all-out hostilities that lasted until the U.S. withdrew in 1975. More than a million combatants and civilians died.

Soviet War in Afghanistan, 1979-1989 (1 million+ deaths). In 1978, Communists seized control of Afghanistan's government. This sparked rebellions throughout the country. In 1979, the Soviet Union sent troops to join the fight against the rebels. Soviet and Afghan government forces bombed many villages, but the rebels used guerrilla tactics to make up for their disadvantage in armaments. For nearly a decade anti-Communist Islamic forces called *mujahideen* fought the invaders. The U.S., U.K., Saudi Arabia and other nations backed the *mujahideen*. When the Soviets withdrew in 1989, the death toll had topped a million, mostly Afghan civilians.

(A list of famous wars in history after the Crucifixion, from A.D. 43 to this writing, is in Appendix "B".)

World Wars III and IV? Albert Einstein was asked by a reporter after World War II ended, "Sir, what type of machinery and weapons do you think will be used in World War III?" He answered with a smile, "I don't know about World War III, but if there is a World War IV, then it will surely be fought with sticks and stones."

Third seal – black horse.

The symbolism of the third horse and horseman, like those of the two previous horses and riders, is defined by their color, equipment, and circumstances surrounding them. *"And when he had opened the third seal, I heard the third beast say, Come and see. And I beheld, and lo a black horse; and he that sat on him had a pair of balances in his hand. And I heard a voice in the midst of the four beasts say, A measure of wheat for a penny, and three measures of barley for a penny; and see thou hurt not the oil and the wine"* (Rev 6:5).

Black is the color of death; the pair of balances in this context is a symbol of commerce; and the voice that spoke told of the exorbitant increases in the prices of staple food items. (In John's time, a penny was a man's wage for a day's work – Matt 20:1-10.) These imply food shortages and, in the extreme, famines – confirmed by Christ in the parallel prophecy in the gospel of Matthew – *"...and there shall be famines..."* (Matt 24:7b).

Famines. These are not rare events, as many of us in these times of plenty may think. Throughout history, famine has afflicted many areas of the world. As you read this, some countries have barely enough food for their people. Certain regions of Africa and Asia have always been hardest hit by famine. These have large areas near deserts, where the rainfall is light and variable. In a dry year, crops may fail, resulting in famines. On the other hand, rivers swollen by heavy rains in fertile regions overflow and destroy farmlands.

The following are 13 of the worst famines since the start of the twentieth century. (A more complete list of famines, from A.D. 400 to the present time, is in Appendix "C".)

Chinese Famine, 1907 (circa 25 million deaths). East-central China was still suffering from a series of poor harvests when a typhoon flooded 40,000 square miles of farmlands, destroying all of the crops in the region. Food riots took place daily. The famine was short-lived, but it took the lives of nearly 25 million people.

Russian Famine, 1921 (c. 5 million deaths). The early 20th century was a terrible time for the Russians: they lost millions of lives in World War I, a revolution in 1917, and several civil wars. All throughout the conflicts, the Bolshevik soldiers often forced peasants to give up their food, leading many farmers to stop planting and eat seeds as they knew they could not eat any crops they would grow. This resulted in a widespread shortage of food and seed. By the year 1921, millions of Russians had died.

Chinese Famine, 1929-1930 (c. 2 million deaths). The Huang He River in northern China is called "China's Sorrow," because it often floods, destroying crops and bringing famine. In 1929 and 1930, heavy rains caused the waterway to overflow its banks and devastate farmlands. Crops rotted in the fields, and famine killed millions of Chinese.

Soviet Famine, 1932-1933 (c. 10 million deaths). The primary cause was the collectivization program of Josef Stalin. He destroyed peasants' farms, crops, and livestock, forcibly taking farmers' lands to convert into collective farms. Reports of peasants hiding crops for private consumption led to wide-scale searches, and hidden crops found were destroyed, many of which were seeds for planting. The forced collectivization of land and destruction of seeds brought mass starvation and millions of deaths.

Bengal Famine, 1943 (c. 7 million deaths). During World War II, the Japanese invaders suspended trade between Bengal and its largest trading partner – Burma (present-day Myanmar), from where the bulk of the Bengalis' food was imported. Then, in 1942, a cyclone and three separate tidal waves hit Bengal. The floods destroyed 3,200 square miles of farmland. Next, a fungus destroyed 90% of all rice crops. At the same time, millions of refugees fleeing from the Japanese in Burma entered the region, increasing the competition for food. By December 1943, millions of Bengalis and Burmese refugees were dead.

Henan Famine, China; 1943 (3-5 million deaths). As a result of food shortages brought about by World War II (1939-1945), millions of people died in China's Henan Province.

Vietnamese Famine, 1943 (c. 2 million deaths). As the Japanese expansion began in Indochina during World War II, Vietnam, a French protectorate, was taken over with the agreement of a collaborationist French government. Agricultural production shifted from food to war-materials, specifically rubber. Moreover, the invading forces seized for their troops what little food crops remained. This, combined with a drought followed by flooding, caused mass starvation and death across much of northern Vietnam.

Great Chinese Famine, 1958-1962 (c. 43 million deaths). As part of Red China's "Great Leap Forward," private ownership of land was outlawed in 1958. Communal farming was introduced in an attempt to increase crop production. Moreover, as the Communist regime placed more importance on iron and steel manufacture, millions of farm workers were sent to metal factories. In the communal farms, Chinese officials ordered seeds planted extremely close together to maximize production. However, the seeds that sprouted were stunted due to overcrowding. A flood in 1959 and a drought in 1960 worsened the food shortages. When the Great Leap Forward ended in 1962, tens of millions of Chinese had died.

Biafra Famine, 1967-1970 (c. 1 million deaths). In May 1967, Nigeria's Eastern Region proclaimed its independence as the Republic of Biafra. A civil war ensued. The Nigerian government imposed blockades around Biafra, effectively cutting off the secessionist state's food supply. The resulting famine lasted until January 1970, when the Biafrans signed a formal surrender. As many as a million people died from the artificial famine.

Sahel Famine: Mauritania, Mali, Chad, Niger, Burkina Faso; 1968-1972 (1 million+ deaths). The disaster was attributed to desertification, which refers not to the advance of deserts, but to the expansion of degraded soil. Although it occurs in every continent, the problem had its gravest effects on the Sahel region in northern Africa to the south of the Sahara desert. Severe lack of rains brought widespread drought in the late 1960s to the early 1970s, spawning a famine that ultimately killed more than one million Africans in five countries.

Bangladesh Famine, 1974 (c. 1 million deaths). The famine was precipitated by widespread flooding. That year also, the United States stopped routine food aid over its objections to Bangladesh's trade with Cuba. The situation was made worse by the country's food rationing system, which provided rationed food to the urban population only. The rural Bangladeshis were gravely afflicted, resulting in famine and some one million deaths.

North Korean Famine, 1994-1998 (2.5-3 million deaths). The isolated hermit nation suffered from a stagnating economy and was both unable and unwilling to import food. As a result, the childhood mortality rate rose to 93 out of 1,000 children, and the mortality rate of pregnant women increased to 41 out of 1,000 mothers. Torrential rains in 1995 flooded the farming regions and destroyed around 1.5 million tons of grain reserves. Korean leader Kim Jung-Il implemented a "Military First" policy, which placed the needs of the military above the needs of the common people, food rations included. Over a four-year period, millions of North Koreans died.

Second Congo War Famine, 1998–2004 (c. 3.8 million deaths). In 1998, rebels backed by Rwanda and Uganda took up arms in eastern Congo against the Congolese government. Forces from Angola, Namibia, and Zimbabwe fought on the side of the government. A ceasefire agreement was signed in 1999, but was violated by all those involved. Millions of fighters and civilians died as a result of the six-year war, mostly from starvation and disease.

Pestilences.

In most famines only a small proportion of deaths are the direct result of starvation. The chief cause of death is usually disease, which can continue long after the famine has ended. Christ had foretold in Matthew 24:7 – *"For nation shall rise against nation, and kingdom against kingdom: and there shall be famines, and pestilences..."*

By "pestilences" Christ seems to refer to what we call today "epidemics" – outbreaks of contagious diseases spreading rapidly, affecting large numbers of people, and causing many deaths. An epidemic can turn into a "pandemic" by spreading over an entire country, continent, or even the whole world.

Here are some of the deadliest pandemics in history.

Plague. The earliest recorded incidence was about 1000 B.C. in Ashdod, described in the Bible (1 Samuel 5:6,12). In the mid-500s A.D., plague struck the Byzantine Empire, from the Black Sea across Europe, killing up to one-half the population of Constantinople. The deadliest on record was the bubonic plague, or Black Death, which raged throughout Europe, Africa, and Asia starting 1347. By 1400, it had killed 20-30 million people, about one-third of Europe's population. An outbreak occurred in China in the mid-1800s and, in the next 75 years, the plague spread to every continent and killed up to another 20 million people.

Smallpox. In the 16th and 17th centuries, European explorers unwittingly spread smallpox. It reached the Americas in 1518 on a Spanish ship and killed half of the native people of Hispaniola (now the Dominican Republic and Haiti). In 1520, when Hernan Cortes conquered the Aztec Empire under Montezuma in what is now Mexico, an infected conquistador triggered an epidemic that killed an estimated 3 million Aztecs, a third of the population. A like contagion hit the Inca Empire of Huayna Capac in 1525, and an estimated 100,000 Incas died in the capital city of Cuzco. Scientists believe that in recent times – in the 1900s alone – smallpox killed more than 300 million people worldwide.

Influenza. Large-scale outbreaks took place in Europe in 1510, 1557, and 1580, spreading into Africa and Asia, making it the first so-called pandemic. (Similar contagions broke out in 1729, 1732, 1781, 1830, 1833, and 1889, the last being called "Russian flu" because it reached Europe from the east.) In the 20th century, the pandemic in 1918-1919 after World War I was the most deadly in history, claiming some 75 million victims worldwide, more lives than those lost in the war (50 million). As Spain suffered the first outbreak, it was called "Spanish flu".

The 1957-1958 outbreak in Guizhou, southwest China, became known as "Asian flu," affecting an estimated 10-35% of the world population. In 1968-1969, a variant from Guizhou or Yunnan in south China, first identified in Hong Kong, was called "Hong Kong flu"; some 30 million people were infected in the US alone. In recent times, more new strains have appeared, such as swine flu, dog flu, horse flu, and avian or bird flu.

Cholera. From 1899 to 1923, more than 800,000 people died of cholera in Europe, Asia, and Africa. Epidemics also occurred in 1953 in Calcutta, India; 1964-1967, in South Vietnam; 1971, during the Bangladeshi civil war, among refugees fleeing to India; 1991, in Latin America; 1994, in the Democratic Republic of the Congo, where the epidemic deaths were estimated at 23,800 in just one month.

AIDS (Acquired Immunodeficiency Syndrome). It is the final, life-threatening stage of infection with HIV (Human-Immunodeficiency Virus). HIV severely damages the immune system, the body's defense against disease. In 1991, about 24 million people across the globe were living with HIV or AIDS. By 2001, the number had gone up to 36 million, an increase of 50%. Per UNAIDS estimates in 2016, 36.7 million people worldwide were living with HIV/AIDS (1.8 million were children under 15 years old); 2.1 million were newly infected. Around 25 million people have died since 1981.

Modern-day menaces. Many mass-killers that wrought havoc in the past have gone underground, but new ones, including a few old ones, are rearing their ugly heads, causing global apprehensions. The following is a list of some of them:

Potentially Pandemic Diseases in the Last 40+ Years

Outbreak	Period	Location	Fatalities
Smallpox	1974	India	c. 15,000
Plague	1994	Surat, India	52
	2014–present	Madagascar	40
SARS coronavirus	2002–2003	Asia	775
Leishmaniasis	2004	Afghanistan	n.a.*
Dengue Fever	2005	Singapore	19
	2006	India	>50
	2006	Pakistan	>50
	2009	Bolivia	18
	2011–present	Pakistan	>350
Chikungunya	2006	India	n.a.*
	2013–2015	Americas	183
Cholera	2007	Iraq	10
	2008	India	49
	2008–2009	Zimbabwe	4,293
	2010–present	Hispaniola, Haiti	>8,500

Ebola	2007	Uganda	n.a.*
	2013–present	West Africa, worldwide	11,232
Hepatitis B	2009	Gujarat, India	49
Hong Kong Flu	2009	Worldwide	14,286
Meningitis	2009–2010	West Africa	931
Measles	2011–present	Congo	>4,500
Hand, foot and mouth disease	2011–present	Vietnam	170
Yellow Fever	2012-2013	Darfur, Sudan	847
MERS coronavirus	2012–present	Worldwide	449
Hepatitis E and A	2014–present	India	36
Swine Flu	2015–present	India	2,035

*(no available data)

Earthquakes.

Christ mentioned one last scourge in Matthew 24:7 – *"For nation shall rise against nation, and kingdom against kingdom: and there shall be famines, and pestilences, and earthquakes, in divers places."*

Earthquakes are seldom mentioned in historical records. Less than 10 major tremors were recorded in the 9th-18th centuries, a period of 900 years. The temblors were few, averaging just one every 100 years, but are chiefly remembered for the number of casualties they inflicted.

Deadliest Earthquakes in History

Year	Magnitude*	Location	Deaths
856	8.0	Damghan, Iran	c. 200,000
1138	8.5	Aleppo, Syria	c. 230,000
1290	6.8	Chihli, China	c. 100,000
1498	8.6	Nankaido, Japan	c. 31,000
1556	8.0	Shaanxi, China	c. 830,000
1667	6.9	Shemakha, Azerbaijan	c. 80,000
1693	7.4	Sicily, Italy	c. 60,000
1721	7.7	Tabriz, Iran	c. 80,000
1755	8.5-9.0	Lisbon, Portugal	c. 100,000

*estimated

Earthquakes, however, have greatly increased in frequency and intensity in the 20th century. Some analysts attribute the higher statistics to the development of more sensitive instruments and advanced communication systems, but the figures nonetheless appear to confirm the prophetic words of Christ.

Below are the major earthquakes from the beginning of the 20th century to this writing. (Earthquakes with magnitudes lower than 7.0 and fatalities less than 1,000 have not been included.)

Major Earthquakes since early 20th Century

Year	Magnitude	Location	Fatalities
1908	7.1	Messina, Italy	c. 200,000
1920	8.3	Haiyuan, Ningxia, China	c. 240,000
1923	7.9	Kanto, Japan	c. 93,000
1927	7.9	Xining, China	c. 200,000
1948	7.3	Ashgabat, Turkmenistan	c. 110,000
1960	9.5	Valdivia, Chile	c. 6,000
1970	8.0	Yungay, Peru	74,194
1976	8.2	Tangshan, China	c. 655,000
1990	7.4	Rudbar, Iran	c. 40,000
1990	7.9	Izmit, Turkey	c. 45,000
2004	9.1-9.3	Sumatra, Indonesia	>230,000
2005	7.6	Kashmir, Pakistan	c. 100,000
2008	8.0	Sichuan, China	69,197
2010	7.0	Port-au-Prince, Haiti	c. 316,000
2011	9.0	Tohoku, Japan	18,184
2015	7.8	Nepal	9,018

Sesmoi. The word "earthquakes" in the New Testament had been translated from the Greek *seismoi* (sing., *seismos*), from which we derive the English words "seismic," "seismology," etc. However, it does not only mean "earthquake." *Seismos* comes from the root-word *seio* ("to rock, agitate"), a commotion of the air (gale) or of the ground (earthquake).³ Thus, in the KJV, depending on the context, *sesmoi* is translated as either "earthquake" or "tempest" (storm).

Storms. Violent atmospheric commotions or weather disturbances are generally called storms. Storms called hurricanes and typhoons are the same, known collectively as tropical cyclones, Hurricanes form in the Atlantic and eastern Pacific Ocean, while typhoons form in the Western Pacific. (A list of the strongest storms since the early 20th century is in Appendix "D".)

Related phenomena. Similar or corollary disturbances resulting from atmospheric or terrestrial disorders can cause heavy, and sometimes even worse, collateral damages, such as –

Floods (Appendix "E");

Landslides, mudflows and avalanches (Appendix "F"), which are triggered by storms, heavy rains, or earthquakes;

Tsunamis (Appendix "G"), which are spawned by either earthquakes or…

Volcanic eruptions (Appendix "H");

Tornadoes (Appendix "I") or whirlwinds, which are very much related to storms, but usually without the accompanying rains.

These have all increased in frequency and destructive power since the beginning of the twentieth century.

Fourth seal – pale horse.

The fourth and last horse of the Apocalypse and its rider are frighteningly enigmatic. *"And when he had opened the fourth seal, I heard the voice of the fourth beast say, Come and see. And I looked, and behold a pale horse: and his name that sat on him was Death, and Hell followed with him. And power was given unto them over the fourth part of the earth, to kill with sword, and with hunger, and with death, and with the beasts of the earth."* (Rev 6:7-8).

The name of the rider of the pale horse is Death, and Hell (translated from *Hades* in Greek – the region of the dead) is close on their heels. The verse says that the horse and its rider will have power over one-fourth of the world, and their power to kill includes those of the second and third horsemen – war and famine, respectively – plus an unnamed kind of death (identified in the parallel prophecy of Matt 24:7 as "pestilences"), and wild animals, thrown in for good measure. This last horseman is the deadliest one of all.

"Green horse." Unlike the first three horses, there is something ambiguous about the color of the fourth horse. "Pale" means "lacking in color." But if we read the original Greek text, we will see that "pale horse" was translated from *hippos chloros*, which really means "green horse" (as in chlorophyll – green leaf). The English translators of the King James Version (1611) probably used the word "pale" as a substitute, inasmuch as no horse is actually colored green. Other Bible translations, such as the New American Standard (NAS), use the word "ashen," which means "pale" and at the same time can literally mean "ash-gray." But, considering that the Revelation is a book of prophecy which frequently uses symbolic language and imagery, what could the "green horse" really represent?

Muslim countries? Green is the traditional color of Islam and the Arabs, adopted by Muslims of other nationalities. Most nations whose populations are about 50% Muslim or higher have or had the color green in their flags. Let us verify this:

Flags with a dominant green field or background: Arab League, Bangladesh, Comoros, Libya, Mauritania, Saudi Arabia.

Flags approximately two-thirds of which are green: Nigeria, Pakistan.

Flags approximately one-half of which is green: Algeria, Western Sahara.

Flags approximately one-third of which is green: Afghanistan, Djibouti, Gambia, Guinea, Iran, Mali, Niger, Oman, Senegal.

Flags approximately one-fourth of which is green: Jordan, Kuwait, Palestinian Authority, Sudan, United Arab Emirates.

Flags with prominent green element(s): Iraq, Maldives, Syria, North Yemen.

"Fourth part of the earth." Let us more closely study the phrase: *"power was given unto them over the fourth part of the earth"*. It looks like it foretells four possible scenarios:

1. Muslims will comprise one-fourth of the world population. Islam is today the world's fastest growing religion – both in terms of birth rate and conversions. According to *Wikipedia*, a 2015 study found that Islam had 1.8 billion adherents, about 24% of the world population. Of these, 80-90% were Sunni, 10–20% Shiite.

2. Muslims will populate one-fourth of the countries of the world. Muslims today reside in virtually all parts of the globe in varying densities. Of the some 193 independent states in the world, countries whose populations consist of 40% Muslims or more number 49 – almost exactly one-fourth! They are listed below:

Countries	**Percent Muslim**
1. Afghanistan	99%
2. Albania	70%
3. Algeria	98%
4. Azerbaijan	84%
5. Bahrain	85%
6. Bangladesh	89%
7. Bosnia-Herzegovina	40%
8. Brunei	62%

END TIME DECODED

9.	Burkina Faso	49%
10.	Chad	52%
11.	Comoros	98%
12.	Djibouti	94%
13.	Egypt	90%
14.	Ethiopia	45%
15.	The Gambia	85%
16.	Guinea	69%
17.	Indonesia	88%
18.	Iran	98%
19.	Iraq	95%
20.	Jordan	90%
21.	Kazakhstan	43%
22.	Kosovo	90%
23.	Kuwait	85%
24.	Kyrgyzstan	61%
25.	Lebanon	70%
26.	Libya	96%
27.	Malaysia	48%
28.	Maldives	100%
29.	Mali	81%
30.	Mauritania	100%
31.	Morocco	98%
32.	Niger	93%
33.	Nigeria	48%
34.	Oman	88%
35.	Pakistan	97%
36.	Qatar	85%
37.	Saudi Arabia	100%
38.	Senegal	87%
39.	Sierra Leone	46%
40.	Somalia	99%
41.	Sudan	97%
42.	Syria	90%
43.	Tajikistan	84%
44.	Tunisia	98%
45.	Turkey	99%
46.	Turkmenistan	87%
47.	United Arab Emirates	76%
48.	Uzbekistan	76%
49.	Yemen	99%

3. Muslims will rule the world? Planet Earth is approximately one-fourth dry land and three-fourths water. If the Muslims dominate most, even if not all, of the countries in the world, they would in effect be the masters of the planet. In the 700s the Muslim empire, with its seat in Baghdad (Iraq), used to rule over the Middle East, Rhodes (Greece), Sicily (Italy), northern Africa, and parts of Spain, India, and China. Should the prophecy prove true, history will just be repeating itself on a larger scale!

4. Muslims will cause the death of one-fourth of humanity? Accordingly, a quarter of all the people in the world could lose their lives by war, famine, pandemics, and wild animals if the global spread of Islamic jihadist terrorism continues without letup.

"Kill with the sword". In October 2006, Sunni Muslim insurgent groups formed the Islamic State of Iraq (ISI). On April 8, 2013, having expanded into Syria, ISI modified its name to "Islamic State of Iraq and the Levant" (ISIL; "Levant" meaning Greater Syria, including Lebanon and Israel) or "Islamic State of Iraq and Syria" (ISIS). They gained prominence when they drove Iraqi government troops out of key cities in western Iraq in early 2014. They also seized vast tracts of northern Syria. The territorial loss of Iraq prompted a renewal of US military action in the beleaguered country.

On June 29, 2014, first day of Ramadan, ISIS formally declared the establishment of a caliphate, the government of a global Islamic transnational state. They also shortened their name to simply Islamic State (IS). The group's leader, previously known by his *nom de guerre* Abu Bakr al-Baghdadi, became Caliph Ibrahim.

As a global caliphate, the IS claims religious, political and military authority over all Muslims worldwide. By March 2015, it had control over territory with 10 million people in Iraq and Syria, as well as nominal control over some areas of Libya. Terrorist Muslim groups in other countries have affiliated with the IS, such as Boko Haram in Nigeria, and the Abu Sayyaf and Maute Groups in the Philippines.

Joseph Farah, editor-in-chief of WND (WorldNetDaily) compares the speed of the ISIS conquest with the original spread of Islam and even that of Alexander the Great. He adds: "the modus operandi of ISIS… calls for a scorched earth policy against its enemies – which includes Christians, Shiites, Alawites, Jews, non-believers and all non-Sunnis. ISIS leadership advocates and practices barbarism designed to strike fear into the hearts and minds of its opponents and anyone who doesn't stand with them in their strict Shariah Sunni code… Already the IS marauders have crucified victims, beheaded them and conducted mass executions of Iraqi soldiers and civilians. No atrocity is beneath them."[4]

"Kill with hunger'. Will the widening attacks carried on by Muslim jihadists and the resulting economic disruptions, lead to global food shortages and, eventually, famine? Wars often bring about famines – either farmers become victims in the crossfire, leave their fields to join the combatants, or flee to safer areas from the battle zones. Sometimes, a besieging army may deliberately initiate a famine by setting up blockades to cut off the food supply and starve the defenders into surrendering. Invading troops may also destroy stored food and growing crops.

"Kill with death". As we have seen, "death" here corresponds to pestilences. The *Encarta Encyclopedia* notes, "Wars and foreign invasions have traditionally provided breeding grounds for epidemic disease. Prior to the 20th century, every European war produced more deaths from disease than from the use of weaponry."[5]

Will the jihadists make use of "pestilences" or biological weapons as an instrument of war? Contagious diseases were occasionally used as weapons in war. In the 14th century, plague-infected cadavers were catapulted into an enemy camp in the Russian Crimea.[6] Historians believe that smallpox was used as a biological weapon by British forces in North America during the French and Indian wars (1689-1763) by distributing blankets that had been used by smallpox victims to cause outbreaks among the Indians.

Today, some nations and terrorist groups are known or suspected to be developing biological weapons. In 1979, the accidental release of anthrax spores from a military facility in the Soviet Union caused 68 deaths. In 2001, after 9/11, anthrax spores were sent by mail to several US business and government offices in several states, where people became ill with inhalational anthrax and several died; others contracted cutaneous anthrax (skin sores).[7] In May 2015, the US Defense Department said it had accidentally sent shipments of live anthrax bacteria from Dugway Proving Ground facility in Utah to labs in nine US states and a US air base in South Korea.[8]

"Kill with the beasts of the earth". Aside from well known wild animals, like lions and tigers, crocodiles and alligators, venomous snakes and boa constrictors, etcetera, could these "beasts" be hunger-crazed packs of former pet cats and dogs whose previous owners will have run out of food to feed them or will have died in the coming wars, famines, and pestilences?

Apocalyptic vision. These scenarios appear to mirror an apocalyptic world in ruins told to the prophet Ezekiel: *"Thus saith the Lord GOD; As I live, surely they that are in the wastes shall fall by the sword, and him that* *is in the open field will I give to the beasts to be devoured, and they that be in the forts and in the caves shall die of the pestilence"* (Ezek 33:27).

Parallel prophecies.
At this point, let us review how the parallel prophecies in the verses of Revelation 6 and Matthew 24 have been matching up. In the table below, it appears that Revelation 6:8 is a repetition of Matthew 24:5-7,11 and Revelation 6:1-7, the only differences being the insertion of earthquakes after pestilences in Matthew and the addition of beasts after "death" (pestilences) in Revelation.

Parallel Prophecies of Matthew 24 and Revelation 6

Matthew 24:5-7,11	Revelation 6:1-7	Revelation 6:8
For many shall come in my name, saying, I am Christ; and shall deceive many... And many false prophets shall rise, and shall deceive many.	First seal – white horse (false Christs and prophets)	Fourth seal – pale or green horse. (The founder of Islam was called the last prophet of God.)
For nation shall rise against nation, and kingdom against kingdom:	Second seal – red horse (wars)	*And power was given unto them over the fourth part of the earth, to kill with sword,*
and there shall be famines,	Third seal – black horse (famines)	*and with hunger,*
and pestilences,	(pandemics)	*and with death,*
and earthquakes, in divers places.	(including storms, etc.)	
	(starving animals)	*and with the beasts of the earth.*

Ghostly green horseman. Incredibly, on the night of February 3, 2011, during an "Arab Spring" riot in Tahrir Square, Egypt, a news camera of MSNBC caught the image of a ghostly green horse and rider galloping through the mob of rioters before vanishing into thin air. (Egypt is the largest Muslim Arab country.) Was it an omen that the fourth horseman of the Apocalypse has arrived and we are now in the period under the influence of the green horse and its rider?

The video can be seen on the internet by typing in key words such as "green horse, Arab Spring riot, Egypt", etc.

Primary terrorist target.
The very first target of Muslim Arab terrorists were the Jews. Their goal: expel the Jews from the Holy Land and destroy the state of Israel. Why? Let us look back briefly on Israel's history.

Promised Land. About 1921 B.C., a man in Mesopotamia named Abram heeded God's call to go to an unknown land (Canaan), which was thereafter promised to him and his descendants (Gen 15:18). Childless, he was told that he would have a son by his wife Sarah. Yet, impatient, he sired a son (Ishmael) by his wife's Egyptian handmaid. Sarah later gave birth to the promised son – Isaac. Ishmael became the ancestor of the Arabs; while Isaac begat twin sons: Esau, progenitor of the Edomites (Idumeans), and Jacob (later renamed Israel), patriarch of the twelve tribes of Israel.

During a famine, Jacob and his family moved to Egypt, where his descendants became slaves. About 1591 B.C, Moses led the Israelites in the Exodus from Egypt to return to Canaan, the Promised Land. The Israelites settled Canaan in 1551 B.C. Around 1000 B.C., King David captured Jerusalem and made it the capital of Israel. After his son and successor, King Solomon, died, the kingdom was divided into the ten-tribe kingdom of Israel in the north and the two-tribe kingdom of Judah in the south. Assyria destroyed Israel in 721 B.C., while Babylon conquered Judah in 606 B.C. and took the Jews captive. When the Persians captured

Babylon in 539 B.C., they allowed the Jews to return and rebuild Jerusalem.

Foreign rulers. Alexander the Great defeated Persia in 332 B.C. and the Greeks ruled over the land. In 165 B.C., the Jews recaptured Jerusalem and established an independent state. In 63 B.C., the Romans came and made the territory a province of their empire, calling it Judea. In 37 B.C., the Romans made Herod, an Idumean, king of Judea. In 135 A.D., after crushing the last Jewish revolt, Emperor Hadrian, expelled all surviving Jews, prohibited their return and, to erase their memory, renamed Judea "Aelia Palaestina" (after Aelius, his clan name, and the ancient Philistines, who had passed away as a nation around 500 B.C.). Idumeans repopulated what later became known as "Palestine."

The Byzantine Empire (Eastern Roman Empire) became the sole power in the region when the Western Roman Empire collapsed in 476 A.D. In 614-629, the Persians held Jerusalem. The Byzantines regained control, but lost it again in 638 to Muslim Arabs. In 1099, the Crusaders captured the Holy City and set up the Kingdom of Jerusalem. Arabs reconquered the city in 1187. Muslims and Jews began returning. The Mamelukes (former slaves-turned-rulers of Egypt) had control from 1250 until 1517, the year the Ottoman Empire (Turkey) took over. The Turks surrendered the city to the British in 1917, near the end of World War I.

Return of the Jews. In the late 1800s, oppression of the Jews in Eastern Europe set off a mass emigration of Jewish refugees. Some Jews called Zionists wanted an independent Jewish nation and set up farm colonies in Palestine. Increasing numbers of Jews retuned. At first, most of Jerusalem's residents were Muslims; even Christians greatly outnumbered Jews. By 1870, Jews had become the majority group. In 1880, about 24,000 Jews were living in Palestine.

At the same time, the Arab population grew rapidly. By 1914, the total population of Palestine was about 700,000 – some 615,000 were Arabs and 85,000 were Jews.

Arab-Jewish conflict. During World War I (1914-1918), the British offered to back Arab demands for independence from the Ottomans in return for Arab support for the Allies. In 1916, some Arabs revolted against the Ottomans. In November 1917, to gain Jewish support in the war, the United Kingdom issued the Balfour Declaration supporting a Jewish national homeland in Palestine. (The Arabs later claimed that Palestine was included in the area promised to them, but the British denied this.) In December 1917, British troops captured Jerusalem from the Ottomans. The League of Nations made Palestine a mandated territory administered by Britain in preparation for self government.

Jewish immigration increased further during the 1920's-1930's. Anti-Zionist sentiments grew among the Arabs who wanted their own Arab state in Palestine. In the 1930s, anti-Jewish riots broke out. On November 25, 1940, a terrorist bomb sank a ship carrying Jewish immigrants off the coast of Haifa, Palestine, claiming 267 lives.

Independence of Israel. In 1947, the United Nations (UN) voted to divide Palestine into an Arab state and a Jewish state. The Jews accepted the decision, but the Arabs rejected it. They immediately resumed terrorist attacks on the Jews.

On May 14, 1948, the Jews proclaimed the independence of Israel. Next day, five neighboring Arab countries attacked the new state. When the fighting ended in 1949, Israel held territories beyond the borders set by the UN plan.

Continuing attacks. Terrorist attacks continue. Since 1960, such groups as Hamas, Islamic Jihad and others have carried out terrorist attacks against the Jews. These have widened and today involve terrorists of other nationalities, as well as targets other than the Jews and Israel. These include nations perceived to be supporting or friendly to Israel.

The attacks occur sans any warning in different parts of the globe. Hardly a week passes without a terrorist incident being reported in the mass media. The press and the public have become so inured, occurrences in the usual flash points are now treated as minor news.

(List of worst terrorist attacks since 1940 in Appendix "J".)

3

End-Time Kings and Beasts

And in the days of these kings shall the God of heaven set up a kingdom, which shall never be destroyed...

- Daniel 2:44a

Most of the principal protagonists in the last days are empires and their rulers whose origins come from ancient kings and their kingdoms. In the end-time prophecies of the books of Daniel and the Revelation, they are at times metaphorically represented as "beasts" and their "horns," and at other times by inanimate objects, such as a statue and its parts. Let us get acquainted with them.

A great image

Around 603 B.C., King Nebuchadnezzar of Babylon, destroyer of Jerusalem and captor of the Jews, had a dream he could not recall. The young Jewish prophet Daniel, a captive in Babylon, recalled the vision for the king. *"Thou, O king, sawest, and behold a great image. This great image, whose brightness was excellent, stood before thee; and the form thereof was terrible. This image's head was of fine gold, his breast and his arms of silver, his belly and his thighs of brass, His legs of iron, his feet part of iron and part of clay"* (Dan 2:31-33).

Head of gold.

Daniel explained the prophetic symbols to King Nebuchadnezzar. *"Thou, O king, art a king of kings: for the God of heaven hath given thee a kingdom, power, and strength, and glory. And wheresoever the children of men dwell, the beasts of the field and the fowls of the heaven hath he given into thine hand, and hath made thee ruler over them all. Thou art this head of gold"* (Dan 2:37-38).

That the head of the image was of fine gold symbolized the great wealth of Babylon. According to the *Encarta Encyclopedia*, Babylon "was at that time the largest city of the known world, covering more than 1,000 hectares (about 2,500 acres)."[1] The *World Book* adds that it was also the largest business center in the Middle East in its time.[2] Babylon's great wealth enabled Nebuchadnezzar to build the famous Hanging Gardens, one of the Seven Wonders of the Ancient World.

Breast and arms of silver.

Another kingdom would take over Babylon's supremacy. *"And after thee shall arise another kingdom inferior to thee... his breast and his arms of silver"* (Dan 2:39a, 32b). The foretold nation which succeeded Babylon as the greatest power in the ancient world was Persia. *Nelson's Illustrated Bible Dictionary* notes: "During the reign of Nabonidus (555-539 B.C.), while Belshazzar was co-regent (Dan 5), the city surrendered to the Persians without opposition."[3]

Persia, although not as rich as Babylon, also possessed great wealth. One of its kings, Xerxes, was able to organize an army and auxiliaries of over 5 million people to invade Greece.[4] The two arms symbolized the unified kingdoms of Media and Persia.

Belly and thighs of brass.

In turn, another kingdom would replace Persia as the dominant power in the ancient world: *"...and another third kingdom of brass... shall bear rule over all the earth... his belly and his thighs of brass"* (Dan 2:39b, 32c). *Nelson's Illustrated Bible Dictionary* relates: "Eventually the balance of power passed from the Persians to Alexander the Great of Greece... in 331 B.C."[5] He defeated the Persians. The two thighs point to the allied kingdoms of Macedonia and Greece. (Alexander was a Macedonian, but his father, Philip of Macedon, conquered the Greeks in 338 B.C.)

"Brass" is a translation of *nechash*, the Hebrew word for copper. Other Bible translations, such as the NIV, render it as "bronze," because both brass and bronze are alloys made with copper. The Bronze Age began in the Aegean civilization of the Greeks (3000-1100 B.C.), who were widely famous for their bronze utensils and ornaments, tools and armaments.

Legs of iron.

The next kingdom that would supplant Greece as world power would be associated with iron. *"And the fourth kingdom shall be strong as iron: forasmuch as iron breaketh in pieces and subdueth all things: and as iron that breaketh all these, shall it break in pieces and bruise… His legs of iron…"* (Dan 2:40, 33a).

The Iron Age began between 1500 and 1000 B.C. with the widespread use of iron for tools and weapons. However, the iron working process remained primitive for a long time, keeping the metal expensive; such that only kings and warriors could afford it. Armies using iron armaments, particularly the Roman legions, sped up the widespread utilization of iron. According to the *World Book*, "the people of Scandinavia knew little about iron before the time of Julius Caesar."[6]

The Wycliffe Bible Commentary concludes: "…the fourth stage of empire is Roman."[7] The two legs of the great image foreshadowed the division of the Roman Empire into two parts: the Latin-speaking Western Roman Empire with its capital in Rome and the Greek-speaking Eastern Roman Empire with its seat in Constantinople.

Feet of iron and clay.

The fifth and last part of the great image in the king's dream consists of the feet: *"…his feet part of iron and part of clay… And whereas thou sawest the feet and toes, part of potters' clay, and part of iron, the kingdom shall be divided; but there shall be in it of the strength of the iron, forasmuch as thou sawest the iron mixed with miry clay. And as the toes of the feet were part of iron, and part of clay, so the kingdom shall be partly strong, and partly broken. And whereas thou sawest iron mixed with miry clay, they shall mingle themselves with the seed of men: but they shall not cleave one to another, even as iron is not mixed with clay"* (Dan 2:33b, 41-43).

As there are two feet, it looks like the last end-time kingdom will have two distinct divisions. The ten toes must be ten kings or rulers. And because the feet will be partly made of iron, it seems that they will be much like the Roman Empire; but being also partly made of clay suggests the addition of a new element to their original nature. What empire could this be? Ever since the fall of the Western Roman Empire in 476 and demise of the remaining Eastern Roman Empire in 1453, no new emergent empire, or even an alliance of kingdoms appears to have matched the metaphorical description. This last kingdom, therefore, must still be future.

Broken by a stone. Eventually, a stone will destroy the great image. *"Thou sawest till that a stone was cut out without hands, which smote the image upon his feet that were of iron and clay, and brake them to pieces.*

Then was the iron, the clay, the brass, the silver, and the gold, broken to pieces together, and became like the chaff of the summer threshingfloors; and the wind carried them away, that no place was found for them: and the stone that smote the image became a great mountain, and filled the whole earth" (Dan 2:34-35). Most Bible commentators agree that "The references to the cut stone from the mountainside in Dan 2:34-35,45 have been interpreted to represent Christ and the church."[8]

The next verse leaves no doubt about its identity. *"And in the days of these kings shall the God of heaven set up a kingdom, which shall never be destroyed: and the kingdom shall not be left to other people, but it shall break in pieces and consume all these kingdoms, and it shall stand for ever."* Inasmuch as the establishment of God's kingdom on earth has not happened yet, the feet of iron and clay must be symbolic of an end-time empire or confederation of states that will ultimately be replaced by the kingdom of God. We shall examine this more closely in Chapter 6 to identify the fifth and last end-time empire and its component kingdoms.

The ram and the he-goat

Around 538 BC, Daniel, now an old man in Babylon, had still another metaphorical view of the future. *"Then I lifted up mine eyes, and saw, and, behold, there stood before the river a ram which had two horns: and the two horns were high; but one was higher than the other, and the higher came up last. I saw the ram pushing westward, and northward, and southward; so that no beasts might stand before him, neither was there any that could deliver out of his hand; but he did according to his will, and became great"* (Dan 8:3-4).

The angel Gabriel unravels the mystery of the ram for Daniel in a following verse. *"The ram which thou sawest having two horns are the kings of Media and Persia"* (Dan 8:20). The two allied kingdoms invaded other kingdoms *"westward, and northward, and southward,"* including Babylon (west of Persia). The "higher" of the two horns represented Persia, which came to power later but became more powerful than Media.

He-goat with horn between eyes.

Another odd-looking animal entered the scene. *"And as I was considering, behold, an he goat came from the west on the face of the whole earth, and touched not the ground: and the goat had a notable horn between his eyes. And he came to the ram that had two horns, which I had there seen standing before the river, and ran unto him in the fury of his power. And I saw him come close unto the ram, and he was moved with choler against him, and smote the ram, and brake his two horns: and there* was no power in the ram to stand before him, but he cast him down to the ground, and stamped upon him: and there was none that could deliver the ram out of his hand"* (Dan 8:5-7).

Gabriel again identified the second strange animal for Daniel, as well as for us future Bible readers. *"And the rough goat is the king of Grecia: and the great horn that is between his eyes is the first king"* (Dan 8:21). The *"he goat from the west"* (of Persia) was Greece. That it *"touched not the ground"* denoted the speed of its advance. The *"great horn between his eyes"* was its king, Alexander the Great, under whose leadership Greece subjugated the Persian Empire in 331 B.C.

Four new horns branch out.

For an unknown reason, the horn between the eyes of the he-goat broke. *"Therefore the he goat waxed very great: and when he was strong, the great horn was broken; and for it came up four notable ones toward the four winds of heaven"* (Dan 8:8). At the height of his conquests, Alexander suddenly died at the young age of thirty-three in 323 BC. *"Now that being broken, whereas four stood up for it, four kingdoms shall stand up out of the nation, but not in his power"* (Dan 8:22).

After the untimely death of Alexander, his top generals fought among themselves for control of the empire. At first, Perdiccas seized Asia the Less and parts of present-day Turkey, Syria, and Iraq. He was succeeded by Antigonus, who tried to take more territories, but was killed in battle in 301 B.C.[9] Four other generals then divided the Greek dominions among themselves (*"toward the four winds of heaven"*): Ptolemy (south); Cassander (west); Lysimachus (east); and Seleucus Nicanor (north).[10] None of them, however, became as powerful as Alexander (*"but not in his power"*).

A "little horn."

A new power would arise in the territory of one of the four generals. *"And out of one of them came forth a little horn, which waxed exceeding great, toward the south, and toward the east, and toward the pleasant land"* (Dan 8:9).

Parts of Italy belonged to Cassander's western domain. Greek legend told of the hero Aeneas founding a settlement in central Italy after the destruction of Troy by the Greeks in the Trojan War. In 275 B.C., the Greek colony of Tarentum in southern Italy was taken by a newly expanding city-state, Rome, which thereafter began to rule over most of the Italian Peninsula. In 168 B.C., Rome defeated Macedonia and made it part of its growing domain. Then, initially posing as the protector of the Greeks, by the 140s B.C. Rome had also taken control of Greece ("*the south*"), with its eyes turning next on Thrace ("*the east*") and Jerusalem ("*the pleasant land*"). It thus becomes apparent that the "little horn" which grew from one of the four new horns of the he-goat was Rome.

Christ crucified, Temple destroyed.

The "little horn" would become very powerful. "*And it waxed great, even to the host of heaven; and it cast down some of the host and of the stars to the ground, and stamped upon them. Yea, he magnified himself even to the prince of the host, and by him the daily sacrifice was taken away, and the place of his sanctuary was cast down*" (Dan 8:10-11).

Rome, through Pontius Pilate, its procurator (administrator) in Judea, sentenced Christ to death in 30 A.D. ("*magnified himself even to the prince of the host*" – head of the army of angels in heaven). Forty years later, Roman legions crushing a Jewish revolt, destroyed the Temple in Jerusalem in 70 AD, thus stopping the daily offering of sacrifices ("*and by him the daily sacrifice was taken away, and the place of his sanctuary was cast down*"). About 1,100,000 Jews were killed, while over 100,000 survivors were sold in slave markets

Four beasts from the sea

About two years earlier, in 540 B.C., Daniel dreamt of the sea. "*Daniel spake and said, I saw in my vision by night, and, behold, the four winds of the heaven strove upon the great sea*" (Dan 7:2).

The prophetic dream also came in symbols. Let us endeavor to decipher their meanings.

"**Wind**." We get clues from Jeremiah and Ezekiel. "*I will scatter them as with an east wind before the enemy; I will shew them the back, and not the face, in the day of their calamity*" (Jer 18:17; cf. 49:36). "*And all his fugitives with all his bands shall fall by the sword, and they that remain shall be scattered toward all winds: and ye shall know that I the LORD have spoken it*" (Ezek 17:21).

Judging from these verses, the word "wind" appears to be a metaphor descriptive of war and destruction.

"**Great sea.**" According to the *International Standard Bible Encyclopaedia*, "The Mediterranean is called *ha-yam ha-gadhol*, 'the great sea' (Num 34:6; Josh 1:4; Ezek 47:10)."[11] The *Wycliffe Bible Commentary* agrees: "Dan 7:2. Upon the great sea. Not just any sea, but, as Lang has ably demonstrated (*Histories and Prophecies of Daniel*, p. 86 ff.), the Mediterranean (see esp. Num 34:6-7; Josh 1:4; 9:1; 15:11-12,47; 23:4;

Ezek 47:10-15,19-20; 48:28)"[12] The word "Mediterranean" means "in the middle of land" (Latin *medius*, "middle" + *terra*, "land"), inasmuch as land almost totally encloses that sea. The Mediterranean Sea is bounded by Europe in the north, Asia in the east, and Africa in the south. In the west, the narrow Strait of Gibraltar connects the Mediterranean to the Atlantic Ocean.

The phrase *"four winds of the heaven strove upon the great sea"* therefore signified the wars waged by the ancient empires and kingdoms that rose and fell around the Mediterranean Sea.

Four uncanny creatures.

"And four great beasts came up from the sea, diverse one from another" (Dan 7:2-3).

The four beasts had different bizarre appearances in Daniel's nightmare. Obviously, they were prophetically symbolic creatures. A bystander in the vision, probably an angel, told Daniel what they stood for. *"I came near unto one of them that stood by, and asked him the truth of all this. So he told me, and made me know the interpretation of the things. These great beasts, which are four, are four kings, which shall arise out of the earth"* (Dan 7:16-17).

The four beasts stood for kings and their empires. They were personified by powerful predators that preyed on and devoured smaller, weaker creatures – suggesting those empires conquered smaller, weaker kingdoms.

Lion with eagle's wings.

"The first was like a lion, and had eagle's wings: I beheld till the wings thereof were plucked, and it was lifted up from the earth, and made stand upon the feet as a man, and a man's heart was given to it" (Dan 7:4).

The Wycliffe Bible Commentary identifies the first beast. "The lion symbolizes Babylon here and also in Jer 4:6-7. The eagle's wings speak of swiftness, as the lion of strength."[13] The lion's wings were plucked when Media-Persia invaded Babylon, which gave up without a fight. That *"a man's heart was given to it."*, Matthew Henry's Commentary on the Whole Bible explains: "…this monstrous animal, this winged lion, is made to stand upon the feet as a man, and a man's heart is given to it. It has lost the heart of a lion, which it had been famous for… lost its courage and become feeble and faint… they are put in fear, and made to know themselves to be but men. Sometimes the valour of a nation strangely sinks, and it becomes cowardly and effeminate…"[14]

Bear with three ribs in its mouth.

"And behold another beast, a second, like to a bear, and it raised up itself on one side, and it had three ribs in the mouth of it between the teeth of it: and they said thus unto it, Arise, devour much flesh" (Dan 7:5).

Matthew Henry saves us the trouble of puzzling over what the bear represents. "This was the Persian monarchy, less strong and generous than the former (Babylon), but no less ravenous. This bear raised up itself on one side against the lion, and soon mastered it. It raised up one dominion; so some read it. Persia and Media, which in Nebuchadnezzar's image were the two arms in one breast, now set up a joint government. This bear had three ribs in the mouth of it between the teeth, the remains of those nations it had devoured…"[15] The *"three ribs in the mouth of it between the teeth"* point to the three kingdoms Persia defeated one after another: Lydia in Asia Minor (545 B.C.), Babylon (539 B.C.), and Egypt (525 B.C.).

Leopard with four wings and four heads.

"After this I beheld, and lo another, like a leopard, which had upon the back of it four wings of a fowl; the beast had also four heads; and dominion was given to it" (Dan 7:6).

The first two beasts being historical empires, identifying the third becomes an easy task. *The Wycliffe Bible Commentary* states: "The sinewy four-winged leopard speaks, without doubt, of Alexander's Grecian (Macedonian) kingdom. Rulership passed from Nineveh (Assyria) to Babylon in 612 B.C.; from Babylon to Persia in 539 B.C., and from Darius III (Persia) to Alexander (Greece) in 331 B.C."[16]

Matthew Henry adds: "This was the Grecian monarchy, founded by Alexander the Great, active, crafty, and cruel, like a leopard. He had four wings of a fowl; the lion seems to have had but two wings; but the leopard had four, for though Nebuchadnezzar made great dispatch in his conquests Alexander made much greater. In six years' time he gained the whole empire of Persia, a great part besides of Asia, made himself master of Syria, Egypt, India, and other nations"[17]

The leopard had four heads. Same as the four horns that grew out of the broken horn between the eyes of the he-goat, these were the four divisions of Alexander's empire after his death. We read in the book *Daniel and the Revelation* (1944): "Upon Alexander's death, his empire was eventually divided among four of his generals. Ptolemy had Egypt, Libya, Arabia, Coele-Syria, and Palestine; Cassander held on to Macedonia and Greece; Lysimachus took Thrace, Bithynia, and some provinces beyond the Hellespont and Bosphorus; and Seleucus Nicanor held Asia the Great and the rest of the territories."[18]

Terrible beast with iron teeth.
"After this I saw in the night visions, and behold a fourth beast, dreadful and terrible, and strong exceedingly; and it had great iron teeth: it devoured and brake in pieces, and stamped the residue with the feet of it..." (Dan 7:7a).

The fourth beast resembled no creature, but is only described as *"terrible and strong"* and *"had great iron teeth: it devoured and brake in pieces"*. Even *Matthew Henry* is unsure. "The learned are not agreed concerning this anonymous beast; some make it to be the Roman empire."[19] Its teeth, which were of iron, however, are a strong clue. Remember, the great image's legs which stood for Rome were also made of iron.

Rome succeeded Greece as the next preeminent empire in the ancient world. After annexing the Greek colony of Tarentum in southern Italy in 275 B.C., successive conquests during the 200s and 100s B.C. made Rome a mighty empire. At its peak in the A.D. 100s, Rome's domain covered about half of Europe, much of the Middle East and the north coast of Africa. *The Wycliffe Bible Commentary* affirms that the fourth beast was Rome. "As in chapter 2, the fourth stage of empire is Roman."[20]

"Diverse" from the others. *"The fourth beast shall be the fourth kingdom upon earth, which shall be diverse from all kingdoms, and shall devour the whole earth, and shall tread it down, and break it in pieces"* (Dan 7:23).

Rome was indeed "diverse" or different from the other powers that preceded it. Whereas most ancient empires were ruled by kings, Rome was a republic under two consuls elected to rule jointly every year by the Roman Senate. (Rome did not have its first emperor until August Caesar, who became absolute ruler in 27 B.C.)

Ten horns. *"...and it had ten horns."* (Dan 7:7b). In prophecy, "beasts" mean empires, while "horns" signify subordinate kingdoms. *"And the ten horns out of this kingdom are ten kings that shall arise..."* (Dan 7:24a). History helps to identify these ten kingdoms.

After the fall of the Western Roman Empire in 476 A.D., "The historian Machiavelli, without the slightest reference to this prophecy, gives the following list of the nations which occupied the territory of the Western Empire at the time of the fall of Romulus Augustus, the last emperor of Rome: the Lombards, the Franks, the Burgundians, the Ostrogoths, the Visigoths, the Vandals, the Heruli, the Suevi, the Huns, and the Saxons: ten in all."[21] (Some commentators name the Alamanni or Germans instead of the Huns.)

Another "little horn".

Like the he-goat in Daniel 8, the terrible beast with great iron teeth also grew an additional, little horn. *"I considered the horns, and, behold, there came up among them another little horn, before whom there were three of the first horns plucked up by the roots: and, behold, in this horn were eyes like the eyes of man, and a mouth speaking great things."* (Dan 7:8). (This "little horn" actually was the eleventh horn of the beast with great iron teeth.)

Do this little horn and the little horn of the he-goat represent the same thing? Let us take a closer look. The little horn that grew out of one of the four horns of the he-goat was Rome. On the other hand, the terrible beast with iron teeth was Rome itself. So, this other little horn was an eleventh kingdom or king that would arise within the Roman Empire – in addition to the first ten kingdoms.

A religious power?

"And of the ten horns that were in his head, and of the other which came up, and before whom three fell; even of that horn that had eyes, and a mouth that spake very great things, whose look was more stout than his fellows. I beheld, and the same horn made war with the saints, and prevailed against them; Until the Ancient of days came, and judgment was given to the saints of the most High; and the time came that the saints possessed the kingdom" (Dan 7:20-22).

The "little horn" or eleventh king would fight and defeat faithful believers (*"made war with the saints, and prevailed against them"*). This suggests warfare with religious undertones. It seems that the "little horn" would have deep-seated religious beliefs contrary to those of the saints. These would lead it to seek the destruction of the saints. In view of this, we are inclined to conclude that the little horn would be a ruler or a kingdom that is deeply religious in nature. The lines *"Until the Ancient of days came, and... the saints possessed the kingdom"* are very telling. The little horn would fight and oppress faithful believers for a long time – from its emergence during the time of the ancient Roman Empire (the terrible beast with great iron teeth) until God comes to establish His kingdom on earth and the saints take over it. It will be in power until the time of the end!

Most powerful force. It thus follows that the little horn (and its descendants) has been in existence for thousands of years now up to our present time. Most of us probably know that "little horn"; we simply never realized that he is the little horn in prophecy!

Who or what could this religious power be? The *World Book Encyclopedia* gives us a good lead: "The Middle Ages was a period in western Europe that began with the fall of the West Roman Empire and lasted through the 1400's. The strong governments established by the Romans disappeared during this period. They were replaced by many small kingdoms and states. The Roman Catholic Church became the most powerful force on the continent, not only in religious matters, but also in politics, learning, and the arts."[22]

Is the little horn or religious power that we are discussing the Roman Catholic Church? Can you think of any other entity, religious or at least somehow similarly oriented, which arose in the time and domain of the ancient Roman Empire and continues to exercise power and influence until this very day?

Eyes and mouth of a man. It was twice mentioned that the little horn has eyes (*"like the eyes of man"*) and a mouth that speaks, as though to stress the idea that it is also a man. Hence, the "little horn" must be a kingdom and also its ruler. So, if the "little horn" is actually the Roman Catholic Church, who is its ruler?

In the early Christian Church, the bishop of Rome was regarded as supreme bishop, later called "pope" (Latin *papa*, "father") – although Christ had said, *"And call no man your father upon the earth: for one is your Father, which is in heaven"* (Matt 23:9).

The Papacy? In A.D. 330, Emperor Constantine transferred the capital of the Roman Empire from Latin-speaking Rome in the west to Greek-speaking Byzantium in the east (renamed Constantinople in his honor; today Istanbul, Turkey). The Pope, left in the seat of the Caesars, came to be regarded as the greatest man in the West. In the last 1,500 years or so, the office of the Pope has been referred to as the Papacy.

War with the saints. Why would the Papacy wage war against the saints, faithful believers and adherents of the same religion it heads? It is hard to imagine that the Roman Catholic Church would fight with some of its own members; but historians have recorded that those who disobeyed the tenets promulgated by the Papacy were indeed persecuted. Here are a few excerpts from recorded history.

A Roman Catholic writer in *The Western Watchmen* admitted – "The church has persecuted. Only a tyro in church history will deny that… one hundred and fifty years after Constantine, the Donatists were persecuted and sometimes put to death… Protestants were persecuted in France and Spain with the full approval of the church authorities… When she thinks it good to use physical force, she will use it."[23]

Author T.R. Birks wrote in *The First Two Visions of Daniel* (1845) that "persecutions were carried on, from the eleventh and twelfth centuries almost to the present day, which stand out on the pages of history. After the signal of open martyrdom had been given in the canons of Orleans, there followed the extirpation of the Albigenses under the form of a crusade, the establishment of the Inquisition, the cruel attempts to extinguish the Waldenses, the martyrdom of the Lollards, the cruel wars to exterminate the Bohemians, the burning of Huss and Jerome, and multitudes of other confessors… the extinction by fire and sword of the Reformation in Spain and Italy, by fraud and open persecution in Poland, and the massacre of Bartholomew… besides the slow and secret murders of the holy tribunal of the Inquisition."[24]

We also learn that "(t)he number of the victims of the Inquisition in Spain, is given in *'The History of the Inquisition in Spain,;* by Llorente, (formerly secretary of the Inquisition), pgs. 206-208. This authority acknowledged that more than 300,000 suffered persecution in Spain alone, of whom 31,912 died in the flames. Millions more were slain for their faith throughout Europe."[25]

We further read in an order issued by the Papacy at the Council of Toulouse: "The lords of the districts shall carefully seek out the heretics in dwellings, hovels, and forests, and even their underground retreats shall be entirely wiped out."[26]

Papal admission and apology. Even though previous popes had made allusions to persecutions committed by the papacy, reigning Pope Francis (2013-), after making a broad admission, asked for forgiveness. On January 25, 2016, he concluded an annual weeklong prayer for Christian unity by making a sweeping apology for Catholic wrongs committed against other Christians and by announcing that he would visit Sweden to mark the 500th anniversary of the start of the Protestant Reformation.

Francis was following in the footsteps of his predecessors who encouraged efforts to heal the rifts with Anglicans, Lutherans, Orthodox, evangelicals and other Christian denominations. In his homily, he asked forgiveness for the "sin of our divisions" – an appeal he made in June 2015 during a visit to a small evangelical house of worship in northern Italy. "As the bishop of Rome and pastor of the Catholic Church, I would like to invoke mercy and forgiveness for the non-evangelical behavior of Catholics toward Christians of other churches," Francis said. "We cannot cancel what has happened, but we don't want to let the weight of past harm continue to pollute our relations."[27]

Different from other kings.
Like Rome, this "little horn" would also be different from the "horns" or kings that preceded it. *"And the ten horns out of this kingdom are ten kings that shall arise: and another shall rise after them; and he shall be diverse from the first..."* (Dan 7:24a).

Whereas the first ten kings ruled over secular kingdoms that were formed and held together by tribal or national loyalties, the eleventh king would rule over a religious kingdom of various nationalities held together by a common belief in a particular set of spiritual doctrines. (Christianity is the religion with the largest number of followers – approximately one-third of the world population, with Roman Catholics comprising nearly 60%.)

Subdued three kings.
The little horn or eleventh king would destroy three of the first ten kings and their kingdoms: *"...another little horn, before whom there were three of the first horns plucked up by the roots..."* (Dan 7:8b); *"...and he shall subdue three kings"* (Dan 7:24b).

Of the ten kingdoms recorded to be in existence after the fall of the Western Roman Empire in 476, seven are still extant today: those of the Saxons (Britain), Visigoths (Spain), Suevi (Portugal), Franks (France), Alamanni (Germany), Burgundians (Switzerland), and Lombards (Italy). Three kingdoms disappeared from the late 5th to the early 6th centuries. These were, as "Elliott summarizes: 'I might cite *three* that were eradicated from before the pope out of the list first given, viz., the *Heruli* under Odoacer, the *Vandals*, and the *Ostrogoths*.'"[28] Author Uriah Smith listed the years of their respective demise. "From the historical testimony above cited, we think it clearly established that the three horns plucked up were the powers named: the Heruli, A.D. 493, the Vandals, in 534, and the Ostrogoths finally in 553..."[29]

The Heruli were defeated and dispersed by the Lombards; the Vandals were vanquished by the Byzantine general Belisarius; and the Ostrogoths were also overthrown by the Byzantine (East Roman) Empire. What did the Papacy have to do with those events? It must be explained that the Herulian, Vandal, and Ostrogoth kings were all Arians, followers of Arius (256-336), a priest of Alexandria, Egypt, who challenged the Church doctrines of the Holy Trinity and divinity of Christ. As Arians, the three kings were considered heretics by the Papacy, which actively supported their destruction in the hands of forces under its influence.

Speaking against God.
The little horn would utter grandiose things against the Creator. *"And he shall speak great words against the most High, and shall wear out the saints of the most High..."* (Dan 7:25a). The line sounds ludicrous – the head of the Church himself assailing God? However, it seems to have truly happened; with the Church outlawing the very "word of God" – the Bible.

The Bible forbidden. The Roman Catholic Church prohibited the possession of the Scriptures by its members. Jan Marcussen quotes in his book (*National Sunday Law*, 96th printing, 2007) that in the Council of Toulouse in 1229, the church leaders under the Pope ruled that – "We prohibit laymen possessing copies of the Old and New Testament... We forbid them most severely to have the above books in the popular vernacular."[30]

Moreover, D. Lortsch, author of *Histoire de la Bible en France* (1910), added – "The church Council of Tarragona ruled that: 'No one may possess the books of the Old and New Testaments in the Romance language, and if anyone possesses them he must turn them over to the local bishop within eight days after the promulgation of this decree, so that they may be burned.'"[31]

The Church policy against Bible owners persisted throughout the centuries. "After the Bible societies were formed they were classed with Communism in an amazing decree. On December 8, 1866, Pope Pius IX, in his encyclical *Quanta Cura* issued the following statement: 'Socialism, Communism, clandestine societies, Bible societies... pests of this sort must be destroyed by all means.'"[32]

Instead of using the Bible, the Church teaches its members and converts with the use of Catechism, a manual containing a summary of religious doctrine, often in the form of questions and answers. A Bible teacher notes, "Although the ten commandments are found in the Roman Catholic Versions of the Scriptures, yet the faithful are instructed from catechisms of the church, and not from the Bible."[33]

Changed times and laws.
The little horn would dare *"think to change times and laws..."* (Dan 7:25b). The Papacy would change the laws God has given in the Bible. The Catechism became the primary instrument of the Church in promoting the change of Biblical times and laws. We find in *Bible Readings for the Home* (1942): "As it appears (in these catechisms), the law of God has been changed and virtually re-enacted by the Papacy."[34]

A church decree, *Decretal, de Tranlatic Episcop*;, boastfully declares: "The Pope has power to change times, to abrogate laws, and to dispense with all things, even the precepts of Christ."[35]

Images in church. The second of the Ten Commandments warns against the making and worship of graven images (Ex 20:4-6). Yet, the Church has dispensed with it, although it probably began with good intentions. Religious researcher J. Mendham noted: "Images were first introduced into churches, not to be worshipped, but either in place of books to give instruction to those who could not read, or to excite devotion in the minds of others... but it was found that images brought into churches darkened rather than enlightened the minds of the ignorant – degraded rather than exalted the devotion of the worshiper."[36]

The Church later institutionalized the veneration of images. "The second Council of Nicea, A.D. 787, was called to establish image worship in the church. This council is recorded in *Ecclesiastical Annals*, by Baronius, Vol. 9, pp. 391-407. (Antwerp, 1612); and Charles J. Hefele, *A History of the Councils of the Church from the Original Documents*, book 18, chapter 1, secs. 332, 333; chapter 2, secs. 345-352 (T. and T. Clark ed., 1896), Vol. 5, pp. 260-304, and 342-372."[37]

As time went by, the error, instead of being corrected, was made worse by attempts to justify it through omission. *Bible Readings for the Home* (1942) related: "The second commandment, which forbids the making of, and bowing down to images, is omitted in Catholic catechisms..."[38]

Seventh-day Sabbath changed. The fourth commandment reminded men to keep the Sabbath holy by resting on the seventh day of the week, Saturday (Ex 20:8-11). But it, too, was changed. To unite the two largest groups of people in the Roman Empire – sun-worshippers, who regarded Sun-day as holy, and Christians, who venerated Sunday as the Resurrection day – Emperor Constantine in 321 A.D. decreed: "Let all the judges and town people, and the occupation of all trades rest on the venerable day of the sun."[39]

The bishop of Rome and other Church leaders agreed for the following reasons: (1) it would separate Christians from the hated Jews, and (2) it would become easier for pagans to come into the Church. Subsequently, Pope Sylvester (314-335) declared Sunday as the "Lord's Day". In 364, the Council of Laodicea transferred the solemnity of the Sabbath from Saturday to Sunday."[40]

A Catholic catechism teaches: "Question – Have you any other way of proving that the church (Roman Catholic) has power to institute festivals of precept? Answer – Had she not such power, she could not have done that in which all modern religionists agree with her – she could not have substituted the observance of Sunday, the first day of the week, for the observance of Saturday, the seventh day, a change for which there is no scriptural authority."[41]

Father Enright, a Roman Catholic priest, wrote: "The Bible says, 'Remember that thou keep holy the Sabbath day.' The Catholic Church says, No! By my divine power I abolish the Sabbath day, and command you to keep the first day of the week. And lo, the entire civilized world bows down in reverent obedience to the command of the holy Catholic Church!"[42]

Biblical feast days changed. Through Moses, God commanded the Israelites to observe other holy days which foreshadowed the life and mission of the Messiah (Col 2:16-17). *"The LORD said to Moses, 'Speak to the Israelites and say to them: "These are my appointed feasts, the appointed feasts of the LORD, which you are to proclaim as sacred assemblies"* (Lev 23:1-2 ff., NIV). The Papacy has changed them as well.

Passover to Good Friday. *"In the fourteenth day of the first month at even is the LORD's Passover"* (Lev 23:5). The feast, which centered on the killing of a sacrificial lamb, was a prophecy of the sacrificial death of the Lamb of God, Christ, who was crucified exactly on the 14th day, just before the evening of the Passover.

The Catholic Church has replaced Passover on the 14th day of the first month (which begins on the evening of the first new moon after the spring equinox) with Good Friday – to keep the yearly observance always on a Friday. However, Good Friday hardly ever coincides any longer with Passover, and the prophetic significance of the crucifixion has thus been lost – that is, *"Christ (is) our Passover"* (1 Cor 5:7).

Feast of Firstfruits to Easter. *"When ye be come into the land which I give unto you, and shall reap the harvest thereof, then ye shall bring a sheaf of the firstfruits of your harvest unto the priest: And he shall wave the sheaf before the LORD, to be accepted for you: on the morrow after the sabbath the priest shall wave it"* (Lev 23:10b-11). Another prophetic holy day, the feast foreshadowed Christ as the "firstfruits" of the resurrection (1 Cor 15:20). It has been replaced with Easter Sunday (named after the pagan goddess Ishtar, Astarte, or Ashtoreth), replete with the pagan fertility traditions of Easter eggs and bunnies. The Feast of Firstfruits fulfilled the prophecy of the resurrection of Christ (1 Cor 15:20,23), but Easter hardly ever falls on the true Biblical day anymore.

Feast of Tabernacles to Christmas. *"The fifteenth day of this seventh month shall be the feast of tabernacles for seven days unto the LORD"* (Lev 23:34). There are Biblical indications that Christ was born during this week-long autumn festival in late September or early October. This is also hinted at in John 1:14 (*"And the Word was made flesh, and dwelt [tabernacled] among us..."*). A factual account can be gleaned from the story of the priest Zacharias and the birth of his son John the Baptist (Christ's cousin, who was six months older) in Luke 1:5-42 (with 1 Chron 24:1-19).

December 25, popularly known today as Christmas, was in the Julian calendar the day after the winter solstice, celebrated as the "Birth of the Invincible Sun" (*Natalis Invicti*) by worshippers of the sun-god Mithras. There could have been no *"shepherds abiding in the field, keeping watch over their flock by night"* during winter in Judea (Luke 2:8); and *"there was no room for them in the inn"* (Luke 2:7) in view of the overcrowding of pilgrims in Jerusalem and even in Bethlehem during the Feast of Tabernacles in autumn.

God's law immutable. The Papacy changed what Christ said could not be altered even just one bit until the time of the end. *"For verily I say unto you, Till heaven and earth pass, one jot or one tittle shall in no wise pass from the law, till all be fulfilled"* (Matt 5:18).

"Three-and-a-half times" in power.

We are told in the Bible how long the little horn would wield power, albeit again in cryptic terms: *"...and they shall be given into his hand until a time and times and the dividing of time"* (Dan 7:25b). How long could this mysterious period be?

Fortunately, we need not grope in the dark. As we now know, Scripture has ways of explaining its mysteries to us. The last book of the Bible, with a nearly identical term, does the conversion for us. *"And to the woman were given two wings of a great eagle, that she might fly into the wilderness, into her place, where she is nourished for a time, and times, and half a time, from the face of the serpent"* (Rev 12:14). The archaic timeframe is actually the paraphrase of an earlier passage: Revelation 12:6. *"And the woman fled into the wilderness, where she hath a place prepared of God, that they should feed her there a thousand two hundred and threescore days."*

The two linked verses reveal that *"a time, and times, and half a time"* are equivalent to *"a thousand two hundred and threescore days"* (1,260 days). So, the similar timeframe *"a time and times and the dividing of time"* in Daniel 7:25c must also be equivalent to 1,260 days. But... there must be a mistake. The little horn, if it is indeed the Papacy, did not hold power for just 1,260 days.

"**A day for a year**". Again, the Bible provides an explanation. A "day" in prophecy is sometimes tantamount to one year, as in – *"After the number of the days in which ye searched the land, even forty days, each day for a year, shall ye bear your iniquities, even forty years..."* (Num 14:34a); as well as *"And when thou hast accomplished them, lie again on thy right side, and thou shalt bear the iniquity of the house of Judah forty days: I have appointed thee each day for a year"* (Ezek 4:6).

Hence, the 1,260 days can also mean 1,260 years – a very long period indeed. Did the little horn or Papacy really stay in power for exactly that number of years? Let us see.

1,260-year sovereignty. Beginning about 526, conditions in Italy became so violent that in 535 the Byzantine emperor Justinian I sent his general Belisarius to conquer the peninsula. Three years later, in 538, Belisarius defeated the Ostrogoths and secured Rome. Justinian gave the city to Pope Vigilius as "head of all the holy churches." The Papacy thus "inherited" the "seat of the Caesars".

More than 1,000 years later, during the "Age of Enlightenment" (1600s to late 1700s), philosophers and intellectuals placed reason and science above religion and blamed the Church for enslaving the human mind during the Dark and Middle Ages. With the outbreak of the French Revolution (1789-1799), all church properties in France were confiscated. In 1798, French General Louis Alexandre Berthier entered Rome, earlier declared a republic by Roman revolutionaries, and took Pope Pius VI prisoner to France. The pope died a year later, and Napoleon Bonaparte decreed that no election should be held to elect a new pope. It looked like the death of the Papacy.

From 538, when Belisarius secured Rome for the Pope, to 1798, when Berthier took Pius VI prisoner, leaving the Church without a head, was exactly 1,260 years – the prophesied period that the little horn or eleventh king would be in power!

Deadly wound healed. *"And I saw one of his heads as it were wounded to death; and his deadly wound was healed..."* (Rev 13:3a). In 1929, more than a hundred years after the pope's capture, the Italian government recognized Vatican City as an independent state. The *San Francisco Chronicle* published a news account of the document signing on its front page. It headlined the event with these words: "Mussolini and Gaspari Sign Historic Pact... Heal Wound of Many Years." The newspaper seemed to confirm the fulfillment of prophecy with almost exactly the same words!

The eight kings

The book of Revelation gives a summary of the end-time kings. *"And there are seven kings: five are fallen, and one is, and the other is not yet come; and when he cometh, he must continue a short space. And the beast that was, and is not, even he is the eighth, and is of the seven, and goeth into perdition. And the ten horns which thou sawest are ten kings, which have received no kingdom as yet; but receive power as kings one hour with the beast"* (Rev 17:10-12). Another mind-boggling conundrum. But we are not completely in the dark, the descriptions of some of the kings are telltale.

"One is".

Barnes' Notes explains: "[And one is] That is, there is one – a sixth – that now reigns. The proper interpretation of this would be, that this existed in the time of the writer; that is, according to the view taken of the time of the writing of the Apocalypse (see Intro., section 2), at the close of the first century."[43]

Rome. And *"one is"* therefore means that the sixth king was extant and ruling at that time that the apostle John wrote the book of Revelation in about A.D. 95. That was the Roman Empire.

Five fallen kings.

That *"five are fallen"* tells us that five kings or kingdoms which preceded Rome had already passed on to history in John's time. We are now familiar with the four ancient empires that held power one after another, culminating in Rome. Let us make a quick review.

Greece. Rome took over the hegemony of Greece (the "he-goat with a horn between its eyes") in the ancient world. Hence, the fifth of the five fallen kings was Greece.

Persia. Greece defeated Persia ("ram with two uneven horns") to become the dominant power in the then known world. Therefore, Persia was the fourth of the five fallen kings.

Babylon. Babylon had been overthrown by Persia. That makes Babylon the third fallen king . And, logically, an earlier king must have been toppled by Babylon. History tells us its name.

Assyria. "About 633 B.C. they (the Medes) began attacking Assyria, at first unsuccessfully; but Cyaxares the Mede having gained the Babylonians under Nabopolassar, the Assyrian viceroy of Babylon, as allies, about 625 B.C. besieged Nineveh… Zeph 2:13-15 shortly before the catastrophe foretold it; and Ezekiel (Ezek 31) shortly afterward about 586 B.C. attests how completely Assyria was overthrown…"[44] Additionally, "After

Esarhaddon, the Assyrian stranglehold on the ancient world began to give way... till 612 B.C., when Nineveh fell and Assyrian civilization was suddenly snuffed out... The neo-Babylonian Empire arose on the ruins of Assyria, and a new historical epoch dawned"[45] To sum up, "Rulership passed from Nineveh (Assyria) to Babylon in 612 B.C..."[46]

The kingdom which reigned supreme before Babylon was thus Assyria. That accounts for the second fallen king – just one more king to complete the list, the kingdom Assyria defeated.

Egypt. *New Unger's Bible Dictionary,* as usual, is very helpful. "Thutmose III (was) the great conqueror and builder, c. 1482-1450. This warrior conducted seventeen campaigns and extended the empire to its widest limits in Palestine, Syria, and the regions of the upper Euphrates and on the Nile up to the Fourth Cataract. At the battle of Megiddo, c. 1482 B.C., he defeated the Hittites.

"Around 680 B.C. Egypt became imperiled by the Assyrians. Esarhaddon conquered the Delta, and Taharka surrendered Lower Egypt. When the Assyrian army was withdrawn, Taharka once more became ruler of the whole country. Under Ashurbanipal the Assyrians made a new invasion (c. 667 B.C.). Ashurbanipal's second campaign eventuated in the sacking of Thebes (c. 663, Nah 3:8-10).

"Dynasty XXVI (c. 663-525) was founded by Psamtik (Psammetichus). It is sometimes called the Saite Dynasty, since the capital was at Sais in the Delta. He was a practical vassal of the Assyrians until about 650, when the Assyrians had to withdraw their occupational forces because of a Babylonian revolt."[47]

So, the ancient power that Assyria dethroned was Egypt. That completes our list of the first six empires of the ancient world: (1) Egypt, (2) Assyria, (3) Babylon, (4) Persia, (5) Greece, and (6) Rome.

You might ask, what do these ancient empires have to do with the end-times? The answer is, they are the keys to the identities of the world empires at the time of the end. You will see soon enough.

The seventh king.

King No. 7 was still future in John's time. "*...and the other is not yet come; and when he cometh, he must continue a short space*" (Rev 17:10b).

Obviously, the seventh king would come after the fall of the Roman Empire, the sixth king. Which Roman Empire? The Roman Empire broke up into two after the death of Emperor Theodosius in 395 A.D. – with one division in the west and the other in the east. The Western Roman Empire collapsed in 476, when rebellious Germanic troops led by Odoacer bloodlessly overthrew the last emperor in Rome, Romulus Augustulus. The Byzantine or East Roman Empire fell almost a thousand years later when the Turks conquered Constantinople in 1453.

The seventh king, therefore, must appear, or might have already appeared, after that. Who could he be? To answer that, we must remember that the first six kings had all oppressed Israel, God's chosen people. So, the seventh king would probably be similarly minded.

The eighth king.

"And the beast that was, and is not, even he is the eighth, and is of the seven, and goeth into perdition. And the ten horns which thou sawest are ten kings, which have received no kingdom as yet; but receive power as kings one hour with the beast" (Rev 17:10-12).

The eighth king is the end-time beast or empire. He will be from the first seven empires or, perhaps, a composite made up of elements from several or all of the first seven empires.

Ten horns. The ten horns of the beast probably correspond to the great image's two feet and ten toes of mixed iron and clay. They seem to be ten end-time kingdoms which will become vassal-states of the very last empire – the eighth king.

We will identify them all in succeeding chapters. In the meantime, for easy review, on the next page is a table enumerating the eight kings or kingdoms alongside their prophetic descriptions.

End-Time Kings and Beasts

The Great Image	The Ram and the He-goat	The Four Great Beasts	The Eight Kings
Daniel 2	Daniel 8	Daniel 7	Revelation 17
			1. Egypt
			2. Assyria
Head of gold		Lion with eagle's wings	3. Babylon
Breast and 2 arms of silver	Ram with 2 uneven horns	Bear with 3 ribs in mouth	4. Persia (w/ Media; conquered Lydia, Babylon, and Egypt)
Belly and 2 thighs of brass	He-goat; horn between eyes	Leopard with 4 wings	5. Greece (Alexander king of Macedonia)
	Horn broken, 4 horns grow out	and 4 heads	(Alexander died; 4 generals split empire)
2 legs of iron	Little horn grows from 1 of 4 horns	Terrible beast with iron teeth	6. Rome (arose from Greek empire; split into west and east)
		and 10 horns	(10 nations in the Roman Empire)
		11th/little horn sprouted, uprooted 3 horns	(Papacy; destroyed 3 nations/kingdoms)
			7. (penultimate, short-lived kingdom)
2 feet, 10 toes of iron & clay			8. (10 horns of beast; vassals of last empire)

4

Two Women and Their Daughters

As is the mother, so is her daughter.

- Ezekiel 16:44b

Prophecy makes quantum leaps from ancient times to the modern era in the blink of an eye. The prophetic events we will discuss in this chapter are of this sort – beginning thousands of years ago and moving on to our modern-day era on the eve of the end of the age.

"Woman clothed with the sun"

John saw a wondrous vision in the sky. *"And there appeared a great wonder in heaven; a woman clothed with the sun, and the moon under her feet, and upon her head a crown of twelve stars"* (Rev 12:1). Some churches teach that the woman is the Virgin Mary. Others say she is the Church. But that is jumping to conclusions without a leg to stand on. Let us again make use of the principle that the Bible interprets itself.

Woman. A "woman" in prophecy symbolizes a faith, church, or religion. Thus, the faith that began with Abraham is the "daughter of Zion" or "daughter of Jerusalem" (Jer 6:2; Isa 62:11; Zech 9:9); the Church is the "bride of Christ" (Rev 21:2,9); the body of saintly Christians is a "chaste virgin" (2 Cor 11:2). On the other hand, a sinful church is called a "whore" or "harlot" (Rev 17:1,5,16; 19:2).

Sun. The *"sun"*, as in Malachi 4:2 (*"the sun of righteousness"*) and Matthew 13:43 (*"Then shall the righteous shine forth as the sun in the* *kingdom of their Father"*), connotes righteousness – the holy and upright living of faithful followers in obedience to God's will.

Moon. The moon was the symbol of the "queen of heaven" (Jer 7:18,44:17), a pagan deity. *Fausset's Bible Dictionary* states: "The moon was worshipped as Isis in Egypt; as Karnaim, 'two horns,' of Ashtoreth, wife of Baal the king of heaven..."[1] The practice had been adopted in Israel. *"And they forsook the LORD, and served Baal and Ashtaroth"* (Judg 2:13). In short, the moon signifies idolatry (Jer 8:2).

Twelve stars. In Joseph's dream (Gen 37:9-10), eleven "stars" stood for his eleven brothers, who, together with him, fathered the twelve tribes of Israel. The twelve stars, therefore, represent the nation of Israel.

To sum up, the *"woman"* symbolizes the faith or religion of Israel which began with the covenant between God and Abraham. It is a righteous religion, being *"clothed with the sun"*; the *"the moon under her feet"* betokening the superiority of the Abrahamic faith over idolatry.

Dragon with seven heads.

An antagonist enters the scene. *"And there appeared another wonder in heaven; and behold a great red dragon, having seven heads and ten horns, and seven crowns upon his heads"* (Rev 12:3). We do not have to puzzle too long over its identity, because six verses later Revelation 12:9a positively identifies the dragon for us. *"And the great dragon was cast out, that old serpent, called the Devil, and Satan, which deceiveth the whole world...* (cf. Rev 20:2). With many aliases, Lucifer (Latin, "light-bearing"/Hebrew, *heylel*/"brightness", Isa 14:12) is also called dragon; he was the serpent in the Garden of Eden (Gen 3); he is the devil ("accuser"/Greek *diabolos*, Rev 12:10), who accuses the brethren before God day and night; and he is Satan ("adversary"/Hebrew *satan*), who persecuted Job without cause (Job 1-2). Moreover, the "dragon" appears to also symbolize an empire.

Seven heads. The dragon has seven heads. The mystery is unveiled for us five chapters later in Revelation 17:9a: *"And here is the mind which hath wisdom. The seven heads are seven mountains..."*

The Greek word translated "mountains" is *oree* (sing. *oros*), which, according to *The New Unger's Bible Dictionary*, "is sometimes rendered 'hill' and sometimes 'mountain' (cf. Matt 5:1 to 5:14; Luke 4:29 to 9:37; etc.)."[2] Have you heard of a world-famous city known as the "City of Seven Hills"? Yes? You are correct if you said, "Rome."

Now, if Rome is symbolized by the seven heads of the dragon (Satan), then Rome must the "head" or capital of the devil. (Incidentally, Rome is often used synonymously for "Vatican".)

Satan's residence? A *The Telegraph* news item was headlined "Chief exorcist says Devil is in Vatican" (June 16, 2016). "The Devil is lurking in the very heart of the Roman Catholic Church, the Vatican's chief exorcist claimed on Wednesday." He is Father Gabriele Amorth, long-time president of the International Association of Exorcists (IAE).

"The Devil resides in the Vatican and you can see the consequences,' said Father Amorth, 85, who has been the Holy See's chief exorcist for 25 years. The evil influence of Satan was evident in the highest ranks of the Catholic hierarchy, with 'cardinals who do not believe in Jesus and bishops who are linked to the demon,' Father Amorth said.

"The attempted assassination of Pope John Paul II by a Turkish gunman in 1981 and recent revelations of 'violence and paedophilia' committed by Catholic priests against children in their care was also the work of the Devil, said Father Amorth, who has written a book about his vocation, *Memoirs of an Exorcist*, which was published recently."[3]

Ten horns. The dragon has ten horns, just like the terrible beast with great iron teeth that we have identified in Daniel 7 as the ancient Roman Empire. Is there a connection?

Both the dragon and the beast personify Rome. The ten horns were the ten kingdoms in the Roman Empire. The seven crowns signify the seven kingdoms that would survive after three of the ten kingdoms would have been "uprooted" (destroyed) by the little horn or eleventh king (Papacy), as we have seen in the preceding chapter.

Advent of the Messiah.

The dragon, representing both Rome and the devil, was waiting for the woman clothed with the sun (religion of Israel) to give birth: "*…and the dragon stood before the woman which was ready to be delivered, for to devour her child as soon as it was born*" (Rev 12:4b). The dragon was keenly watching for the prophesied Messiah to be born with the intention of ("devouring") killing it immediately after birth.

"*And she brought forth a man child, who was to rule all nations with a rod of iron: and her child was caught up unto God, and to his throne*" (Rev 12:5). The "woman" gave birth to the Jewish Messiah. Satan then used Herod, the Idumean king of Judea appointed by Rome, to order the massacre of innocent children in the hope of killing the Christ-child. They failed. Yet, Satan later succeeded in getting the Jews and the Romans to crucify the grownup Christ. However, after the crucifixion and the resurrection, Christ ascended to heaven to take His place at the right hand of the Father ("*caught up unto God, and to his throne*").

Usurper in heaven. The devil did not accept his failure on earth to thwart the Almighty Father's plan. He attempted to take the Messiah's place on the right hand of God. The veiled prophecy in Zechariah 3:1 reads: *"And he shewed me Joshua the high priest standing before the angel of the LORD, and Satan standing at his right hand to resist him."*

Joshua personifies Christ. (The names "Joshua" and "Jesus" both came from the same ancient, original Hebrew name – "Yahushua". See Appendix "K".) The "angel of the LORD" was the visible manifestation of the invisible God (Col 1:15a), whose form no man has ever seen (John 1:18a; 5:37b) or can see (1 Tim 6:16). The devil had raced ahead and positioned himself at the right hand of the angel representing God before Christ arrived (to be high priest in heaven – Heb 4:14).

Zechariah 3:3-4 continues: *"Now Joshua was clothed with filthy garments, and stood before the angel. And he answered and spake unto those that stood before him, saying, Take away the filthy garments from him. And unto him he said, Behold, I have caused thine iniquity to pass from thee, and I will clothe thee with change of raiment."* The *"filthy garments"* symbolize the sins of mankind that Christ had taken upon Himself; the *"change of raiment"* means He was made spotless or sinless once again in the sight of God.

Satan's attempt to usurp the place of Christ at the right hand of God precipitated hostilities in the celestial realms. *"And there was war in heaven: Michael and his angels fought against the dragon; and the dragon fought and his angels, And prevailed not; neither was their place found any more in heaven. And the great dragon was cast out, that old serpent, called the Devil, and Satan, which deceiveth the whole world: he was cast out into the earth, and his angels were cast out with him"* (Rev 12:7-9). Satan and his minions lost, and were expelled from heaven.

The "woman" persecuted.

"And when the dragon saw that he was cast unto the earth, he persecuted the woman which brought forth the man child" (Rev 12:13). Frustrated, Satan vented his wrath on the "woman" – the Jews and their religion. (The Jewish religion, which uses the Hebrew Scriptures only, is known as Judaism. Christianity, which began with Christ, the Jewish Messiah, uses both the Old [Hebrew] and New [Greek] Testaments, and is thus sometimes called the Judeo-Christian faith.)

Through Rome, the devil destroyed Jerusalem and the Holy Temple in 70 A.D. at the defeat of a Jewish revolt and ultimately drove the Jews into worldwide dispersion in 135 A.D. when the last Jewish uprising was crushed. To erase the memory of the Jews, Emperor Hadrian ordered

Jerusalem plowed with salt, forbade Jews to return, then renamed Jerusalem "Aelia Capitolina" (after his clan name Aelius) and Judea, "Syria Palaestina" (after the Philistines who had vanished after 500 BC).

Anti-Semitic persecutions. After the Jews' dispersion (*diaspora*) from Judea, their persecution continued in the various countries they escaped to. The oppressive actions taken against them were at first moderate, but grew worse through the centuries. Some major instances:

In A.D. 300, the Council of Elvire in Spain prohibited social contact with Jews. Twenty-five years later, the Council of Nicea prohibited Jews from making converts and intermarrying with Christians. The Justinian Code of 527 laid the groundwork for anti-Semitism as a permanent Christian state policy. In 624-628, Muhammad expelled or killed Jews in Medina (Arabia), beheading and mutilating thousands.

The mass expulsion of Jews from European countries also began in 628 in the Christian kingdom of the Franks. In 1010 and 1012: Jews were expelled from Limoges, France, and Mainz, Germany. In 1066, they were massacred in Granada, Spain.

After Pope Urban II called for the first Crusade in 1096, Crusaders on the way to the Holy Land massacred Jews in England, France, Germany, Austria and all across Europe, shouting "Christ-killers, embrace the cross or die!" Later, the slaughter became more systematic. The first pogrom (organized massacre) of the Jews took place in 1113 in Kiev, Russia.

False charges, oppressive laws. The Papacy countenanced the anti-Semitic persecutions. A rumor called "blood libel" first circulated in Norwich, England, in 1144 – accusing Jews of murdering Christian children at Passover to use their blood for *matzot* (unleavened bread). During the Second Crusade: (1147-1149), hundreds of Jews suspected of blood libel were murdered in Troyes, France; Bohemia; Halle, Germany; Carinthia, Austria. In 1171, the Jews first formally accused of blood libel in Blois, France, were burned alive *en masse*.

In 1198, Pope Innocent III ordered all Jews in his realm imprisoned. At the Fourth Lateran Council of 1215, he decreed that all Jews should wear a badge or hat for identification. In the 13th-14th centuries, 40 Church councils in Western and Central Europe adopted the decree.

In 1243, Jews were accused of "desecration of the host" – piercing the communion wafer to draw blood from the body of Christ. In 1298, six months after the Jews were accused of the crime in Gottingen, mobs destroyed 146 Jewish communities in Germany and Austria – killing over 100,000 Jews. Earlier, in 1266 the Church Council of Breslau (Wroclaw), Poland, had set up one of the first ghettos (quarters Jews were forced to live in, segregated from Christians).

As the Black Death plagued Europe, another unfounded rumor in 1348 accused Jews of poisoning wells. Mobs destroyed over 350 Jewish communities from the Mediterranean Sea to Germany, Spain, Portugal and Switzerland.

In 1492, King Ferdinand and Queen Isabella of Spain issued the infamous Edict of Expulsion of the Jews from Castile and Aragon. More than 100,000 Jews sought refuge in Portugal, but were forced into baptism, sold into slavery, or killed.

In 1555, Pope Paul IV issued a bull that Jews in Papal States could not own land and should be segregated in quarters or streets with only one gate. In 1750, Frederick II of Prussia issued a law prohibiting Jews to marry (to reduce their number). In 1775, Pope Pius VI issued an edict forbidding Jews to ride in carriages and erect tombstones on their graves.

In 1878, Romania issued 200 discriminatory laws keeping Jews out of various trades and restricting them in ghettos; 125,000 Jews left to avoid starvation. In 1884-1893, in fear of pogrom-like laws, 700,000 Jews fled Russia and Poland; 600,000 more followed within 15 years.

In 1921, with the blessings of the Pope and sanction of King Carol, anti-Semitism became a legal and patriotic movement in Romania. Jews were beaten up in the streets, killed at work or at home, their houses burned, and synagogues desecrated. For the sake of brevity, we will just summarize these and many other major expulsions and massacres that the Jews went through across the centuries, listed below:

Anti-Semitic Persecutions[4]
(Middle Ages to the Twentieth Century)

Expulsions, etc:
628: Kingdom of the Franks
1010: Limoges, France
1012: Mainz, Germany
1182: France, ordered by Philip II
1198: Pope Innocent III ordered all Jews imprisoned
1306, 1322: France
1367: Hungary
1394: France
1420: Mainz, Germany, Lyon, France
1421: Austria
1453: Wroclaw, Poland
1483: Warsaw, Poland

Massacres:
624-628: Medina, Arabia (Jews beheaded, mutilated)
1066: Granada, Spain
1096: England, France, Germany Austria, Europe (First Crusade)
1113: Kiev, Russia (first pogrom)
1147-1149: Troyes, France; Bohemia; Halle, Germany; Carinthia, Austria (Second Crusade; hundreds of Jews suspected of "blood libel" murdered)
1171: Blois, France (Jews first formally accused of blood libel)

Two Women and Their Daughters | 71

Expulsions, etc:
1492: King Ferdinand and Queen Isabella expelled all Jews (over 100,000) in Castile and Aragon
1495: Lithuania (instigated by the Shlakhta, business rivals of the Jews and allies of the Church)
1496: Portugal (ordered by King Emanuel on the insistence of other Catholic monarchs)
1499: Nuremberg, Germany
1510: Brandenburg, Germany
1519: Regensburg, Germany
1541: Naples, Prague, and some Austrian cities
1550: Genoa, Italy
1551: Bavaria, Germany
1567: Republic of Genoa
1569: Papal States
1597: Milan, Italy
1615: Worms, Germany
1622: Switzerland (no Jews left after expulsions in the 15th and 16th centuries)
1649: Hamburg, Germany
1670: Vienna, upper and lower Austria (ordered by Emperor Ferdinand III)
1712: Sandomierz, Poland (Jews accused of blood libel)
1727: Russia (ordered by Tsarina Catherine)
1744-1753: Russia (35,000 Jews ordered expelled by Tsarina Elizabeth Petrovna)
1745: Prague (ordered by Empress Maria Theresa)
1878: Romania (125,000 Jews left after being prohibited from trades and restricted to ghettos)

Massacres:
1189-1192: York, England (Third Crusade)
1298: Gottingen, Germany, and Austria (100,000 Jews accused of desecrating the host killed)
1389: Prague (3,000 ghetto residents murdered)
1391: Seville, Spain (tens of thousands of Jews killed)
1407: Krakow, Poland (Jews accused of blood libel killed)
1411: Castile, Spain (thousands of Jews killed at the start of the Inquisition in Spain)
1435: Majorca, Baleares Islands, Spain
1453: Wroclaw, Poland
1473: Cordoba, Spain
1474: Segovia, Spain
1506: Lisbon, Portugal
1556: Ancona, Italy
1648: Ukraine and Galacia (Cossack rebels, aided by Tartars, destroyed 300 Jewish communities; killed 200,000-400,000 Jews, about half of the Jewish population)
1650: Lithuania (Jews massacred by Russian soldiers)
1655-1656: Poland (Jews killed in 700 Jewish communities)
1664: Lemberg (Lvov), Russia
1680: Brest-Litovsk, capital of Polesie province in Poland
1682: Krakow, Poland
1720: Jerusalem (Azkenazi Jewish community destroyed)
1768: Haidamak, Poland
1824: Odessa, Russia (first government-approved pogrom)

Expulsions, etc:
1884-1893: Russia and Poland (700,000 Jews fled from pogrom-like laws; 600,000 more followed within the next 15 years)
1885: Germany (Jewish-Russian refugees expelled)
1891: Russia (most of 35,000 Jews expelled)
1910: Kiev, Russia (Jews expelled)

Massacres:
1881: Elizavetgrad, Russia (pogroms; spread to Kiev, Odessa, Volhynia, Podolia, Chernigov, and Poltava)
1903: Kishinev, Russia (pogrom)
1905: Russia (pogroms)
1918: Hungary, Poland, and the Ukraine (pogroms)
1929: Jerusalem (Arab riots)
1941-1945: Nazi Holocaust (some 6 million Jews exterminated)

Flight of the woman.

"And to the woman were given two wings of a great eagle, that she might fly into the wilderness, into her place, where she is nourished for a time, and times, and half a time, from the face of the serpent" (Rev 12:14). Let us decipher the metaphors in this puzzling passage.

"Great eagle". The eagle has long been used a symbol of power in the flags, seals, and coats of arms of many nations. The Persians under Cyrus had a golden eagle on a spear as their standard (Isa 46:11). The eagle is represented in Assyrian sculptures as an icon accompanying their armies; Nisroch, their god, had an eagle's head. The Romans had an eagle in their standard, to which the swiftness of their conquests was compared (Deut 28:49).[5]

In modern times, some nations that still use the eagle as an emblem are Albania, Austria, Germany, Mexico, Russia, the United States. Since the "wings of the great eagle" enabled the "woman" to escape, a nation symbolized by an eagle is very likely that helper of the Jews.

From the nations mentioned, the most help came from the United States, whose national seal depicts a great eagle with outspread wings.

"Wilderness". The word means a sparsely populated place. It was in this condition that the European explorers found the Americas when they first came to the New World. So, was it Mexico in Central America or the U. S. in North America? Between the two, "wilderness" is probably more descriptive of the U.S. in the 15th-16th centuries.

Did the U.S. ("eagle") really help save the "woman" (religion of the Jews)? During World War II, many thousands of Jews escaped death when they fled from Nazi-occupied areas to places of refuge in other countries, foremost among them the United States, where their lives and their faith were preserved and nurtured (*"nourished"*).

The *Encyclopaedia Britannica* has on record that as the persecution of the Jews intensified prior to the Holocaust, "(a)round 102,000 Jewish refugees escaping Nazi Germany were admitted into the United States before the outbreak of World War II."[6]

Hitler launched the systematic genocide of the Jews and other people he considered racially inferior or undesirable in early 1941. They were rounded up and imprisoned in death camps in Eastern Europe, where they were killed or died from starvation and disease.

War Refugee Board. When the Holocaust became apparent during the war, on January 22, 1944, U.S. President Franklin D. Roosevelt established the War Refugee Board (WRB), an agency charged with taking all measures within its power to rescue victims of the Nazis – mainly Jews – from death in German-occupied Europe.

According to the *Encarta Encyclopedia*, "The WRB financed the rescue operations of Raoul Wallenberg, a Swedish businessman and diplomat in Budapest, Hungary, who helped save about 100,000 Hungarian Jews from being killed by the Nazis…"[7]

Despite these, some 11 million victims, including about 6 million Jewish men, women, and children (two-thirds of all the Jews in Europe) lost their lives in the Holocaust. Needless to say, Jews who believed in Christ, though a very small minority, inevitably went through the same afflictions inflicted on their orthodox brethren.

More Jewish refugees, many of them survivors of the Holocaust, migrated to America after the war. "More than 93,000 Jews immigrated to the United States from 1946 to 1949."[8]

"A time, and times, and half a time".

We are told how long the "woman" would be protected from the wrath of Satan in Revelation 12:14b – "*…she is nourished for a time, and times, and half a time, from the face of the serpent.*" We have seen in Chapter 3, how long that period is in more understandable terms. Revelation 12:6b provided the interpretation: "*…that they should feed her there a thousand two hundred and threescore days*" (1,260 days).

In the account of the "little horn" or eleventh king (Dan 7), we saw that 1,260 days was prophetically equivalent to 1,260 years. However, the seventh king would be in power for just a short while (Rev 17:10c – "*…the other is not yet come; and when he cometh, he must continue a short space*"). Hence, the 1,260 days must be literal.

Three-and-a-half years. 1,260 days are equivalent to three-and-a-half Biblical years or 42 Biblical months of exactly 30 days each. Did that actually come to pass? The insight on the matter of Martin Hunter of the National Institute for Inventors (NIFI) is definitely a big help.

In the early stages of World War II, the United States kept away from the conflict. However, on November 26 (25, Washington time), 1941, a Japanese war fleet under Vice Admiral Nagumo Chuichi, with 6 aircraft carriers, 2 battleships, 3 cruisers, and 11 destroyers, sailed to a point about 275 miles (440 km) north of Hawaii. From there, they launched some 360 warplanes on December 7, 1941.[9]

In a surprise air attack, the Japanese ravaged the U.S. Pacific Fleet anchored at Pearl Harbor. The United States was forced to declare war on Japan the following day. Three-and-a-half years later, in Europe, Nazi General Alfred Jodl, signed an unconditional surrender of all German armed forces on May 7, 1945, at U.S. General Dwight Eisenhower's headquarters in Reims, France. The U.S. and British governments declared May 8 as V-E (Victory in Europe) Day. (The full unconditional surrender took effect at one minute past midnight after a second signing in Berlin with Soviet participation.)[10]

From November 25, 1941, to May 8, 1945, there were exactly 1,260 days ("*a time, and times, and half a time*"), the length of time that the United States ("*great eagle*") fought with the leaders of the Axis Powers –primarily the Nazi perpetrators of the Holocaust and persecutors of the Jews and their religion ("*the woman*").[11]

"Flood after the woman".

"*And the serpent cast out of his mouth water as a flood after the woman, that he might cause her to be carried away of the flood. And the earth helped the woman, and the earth opened her mouth, and swallowed up the flood which the dragon cast out of his mouth*" (Rev 12:15-16). Let us decipher the metaphors in this puzzling passage.

"Flood". In Bible prophecy, "*flood*" can mean "invading armies", as in Isaiah 59:19 – "*When the enemy shall come in like a flood, the Spirit of the LORD shall lift up a standard against him*"; and Jeremiah 46:7-8 – "*Who is this that cometh up as a flood, whose waters are moved as the rivers? Egypt riseth up like a flood, and his waters are moved like the rivers; and he saith, I will go up, and will cover the earth; I will destroy the city and the inhabitants thereof.*" The "flood", therefore, in the prophecy of the "woman clothed with the sun" was the Nazi armies threatening to obliterate the Jews and their religion.

"Earth". "*Earth*" is the opposite of "*sea*", as suggested in Genesis 1:10, wherein the world had only two kinds of surface – earth and seas. ("*And God called the dry land Earth; and the gathering together of the waters called he Seas…*").

Revelation 17:15 says that "waters" or "sea" is symbolic of a place with many peoples speaking many different languages (the Old World). If so, then "earth", its opposite, is an uninhabited or sparsely populated place – the condition of the Americas when the first European colonizers arrived. *"Earth"* therefore signifies the New World, whose most powerful nation today is the United States.

"Swallowed". The United States helped save the Jews and their religion (*"the earth helped the woman"*) when it *"swallowed up the flood"* (to "swallow" is to "eat" or "devour", which prophetically means to defeat or to conquer, as in Deut 32:42; Isa 9:12; Jer 46:14; Dan 7:23). In other words, as leader of the Allied forces, the United States (*"earth"*) defeated (*"swallowed"*) the armies (*"flood"*) of Nazi Germany (*"which the dragon* [Satan] *cast out of his mouth"*).

The "seventh king".

We thus discern the identity of the "seventh king". He was the Nazi dictator Adolph Hitler and his Nazi party, who were in power for just some twelve years (*"a short space"*) – from January 30, 1933, when Hitler was named Chancellor of Germany, to May 8, 1945, when the defeated Nazi armies unconditionally surrendered to the Allied forces.

"Remnant of her seed".

"And the dragon was wroth with the woman, and went to make war with the remnant of her seed, which keep the commandments of God, and have the testimony of Jesus Christ" (Rev 12:17).

Interestingly, the *"remnant of her seed"* does not refer to *all* the Jews living today, or even the survivors of the Holocaust. The *"remnant"* is qualified as only those who *"keep the commandments of God, and have the testimony of Jesus Christ"*. It thus points exclusively to the Jews who obey the commandments God gave through Moses (the Mosaic law or *Torah*) and, in addition, believe in the Gospel (good news) of Yeshua (Jesus Christ), the Jewish Messiah. They are called "remnant", because most of the other Jews did not accept Yeshua as the prophesied Messiah. As a result, Jews in general also rejected the New Testament.

Jewish Christians. The first followers of Christ were Jews. Most of the converts to the faith following His death were Jews. They are mentioned in Acts 21:20b: *"Thou seest, brother, how many thousands of Jews there are which believe; and they are all zealous of the law."* As a matter of fact, Christianity was initially considered a sect of the Jews, as we can read in Acts 24:5 – *"For we have found this man a pestilent fellow, and a mover of sedition among all the Jews throughout the world, and a ringleader of the sect of the Nazarenes"* (cf. Acts 28:22).

"Nazarenes" was one of the names given to the early Christians. We read in the *Encyclopaedia Britannica:* "Even after Paul proclaimed his opposition to observance of the Torah as a means of salvation, many Jewish Christians continued the practice. Among them were two main groups: the Ebionites – probably the people called *minim*, or 'sectaries' (sect members) in the Talmud – who accepted Jesus as the messiah but denied his divinity; and the Nazarenes, who regarded Jesus as both messiah and God yet still regarded the Torah as binding upon Jews... there were relatively few Jewish converts, though the Christian movement had some success in winning over Alexandrian Jews."[12]

Survival through the centuries. Although few in number, the Jewish Christians kept their faith alive throughout the centuries. Early Church Father "Epiphanius (c. 315-402) described the Nazarenes of his time... 'They make use not only of the New Testament, but they also use in a way the Old Testament of the Jews... the Nazarenes do not differ in anything, and they profess all the dogmas pertaining to the prescriptions of the Law and to the customs of the Jews, except that they believe in Christ...'"[13] He added that "this sect of the Nazarenes thrives most vigorously in the state of Berea, in Coele-Syria, in Decapolis, around Pella, and in Bashan (the Golan)..."[14]

From 325 A.D., "(t)here was a tremendous amount of persecution that resulted from the very anti-Semitic Council of Nicea. As a result, Messianic Judaism became an underground movement."[15] According to the *Encarta Encyclopedia*, "Until the 5th century, remnants of the sect were known to have existed in Palestine and Syria."[16] The remnants survived in Europe as well. *Wikipedia* relates: "As late as the eleventh century, Cardinal Humbert of Mourmoutiers still referred to the Nazarene sect as a Sabbath-keeping Christian body existing at that time."[17]

However, they led lives like those of fugitives, "...beginning with the Council of Verona in 1184... these Jewish believers in Messiah... were 'persecuted and hunted down like wild game by the Romish Church.'"[18]

Spread of the movement. "Often mentioned are the Pasaginians, beginning with the Council of Verona in 1184... so named by the Italians from the Latin word *passagium*, meaning 'passage' for the wandering, unsettled life of these Jewish believers in Messiah... They were also called *Circumcisi*."[19] "The Catholic writing of Bonacursus (was) entitled 'Against the Heretics Who Are Called Pasagii,' in about 1185... Gregorius of Bergamo, about 1250, writes this against the Pasaginians... 'The Pasaginian "heresy" had spread to Hungary, Bulgaria, France, and even into England and Italy.'"[20]

Moreover, "(n)otable converts from Judaism who themselves attempted to convert other Jews are more visible in historical sources beginning around the 13th century, when Jewish convert Pablo Christiani attempted to convert other Jews… In the 15th and 16th centuries, Jewish Christians occupying professorships at the European universities began to provide translations of Hebrew texts…"[21]

On the other side of the coin, 18th century Neander, a German church historian born of Jewish parents, in 1789 wrote disparagingly about his Pasaginian contemporaries.[22]

Hebrew Christians. "In the 19th century, some groups attempted to create congregations and societies of Jewish converts to Christianity, though most of these early organizations were short-lived."[23] As they grew in number in modern times, more Jews who believed in Yeshua haMashiach ("Jesus Christ") became more visible, calling themselves Hebrew Christians around the mid-1800s.

Beginning in the late 1800s, there were more signs of a resurgence of the movement. "Rabbi Isaac Lichtenstein of Hungary became a believer in Yeshua, and remained a practicing Jew until he died."[24]

Messianic Jews. In the late second half of the twentieth century, members of the movement became better known as Messianic Jews. "Messianic Judaism as we know it today began in the early 1970s, with congregations like Beth Yeshua in Philadelphia and Beth Messiah, in the suburbs of Washington D.C."[25]

"The earliest record of the terms 'Messianic Jew' and 'Messianic Judaism' being used for Jewish believers in Yeshua was in a publication called *Our Hope*, published by Dr. A.C. Gabelein in March 1985."[26]

Messianic Gentiles?

We have seen in Revelation 12:17 that *"The dragon was wroth with the woman, and went to make war with the remnant of her seed, which keep the commandments of God, and have the testimony of Jesus Christ."* We have identified that remnant as the Messianic Jews.

Surprisingly, Revelation 14:12 introduces us to a second group of believers who do exactly the same things, but not identified as remnants of the woman's seed: *"Here is the patience of the saints: here are they that keep the commandments of God, and the faith of Jesus."*

The "saints", as Daniel 7:22 and 27 describe, are all those who will inherit the kingdom of God. As the remnants of the woman's seed are "saints" who will be heirs of the kingdom, there must be Gentiles who will also be "saints" and heirs. These *"are they that keep the commandments of God, and the faith of Jesus."* What shall we call them… Messianic Gentiles? But that simply means "Christians".

A Messianic is one who believes in the Messiah. Hence, all Christians are Messianics. (Messiah is from Hebrew *mashiach*, meaning "anointed";

Christ is from *christos*, Greek translation of *mashiach*.) So, what should we call Gentile Christians who keep the law (Torah) God gave through Moses, Torah Christians or Mosaic Christians?

A whorish mother of harlots

A second woman, the antithesis or direct opposite of the first, enters the picture. *"And there came one of the seven angels which had the seven vials, and talked with me, saying unto me, Come hither; I will shew unto thee the judgment of the great whore that sitteth upon many waters. With whom the kings of the earth have committed fornication, and the inhabitants of the earth have been made drunk with the wine of her fornication"* (Rev 17:1-2). Let us examine the prophetic symbols.

"Whore". *The Wycliffe Bible Commentary* gives us a clue to her identity. "To whom or what does this woman refer? ...She is definitely some vast spiritual system that persecutes the saints of God, betraying that to which she was called. She enters into relations with the governments of this earth, and for a while rules them. I think the closest we can come to an identification is to understand this harlot as symbolic of a vast spiritual power arising at the end of the age, which enters into a league with the world and compromises with worldly forces. Instead of being spiritually true, she is spiritually false, and thus exercises an evil influence in the name of religion...

"The majority of commentators, since the time of the Reformation, identify her with the papacy, as Luther, Tyndale, Knox, Calvin (Institutes, IV, 2,12), Alford, Elliott, Lange, and many others. The Roman Catholic Church itself identifies this woman with Rome – but of course pagan Rome, now past."[27]

"Many waters". The woman is said to be sitting on "many waters." The term can mean a large body of water, such as a lake or a sea. A latter verse, Revelation 17:15, tells us that "many waters" is a metaphor for a place with many peoples speaking various languages. *"And he saith unto me, The waters which thou sawest, where the whore sitteth, are peoples, and multitudes, and nations, and tongues."*

In the last chapter we saw that the "great sea" is the Mediterranean Sea, which is almost entirely enclosed by three continents. Along its African shores in the south are Morocco, Algeria, Tunisia, Libya and Egypt, all of which have only one major language – Arabic. On the eastern, Asian end are Cyprus, Israel, Lebanon, Syria, ad Turkey. Cyprus speaks Greek and Turkish; Israel, Hebrew; Lebanon and Syria, Arabic; Turkey, Turkish and Arabic – just four main languages. On the northern, European coastline fronting the sea are Spain, France, Italy and Greece, with 47 other European nations farther north and east. Europe occupies just about 7%

of the earth's land area, but some 50 languages and over 100 dialects are spoken there. It looks like the "many waters" with many peoples and languages refers to Europe.

After the discovery of new lands (the "New World") by European voyagers during the Age of Exploration (1400s-1800s), their homeland, specially Western Europe and its civilization and culture, was referred to as the Old World. Hence, "many waters" point to the Old World.

"Fornication with kings".

The "whore" here is not an ordinary prostitute waiting for clients on street corners. Her patrons come from the ranks of blue-blooded royalty. *Barnes Notes* makes no bones about her profession. "Spiritual adultery. The meaning is, that papal Rome, unfaithful to God, and idolatrous and corrupt, had seduced the rulers of the earth, and led them into the same kind of unfaithfulness, idolatry, and corruption. Compare Jer 3:8-9; 5:7; 13:27; 23:14; Ezek 16:32; 23:37; Heb 2:2; 4:2. How true this is in history need not be stated. All the princes and kings of Europe in the dark ages, and for many centuries were, and not a few of them are now, entirely under the influence of papal Rome."[28]

Since the Dark Ages, kings and emperors have been traditionally crowned by popes, archbishops, bishops, or some other high ranking prelate of the Roman Catholic Church. How did this tradition begin?

Donation of Constantine. Emperor Constantine the Great legalized Christianity in A.D. 313. The following year, Sylvester I was elected bishop of Rome. According to one legend, Constantine converted to Christianity after Sylvester miraculously cured him of leprosy. In his gratitude, the emperor conferred on Sylvester and all his successors ecclesiastical primacy over the great patriarchates, as well as temporal sovereignty over Italy and all the regions of the Western Roman Empire, documented in the so-called "Donation of Constantine".[29]

Significantly, the document also conveyed the idea that the bishop of Rome (later called "Pope") had the right to appoint secular rulers in the Western Empire. Thus, emperors, kings, and other rulers did not officially become sovereigns unless they were crowned by a primate of the Roman Catholic Church.

Forgery. The document had great influence on political and religious affairs in medieval Europe. However, in 1440, it was exposed as forgery. Lorenzo Valla showed that the Latin used in the document was not that of the 4th century, but of the 8th century. Consensus: the "Donation" was written in the 750s or 760s by a cleric of the Lateran in Rome, possibly with the knowledge of Pope Stephen II (or III; 752–757).[30]

Scarlet-colored beast.
"So he carried me away in the spirit into the wilderness: and I saw a woman sit upon a scarlet coloured beast, full of names of blasphemy, having seven heads and ten horns" (Rev 17:3). As we now know, a "beast" in prophecy stands for an empire; while "horns" are symbolic of subordinate kingdoms. Does the color "scarlet" mean anything?

The prophet Isaiah tells us: *"Come now, and let us reason together, saith the LORD: though your sins be as scarlet, they shall be as white as snow; though they be red like crimson, they shall be as wool"* (Isa 1:18). Scarlet is a color of sin! Hence, the *"scarlet coloured beast"* represents a sinful empire.

"Blasphemy". Let us try to get a clear idea of what blasphemy is. *The New Unger's Bible Dictionary* states: "There are two general forms of blasphemy: (1) Attributing some evil to God, or denying Him some good that we should attribute to Him (Lev 24:11; Rom 2:24); (2) Giving the attributes of God to a creature – which form of blasphemy the Jews charged Jesus with (Matt 26:65; Luke 5:21; John 10:36)."[31]

For example: *"And the high priest answered and said unto him, I adjure thee by the living God, that thou tell us whether thou be the Christ, the Son of God. Jesus saith unto him, Thou hast said: nevertheless I say unto you, Hereafter shall ye see the Son of man sitting on the right hand of power, and coming in the clouds of heaven. Then the high priest rent his clothes, saying, He hath spoken blasphemy; what further need have we of witnesses? behold, now ye have heard his blasphemy"* (Matt 26:63b-65; cf. Mark 14:61-64; John 10:33,36).

Another instance: *"And when he saw their faith, he said unto him, Man, thy sins are forgiven thee. And the scribes and the Pharisees began to reason, saying, Who is this which speaketh blasphemies? Who can forgive sins, but God alone?"* (Luke 5:20-21; cf. Matt 9:2-3).

Nelson's Illustrated Bible Dictionary comments that "The unbelieving Jews of Jesus' day charged Him with blasphemy because they thought of Him only as a man while He claimed to be God's Son (Matt 9:3)."[32]

"Seven heads". The "beast" also has seven heads. As in the dragon with seven heads, they signify seven mountains or hills and thus point again to the famous "city of seven hills" – Rome.

That the "woman" is sitting on the "beast" indicates to us that the church or religion is based or located in the end-time empire, where the city of seven hills is found.

"Ten horns". The beast also has ten horns. *"And the ten horns which thou sawest are ten kings, which have received no kingdom as yet; but receive power as kings one hour with the beast. These have one mind,* *and shall give their power and strength unto the beast. These shall make war with the Lamb, and the Lamb shall overcome them: for he is Lord of lords, and King of kings: and they that are with him are called, and chosen, and faithful"* (Rev 17:12-14). The narrative has suddenly shifted to the time of the end. The ten kings symbolized by the ten horns are ten nations who will support the end-time beast and fight against Christ at His Second Coming.

"And the ten horns which thou sawest upon the beast, these shall hate the whore, and shall make her desolate and naked, and shall eat her flesh, and burn her with fire" (Rev 17:16). The ten end-time kings will destroy the Roman Catholic Church. It is interesting to note that one of the first declarations of the Islamic State caliphate after its establishment in 2014 was that it would destroy the Vatican.

Richly dressed and bejeweled.
"And the woman was arrayed in purple and scarlet colour, and decked with gold and precious stones and pearls, having a golden cup in her hand full of abominations and filthiness of her fornication" (Rev 17:4). The Church represented by the "woman" is extremely wealthy.

Purple and scarlet. According to the *World Book*:, "The Phoenicians and Romans made a purple dye from murex sea snails. They believed that cloth colored with this dye was more valuable than gold."[33]

The expensive purple dye was used to color the clothes of wealthy people in the ancient world around the Mediterranean Sea. Hence, the religious system represented by the woman is truly a very rich church.

The woman is also dressed in scarlet-colored garments. As we have seen earlier, scarlet can signify sin. Thus, the woman personifies a church or religion that is both very wealthy and sinful.

Gold and gems. Author Dave Hunt quotes from the book *Vicars of Christ: The Dark Side of the Papacy* (Peter de Rosa, 1988): "Of Rome's wealth in the Middle Ages de Rosa says: 'The cardinals had huge palaces with countless servants. One papal aide reported that he never went to see a cardinal without finding him counting his gold coins. The *Curia* was made up of men who had bought office and were desperate to recoup their enormous outlay… For every benefice of see, abbey and parish, for every indulgence there was a set fee. The pallium, the two-inch-wide woolen band with crosses embroidered on it… paid for by every bishop… brought in… hundreds of millions of florins to the papal coffers… the Council of Basle in 1432 was to call it "the most usurious contrivance ever invented…"'[34]

By the end of the 15th century, the Roman Catholic Church, with its numerous parishes, monasteries and convents, had become the largest landowner in Europe – possessing close to half the land or more in France, Germany, Sweden and England.

In our modern time, "Nino Lo Bello, former Rome correspondent for *Business Week*, calls the Vatican 'the tycoon of the Tiber' because of its incredible wealth and worldwide enterprises. His research indicates that it owns fully one-third of Rome's real estate and is probably the largest holder of stocks and bonds in the world, to say nothing of its ownership of industries from electronics and plastics to airlines and chemicals and engineering firms."[35]

"Babylon, Mother of Harlots".

The "whore" has a name and title: *"And upon her forehead was a name written, MYSTERY, BABYLON THE GREAT, THE MOTHER OF HARLOTS AND ABOMINATIONS OF THE EARTH"* (Rev 17:5). The "woman" is not really Babylon, but a religion very much like that of ancient Babylon. *Matthew Henry* cautions us to "not take it for the old Babylon literally so called, we are told there is a mystery in the name; it is some other great city resembling the old Babylon.

"She is named from her infamous way and practice; not only a harlot, but a mother of harlots, breeding up harlots, and nursing and training them up to idolatry, and all sorts of lewdness and wickedness – the parent and nurse of all false religion and filthy conversation."[36]

Barnes' Notes echoes the thought: "[Babylon the great] papal Rome, (is) the nominal head of the Christian world, as Babylon had been of the pagan world."[37]

"Drunken with blood".

The woman is also a drunkard, but not the usual kind of alcoholic hooked on wine or hard liquor. *"And I saw the woman drunken with the blood of the saints, and with the blood of the martyrs of Jesus: and when I saw her, I wondered with great admiration"* (Rev 17:6).

Saints persecuted. Historians have recorded that church members who disobeyed the tenets promulgated by the Papacy were persecuted. As we have discussed in Chapter 3, the "little horn" in Daniel 7 oppressed, hunted, and all but wiped out Christians who did not conform to Catholic teachings. Whereas the "little horn" personifies the Papacy in Old Testament prophecy, the "whore" embodies the Roman Catholic Church in New Testament prophecy.

A Catholic priest bragged in the *Western Watchman*, a turn-of-the-century Catholic publication: "During the 2,000 years the Church has been on earth, she has warred with nearly every government in the world. The world is full of their ruins. Their thrones have toppled over and fallen, their dynasties have come to dust. And the governments of the world today will meet the same fate if they challenge the hostility of the church of God... she is the invincible church of God. God help the state that attacks her; God help the king that provokes her hostility."[38]

"That great city".

"And the angel said unto me, Wherefore didst thou marvel? I will tell thee the mystery of the woman, and of the beast that carrieth her, which hath the seven heads and ten horns... And the woman which thou sawest is that great city, which reigneth over the kings of the earth" (Rev 17:7,18). The "woman" is described as a "great city". Get it?

"Habitation of devils".

"And after these things I saw another angel come down from heaven, having great power; and the earth was lightened with his glory. And he cried mightily with a strong voice, saying, Babylon the great is fallen, is fallen, and is become the habitation of devils, and the hold of every foul spirit, and a cage of every unclean and hateful bird" (Rev 18:1-2).

The chief exorcist of the Vatican and president of the International Association of Exorcists (IAE), Fr. Gabriele Amorth, who claims to have conducted some 160,000 rites of exorcism, was quoted some years ago in the "Watching the World" section of *Awake!* magazine as saying that the city with the highest number of demonic possessions in the world was... you guessed it, Rome.

That the great city prophetically referred to as "Babylon" is infested by demons is confirmed by other members of the Catholic clergy. "Just in the dioceses of Rome, around a third of calls that are received are requests for the services of an exorcist," said Fr Cesar Truqui, a priest and exorcist from Switzerland and a member of the Legionaries of Christ, a conservative Catholic order. It is said that the "Pope continues to complain about the problem of the devil, and incidents of demonic possession are on the rise, especially in Rome."[39]

"It seems that the Church's attitude today toward Satan's work in the world is embarrassment: she is ashamed to admit its reality," stated Italian Fr. Raul Salvucci, an exorcist since 1975, who has just published a book on his experiences (*What to Do with These Demons?*, Ancora, available only in Italian).[40]

Just the same, exorcism has become big business in Rome and all Italy. Fr. Salvucci adds: "Eight years ago, a University Congress held in Perugia discovered that in Italy the esoteric has a following of some 12 million. There were about 170,000 wizards (who perform exorcisms), with income amounting to $600 million. Today, however, the income from these practices has risen to close to $3 billion."[41]

Dealing in souls of men.
The great city of the "whore" would become a wealthy world trade center, dealing in various luxurious goods – including the souls of men. *"And the merchants of the earth shall weep and mourn over her; for no man buyeth their merchandise any more: The merchandise of gold, and silver, and precious stones, and of pearls, and fine linen, and purple, and silk, and scarlet, and all thyine wood, and all manner vessels of ivory, and all manner vessels of most precious wood, and of brass, and iron, and marble, And cinnamon, and odours, and ointments, and frankincense, and wine, and oil, and fine flour, and wheat, and beasts, and sheep, and horses, and chariots, and slaves, and souls of men"* (Rev 18:11-13).

Payments for prayers. The Roman Church, without any Biblical basis, has classified sins according to gravity – for which priests prescribe penances for atonement. Author Ralph Woodrow (*Babylon Mystery Religion, 1981 Edition*) tells us that "the giving of money and prayers for the dead go hand in hand.

"High Mass can be very expensive, depending on the flowers, candles, and number of priests taking part. It is sung in a loud tone of voice. The low Mass, on the other hand, is much less expensive – only six candles are used and it is repeated in a low voice. The Irish have a saying, 'High money, HIGH Mass; low money, LOW Mass; no money, NO MASS!'

"Those who die without anyone to pay for Masses in their behalf are called the 'forgotten souls in Purgatory'... If a Catholic fears he might become one of the 'forgotten souls', he may join the Purgatorian Society which was established in 1856. A contribution each year to the society will assure him that, upon his death, prayers will be said for his soul."[42]

Salvation for sale. "Another source of money was the selling of indulgences. *The Catholic Encyclopedia* explains that sins committed *after* baptism (which for a Catholic is usually in infancy!) can be forgiven through the sacrament of penance, 'but there still remains the *temporal punishment* required by Divine justice, and this requirement must be fulfilled either in the present life or in the world to come, i.e. in Purgatory. An indulgence offers the penitent sinner the means of discharging this debt during this life on earth."[43]

"The sale of relics, church offices, and indulgences became big business within the church in the Middle Ages. Pope Boniface VIII declared a jubilee for the year 1300 and offered liberal indulgences to those who would make a pilgrimage to St. Peter's. An estimated 2,000,000 people came within that year and deposited such treasure before the supposed tomb of St. Peter that two priests with rakes in their hands were kept busy day and night raking up the money."[44]

"**Dispensations** were another source of papal revenue. Extremely severe, even impossible, laws were passed so that the Curia could grow rich by selling dispensations… (such as) from fasting during Lent… Marriage in particular was a rich source of income. Consanguinity was alleged to hold between couples who had never dreamed they were related. Dispensations from consanguinity in order to marry amounted to a million gold florins a year."[45]

"Come out of her!"

Many innocent believers have become members of the sinful church. No wonder, a cry had to issue from heaven. *"And I heard another voice from heaven, saying, Come out of her, my people, that ye be not partakers of her sins, and that ye receive not of her plagues"* (Rev 18:4).

The heavenly voice warns God's people to get out and dissociate themselves from the sinister religion before it becomes too late.

Eastern Orthodox churches

In 330, Emperor Constantine transferred his capital from Rome to the site of an ancient Greek city in the east, Byzantium, which he renamed Constantinople in his honor (today Istanbul, Turkey).

"Rome of the east". Called "Rome of the east", Constantinople was at the intersection of Europe and Asia, and on the route linking the Mediterranean to the territory of Rome's great enemy, Persia.

After Constantine died in 337, his three sons and two of his nephews fought for control of the Roman Empire. One of his nephews, Julian, became emperor in 361. (He tried, without success, to stop the spread of Christianity in order to restore the traditional Roman religion.)

The last ruler in Constantine's line, Theodosius I (379–395), made Christianity the official religion of the empire in 392 and prohibited all pagan practices. He was the last emperor to rule over a unified Roman Empire. At his death in 395, the empire was divided between his sons Honorius and Arcadius into the Eastern and Western empires. The city of Constantinople became the center of eastern Christendom.

East-west disagreements.

The Eastern and Western churches were at odds on, among others, two major religious issues: first, the Nicene Creed and the doctrine of the Holy

Trinity; and second, the doctrine of papal infallibility and the pope's claim to authority over the entire church. Eastern Christians use the original text of the Nicene Creed, which states that the Holy Spirit proceeds from the Father, based on a passage in the Gospel of John (15:26 – *"But when the Comforter is come, whom I will send unto you from the Father, even the Spirit of truth, which proceedeth from the Father, he shall testify of me."*).

However, in 589 the Third Council of Toledo in Spain added the phrase *filioque*, a combination of Latin words meaning "and from the Son", denoting that the Holy Spirit comes from both the Father and the Son. Most Byzantine theologians objected because the addition was made unilaterally, altering a creed approved by early ecumenical councils, and also because the formula reflected a particular Western concept of the Trinity which Easterners considered heretical. In 867 and 879, the patriarch of Constantinople assailed *filioque*. Just the same, the Roman Catholic Church authorized its general liturgical use early in the 11th century.

Christianity divided. In 1043 Michael Cerularius became patriarch of Constantinople and, in reaction to the pope's meddling in the affairs of Byzantine churches in southern Italy, began a campaign against Latin churches in his own city, eventually closing them down. Pope Leo IX sent Cardinal Candida to Constantinople in 1054 to deal with the problem, but the cardinal ended up issuing an anathema (solemn curse of excommunication) against Cerularius, who then summoned a synod and excommunicated the papal delegate.

In what is known as "The Great Schism", churches under the pope in Rome severed their relationships with the churches affiliated with the patriarch of Constantinople. The latter group is today collectively called the Eastern Orthodoxy. (The word "orthodoxy" simply means "correct teaching," or "right belief.")

Eastern Orthodox Churches are the major Christian churches today in Greece, Russia, eastern Europe, and western Asia. Unlike the Pope, the Patriarch of Constantinople does not exercise administrative powers beyond his own territory or patriarchate. His position is simply a primacy among equals.

Although Eastern Orthodox churches have no statues or other three-dimensional images, they are richly decorated with religious art. Icons (holy images) form an essential part of Orthodox worship, as these are said to stimulate the faith and piety of the worshippers.

Today, while the Roman Catholic Church has well over 1.2 billion members, the Eastern Orthodox Churches count just 225-300 million adherents.

The Reformation

In the 14th century, John Wycliffe (1330-1384), a priest and Oxford theology professor (later called the "Morning Star of the Reformation"), criticized papal taxation, transubstantiation (literal transformation of the Eucharist wafer into the body of Christ), and neglect in teaching the Bible. With Nicholas of Hereford, he translated the Latin Vulgate into the first Bible in English. Portions were distributed by the barefoot Poor Priests, who later gave rise to the Lollards.

After Wycliffe's death, his followers were imprisoned, tortured and burned to death. His bones were also dug up and burned. In 1415, Bohemian (Czech) Jan Hus, priest and University of Prague rector who preached Wycliffe's doctrines, was burned at the stake for speaking about Church corruption and the importance of reading the Bible. In1498, Girolamo Savonarola, an Italian monk who dared criticize the Church, was hanged.

Lutheranism.

In 1517, protesting the sale of indulgences and other unbiblical Church practices, German monk Martin Luther (1483-1546) nailed 95 theses (topics for debate) on the door of Castle Church in Wittenberg, Germany. Aided by the newly invented movable type printing press, his ideas quickly spread across the Holy Roman Empire, marking the start of the Reformation.

In 1519, Luther asserted in debate that the Pope and ecclesiastical councils could make mistakes. The Pope issued a bull forbidding Luther to preach, but Luther burned it in public. He also criticized pilgrimages and devotion to saints, which he said stressed works instead of faith. In 1521, the Pope excommunicated Luther. The Holy Roman Emperor gave him a chance to retract in a trial at the Diet (assembly) of Worms, but Luther refused. Declared an outlaw, he was taken by his supporters into hiding, during which time he translated the Bible into German.

As the Reformation spread, Emperor Charles V gave each German state the right to choose between Catholicism and Lutheranism. He, however, reversed his decision in 1529, causing the German state rulers to protest, giving rise to the term "Protestant". At the Diet of Augsburg in 1530, the Holy Roman Emperor tried to reconcile the two sides. The Lutherans presented a conciliatory document called the "Augsburg Confession", but the Catholic Church rejected it. Many German state rulers sided with Luther. Church members in the Scandinavian countries soon joined the Lutherans.

Luther, though, thought that, based on his understanding of Paul's epistles, Christ had abolished the law of God. He thus taught that a simple belief in Christ as Savior was sufficient for salvation. Moreover, he retained the observance of the holidays instituted by the Roman Catholic Church, such as Sunday sabbath of rest, Christmas, Good Friday, Easter Sunday, All Saints Day and others, which have little or no Biblical basis, but, rather, much pagan influence.

Anglicanism.

King Henry VIII of England asked Pope Clement VII to annul his first marriage so he could remarry in the hope of producing a male heir. When the pope refused, in 1534 the king issued his Act of Supremacy, breaking away from the Roman Catholic Church and making himself head of the new Church of England. As supreme head of the church, he ordered Bibles placed in all churches; priests were allowed to marry; and the shrines of saints were destroyed.

William Tyndale (1494-1536), a priest following in the footsteps of John Wycliffe and a friend of Martin Luther, had earlier translated the New Testament from Greek and parts of the Hebrew Scriptures into English in 1526. (His beautifully lyrical translation later became the basis of the King James Version.) He was able to have it published in Germany and had copies smuggled into England. He was, however, betrayed and the Roman Catholic authorities put him to death by strangling as a heretic in Antwerp, Belgium, in 1536.

Miles Coverdale finished the work of Tyndale by translating the rest of the Old Testament. It became the single most powerful factor in the Reformation movement in England.

Calvinism.

John Calvin (1509-1564), a Protestant student persecuted in Paris, moved to Switzerland in 1534. In defense of Protestants, he wrote *Institutes of the Christian Religion*, summarizing the ideas of the early Church Fathers, medieval theologians, Martin Luther, and Ulrich Zwingli, a Swiss reformer priest. (The book later became the doctrinal foundation of all Reformed Churches in Europe and America.)

Teaching predestination and urging his followers to abstain from pleasure, Calvin, with William Farel, turned the city of Geneva into a strict theocracy. Yet, although Calvin believed in God's commandments, he kept a Sunday sabbath of rest.

Other Protestant reformers who fled to Geneva brought Calvinism back to their homelands, where they established new churches and were known under new names, such as: Puritans (England), Huguenots (France), Reformed Church (the Netherlands), Presbyterians (Scotland).

While Luther set the Reformation movement in motion, it was Calvin who greatly influenced its development.

Counter-Reformation.

A movement seeking to oppose Protestantism, as well as revitalize the Roman Catholic Church, became active in the 16th and 17th centuries. Pope Paul III initiated the Counter-Reformation in response to the growth of Protestant Christianity and to promote reform within the Church. He named reformers to the College of Cardinals and advocated the founding of new Catholic religious orders.

Jesuits. Spaniard Ignatius of Loyola formed the Society of Jesus in 1534 as part of the move to reclaim Europe for Roman Catholicism. Called Jesuits, his followers engaged in foreign missionary work and education.

In 1542, the church reorganized the infamous Inquisition in Italy to help the courts fight Protestantism more effectively.

Council of Trent. In 1545 Paul convened the Council of Trent, which instituted general reforms and more accurately defined the doctrines of the Church. The council met in sessions between 1545 and 1563 in Trent, Italy. It clarified Catholic doctrine on questions disputed by Protestant theologians, such as original sin, grace, free will, the seven sacraments, the Mass, and the relation between Scripture and tradition. The council arranged for the pope to issue a catechism and books on liturgy (forms of worship) for greater uniformity in church teachings.

Forbidden books. The Church also published a list of books Catholics were forbidden to read, because they were considered harmful to faith or morals.

Five major groups.

The breakup of the Christian Church resulted in five major groups of churches in Europe:
1. Roman Catholic (Italy, Spain, Austria, Ireland, parts of France)
2. Eastern Orthodoxy (Greece, Russia, east Europe, west Asia)
3. Lutheran (Germany, Scandinavian countries)
4. Anglican (England, Wales, Northern Ireland)
5. Calvinist (Switzerland, Netherlands, Scotland, parts of France)

Protestant denominations.

Historical Protestants established a number of other new churches – often called denominations – including the Baptist, Methodist, and Presbyterian churches.

Modern-day Protestants include Pentecostals, Born Again Christians, Seventh-Day Adventists, Latter-Day Saints, Jehovah's Witnesses, and many others.

5

The Beasts of the Apocalypse

And the beast that was, and is not, even he is the eighth, and is of the seven, and goeth into perdition.

- Revelation 17:11

Bible prophecy points to a final "beast" or empire that will wield power in the last days. It is a hybrid, chimeric creature made up of a combination of several other animals – each one corresponding to one of the four symbolic beasts or ancient empires that we saw in the book of Daniel, chapter 7. In this chapter, we will see how they have converged into one single monstrous entity.

The beast from the sea

The monster comes into full view in the thirteenth chapter of the book of Revelation (*Apokalypsis* in the original Greek text, meaning "unveiling" or "disclosure" of hidden things known only to God. Today, the word "apocalypse" has come to mean a cataclysmic world upheaval.) *"And I stood upon the sand of the sea, and saw a beast rise up out of the sea, having seven heads and ten horns, and upon his horns ten crowns, and upon his heads the name of blasphemy"* (Rev 13:1).

Seven heads.

The "seven heads", *Barnes Notes* states, are "the seven hills on which the city of Rome was built,"[1] namely, the Aventine, Caelian, Capitoline, Esquiline, Palatine, Quirinal, and Viminal hills. The *Encarta Encyclopedia* says: "The original city of Romulus was built upon Palatine Hill (*Mons*

Palatinus). The Capitoline Hill (*Monte Capitoline*) was long the seat of Rome's government, and the Palatine Hill was the site of such great structures as the Palace of the Flavians, built by the Roman emperor Domitian."[2]

Ten horns.

The beast from the sea and the red dragon in heaven (Rev 12:3) are dead-ringers – both have seven heads and ten horns. Are they one and the same, or two different creatures? Let us see. Under close scrutiny, it appears they are mere look-alikes.

The red dragon, as we have seen earlier, was both the devil and ancient Rome with ten nations in its domain. The beast from the sea, though, is the end-time empire that will arise in place of the fallen Roman Empire with ten new nations. Revelation 17:12-13 affirms this. *"And the ten horns which thou sawest are ten kings, which have received no kingdom as yet; but receive power as kings one hour with the beast."* They likely correspond to the "ten toes" of the two feet of mixed iron and clay of the great image that we saw in Daniel chapter 2 – a prophetic representation of the very last empire.

Ten and seven crowns.

The numbers of their crowns further differentiate the two beasts. The beast from the sea has ten crowns – one on each of its ten horns. The red dragon, on the other hand, has only seven crowns – one each on its seven heads. The difference is explained by the fact that three of the ten kingdoms in the Roman Empire had been destroyed by the "little horn" or eleventh king in Daniel 7:8,24, who, as we have determined earlier, was the Papacy.

"Name of blasphemy".

The beast from the sea has a distinctive marking on its seven heads: *"...and upon his heads the name of blasphemy"* (Rev 13:1). As we have seen in the preceding chapter, blasphemy can refer to a man claiming to be God or, at least, to have some attributes of God (Matt 26:65; Luke 5:21; John 10:36).

The end-time empire

In Revelation 17:8, the beast from the sea is further described in vague, cryptically enigmatic terms that further shroud it in mystery. *"The beast that thou sawest was, and is not; and shall ascend out of the bottomless pit, and go into perdition: and they that dwell on the earth shall wonder, whose names were not written in the book of life from the foundation of the world, when they behold the beast that was, and is not, and yet is."* Befuddling? We nonetheless find clues to the meanings of its intriguing descriptions,

"Was, is not, yet is".

The beast or empire "*was*", meaning it had existed before John wrote the book of Revelation around A.D. 95. That it "*is not*" goes to say that it no longer existed during that time (it was therefore not the Roman Empire, which had exiled John to the rocky, mining island of Patmos, where he wrote the book). However, the beast "*yet is*", implying that its presence or influence could still be felt very strongly in those closing years of the first century.

That the beast "*shall ascend out of the bottomless pit*" seems to say that the empire will come back to life. According to *Nelson's Illustrated Bible Dictionary*, "In the New Testament, the phrase the bottomless pit refers to the abode of the demons. (Rev 20:2-3)."[3] The end-time empire will come back from hell!

Eighth king.

"*And there are seven kings: five are fallen, and one is, and the other is not yet come; and when he cometh, he must continue a short space*" (Rev 17:10). We have already identified the "seven kings". In Chapter 3, the five fallen empires were Egypt, Assyria, Babylon, Persia, and Greece; the "one (that) is" (existing) at the time John penned the book of Revelation was Rome; and the seventh "not yet come," but must continue just "*a short space*", we have identified in Chapter 4 as Nazi Germany.

"*And the beast that was, and is not, even he is the eighth, and is of the seven, and goeth into perdition*" (Rev 17:11). Since we already know that the seventh king was Nazi Germany, it follows that the eighth king will appear after Hitler's regime. That he "*is of the seven*" means the eighth king or empire will be an offshoot or descendant of the first seven empires. It will, however, be ultimately destroyed ("*goeth into perdition*").

A composite creature

John saw a chimera, a grotesque creature combining the parts of several animals – those of the predators in Daniel 7. "*And the beast which I saw was like unto a leopard, and his feet were as the feet of a bear, and his mouth as the mouth of a lion: and the dragon gave him his power, and his seat, and great authority*" (Rev 13:2). (The dragon here stands for the terrible beast with great iron teeth).

"Like a leopard".

The beast from the sea looks like a leopard, apparently from the tops of its heads to the tip of its tail. In Daniel ch. 7, a bizarre four-headed leopard with four wings represented Greece. Bible references agree, such as *The Wycliffe Bible Commentary*: "The sinewy four-winged leopard speaks, without doubt, of Alexander's Grecian (Macedonian) kingdom."[4]

But, without the four wings and four heads, in what way could the end-time beast from the sea possibly be like ancient Greece?

Democracy? Ancient Greece is well known in history as the birthplace of democracy, which began to develop in the Greek city-state of Athens as early as the 500s B.C. The term democracy (*demokratia*) is formed by the Greek words *demos* ("people") and *kratos* ("rule" or "authority") – in short, "rule of the people".

Led by the statesman Cleisthenes (570?–508? B.C.), the citizens of Athens developed a democracy that lasted for almost 200 years. The concept of democracy or "rule of the people" spread to the other city-states of classical Greece, as well as to Rome in its early years as a republic. When the Roman Republic ended under the rule of emperors, the free cities of Italy, Germany, and Flanders carried on the democratic tradition, making use of some principles of democracy during the Middle Ages.[5]

Democracy undermined the authoritarian rule of kings. Before the close of the nineteenth century, every major Western European monarchy had adopted a constitution limiting the power of the Crown and giving a substantial share of political power to the people through a representative legislature, often modeled on the British Parliament.[6]

The end-time empire being like a leopard strongly suggests that its government would probably be democratic in nature.

Leopard spots. The leopard is distinguished from other big cats, such as lions and tigers, by its light tan coat of fur that is marked with many dense black spots. Its body markings appear to be symbolic, too, as verses in the Scriptures imply.

"Can the Ethiopian change his skin, or the leopard his spots? then may ye also do good, that are accustomed to do evil" (Jer 13:23); *"But with the precious blood of Christ, as of a lamb without blemish and without spot"* (1 Peter 1:19); *"Wherefore, beloved, seeing that ye look for such things, be diligent that ye may be found of him in peace, without spot, and blameless"* (2 Peter 3:14); *"That he might present it to himself a glorious church, not having spot, or wrinkle, or any such thing; but that it should be holy and without blemish"* (Eph 5:27). (See also Deut 32:5; Heb 9:14).

Judging from the above verses, "spots" signify "sins". Hence, the leopard-like empire would likely be also sinful in character!

Determining right and wrong. Abraham Lincoln, 16th president of the United States, defined democracy as a "government of the people, by the people, for the people." Thus, in most democracies people elect their representatives to an assembly called a council, parliament, or congress, which makes laws in their behalf. So, although indirectly, it is the people themselves who determine what should or should not be done, what is right and what is wrong.

Is that good in the eyes of God? Let us view the effects of some laws and court decisions in America that have impacted the lifestyles of their citizens and influenced those of other democratic nations.

Sex and violence are usual fare in entertainment and the mass media. Some believe that censorship of obscenity and pornography violates civil liberties like freedom of speech and of the press, which are guaranteed by the First Amendment to the U.S. Constitution. Yet Christ has said, *"…whosoever looketh on a woman to lust after her hath committed adultery with her already in his heart"* (Matt 5:28b); and *"Do violence to no man…"* (Luke 3:14b).

Fornication between consenting adults is widely practiced and regarded as a normal way of life. Prostitution is legal in some states or countries, whereas Paul had said: *"Flee fornication. Every sin that a man doeth is without the body; but he that committeth fornication sinneth against his own body"* (1 Cor 6:18).

Divorce is prevalent and often resorted to for the slightest reason. Christ's words are thus disregarded: *"And I say unto you, Whosoever shall put away his wife, except it be for fornication, and shall marry another, committeth adultery: and whoso marrieth her which is put away doth commit adultery"* (Matt 19:9). Only two states in the world today have no divorce law: the Vatican and the Philippines.

Abortion has become legal in many countries. Lawmakers and judges forget what God commanded Adam and Noah: *"Be fruitful, and multiply, and replenish the earth"* (Gen 1:28a; 9:1).

Same sex marriage is now permissible in many countries. This violates God's law: *"Thou shalt not lie with mankind, as with womankind: it is abomination"* (Lev 18:22); and *"For this cause God gave them up unto vile affections: for even their women did change the natural use into that which is against nature"* (Rom 1:26).

Sex change procedures are done in many countries; transvestites who have not been operated on cross-dress. God's words are thus set aside. *"The woman shall not wear that which pertaineth unto a man, neither shall a man put on a woman's garment: for all that do so are abomination unto the LORD thy God"* (Deut 22:5).

Prayers in public schools are forbidden, inasmuch as the U.S. Supreme Court has ruled that group prayer in classrooms violates the Constitution. That is a great irony, considering that the United States is the world's largest Christian nation. *"And whatsoever ye do in word or deed, do all in the name of the Lord Jesus, giving thanks to God and the Father by him"* (Col 3:17).

Ten Commandments monuments are removed from many public schools because courts of law have ruled them to be unconstitutional. It is as if they do not know Christ has said: *"For verily I say unto you, Till heaven and earth pass, one jot or one tittle shall in no wise pass from the law, till all be fulfilled"* (Matt 5:18).

Democracy or theocracy? Christians are citizens of two realms – the kingdom of God and government of men. No state can demand complete loyalty from its Christian citizens, because, apart from man-made laws, they also have to obey the commandments of God. However, in many instances, the laws of men come into conflict with the law of God.

From a Biblical standpoint, there is no need for men to pass laws for their governance. Through Moses, God has given us His law (the Torah), comprising 613 commandments which cover virtually all aspects of human life. It therefore boils down to a choice between democracy and theocracy (*theokratia: theos/"God"+kratia*), between "rule of the people" and "rule of God", between life and death – as we are warned in Deuteronomy 30:16, 19. *"I command thee this day to love the LORD thy God, to walk in his ways, and to keep his commandments and his statutes and his judgments, that thou mayest live and multiply: and the LORD thy God shall bless thee in the land whither thou goest to possess it… I call heaven and earth to record this day against you, that I have set before you life and death, blessing and cursing: therefore choose life, that both thou and thy seed may live."*

"Feet of a bear".

The beast from the sea has feet like those of a bear – *"…and his feet were as the feet of a bear"* (Rev 13:2b). In Daniel 7, the second predator in the prophet's vision was a bear with three ribs in its mouth. Bible commentators concur that the bear personifies Persia. "The bear is an apt symbol of the Medo-Persian kingdom. Strength and ferocity figure in almost every Biblical use of the bear. The ponderous bulk fits the massive Persian armies. Xerxes is said to have moved two and one-half million men to attack Greece. Duality (union of two kingdoms) may be suggested by reference to the beast's side."[7] In what imaginable way could the end-time empire possibly be like Persia?

Sun worship? The *Encyclopaedia Britannica* states: "The Persians worshipped Mithra, or Mithras, the same god as Mitra, the sun god in the ancient literature of Hinduism called the Vedas. The first written mention of the Vedic Mitra dates to 1400 B.C. Mithra was said to be the god of light."[8] The Persians spread the worship of Mithra, called Mithraism, throughout Asia Minor.[9] The defeat of the Persians by Alexander the Great (333-331 B.C.) further paved the way for the worship of Mithra to proliferate throughout the Hellenic world.[10]

The Mithraic cult was brought to Rome about 68 B.C. by Cilician pirates captured by the Roman general Pompey the Great. During the early years of the empire it spread rapidly throughout Italy and the Roman provinces.[11] The cult became popular, specially among Roman soldiers and slaves. By about A.D. 100, it had expanded in Europe.[12] The cult spread to as far west as Germany, Spain, and Great Britain.[13] In the 3rd and 4th centuries A.D., the cult of Mithra, carried and supported by the soldiers of the Roman Empire, was the chief rival to the newly developing religion of Christianity.[14]

Roman day of rest. In A.D. 321, to unify the two largest groups of people in the Roman Empire – sun-worshippers and Christians –Emperor Constantine decreed as the Roman day of rest Sun-day (the first day of the week), which was Mithra's holy day and which Christians also venerated as Christ's resurrection day.

The Gentile bishops and other leaders of the Church, wanting to distance themselves from the seventh-day Sabbath-keeping Jews, whom they often called "Christ-killers", welcomed the imperial decree. Later, Pope Sylvester, bishop of Rome (314-335), declared Sunday as "the Lord's Day". In 364, the Council of Laodicea conferred upon Sunday the holiness of the seventh-day Sabbath (Saturday). (Sabbath in Hebrew is *shabbath*; in Greek, *sabbaton*; in Latin, *sabbatum*; in Italian, *sabato*; in Spanish, *sabado*.)

It was thought that "Mithraism was similar to Christianity in many respects, for example… the adoption of Sundays and of December 25 (Mithra's birthday) as holy days,.. The similarities… made possible the easy conversion of its followers to Christian doctrine."[15]

In the 16th century, when Martin Luther, followed by John Calvin and others, led and spread the Reformation, the Protestant churches that grew out of the movement continued to observe Sunday as the day of rest, along with the other holidays instituted by the Roman Catholic Church that they had broken away from, such as Easter, named after the pagan goddess of spring Eastre, and Christmas, originally the feast of the Saturnalia and birthday of Mithra.[16]

So, although it may not actually worship the sun, the end-time empire with feet like those of a bear would be walking like the bear (Persia) by observing its day of rest on Sun-day, Mithra's holy day.

Pagan practices. Thus have the commandments of God been made of none effect, in defiance of the warning in Deuteronomy 12:30, *"Take heed to thyself that thou be not snared by following them, after that they be destroyed from before thee; and that thou inquire not after their gods, saying, How did these nations serve their gods? even so will I do likewise."*

"Mouth of a lion".

The beast from the sea has the mouth of a lion – *"...and his mouth as the mouth of a lion"* (Rev 13:2c). What could this mean?

In Daniel chapter 7, a lion with wings of an eagle represented Babylon. It is historical. "In the ruins of the ancient city of Babylon, broken statues of lions with two wings have been seen."[17] *The Wycliffe Bible Commentary* explains: "The lion symbolizes Babylon here and also in Jer 4:6-7. The eagle's wings speak of swiftness, as the lion of strength."[18] Granted that the lion represents Babylon, what is its connection to the end-time empire?

Richest business center? According to the *World Book*, Babylon was the wealthiest hub of commerce and industry in the ancient world. "Various agricultural and manufacturing activities flourished in the city. Babylon was the largest business center in the Middle East at that time."[19] *Encarta Encyclopedia* adds: "Nabopolassar founded the Neo-Babylonian dynasty, and his son Nebuchadnezzar II expanded the kingdom until it became an empire embracing much of southwest Asia. The imperial capital at Babylon was refurbished with new temple and palace buildings, extensive fortification walls and gates, and paved processional ways; it was at that time the largest city of the known world, covering more than 1,000 hectares (some 2,500 acres)."[20] No wonder the great image's head of gold also stands for Babylon in Daniel 2:37,38.

Hence, as Babylon, symbolized by the winged lion and the head of gold, was the wealthiest kingdom in its time, the end-time empire with the mouth of a lion will also be the richest in the end-times.

Free enterprise. Babylon thrived on an economic system that was very much like those of the richest countries of the world today – free enterprise. Modern-day "free enterprise" economies are called so, because they allow the people to carry out their economic activities free from, or with minimal, government control.

Laissez faire. The guiding spirit of free enterprise is *laissez faire*. The French term, according to the *Merriam-Webster Dictionary*, means "to let (people) do (as they choose)". Thus, in a free enterprise economic system, producers create and merchants sell whatever goods and services customers will buy. The *World Book* notes that "The theory of laissez faire greatly influenced economic thought and action during the early and mid-1800's."[21]

Evils of *laissez faire*? As sellers offer whatever buyers will buy, the principle of *laissez faire* often violates the commandments of God.

Human reproduction: contraceptives (condoms, IUDs, birth control pills), abortifacient drugs, surgical procedures (ligation, vasectomy) – in violation of God's instructions to the first men and Noah (Gen 1:28; 9:1).

Entertainment and sports: Sex and violence in movies and TV; pornographic publications and videos; sex toys (in disregard of Christ's words in Matt 5:28); violent sports (boxing. wrestling, mixed martial arts) are big business in media, the Olympics and other sports events (taekwondo, wushu, shooting, fencing), ignoring Luke 3:14b.

Fashion; Seductive and revealing clothing (see-through/figure-hugging garments, miniskirts, shorts, bikinis) – oblivious of God's warnings:*"… uncover thy locks, make bare the leg, uncover the thigh, pass over the rivers. Thy nakedness shall be uncovered, yea, thy shame shall be seen…"* (Isa 47:2b-3a); *"'I will lift your skirts over your face. I will show the nations your nakedness and the kingdoms your shame'"* (Nah 3:5b, NIV).

Tattoos have become fashionable, with no one seeming to know that God had said, *"'Do not cut your bodies for the dead or put tattoo marks on yourselves. I am the LORD'"* (Lev 19:28, NIV).

Cosmetic surgery (facelifts, body augmentation, liposuction) is commonplace, unaware of Psalm 139:14 – *"I will praise thee; for I am fearfully and wonderfully made: marvellous are thy works…"*

Alcoholic beverages. Wine is among God's blessings that He had asked to be offered to Him (Num 15:7, etc.); but, wine and other alcoholic drinks, when abused, cause social and medical problems. Solomon knew this. *"Who hath woe? who hath sorrow? who hath contentions? who hath babbling? who hath wounds without cause? who hath redness of eyes? They that tarry long at the wine; they that go to seek mixed wine"* (Prov 23:29-30; cf. Isa 5:11).

Drugs: Illegal drugs are a worldwide scourge, controlled by crime syndicates. The substances include marijuana, cocaine, heroin, methamphetamine, hallucinogens, designer drugs, etc., made and used in ignorance of Revelation 21:8 – *"But the fearful, and unbelieving, and the abominable, and murderers, and whoremongers, and sorcerers, and idolaters, and all liars, shall have their part in the lake which burneth with fire and brimstone: which is the second death."*

The word "sorcerers" in the Greek original is *farmakois*, from *pharmakon* ("drug"), which gave us "pharmacy", "pharmaceutical", etc.; hence, "sorcerers", aside from wizards and witches who brew magic potions, also refers to those who produce, sell, and use illegal drugs in our time.

Capitalism. Free enterprise, the *World Book* notes, is often called "capitalism", because many free enterprise economies operate on the principles of capitalism, which calls for the ownership and control of businesses by private individuals. The capitalist countries of Western Europe, which became the model for latter industrialized countries, such as America and Japan, are today among the most prosperous in the world. In these days of mass production, global markets, and multinational corporations, the richest multibillionaires are capitalists.

Greed for gain. In a capitalist economy, there is no limit, despite taxes, to the profits that entrepreneurs and their companies can accumulate. Yet, the Scriptures say that the desire for wealth can lead to miseries. *"For the love of money is the root of all evil: which while some coveted after, they have erred from the faith, and pierced themselves through with many sorrows"* (1 Tim 6:10).

Paul reminds us: *"For we brought nothing into this world, and it is certain we can carry nothing out"* (1 Tim 6:7; cf. Job 1:21). We will therefore do well to heed Christ: *"Lay not up for yourselves treasures upon earth, where moth and rust doth corrupt, and where thieves break through and steal: But lay up for yourselves treasures in heaven, where neither moth nor rust doth corrupt, and where thieves do not break through nor steal"* (Matt 6:19-20).

Power and seat from the dragon.

The end-time empire will receive its power and seat from Satan – *"... and the dragon gave him his power, and his seat, and great authority"* (Rev 13:2b). Inasmuch as we have already identified both the dragon and the fourth beast with the great iron teeth as ancient Rome, it looks like the beast from the sea or end-time empire will be a modern version of the defunct Roman Empire that will be based in Rome's ancient domain (*"his seat"*).

Features of four creatures.

To summarize, the beast will combine features of the four beasts of Daniel 7 – leopard (Greece), bear (Persia), lion (Babylon), and terrible beast with great iron teeth (Rome). Politically, the empire will be democratic, much like ancient Greece; religiously, it will keep Sunday holy just like Persia; economically, it will be a very wealthy center of free enterprise the way Babylon was; and, geographically, it will be situated in the domain of the ancient Roman Empire.

The European Union?

Do you now have a good idea of who or what the end-time empire could be? Is it the European Union (EU)? To know for sure, let us look back on how the EU came to be.

Coal and Steel Community. In 1951, Belgium, France, Italy, Luxembourg, the Netherlands, and West Germany, all democratic, Christian, and capitalist European countries, established the European Coal and Steel Community (ECSC), which unified the six nations into a single market for the production and trade of coal, steel, iron ore, and scrap metal. The principal focus of the industrial union on steel and iron is reminiscent of the ancient Roman Empire, which was symbolized by the two legs of iron in Daniel 2 and by the terrible beast with great iron teeth in Daniel 7.

(The first five organizers had an ulterior motive: to monitor the economic revival of West Germany and hopefully to prevent its remilitarization and return to its position of power in Europe, which had led to its major roles in World Wars I and II.)

Common Market. In 1957, the six ECSC members signed the Treaties of Rome(!), which created the European Atomic Energy Community (Euratom) for the development of peaceful uses of atomic energy and the European Economic Community (EEC), which came to be known as the Common Market.

European Community. In 1967, the ECSC, Euratom and the EEC merged as the European Community (EC); and in 1968 all tariffs between member states were removed. The success of the EC induced Denmark, Ireland, and the United Kingdom to join in 1973; Greece in 1981; Portugal and Spain in 1986 – bringing the number of member-states to twelve.

European Union. In 1992, the 12 European Community member-countries signed the Maastricht Treaty in the Netherlands, creating the European Union (EU). In 1995, Austria, Finland, and Sweden were admitted as full members. Ten more nations swelled the EU membership in 2004: Cyprus, the Czech Republic, Estonia, Hungary, Latvia, Lithuania, Malta, Poland, Slovakia, and Slovenia. Bulgaria and Romania joined in 2007.

<u>Democratic member-states</u>. All of the countries making up the EU have governments that are basically democratic in nature – thus fulfilling the prophecy that the end-time empire would be like the leopard (Greece, the birthplace of democracy).

Sunday rest day. The vast majority of people in EU are Christians – Roman Catholics, Protestants, Eastern Orthodox and other minor sectarians. Descended from the Roman Church, practically all of them keep Sunday as their day of rest, hence walking in the way of the bear (Persia, ancient home of Mithraic sun-worshippers.)

Biggest business center. The EU is today the world's largest free-trade zone; with the North American Free Trade Agreement (NAFTA), comprising Canada, the USA and Mexico, only second. As such, the EU strongly resembles the lion (Babylon, the richest market and business center in ancient times).

Western European hub. The EU has its headquarters in Brussels, Belgium, part of ancient Gaul in Western Europe under the Roman Empire, thus literally fulfilling the prophecy that it would receive its seat or location from the dragon (imperial Rome).

Deadly wound.

"And I saw one of his heads as it were wounded to death..." (Rev 13:3a). In Daniel 7, we saw that the four heads of the leopard signified the four divisions or parts of Alexander's empire after his death. In Revelation 13, we can thus assume that the fatally injured head is also a part of Western Europe. Which one?

Dismembered. In June 1945, after their victory in World War II, the Allies held western Germany, while the Soviet Union occupied the country's eastern half, together with other eastern European countries. The Soviets imposed barriers on communication, trade, and travel between communist East and democratic West. It became known as the Iron Curtain. Tensions grew, starting what was later called the Cold War.

In 1949, Germany's western zone officially became the Federal Republic of Germany (West Germany); while the Soviet zone was proclaimed as the German Democratic Republic (East Germany). It was, as it were, the death and destruction of the second most populous nation in Europe (next only to Russia).

Recovery. West Germany quickly recovered economically. By 1955, the value of goods it produced was greater than that of all of Germany in 1936 before the war. The "economic miracle" enabled West Germany to absorb over 10 million refugees from Eastern Europe and more than a million workers from the rest of Europe.

The East German economy was also recovering, but the standard of living remained much lower. In the early 1950s, thousands of East Germans were escaping each week to West Germany. Almost 3 million people left, and the labor force fell sharply. In 1961, the Communists built the Berlin Wall between East and West Berlin. From 1961 to 1989, hundreds died trying to escape from East Germany, many in the attempt to go over the Berlin Wall.

Deadly wound healed.
The wound would miraculously heal: *"...and his deadly wound was healed"* (Rev 13:3b). In 1989, the people in many Eastern European countries began demonstrating against their Communist governments. East German citizens also demanded more freedom. On November 9, 1989, in a dramatic change in policy, East Germany's government announced that it would open its borders and permit its citizens to travel freely.

In March 1990, East Germans voted for candidates who favored unification with West Germany. On October 3, 1990, East Germany and West Germany were officially reunited. One month later, on November 9, jubilant East and West Germans tore down much of the Berlin Wall, and more than 200,000 East Germans streamed into West Germany. There was great rejoicing in the free world at the return of democracy and capitalism in all of Germany (*"and all the world wondered after the beast"* – Rev 13:3c).

Formidable in war.
The beast would become a great military power. *"And they worshipped the dragon which gave power unto the beast: and they worshipped the beast, saying, Who is like unto the beast? who is able to make war with him?"* (Rev 13:4).

As early as April 1949, the North Atlantic Treaty Organization (NATO) was organized – to discourage the Soviet Union from invading non-Communist nations in Western Europe. Each NATO member country agreed to treat an attack on any one member as an attack on itself. The first members were Belgium, Canada, Denmark, France, Iceland, Italy, Luxembourg, the Netherlands, Norway, Portugal, the United Kingdom, and the United States. (Greece and Turkey joined in 1952; West Germany, in 1955, later as Germany in 1990; Spain, 1982; Czech Republic, Hungary, and Poland, 1999; Bulgaria, Estonia, Latvia, Lithuania, Romania, Slovakia, and Slovenia, 2004; and Albania and Croatia, 2009.)

NATO's policy is deterrence, namely, to discourage an attack on any one of its members. During the Cold War, NATO relied on US nuclear capability to deter a Soviet attack. The US is NATO's most powerful member with its large arsenal of nuclear weapons.

9/11. On September 11, 2001, terrorists crashed three hijacked jetliners into the twin 110-story towers of the World Trade Center in New York City and the Pentagon near Washington, D.C. Around 3,000 people died in what became known as 9/11. NATO declared it as an attack against all NATO members. In a U.S.-led campaign in Afghanistan on the suspected perpetrators (the al-Qaeda terrorist group led by Osama bin Laden), Canada and the United Kingdom contributed forces to the US effort. The campaign led to the fall of the Taliban, the ruling Afghan party that was said to be coddling al-Qaeda. The mission was NATO's first operation outside Europe.

Sequence and fulfillment of prophecies.
As the reader may have noticed, prophecies in the Bible are not always chronological. In some prophecies we have discussed, latter incidents are mentioned ahead of preceding events. It is as if they had been seen without order in a timeless void.

Moreover, some prophecies have multiple fulfillments, that is, they come true more than once. So, while certain prophesied events may seem to have already taken place, some other future events may appear to be the realization of the same visions. The verses we have just discussed (Rev 13:3-4) are cases in point. Although the wounded "head" that was later healed seems to fit precisely into circumstances descriptive of post-war Germany, it may be that the foretold events also point to an actual person – a political leader on the world stage – the much dreaded "Antichrist". With that in mind, let us continue.

Last 42 months?
"And there was given unto him a mouth speaking great things and blasphemies; and power was given unto him to continue forty and two months" (Rev 13:5). The timeline likely begins at the middle of the last 7 years prophesied in Daniel 9:27 – *"He will confirm a covenant with many for one `seven.' In the middle of the `seven' he will put an end to sacrifice and offering. And on a wing [of the temple] he will set up an abomination that causes desolation, until the end that is decreed is poured out on him"* (NIV).

Forty-two months or three-and-a-half years after ratifying an agreement for 7 years with many others, "he" will stop offerings in a holy place and put an object called "abomination of desolation" there. It looks like Revelation 13:5 refers to the 3-½ years of the Great Tribulation that will serve as a prelude to Armageddon, the Day of the Lord, and the Second Coming of Christ.

End-time Antichrist? *"And he opened his mouth in blasphemy against God, to blaspheme his name, and his tabernacle, and them that dwell in heaven"* (Rev 13:6). As we have seen in Chapter 4, a man commits "blasphemy" by attributing some evil to God, or by denying some good we should attribute to Him, or by claiming to be God or, at least, to be in possession of some traits of God.

"And it was given unto him to make war with the saints, and to overcome them…" (Rev 13:7a). Just like the little horn (eleventh king or Papacy), the end-time empire and its ruler will persecute and defeat faithful believers.

Ruler of the world.
" … and power was given him over all kindreds, and tongues, and nations. And all that dwell upon the earth shall worship him, whose names are not written in the book of life of the Lamb slain from the foundation of the world" (Rev 13:7b-8). The end-time empire and its ruler will become the supreme power on earth. If indeed it is EU, will the European Union overshadow the United States and become the most powerful government in the world?

Lately, the US has been cutting back on its military budget and trimming its armed forces. *USA Today* reported in July 2015 that the "US Army is to cut 40,000 soldiers from its ranks over the next two years at home and abroad… Under the cost-cutting plan, the Army will be down to 450,000 soldiers at the end of the 2017 budget year, even though in 2013 it argued in budgetary documents that going below 450,000 troops might mean it could not win a war."[22]

U.S. Joint Chiefs Chairman Gen. Martin Dempsey, drawing from direct experience gained in the Vietnam War and through two Gulf Wars, said in mid-2015 that the 21st-century American military might have fallen to "the bottom edge of our manageable risk."[23]

The beast from the earth

A second beast enters the world stage. *"And I beheld another beast coming up out of the earth; and he had two horns like a lamb, and he spake as a dragon"* (Rev 13:11). Like the first, the second beast represents an empire ruling over other kingdoms or nations. Let us again decipher the metaphors one after another.

"Earth".
As we have already seen, the "earth" is the opposite of "sea". In Genesis 1:9-10, the surface of the planet was made up of only two kinds – water (sea) and dry land (earth).

So, if "sea" in Revelation 17:15 metaphorically means a place with many nations and languages, then "earth" alludes to its opposite – a place with very few people, the condition in which European voyagers during the Age of Exploration discovered the Americas – the New World (the continental landmasses of North, Central, and South America). In that case, the verse insinuates that the second "beast" or empire will emerge in the New World.

"Like a lamb".
The second beast will have a lamb-like characteristic: *"...and he had two horns like a lamb..."* (Rev 13:11b), so unlike the bizarre first beast. The latecomer's comparison to a lamb, a young sheep, connotes youth; so the second end-time empire must still be young. Moreover, a lamb is gentle and docile, in contrast to the earlier predatory "beasts" (lion, bear, leopard, dragon), which rose to power by devouring or conquering smaller, weaker kingdoms.

The vision thus suggests that the lamb-like empire would attain prominence through generally peaceful means. Moreover, since the biblical Lamb of God is Christ, the second end-time empire must be mainly Christian as regards the religion of its citizens.

Let us try to pinpoint a country that matches all or several of the descriptions: (1) an empire with several other kingdoms, nations or states under it; (2) located in the New World or the Americas; (3) a place with originally very few people; (4) a young country; (5) attained prominence through relatively peaceful means; and (6) a Christian nation. Several modern countries fit the description. Is it Canada, the United States, Mexico, Brazil, Argentina?

Let us try another tack. What is the most prominent country in the Americas today? And when we hear the word "America", which country immediately comes to mind?

The United States? (1) The United States of America, as its name denotes, is composed of many states. (2) It is in the New World, specifically North America. (3) It was originally a "wilderness", sparsely populated by Native Americans. (4) It is young, not yet 250 years old, having been founded in 1776. (5) Although it became embroiled in a few short wars, the USA expanded its territory mostly through peaceful pioneering development and land purchases. It grew wealthy through agriculture and industry, so much so that Thomas Jefferson, the third US president (1801-1809), envisioned his country as "a nation of small farmers – an ideal society wherein the people would lead simple, but productive lives."[24] (6) The USA is predominantly Christian – in fact, the largest Christian, nation in the entire world.

"**Two horns**". The second beast has two horns like those of a lamb. A "horn" in prophecy, as we have become familiar with, is a king or ruler and his kingdom or nation that is part of an empire. What do the "horns" symbolize?

After the discovery of the Americas, Europeans fleeing political and religious repression sailed to the New World to establish colonies or new communities where they could freely practice their beliefs. Puritans (separatists who wanted to purify the Church of England) made up 40% of the Pilgrim Fathers who came on the ship *Mayflower* and founded the Plymouth Colony in 1620. Puritanism was the dominant religious force in New England throughout the 17th and 18th centuries.[25]

A tradition of religious freedom, without any government control, flourished in America. In time, that tradition gave birth to the principle of the "separation of church and state." Thus, the temporal kingdom and the spiritual kingdom are able to function without any interference from one another, as later enshrined in the United States Constitution. Are the church and the state the two "horns" like those of a "lamb"?

"Like a dragon".

Paradoxically, the gentle "lamb" has a sinister side – "*...and he spake as a dragon*" (Rev 13:11c). The dragon, as we have seen in Revelation 12:9, is Satan, who had the temerity to rebel against God. Thus it looks like the "lamb", despite its innocent and harmless appearance, would also defy the Creator. Has the United States been guilty of this behavior?

Bastion of democracy. As the world's stronghold of democracy, the United States is the role-model setting the example in civil liberties that other democratic nations copy. In fact, many new democratic countries have patterned their constitutions after that of the United States. In our earlier discussion about how the end-time empire is like a "leopard" (Greece, the birthplace of democracy), we saw how the United States leads the world in promulgating laws that clash against the commandments of God.

"All the power of the first beast".

The second end-time empire will be as powerful as the first, which has taken the place of ancient Rome. "*And he exerciseth all the power of the first beast before him...*" (Rev 13:12a). It will be a world power just like Rome and its scion, the European Union.

The *New International Version* (NIV) has a slightly different translation, "*He exercised all the authority of the first beast on his behalf...*" (Rev 13:12a, NIV). "*On his behalf*" points to the fact that the second empire, the United States, has on many occasions acted in the interest, and even in defense, of its Western European allies, which later formed the nucleus of the European Union.

The USA became widely recognized as a world power in 1898, after it gained a quick victory over Spain in the Spanish-American War. In the subsequent Treaty of Paris of December 10, 1898, Spain ceded Guam, Puerto Rico, and the Philippines to the United States, which also annexed Hawaii that year. (The US earlier bought Alaska from Russia in 1867.) In the succeeding years of the 20th century, the USA continued to grow and became one of the world's strongest military powers.

"Worship the first beast".

The second beast *"causeth the earth and them which dwell therein to worship the first beast, whose deadly wound was healed"* (Rev 13:12b). Let us try to more clearly understand this.

The word translated "worship" was in the original Greek text *proskuneo* ("to kiss, like a dog licking his master's hand"; "to fawn or crouch to, i.e. [literally or figuratively] prostrate oneself in homage [do reverence to, adore]").[26] It can therefore be synonymous to "idolize", which, in turn, can simply mean to "look up to" a person as, for example, a role model. In short, the second beast or end-time empire will urge other nations to idolize the first empire.

We see this in the many ways the American media pictures the European Union as a paradigm of democracy and capitalism.

"Fire from heaven".

The second empire will be some kind of a miracle worker. *"And he doeth great wonders, so that he maketh fire come down from heaven on the earth in the sight of men"* (Rev 13:13). We can unravel this riddle through both Biblical and scientific terms.

"Fire". In the Bible, fire can be symbolic of God's anger and judgment, as in Deuteronomy 4:24 – *"For the LORD thy God is a consuming fire, even a jealous God"*; and in Amos 5:6 – *"Seek the LORD, and ye shall live; lest he break out like fire in the house of Joseph, and devour it, and there be none to quench it in Bethel."*

In the phrase *"fire from heaven"*, "heaven" was translated from the Greek word *ouranos*, meaning "sky". Uranus was the name of the god of the sky in Greek mythology, from which the modern-day English word "uranium" has been derived. Uranium is a radioactive metallic chemical element, certain isotopes of which can sustain efficient chain reaction. For this reason, it is used as a source of nuclear energy, such as in making atomic bombs.

The United States developed and dropped the world's first two atomic bombs on the Japanese cities of Hiroshima and Nagasaki in World War II to force Japan into surrendering. Today, America continues to maintain a large nuclear arsenal as a deterrent to aggression by its rivals for global hegemony.

Indeed, the second beast or end-time empire has made *"fire come down from heaven on the earth in the sight of men."*

"Deceive the earth".
"And deceiveth them that dwell on the earth by the means of those miracles which he had power to do in the sight of the beast..." (Rev 13:14a). It is flabbergasting to think that the second beast will dare hoodwink the entire world. Has anything even remotely like this actually happened?

Apollo lunar landings? Conspiracy theorists claim that the Apollo 11 moon landing on July 20, 1969, and the next five manned landings (1969–72) were faked. The footages shown on worldwide television, they say, had been shot in a top-secret earthbound studio.

Several books and documentary videos have been produced in the USA, Russia, Germany, and Japan detailing the alleged hoax. (Books: *We Never Went to the Moon: America's Thirty Billion Dollar Swindle,* Bill Kaysing, 1976; *Moongate: Suppressed Findings of the U.S. Space Program*, William L. Brian, 1982; *Antiapollon: Moonlight scam US,* Yury Ignatyevich Mukhin; *Dark Moon: Apollo and the Whistle-Blowers,* David S. Percy and Mary Bennett; *The Americans on the Moon: The Great Breakthrough or Cosmic Scam?,* Alexander Ivanovich Popov; *One Small Step?: The Great Moon Hoax,* Gerhard Wisnewski; *1962-1972: Apollo 11 Has Never Been to the Moon,* Takahiko Soejima, 2004. Videos: *Was It Only a Paper Moon?,* James M. Collier, 1997; *What Happened on the Moon?,* David S. Percy and Mary Bennett; *Did We Go?,* Aron Ranen; *A Funny Thing Happened on the Way to the Moon,* Bart Sibrel, 2001; *Conspiracy Theory: Did We Land on the Moon?,* Fox TV network, 2001.)

After the February 2001 airing of Fox network's TV special seen by some 15 million viewers, opinion polls showed that 6-20% of Americans and 28% of Russians believed that the manned lunar landings were faked.[27] Conspiracists point to allegedly incriminating details that are said to be dead giveaways. Let us examine a few.

No stars. The sky in the still photos and video footages is solid black, there are no stars in the background. (Was the arrangement of the stars too difficult to extrapolate?)

No blast crater. The surface beneath the lunar module is level and undisturbed. (How come the lunar module's engine exhaust made no blast crater?)

Inconsistent shadows. The angles and colors of shadows vary; some point in opposite directions. (Effects of studio lights?)

Identical backgrounds. Horizons and other background details are the same in photos captioned to have been taken miles apart.

Astronauts' footprints. On earth, footprints are preserved by moisture in the soil which keeps the particles adhering together. However, there is no water on the moon.

Deadly cosmic radiations. The Van Allen radiation belts, solar flares, solar wind, coronal mass ejections, etc., make lunar trips very dangerous. (NASA would not risk showing astronauts getting sick or dying on live, worldwide TV.)[28] Detractors say technologies had not been perfected to protect life for long periods in outer space. Thus, instead of increasing and eventually establishing a station on the moon, manned missions decreased and eventually came to a stop.

Probable motives? The US was lagging behind in the space race. The USSR achieved the early milestones: first man-made satellite (Sputnik 1, October 1957); first living creature in orbit (dog Laika, November 1957); first artificial object to orbit the Sun (Mechta, January 1959); first man-made object on the moon (Luna 2, September1959); first photos of the hidden side of the moon (Luna 3, October 1959); first man in space (Yuri Gagarin, April 1961); first woman in orbit (Valentina Tereshkova, June 1963); first spacewalk (Alexei Leonov, March 1965).

In the Cold War, third world countries were being subverted and leaning towards communism. The American Patriot Friends Network claimed in 2009 that the lunar landings helped distract public attention from the unpopular Vietnam War. The moon missions ended about the time that the US ended its involvement in the war. Author Bart Sibrel noted that "the Soviets did not have the capability to track deep space craft until late in 1972, immediately after which the last three Apollo missions were abruptly cancelled."[29]

Rebuttals. Evidence for the landings and detailed rebuttals to the hoax claims have been published. In June 1977, NASA issued a fact sheet debunking claims that the Apollo lunar landings were faked. It was reissued on February 14, 2001, the day before Fox TV broadcast *Conspiracy Theory: Did We Land on the Moon?* Vince Calder and Andrew Johnson, scientists from Argonne National Laboratory, gave detailed answers to the conspiracy claims on their website. They showed the landing was basically accurate, allowing for mistakes such as mislabeled photos and imperfect recollections.

Biblical comments. Two Bible verses, although one talks about a man's lifespan and the other about homelands, may perhaps also apply to man's quest for other worlds beyond this planet we call home. Job 14:5 – *"Seeing his days are determined, the number of his months are with thee, thou hast appointed his bounds that he cannot pass";* and Acts 17:26 – *"And hath made of one blood all nations of men for to dwell on all the face of the earth, and hath determined the times before appointed, and the bounds of their habitation."* In other words, the Creator has ordained preset limits to human existence and dwelling places.

"Image of the beast".

The second end-time empire will exhort other nations to emulate the first: *"…saying to them that dwell on the earth, that they should make an image to the beast, which had the wound by a sword, and did live"* (Rev 13:14b).

"Image" in the original Greek test is *eikon* (icon), meaning "likeness," "resemblance," or "representation." Dictionaries define "image" as "a likeness or copy," "a reproduction or imitation." Hence, to *"make an image to the beast"* means to make a "copy" of the beast.

By its pronouncements and actions the United States has been urging other countries to copy or imitate the characteristics of the countries of the European Union: democratic, capitalist, and Sunday-resting! Truly, America is today the champion of democracy, capitalism, and Sunday-keeping Christianity

Democratic bandwagon. During the 1800's, democracy spread steadily. Many countries copied the American and British models. By the 1920s and 1930s, democracy was firmly established throughout much of Western Europe, as well as in the former British colonies of Australia, Canada, New Zealand. In the 1950's, newly independent nations in Africa and Asia joined the bandwagon by likewise developing their own democratic institutions. By the second half of the 20th century, every independent country in the world, with only a few exceptions, had a government that, in form if not in practice, embodied some of the principles of democracy.[30] In the late 1980s and early 1990s, democracy grew in northern and central Asia, as well as Eastern Europe, as Communists lost control of the states in the USSR and other Eastern European nations.

The democratic system, which began in Greece as "rule of the people", today serves as the paradigm for the rest of the world.

Sunday resting Christianity. The largest Christian nation, the United States, is also the leading missionary-sending country. In the 1800s, the China and slave trades brought American missionaries to East Asia and Africa, where they preached and put up churches, schools and hospitals. Today, about one-third of the world's people are Christians, constituting the largest religious group. At the same time, Christianity's population centers have shifted from the West to Latin America, Africa, Asia, and the Pacific region, where more than half of the world's Christians live today.[31]

Notably, the vast majority of Christians observe Sunday (the Persian sun-god's birthday) as their day of rest (decreed by Emperor Constantine and adopted by the Roman Catholic Church way back in 321 A.D.).

Capitalist economies. The success of capitalism in countries like the United States, the United Kingdom, Germany and Japan is said to be proof of its "superiority" over other economic systems. In imitation, many nations in the "free world" have adopted one form or another of capitalism. The founding member-states of the European Union were all capitalist countries.

The International Monetary Fund (IMF) and the World Bank, of which the United States is principal member, encourage and support the formation of other regional free trade associations that copy the European Union's economic model. These include:

CARIFTA (Caribbean Free Trade Area), 1968
ECOWAS (Economic Community of West African States), 1975
SADC (Southern African Development Community), 1979
NAFTA (North American Free Trade Agreement), 1989
EFTA (European Free Trade Association), 1994
ASEAN (Association of Southeast Asian Nations - Integration), 2016

The modus of these economic cooperation groups traces its roots to the free enterprise market system of Babylon, which made it the wealthiest business center of the ancient world.

Worship the beast or die.

As judge and executioner of the first beast, the second beast *"...had power to give life unto the image of the beast, that the image of the beast should both speak, and cause that as many as would not worship the image of the beast should be killed"* (Rev 13:15).

As we have defined earlier, the English word "worship" is *proskuneo* in Greek and may simply mean "to idolize", "emulate", or "look up to" (as a role model). On the other hand, the word "kill", from the Greek *apokteino,* means "to kill outright"; or, figuratively, "to destroy."[32]

Hence, Revelation 13:15 may be interpreted as follows: *"And he had power* (ability) *to give life unto* (energize) *the image* (copy or imitation) *of the beast* (democratic, Sunday-resting, and capitalist Western Europe), *that the image* (copy) *of the beast should both speak* (make pronouncements), *and cause that as many as would not worship* (idolize, emulate, or copy) *the image of the beast should be killed* (destroyed). The United States, through its policies and agencies, is actively against and deeply committed to bring down or destroy all political regimes opposed to democracy and capitalism, which originated in Western Europe.

The Cold War. After the 1917 Bolshevik Revolution, Russia became a Communist dictatorship and, starting in 1922, formed with its eastern European vassal states the Union of Soviet Socialist Republics (USSR). During the 1920s and 1930s, the Soviets called for a world revolution and the destruction of capitalism. They charged the USA and its Western capitalist allies of attempting to overthrow the Communist form of government.

In 1947, the Truman Doctrine authorized the US to aid any nation threatened by Soviet expansionism. Several confrontations between the superpowers, such as the Berlin Blockade of 1948-49, took place, without deteriorating into actual warfare – thus the term "Cold War". The rivalry led to the formation of the North Atlantic Treaty Organization (NATO) by the West in 1949 and the Warsaw Pact by the Communists in 1955. In 1957, the Eisenhower Doctrine permitted the United States president to "use armed force to assist any… nation… requesting assistance against armed aggression from any country controlled by international Communism."

Although originally centered in Europe, the Cold War drew the USA and the USSR into local conflicts across the globe, such as the Korean War in 1950, wherein the US and the United Nations helped the South Koreans resist North Korea backed by Russia and Red China. In 1961, the USA sponsored the failed invasion of pro-Soviet Cuba by anti-Castro Cubans at the Bay of Pigs. In the 1960's-early 1970s, the Americans backed South Vietnam against the Communist Viet Cong forces. The USA and the USSR also supported opposing sides in Latin America (Dominican Republic) and Africa (Republic of the Congo, Nigeria, Angola, Somalia, Ethiopia). During the Soviet invasion of Afghanistan (1979-89), the Carter presidency considered ways in which the United States could win a nuclear war. The next president, Ronald Reagan, argued that the only way to end the Cold War was to win it by intensifying the arms race. He deployed nuclear ballistic and cruise missiles in Western Europe.

Widespread demands for democratic liberties broke up the Soviet Union in 1991, bringing "the end of the Cold War… challenged the claims of Communism… and enabled supporters of open markets to proclaim the superiority of capitalism. Many nations that formerly followed the theories of German social philosopher Karl Marx abruptly abandoned that philosophy, bringing virtually the entire globe into the orbit of the (capitalist) market."[33]

The "mark of the beast".

"And he causeth all, both small and great, rich and poor, free and bond, to receive a mark in their right hand, or in their foreheads" (Rev 13:16). The second beast or end-time empire will put a "mark" on its citizens. What could that be?

Mark and seal. It seems that a mark is synonymous to a seal. In Ezekiel 9:4 – *"And the LORD said unto him, Go through the midst of the city, through the midst of Jerusalem, and set a mark upon the foreheads of the men that sigh and that cry for all the abominations that be done in the midst thereof."*; while in Revelation 7:2-3 – *"And I saw another angel ascending from the east, having the seal of the living God: and he cried with a loud voice to the four angels, to whom it was given to hurt the earth and the sea, Saying, Hurt not the earth, neither the sea, nor the trees, till we have sealed the servants of our God in their foreheads."*

In Ezekiel, God told the scribe to put a mark on the foreheads of righteous men; while in the Revelation, angels were to put the seal of God in the foreheads of His servants. God's servants are righteous men, so the mark must be in practically the same class as the seal.

The seal of God.

The angels have already accomplished their mission by the time we get to Revelation 14:1 – *"And I looked, and, lo, a Lamb stood on the mount Sion, and with him an hundred forty and four thousand, having his Father's name written in their foreheads."* Does the seal of God solely consist of the name of the Almighty Father and nothing more? The word "seal" implies the presence of other elements aside from a name.

As a rule, seals have a pattern containing at least three elements: (1) name; (2) title; and (3) domain. For example, Elizabeth I (1586-1603): *Elizabetha dei gracia Anglie Francie et Hibernie Regina Fidei Defensor*, meaning "*Elizabeth* (name), by grace of God, *Queen* (title) of *England, France and Ireland* (domain), Defender of the Faith".

In the entire Bible, this pattern can be found only in the Fourth Commandment (Exodus 20:8-11) – *"Remember the sabbath day, to keep it holy. Six days shalt thou labour, and do all thy work: But the seventh day is the sabbath of the LORD (NAME) thy God (TITLE): in it thou shalt not do any work, thou, nor thy son, nor thy daughter, thy manservant, nor thy maidservant, nor thy cattle, nor thy stranger that is within thy gates: For in six days the LORD made heaven and earth, the sea, and all that in them is (DOMAIN), and rested the seventh day: wherefore the LORD blessed the sabbath day, and hallowed it."*

Three elements in the verse form a seal:
1) Name: *"the LORD"* (substituted for "YHWH")
2) Title: *"God"*
3) Domain: *"heaven and earth, the sea, and all that in them is"*

It therefore becomes apparent that the Fourth Commandment enjoining God's people to cease from work and rest on the seventh day of the week is the seal of God!

Memorial to the Creation.

Resting from work on the seventh-day Sabbath is the memorial to YHWH's work of creation. *"And hallow my sabbaths; and they shall be a sign between me and you, that ye may know that I am the LORD your God"* (Ezek 20:20).

For that reason, the fourth commandment begins with the word *"Remember…"* By keeping the seventh-day Sabbath holy, we honor YHWH by remembering that He is the Creator of heaven and earth. Those who ignore or neglect the Sabbath are actually refusing to acknowledge YHWH as the Creator. That is a most grievous insult to the Creator that deserves the supreme punishment. *"Six days may work be done; but in the seventh is the sabbath of rest, holy to the LORD: whosoever doeth any work in the sabbath day, he shall surely be put to death"* (Ex 31:15b; cf. Num 15:32,36).

A counterfeit seal.

Satan or Lucifer, in his desire to *"be like the most High"* (Isa 14:14), arrogates unto himself imitations of attributes which the Creator possesses. These counterfeit traits are typically the opposite of those which God is, has, or does. Let us consider examples.

"The LORD is good" (Ps 34:8, 100:5, 135:3, etc.), whereas the devil is evil (John 17:15, etc.)

"God is light" (1 John 1:5); while Satan is called the "prince of darkness."

The Temple's Holy of Holies was in the west (Ex 27:9-16), but apostate Israelites worshipped the sun facing the east (Ezek 8:16).

The names of 72 angels derived from Exodus 14:19-21, when spelled or pronounced backwards, reveal the names of 72 demons.

The symbol of Christ venerated by Christians is the upright Latin cross; Satanists worship before an inverted Latin cross.

The "black mass" is a ritual characterized by the inversion of the Latin mass celebrated by the Roman Catholic Church.

"Backmasked" rock music and pop songs, recorded deliberately or unintentionally, when played backwards, express Satanic messages.

The "mark of the beast", therefore, must be the reverse of the seal of God. Thus, if the seal of God is resting from work on the seventh and last day of the week (Saturday), the mark of the beast must be the exact opposite – resting from work on the first day of the week (Sunday)!

"Right hand or forehead".
The mark will be *"...in their right hand, or in their foreheads"* (Rev 13:16b). Why specifically on those two parts of the body?

Proverb 10:4 says, *"He becometh poor that dealeth with a slack hand: but the hand of the diligent maketh rich."* Accordingly, we use our hands to work and earn a living. And, since most people are right-handed, having the mark *"in the right hand"* (the usually more active hand) means regular or customary use of the mark.

The alternative spot for the mark is *"in the forehead"*. Note that the word used is "in", not "on", the forehead – suggesting that the mark is placed in the mind, not on the skin of the brow. The "brain's decision-making center, the pre-frontal cortex"[34], is just behind the forehead. Hence, having the mark *"in the forehead"* means that the person understands and willingly accepts the mark.

Widespread acceptance. Labor practices and new laws in modern industrialized countries, with the U.S. setting the example, have facilitated the implementation of the "mark of the beast". "By the end of World War I, the 8-hour day and the 48-hour week prevailed in most industries in the U.S. and Britain."[35] Twenty years later, the "Federal Wage and Hour Law... (was) enacted by the United States Congress in 1938 to eliminate labor conditions injurious to the health and efficiency of workers... A subsequent... decrease in maximum non-overtime hours to 40, was incorporated in the original law."[36] "The practice of limiting the maximum period of work to 5 days and 40 hours or less per week was virtually universal in the U.S. by the beginning of World War II... By the middle of the 20th century most of the countries of the world had legislation limiting the basic work-week in non-agricultural industries to 40-48 hours" (5-6 days).[37]

As a result, it became customary for most workers to start work on Monday and stop working at the end of the day on either Friday or Saturday. In either case, the overwhelming majority, in conformity with the global practice, keep Sunday as their day of rest.

Most horrible punishment. People who accept the mark of the beast infuriate the Creator. A punishment specially reserved for them awaits in the afterlife. *" And the third angel followed them, saying with a loud voice, If any man worship* (idolize) *the beast* (EU) *and his image* *(democratic, capitalist system) and receive his mark (resting on Sunday) in his forehead (mind), or in his hand (practices it), The same shall drink of the wine of the wrath of God, which is poured out without mixture into the cup of his indignation; and he shall be tormented with fire and brimstone in the presence of the holy angels, and in the presence of the Lamb"* (Rev 14:9-10).

The *"number of his name"*.
"And that no man might buy or sell, save he that had the mark, or the name of the beast, or the number of his name. Here is wisdom. Let him that hath understanding count the number of the beast: for it is the number of a man; and his number is Six hundred threescore and six" (Rev 13:17-18). The number of the name of the beast is 666. Can we find a plausible explanation?

Let us try. In modern Hebrew, *demokratia* is spelled as follows (without vowel-marks and written left-to-right, instead of the normal right-to-left, for the convenience of non-Hebrew readers):

ד מ ו כ ר ט י ה
Dalet-Mem-Vav-Kaph-Resh-Tet-Yod-Hey
D (e) M O K R (a) T I A

However, if we spell it in a rudimentary, primeval way, before certain Hebrew letters (ה/H, ו/W, י/Y) were added at the end of words to indicate vowels (10th-late 7th centuries B.C.)[38], *demokratia* can be spelled differently:

ד מ כ ר א ת א
D (e) M (o) K R A T (i) A
Dalet-Mem-Kaph-Resh-Aleph-Tav-Aleph
(4)+(40)+(20)+(200)+(1)+(400)+(1) = 666

Surprisingly, the *gematria* (letter values) of this unconventional spelling adds up to the number of the name of the beast – 666!

Bar code. In the United States and most modern countries, bar codes, which uniquely identify each product, are a ubiquitous part of today's retail business. They appeared on supermarket items in 1973; and similar codes have since been developed for use in factories, warehouses, hospitals, libraries, *et al.* A laser scanner is used to "read" the bar code and transmit it to a computer that translates the code into information about an article. At supermarkets, groceries and other retail stores, one practically cannot buy anything without a bar code printed or attached to it.

Almost any product can be bought in supermarkets – all sorts of fresh and preserved food and beverages, as well as non-food items for home, school, office, personal use, even auto supplies and accessories. In food products alone, supermarkets account for at least 75% of all sales in the United States.[39]

A bar code consists of parallel vertical lines or bars of varying thicknesses that represent the numbers 0 to 9 (also printed at the base of the code). The bar code usually has two parts: the pattern of lines on the left identifies the manufacturer, while the set of lines on the right describes the product. The two parts are marked off by three sets of lines that are not part of the product information, but serve only as separators.

A bar code starts with two thin lines on the left (to inform the computer that the code has started); two identical lines mark the middle (to separate the first part from the second); and the same two lines frame the right edge (to let the computer know that the code has ended). The two thin lines are used, since they are the simplest and most easily read or recognized. They represent the number "six" (6). Together, the three separators spell out the number of the name of the beast – "6-6-6"!

Practical translation. We can now more practically translate Revelation 13:17 for our time: *"And that no man* (nobody) *might buy or sell* (anything), *save* (except) *he that had the mark* (Sunday rest), *or the name of the beast* (democracy), *or the number of his name* (666 in bar codes)."

In simpler terms: "Nobody can buy or sell anything in a Sunday-resting democracy except products with bar codes."

The bar code, a sign of free enterprise and capitalism, likewise confirms to us that the "beast" is part lion, symbol of Babylon, the wealthiest business center in the ancient world.

"Number of a man".

In Biblical numeric symbolism, "six" (6) is the number of man, as we can see in several instances: man was created on the sixth day of creation (Gen 1:26-31); the first six days of the week are the days God allows man to work (Ex 20:8-11); a slave is released after serving for six years (Ex 21:2; Deut 15:12), etc..

In Daniel chapter 7, it was twice mentioned that the *"little horn... in this horn were eyes like the eyes of man, and a mouth speaking great things... that horn that had eyes, and a mouth that spake very great things..."* (Dan 7:8b,20b) as if to emphasize that the "little horn" personifies a man, whom we later identified as the Papacy.

The man called "Pope", according to an April 18, 1915, article in *Our Sunday Visitor*, a Catholic journal, has a crown with the Latin words "VICARIUS FILII DEI", which are translated as "Vicar (Representative) of the Son of God". Latin, like Hebrew and Greek, did not have any characters for numbers; so letters were also used as numbers. Let us add up the applicable numbers on the Pope's crown:

V I C A R **I V** S F **I L I I D** E **I**
5+1+100 + 1+5   +1+50+1+1+500 + 1 = 666

The numbers on the crown of the Pope, although he may not be the beast, likewise add up to the number of the name of the beast – "666"!

6

Adversaries and Antichrists

*Little children, it is the last time:
and as ye have heard that antichrist shall come,
even now are there many antichrists...*

- 1 John 2:18a

Let us now trace the lineages of the other protagonists in the end-time tableau. We will hark back to the days when Persia was at the height of its power, but was threatened by Greece, which was then poised to be the new dominant power in the ancient world.

Persian-Grecian rivalry

After Media-Persia took over Babylon, the Jewish prophet Daniel became an adviser to the king of the invaders. The angel Gabriel told him: *"Also I in the first year of Darius the Mede, even I, stood to confirm and to strengthen him. And now will I shew thee the truth. Behold, there shall stand up yet three kings in Persia; and the fourth shall be far richer than they all: and by his strength through his riches he shall stir up all against the realm of Grecia"* (Dan 11:1-2). Gabriel foretold the emergence of three more kings in Persia, the last of whom would attempt a massive invasion of Greece.

Rise and fall of Alexander.

Gabriel continued: *"And a mighty king shall stand up, that shall rule with great dominion, and do according to his will. And when he shall stand up, his kingdom shall be broken, and shall be divided toward the four winds of heaven; and not to his posterity, nor according to his dominion which he ruled: for his kingdom shall be plucked up, even for others beside those"* (Dan 11:3-4).

Alexander, the "mighty king," defeated the formidable Persian army, crowning his many other previous victories. However, he died shortly thereafter, and his vast empire was divided into four parts (*"the four winds of heaven"*), but not among his heirs (*"not to his posterity"*). As we saw in Daniel 8:22 (Ch. 3), four of Alexander's generals divided the Greek dominions among themselves.

Kings of the north and south.
The two more powerful generals eventually became the king of the north and the king of the south. Seleucus Nicanor, who held Asia the Great, became "king of the north" and started the Seleucid dynasty based in Syria. Ptolemy made Egypt his seat of power and founded the Ptolemaic dynasty there as the "king of the south".

"And the king of the south shall be strong, and one of his princes; and he shall be strong above him, and have dominion; his dominion shall be a great dominion" (Dan 11:5). Ptolemy adopted the name Ptolemy Soter and expanded his southern kingdom's possessions by capturing Cyprus, Phoenicia, Caria, and Cyrene.

History foretold.
The following prophecies may sound like historical accounts, but at the time of the telling they were still future events narrated ahead of time. Prophecy is history foretold before it happens. The litany of prophecies that you will read next were first given in the late 7th century B.C., but their various fulfillments began only in the late 4th century B.C., some 300 years later, and will have great bearing on events at the time of the end. The narratives have been excerpted from *Daniel and the Revelation* by Uriah Smith (revised 1944).

North-south alliance. *"And in the end of years they shall join themselves together; for the king's daughter of the south shall come to the king of the north to make an agreement: but she shall not retain the power of the arm; neither shall he stand, nor his arm: but she shall be given up, and they that brought her, and he that begat her, and he that strengthened her in these times"* (Dan 11:6).

To put an end to the rivalry between north and south, Ptolemy Philadelphus, the second king of Egypt, offered his daughter Berenice to Antiochus Theos, third king of Syria, if the latter would put away his wife Laodice. Antiochus agreed and married Berenice. But Antiochus changed his mind and took back Laodice, dumping Berenice. Nonetheless, Laodice had Antiochus poisoned (*"neither shall he stand,"*) and Berenice murdered (*"she shall not retain the power of the arm"*), including her Egyptian servants (*"they that brought her"*) and her son by Antiochus (*"he that begat her"*; probably better, *"he that she begat"*).

Seesaw warfare. *"But out of a branch of her roots shall one stand up in his estate, which shall come with an army, and shall enter into the fortress of the king of the north, and shall deal against them, and shall prevail: And shall also carry captives into Egypt their gods, with their princes, and with their precious vessels of silver and of gold; and he shall continue more years than the king of the north"* (Dan 11:7-8). Berenice's brother (*"out of a branch of her roots"*), Ptolemy Euergetes, on becoming king of Egypt, attacked the new king of the north, Seleucus Callinicus, to avenge his sister. Defeating the northerners (*"and shall prevail"*), he took 2,500 of their idols (*"carry captives into Egypt their gods"*), as well as 40,000 talents of silver and other treasures (*"with their precious vessels of silver and of gold;"*). He lived 4-5 years longer than Seleucus Callinicus, who died after falling from a horse in exile (*"he shall continue more years than the king of the north"*). *"So the king of the south shall come into his kingdom, and shall return into his own land.*

"But his sons shall be stirred up, and shall assemble a multitude of great forces: and one shall certainly come, and overflow, and pass through: then shall he return, and be stirred up, even to his fortress" (Dan 11:9-10). The sons of Seleucus Callinicus mustered a huge army (*"a multitude of great forces"*) to recover the territories they had lost. The younger son, Antiochus Magnus ("the Great"), won back Seleucia and Syria (*"one shall certainly come, and overflow"*). He was advancing to invade Egypt when he accepted a truce and headed back for home (*"then shall he return... even to his fortress"*).

"And the king of the south shall be moved with choler, and shall come forth and fight with him, even with the king of the north: and he shall set forth a great multitude; but the multitude shall be given into his hand" (Dan 11:11). Ptolemy Euergetes's heir, Ptolemy Philopator, incensed at their losses, mustered a large army to strike back at Antiochus Magnus, who deployed 62,000 foot soldiers and 6,000 horsemen (*"he shall set forth a great multitude"*). It was Ptolemy Philopator, though, who won a resounding victory on the battlefield (*"the multitude shall be given into his hand"*).

"And when he hath taken away the multitude, his heart shall be lifted up; and he shall cast down many ten thousands: but he shall not be strengthened by it" (Dan 11:12). Following his triumph, Ptolemy

Philopator wanted to offer sacrifices in Jerusalem. As victor, he felt privileged to enter the holy of holies of the Temple ("*his heart shall be lifted up*"), but he was prevented by the Jews. Returning to Egypt, he had some 50,000 Jews in Alexandria massacred ("*he shall cast down many ten thousands*"), an act that simply made him more enemies ("*but he shall not be strengthened by it*").

"For the king of the north shall return, and shall set forth a multitude greater than the former, and shall certainly come after certain years with a great army and with much riches" (Dan 11:13). Ptolemy Philopator was succeeded by his son, Ptolemy Epiphanes, then only five years old. Antiochus Magnus, seeing an opportunity, assembled a much bigger army than before ("*the king of the north shall return, and shall set forth a multitude greater than the former*") to invade Egypt.[1]

Emerging power.

A new military power will step into the rivalry between the kings of the north and south. *"And in those times there shall many stand up against the king of the south: also the robbers of thy people shall exalt themselves to establish the vision; but they shall fall"* (Dan 11:14). Several parties plotted against the Egyptian boy-king ("*there shall many stand up against the king of the south*"), such as Philip of Macedon and a seditious Alexandrian faction. But a rising new power intervened in 200 B.C. by placing the young Ptolemy Epiphanes under its tutelage – Rome, whose legions would later loot the Jerusalem Temple in 70 A.D. ("*the robbers of thy people*"). Rome's intrusion into the long-running feud between the two Hellenistic kingdoms of the north and south betrayed its ambition to dominate the region ("*shall exalt themselves to establish the vision*").

The Romans sent the mercenary general Scopas, who succeeded in conquering Judea and Coele-Syria for Egypt. Rome thereafter engaged and defeated Philip of Macedon in the Second Macedonian War (200–196 BC), frustrating the plotters.

Fall of the south. *"So the king of the north shall come, and cast up a mount, and take the most fenced cities: and the arms of the south shall not withstand, neither his chosen people, neither shall there be any strength to withstand"* (Dan 11:15).

Taking advantage of the Romans' war with Philip of Macedon, Antiochus Magnus led his army to recover lost territory. He marched into Coele Syria and, at Panion near the source of the Jordan River, defeated the troops of Scopas, who fled to Sidon ("*but they shall fall*"). Antiochus laid siege to the fortified citadel ("*cast up a mount*") and Scopas, who still had ten thousand men ("*his chosen people*"), but faced with starvation, surrendered (*"the arms of the south shall not withstand... neither shall there be any strength to withstand"*), in the process giving up control of Judea. Antiochus next invaded Egypt. When the war ended in 195 B.C., he was in possession of southern Syria and the Egyptian territories in Asia Minor. Egypt had practically become a Seleucid province of the "king of the north."[2]

New king of the north.
"But he that cometh against him shall do according to his own will, and none shall stand before him: and he shall stand in the glorious land, which by his hand shall be consumed" (Dan 11:16). The next kings of the north, Antiochus Asiaticus and his successors, faced the growing military might of Rome.

In 65 B.C., Roman consul Pompey occupied Syria, making it a province of Rome. With the occupation of Syria, Rome became the new "king of the north" (*"none shall stand before him"*). Two years later, Pompey invaded Jerusalem, killing over 12,000 Jews. He demolished the walls of Jerusalem, imposed a tribute on the Jews, and placed several Jewish cities under Syria (*"he shall stand in the glorious land, which by his hand shall be consumed."*).

Julius Caesar. An outstanding military and political leader came to power in Rome. *"And in the latter time of their kingdom, when the transgressors are come to the full, a king of fierce countenance, and understanding dark sentences, shall stand up. And his power shall be mighty, but not by his own power: and he shall destroy wonderfully, and shall prosper, and practise, and shall destroy the mighty and the holy people"* (Dan 8:23-24).

A *"king of fierce countenance"*, Julius Caesar was said to have captured 1,000 cities and slain 1,192,000 men. He was adept at political intrigue (*"understanding dark sentences"*), using that skill to advance his personal ambitions. He did not wield power and authority on his own; he was initially one of two consuls elected annually by the Roman Senate to jointly govern the republic and its possessions (*"his power shall be mighty, but not by his own power"*).

In 60 B.C., Julius Caesar allied himself with Marcus Crassus and Pompey in the First Triumvirate. Crassus was a man of enormous wealth and political ambition, while Pompey was a great military leader and the idol of the people. Through violence and bribery, Julius Caesar was elected consul in 59 B.C.[3]

In 49 B.C., a struggle for power arose between Julius Caesar and Pompey. It culminated in Pompey's defeat in the battle of Pharsalus. With

Caesar in hot pursuit, Pompey retreated to Egypt, but was poisoned by the Egyptians, who were then embroiled in a dispute of succession between the deceased king's son Ptolemy XII and daughter Cleopatra.

Cleopatra. *"He shall also set his face to enter with the strength of his whole kingdom, and upright ones with him; thus shall he do: and he shall give him the daughter of women, corrupting her: but she shall not stand on his side, neither be for him"* (Dan 11:17).

Caesar, on his arrival in Egypt, found himself surrounded by many unfriendly Egyptian forces and so summoned all his troops in Asia (*"enter with the strength of his whole kingdom"*). He set the Egyptian fleet on fire, accidentally burning the famous library in Alexandria, which housed more than 400,000 volumes. An army of 3,000 Jews (*"upright ones with him"*) under Antipater the Idumaean helped Caesar secure victory.

Cleopatra, backed by a faction against her brother, went to Julius Caesar (*"he shall give him the daughter of women"*), who, smitten by her charms, made her his mistress and the mother of his illegitimate son (*"corrupting her"*). However, she later fell in love with Caesar's rival, Mark Antony, and fought against Rome (*"she shall not stand on his side, neither be for him"*).

Death of the dictator. *"After this shall he turn his face unto the isles, and shall take many: but a prince for his own behalf shall cause the reproach offered by him to cease; without his own reproach he shall cause it to turn upon him"* (Dan 11:18). Caesar left Egypt to fight Pharnaces in Syria and Asia Minor (*"turn his face unto the isles"*; "isles", aside from islands, can also mean "coastlands" or "inhabited places reached by sea").[4]

Victorious (*"shall take many"*), Julius Caesar uttered his famous words, *"Veni, vidi, vinci"* ("I came, I saw, I conquered."). He next attacked the remaining troops of Pompey (*"a prince for his own behalf"*) in Africa under Cato and Scipio, whose continued defiance was a rejection of his supremacy (*"cause the reproach offered by him to cease"*). Caesar defeated them, as well as Labienus and Varus in Spain who had also defied him (*"cause it to turn upon him"*).

"Then he shall turn his face toward the fort of his own land: but he shall stumble and fall, and not be found" (Dan 11:19). Julius Caesar then returned to Rome (*"he shall turn his face toward the fort of his own land"*), where the admiring Romans proclaimed him dictator for life. A group of conspirators, however, fearing Caesar would make himself king, assassinated him on the ides of March (March 15) in the spring of 44 B.C. (*"he shall stumble and fall, and not be found"*).

A raiser of taxes. Another Caesar took over Julius's place. *"Then shall stand up in his estate a raiser of taxes in the glory of the kingdom: but within few days he shall be destroyed, neither in anger, nor in battle"* (Dan 11:20). After a civil war that followed the death of Julius Caesar, he was succeeded as consul by his grandnephew and adopted son Octavian, who took the name Gaius Julius Caesar.

In 27 B.C. the Roman Senate gave Octavian the title Augustus ("the exalted"). It also gave him legal power to direct Rome's religious, civil, and military affairs, with the Senate as an advisory body. He became known as Augustus Caesar, the first Roman Emperor, ending the Roman Republic and replacing it with the Roman Empire.

The empire made great advances under Augustus Caesar. He developed the postal system, harbors, and the highway network connecting Rome to its remote provinces. To fund his projects, he levied taxes throughout the empire (*"a raiser of taxes in the glory of the kingdom"*).

Birth in Bethlehem. It was one such taxation that brought the Jewish couple Joseph and Mary to Bethlehem, where the Messiah was born. *"And it came to pass in those days, that there went out a decree from Caesar Augustus, that all the world should be taxed. (And this taxing was first made when Cyrenius was governor of Syria.) And all went to be taxed, every one into his own city. And Joseph also went up from Galilee, out of the city of Nazareth, into Judaea, unto the city of David, which is called Bethlehem; (because he was of the house and lineage of David:) To be taxed with Mary his espoused wife, being great with child"* (Luke 2:1-5).

Emperor worship. *"And through his policy also he shall cause craft to prosper in his hand; and he shall magnify himself in his heart, and by peace shall destroy many: he shall also stand up against the Prince of princes; but he shall be broken without hand"* (Dan 8:25). Historical records show that "Augustus was a cold, calculating statesman, but he knew how to win popular affection" (*"through his policy also he shall cause craft to prosper in his hand"*).[5]

Becoming Rome's first emperor must have made Augustus extremely proud of himself (*"he shall magnify himself in his heart"*). "His appearance is described by the biographer Suetonius… 'He had clear, bright eyes, in which he liked to have it thought that there was a kind of divine power, and it greatly pleased him, whenever he looked keenly at anyone, if he let his face fall as if before the radiance of the sun.'"[6]

"After the death of Lepidus, Augustus became Pontifex Maximus ("chief priest") with supreme authority over the control of Roman religion."[7] He initiated the worship of emperors. "Caesar's heir Octavian pressed for the declaration of Caesar as divine – which the Senate granted by its vote in

42."⁸ "Julius Caesar's recognition as a god of the Roman state in January 42 BCE enhanced Octavian's prestige as son of a god".⁹

Roman citizens accepted as "many individuals and even whole communities, in Italy and elsewhere, expressed their thanks spontaneously by worshiping Augustus and his family. Emperor worship was also encouraged officially…"¹⁰ "After his death on Aug. 19, A.D. 14, the people of the Roman Empire worshiped him as Divine Augustus."¹¹

Augustus did not die of a lingering illness, but was taken ill in 14 A.D. and died in his bed (*"within few days"*) in his villa at Nola near Naples (*"he shall be destroyed, neither in anger, nor in battle"*).

Emperor worship became a widespread practice. "The Romans worshiped an emperor as a god after his death. Emperor worship provided a common base of loyalty among the empire's peoples, who otherwise observed many different religions and traditions."¹² "Christians were subject to charges of treason for refusing to offer sacrifices before the emperor's image"¹³

Pax Romana. "The reign of Augustus marked the beginning of a long period of stability, which became known as the Pax Romana (Roman Peace)."¹⁴ Moreover, "the empire flourished and added new territories, notably ancient Britain, Arabia, and Dacia (present-day Romania).¹⁵ "Roman peace" covered the civilized world, where even the most remote lands were ransacked in order to supply the wealthy Roman citizens with luxuries and delicacies.¹⁶ Thus was the prophecy fulfilled that he *"by peace shall destroy many"*.

"This peace lasted more than 200 years, from 27 B.C. to A.D. 180. During the Pax Romana, the Roman Empire extended over much of Europe, the Middle East, and northern Africa."¹⁷

Crucifixion of Christ. Following the death of Augustus Caesar, he was succeeded by his stepson and son-in-law Tiberius as emperor. It was during the reign of Tiberius that Christ was sentenced to death in 30 A.D. by Pontius Pilate and crucified in Jerusalem (*"he shall also stand up against the Prince of princes"*). (The "he" now refers to the Roman Emperor, whoever he might be. In Bible prophecy, both the predecessor and any of his successors, and even their kingdom, are referred to as the same personage.)

Fall of Rome. After being the dominant world power for around 750 years, the Western Roman Empire began to decline. It finally crumbled in 476 A.D., when the last emperor, 16-year-old Romulus Augustulus, was eased out by Odoacer, leader of rebelling Germanic troops. The fall was not the outcome of war. As stated in Daniel's prophecy, *"he shall be broken without hand"*.

Kings of the north.
Other empires replaced Rome as "king of the north". Let us trace their lineage from ancient times to our modern era. (These overlap.)

Seleucid Dynasty (312-64 B.C.). After Alexander's death in 323 B.C., Seleucus, one of the Macedonian generals, became the ruler of southwest Asia. The Seleucid Empire he founded, at its height, extended from Asia Minor (now Turkey) to India. In 64 B.C., the last Seleucid territory, Syria, fell to the Romans.

Roman Empire (275 B.C.-476 A.D.). By 275 B.C., Rome held most of the Italian Peninsula. It became the Roman Empire, which, at its peak in the A.D. 100s, covered about half of Europe, much of the Middle East, and the north coast of Africa. In A.D. 476, Germanic rebels deposed the last Western Roman emperor.

Byzantine Empire (395-1453). In A.D. 330, Emperor Constantine transferred his capital from Rome to Byzantium (which he renamed Constantinople; now Istanbul, Turkey). In 395, the empire split into the West Roman Empire and the East Roman Empire. By the 500s, the Byzantine Empire included parts of southern and eastern Europe, northern Africa, and the Middle East. The Empire ended when the Ottoman Turks conquered Constantinople in 1453.

Holy Roman Empire (962-1806). In the mid-900s, King Otto I of Germany gained control of most of northern and central Italy. In 962, he had Pope John XII crown him emperor of what became known in the 1200s as the Holy Roman Empire. In 1438, Albert II of the Habsburg family became Holy Roman emperor. His family ruled until 1806, when the Habsburgs were defeated by Emperor Francis II of France, who declared the end of the Holy Roman Empire.

Spanish Empire (late 1400s-late 1800s). In the late 1400s, Spain established colonies off northwestern Africa and in the Caribbean. Conquistadors conquered the Aztec Empire of Mexico in 1519-1521. By 1588, the Spanish Empire ruled territories in North, Central and South America, Asia, Africa, and Oceania. Spain lost much of Latin America in the independence movements of the early 19th century; as well as Cuba, Puerto Rico, the Philippines, and Guam in 1898 after its defeat in the Spanish-American War.

Napoleonic France (1799-1815). During the French Revolution (1789-1799), a young army officer named Napoleon Bonaparte rose from the ranks, becoming general in 1793. In 1799, he overthrew the revolutionary government and seized control of France. He was voted emperor in 1804. A military genius, Napoleon had conquered most of western and central Europe by 1812. After a series of defeats, however, he abdicated in 1814, but returned to rule France again in 1815. Later that year, Napoleon met his final defeat at Waterloo in what is now Belgium.

British Empire (late 1500s-mid 1900s). The British Empire began in the late 16th century with chartered commercial ventures in North America and the Caribbean Islands. At its height in the late 19th and early 20th centuries, the Empire held power over 20% of the world's land area and more than 400 million people in large parts of Africa, Asia, and North America. After World War II, people in Africa and Asia began agitating for independence. Since the early 1930s, many British possessions have become independent nations.

Nazi Germany (1933-1945). The Nazi Party came to power on January 30, 1933, when Adolf Hitler became Chancellor of Germany. In 1938, Nazi troops invaded Austria, then occupied Czechoslovakia and Poland in 1939. The next year, they overran Denmark, Norway, the Netherlands, Belgium, Luxembourg, and France. In early 1941, Hitler launched the systematic genocide of people he considered racially inferior or undesirable. In the so-called Holocaust, some 11 million victims, including about 6 million Jews (2/3 of those in Europe), were killed. Defeated by the Allied forces, the Nazi armies surrendered on May 8, 1945.

United States (1776-). In 1775, thirteen British colonies in North America revolted against Great Britain. On July 4, 1776, at their Second Continental Congress, the colonists officially declared their independence and formed the United States of America. After years of fighting, the Americans and the British signed the Treaty of Paris on September 3, 1783, ending the Revolutionary War. The USA grew rapidly in the 1800s and 1900s. After spearheading the Allied victories in World Wars I and II, the US became recognized as the most powerful nation in the world.

Kings of the south.

Let us next examine how hegemony passed from one hand to another in the succession of kings of the south during more or less the same timeframe.

Ptolemaic Dynasty (305-30 B.C.). Ptolemy, one of Alexander's generals, gained control of Egypt. About 305 B.C., he took the title of king, founding the dynasty of the Ptolemies. After a long line of kings, his descendant Cleopatra lost the naval Battle of Actium in 31 B.C. to Augustus Caesar, who made Egypt a province of Rome.

(There would be no "king of the south" in the next 600 years.)

Arab Islamic Empire (632-1258 A.D.). When Muhammad, founder of the new religion called Islam, died in 632, Abu Bakr, his friend and father-in-law, was acclaimed *caliph* ("successor" to the Prophet) in Medina, Arabia. From 750, when the Abbasid caliphate overcame its opponents, to the mid-800s, the Arab Muslim caliphs expanded their Islamic state into an empire. They ruled from Damascus, Syria (661-762), and Baghdad, Iraq (762-1258). The last caliph fell when the Mongols captured Baghdad in 1258.

Ottoman Empire (1300-1922). The Ottomans were of nomadic Turkic tribes who migrated to the Middle East from central Asia. In the late 1200s, they began to expand their small territory in the northwest corner of Anatolia (now Turkey). In 1453, they conquered Constantinople, capital of the Byzantine Empire. The Ottomans had the world's most powerful empire during the 1500s and 1600s, controlling what is now Turkey and parts of North Africa, southwest Asia, and southeastern Europe. During World War I (1914-1918), they supported Germany, but were both defeated. In 1922, a new Turkish government abolished the Ottoman Empire.

Egypt (1922-1979). Egypt, an ancient kingdom that is today the largest Arab country, returned to power in 1922, when Great Britain granted its independence. In 1948, Egypt and four other nearby Arab countries attacked newly independent Israel, but were repulsed. Fighting erupted again in June 1967 in the Six-Day War, which was again won by Israel. In October 1973, Egypt and Syria launched a surprise attack against the Israelis; they were driven back when the United States airlifted supplies to Israel. In 1979, the Camp David Accords returned the Israeli-held Sinai Peninsula to Egypt and paved the way for peace with Israel.

Iran (1501-). Iran ("land of the Aryans") had two ancient kingdoms: Media and Persia. Around 550 B.C., the Persians overpowered the Medes. They later fell under the Greeks (331-250 B.C.); Parthians (250 B.C.-224 A.D.); Muslim Arabs (636-900s); Seljuk Turks (mid-1000s-1220); Mongols (1220-1400s). In 1501, Iran became a kingdom again. The monarchy adopted a parliamentary system in 1906, but in the late 1970s opponents of the shah (king) united under Muslim religious leader Ayatollah Khomeini, who led a revolution and declared an Islamic republic after the shah fled in January 1979. In recent years, the United States has accused Iran of supporting terrorism and developing nuclear weapons that might become available to terrorists or be used against Israel.

To summarize, below is a table for the reader's quick reference:

Kings of the North and South

King of the North	King of the South
Seleucid Dynasty (312-64 BC)	Ptolemaic Dynasty (305-30 BC)
Roman Empire (275 BC-476 AD)	
Byzantine Empire (395-1453)	Arab Islamic Empire (632-1258)
Holy Roman Empire (962-1806)	
Spanish Empire (late 1400s-late 1800s)	Ottoman Empire (1300-1922)
Napoleonic France (1799-1815)	
British Empire (late 1500s-mid 1900s)	Egypt (1922-1979)
Nazi Germany (1933-1945)	
United States (1776-)	Iran (1501-)

The "vile person"

The end-time chronicle in Daniel 11 leaps nearly 2,000 years after Augustus Caesar. The succeeding verses talk about a "vile person". *"And in his estate shall stand up a vile person, to whom they shall not give the honour of the kingdom: but he shall come in peaceably, and obtain the kingdom by flatteries"* (Dan 11:21).

"His estate".

The phrase (*"his estate"*) refers to the vast territory of the Roman Empire when Augustus Caesar was emperor. That territory included the region called Mesopotamia ("between rivers" – the Euphrates and Tigris), which came under Roman rule for several periods until A.D. 226, when the Persians seized the area. Mesopotamia is occupied today by the country we know as Iraq.

Arab Muslims defeated the Persians in 637 and in 762, and established Baghdad as the capital of the Arab Empire until 1258, when the Mongols captured the city. The Ottoman Empire began to control Mesopotamia in the early 1500s. British troops took over near the end of World War I and, in 1920, received a mandate from the League of Nations to administer the area. They renamed the country Iraq and set up an Arab king as head of state. The British mandate ended in 1932, and Iraq became an independent state.

Founded by Nimrod. The modern state of Iraq appears to have derived its name from the second city founded by Nimrod after Babel – Erech. *"And the beginning of his kingdom was Babel, and Erech, and Accad, and Calneh, in the land of Shinar"* (Gen 10:10). In turn, Erech may have come from the Hebrew *yareeach* ("moon") as archeologists have found bricks that bear the monogram "the moon". The *New Unger's Bible Dictionary* notes that the largest excavated temple there was devoted to Inanna, Lady of the Heavens (the moon goddess). *Nelson's Bible Encyclopedia* says the Babylonians and the Assyrians called Erech "Uruk". From these, we can glean how the name of the country became Iraq.

Surprisingly, the Scriptures seem to identify the "vile person" as Saddam Hussein, the former president of Iraq. Let us analyze the circumstances and the Biblical verses to find out if this is plausible.

Antichrists.
The name "Saddam" in Arabic means "one who confronts". It reminds us of Nimrod, builder of the Tower of Babel and considered by many Bible scholars as the "first Antichrist". Some writers say Nimrod means "rebel", based on Genesis 10:9 – *"He was a mighty hunter before the LORD: wherefore it is said, Even as Nimrod the mighty hunter before the LORD."* The phrase is stated twice in a single verse, as though for added emphasis. The word "before" in Hebrew is *neged*, meaning "in front," "opposite," or "against". The Greek Septuagint translated *"before the Lord"* as *"against the Lord."* Thus, the phrase can also mean "in defiance of the Lord."

A person who "confronts" (Saddam) and another who is "in front" or "against" (Nimrod) are doing basically the same thing! So, if Nimrod was the first Antichrist, the "vile person" (Saddam or one of his successors) must be the end-time Antichrist! As Nimrod reigned over ancient Erech, Saddam ruled over modern-day Iraq.

Ruthless ruler. Iraq was a monarchy until 1958, when the king was overthrown in a military coup, and Iraq became a republic with a president as the head of government. Thus, when Saddam Hussein became the country's ruler in 1979, he did not become king (*"to whom they shall not give the honour of the kingdom"*), but assumed the title of president. (Later on, though, international media reported that Saddam had a solid gold throne in one of his palaces.)

He would *"obtain the kingdom by flatteries"* (deceit and intrigue). In 1968, when Baath Party officers overthrew the government, Major General Ahmed Hassan al-Bakr became head of the newly formed Revolutionary Command Council (RCC), the country's supreme executive, legislative, and judicial body. Chairman and President Al-Bakr gave Saddam Hussein the second most powerful posts of deputy chairman and vice president. Saddam formed the much-feared Presidential Guard and became the unchallenged leader of internal security. From the early 1970s onward, Saddam Hussein was widely recognized as the power behind President al-Bakr, who after 1977 was little more than a figurehead.[18]

"And with the arms of a flood shall they be overflown from before him, and shall be broken" (Dan 11:22a). Saddam jailed, executed, or assassinated the regime's opponents, then turned against his own opponents inside the ruling party, using ruthless internal security units loyal to him personally.

On July 16, 1979, President al-Bakr resigned (said to have been forced by Saddam, who took over as president, RCC chairman, and commander-in-chief of the armed forces). After a plot to overthrow him was uncovered, Saddam rounded up dozens of officials on charges of treason (they had opposed al-Bakr's resignation and Saddam's succession). A special court sentenced 22 senior officials to death; while many others were sent to prison.[19]

Against Israel. *"...yea, also the prince of the covenant"* (Dan 11:22b). The covenant likely means the agreement between God and Abraham (Gen 17:7-10), wherein God promised to *"give unto thee (Abraham), and to thy seed after thee, the land wherein thou art a stranger, all the land of Canaan, for an everlasting possession"*. The Hebrew word translated "prince" is *nagiyd*, also rendered in the KJV as "captain, chief, governor, leader, noble, ruler, excellent thing".[20] Thus, *"prince of the covenant"* refers to Abraham, patriarch of the Israelites, who were to possess the Promised Land, or to even the promise itself (as an "excellent thing").

Saddam Hussein was rabidly against Israel's possession of Palestine (Canaan). In fact, he led the Arab opposition to the 1979 Camp David Accords intended to end the conflict between Egypt and Israel over Palestine.[21]

Deceitful negotiator. *"And after the league made with him he shall work deceitfully"* (Dan 11:23a). In 1975 Saddam himself negotiated an agreement with Iran that made Iraqi concessions on border disputes in return for the withdrawal of Iranian support to Kurdish rebels in northern Iraq.[22] However, in September 1980 he declared the agreement with Iran null and void, and claimed authority over the entire disputed Shatt al-Arab river and estuary, Iraq's only access to the sea.[23]

"...for he shall come up, and shall become strong with a small people" (Dan 11:23b). Saddam strengthened his grip on power with the support of the Sunni Muslim minority (*"small people"*) of Iraq, which had a Shiite Muslim majority. To his advantage, Sunni Arab urban leaders dominated the Iraqi government and the army.[24]

National development. *"He shall enter peaceably even upon the fattest places of the province; and he shall do that which his fathers have not done, nor his fathers' fathers; he shall scatter among them the prey, and spoil, and riches"* (Dan 11:24a). Customarily, the Arab chieftains in the Iraqi parliament passed laws that mainly benefited themselves.[25] Unlike them, however, Saddam used the revenues from Iraq's vast oil reserves to modernize the country and raise the people's standard of living. Using Iraq's huge petroleum resources, he led a successful development program in the 1970s.

Weapons of mass destruction. *"…yea, and he shall forecast his devices against the strong holds, even for a time"* (Dan 11:24b). Saddam Hussein started to develop nuclear, chemical, and biological weapons of mass destruction (WMDs), raising apprehensions among Iraq's neighbors. "In June 1981, a surprise air attack by Israel destroyed a nuclear reactor near Baghdad."[26]

Iraq-Iran War. *"And he shall stir up his power and his courage against the king of the south with a great army…"* (Dan 11:25a). Iraq invaded Iran in September 1980. "The quarrel (over Shatt al-Arab) flared into a full-scale war. Iraq quickly overran a large part of the Arab-populated province of Khuzistan and destroyed the Abadan refinery."[27] (In our analysis, the "king of the south" today is Iran.)

"…and the king of the south shall be stirred up to battle with a very great and mighty army; but he shall not stand" (Dan 11:25b). "In January 1981 Iran launched its first counteroffensive, but Iraq decimated the assault."[28] *"…for they shall forecast devices against him"* (Dan 11:25c). "…as early as 1983 the (Iraqi) armed forces used poison gas against Iranian troops."[29] "Iraq's Kurds supported Iran against the Iraqi government. In 1987 and 1988, the Iraqi government lashed out against the Kurds. The army released poison gas in Kurdish villages, killing thousands of people."[30]

"Yea, they that feed of the portion of his meat shall destroy him…" (Dan 11:26a). Buyers of Iranian oil extended help to Iraq to defeat Iran. The U.S. was "giving trade credits to Iraq and supplying the Iraqi armed forces with intelligence information through Saudi Arabia."[31] Other leading members of the United Nations (UN) were also importers of Iranian oil, but "the UN refused to come to Iran's aid to repel the Iraqi invasion… Outside the UN, other governments took few constructive steps to end the fighting… partly caused by Iran's international isolation and the mutual hostility between Iran and the West in the wake of Iran's Islamic revolution."[32]

"…and his army shall overflow: and many shall fall down slain" (Dan 11:26b). "Exploiting their superiority in numbers, Iran sent its Revolutionary Guard on the attack, supported by regular military forces. Outnumbered Iraqi forces inflicted heavy losses on the Iranians but ultimately fell back. As soon as the initial Iranian thrust had exhausted itself, however, the Iraqi

army exploited Iranian disorganization and lack of equipment to retake much of the lost territory."[33] "Hundreds of thousands of Iranians were killed or injured, and over a million people were left homeless."[34]

"And both these kings' hearts shall be to do mischief, and they shall speak lies at one table; but it shall not prosper: for yet the end shall be at the time appointed" (Dan 11:27). "In July the United Nations Security Council passed Resolution 598, calling for both sides to stop fighting, withdraw to the prewar border, and submit to an international body to determine responsibility for the war... On August 20, 1988, both sides ceased fighting in accordance with the terms of Resolution 598... A decade after the 1988 cease-fire, Iran and Iraq had yet to settle these differences."[35]

"Then shall he return into his land with great riches; and his heart shall be against the holy covenant; and he shall do exploits, and return to his own land" (Dan 11:28). "Hussein emerged from the war more secure than before; he even claimed the Iranian failure to unseat him represented a tremendous Iraqi victory..."[36] Moreover, his opposition to Israel's possession of the Holy Land would grow even more intense (*"his heart shall be against the holy covenant"*).

Persian Gulf War. *"At the time appointed he shall return, and come toward the south, but it shall not be as the former, or as the latter"* (Dan 11:29). "In August 1990, Iraqi forces invaded and occupied Kuwait. Before the invasion, Hussein had accused Kuwait of violating oil production limits set by the Organization of the Petroleum Exporting Countries (OPEC), thus lowering the worldwide price of oil. In addition, Iraq and Kuwait had disagreed over territory and over Iraq's multibillion-dollar debt to Kuwait."[37] (Kuwait is located just across the southeast border of Iraq.)

However, Saddam would not be as formidable in this new aggression as he was in the war with Iran. *"For the ships of Chittim shall come against him: therefore he shall be grieved, and return..."* (Dan 11:30a). What or who is Chittim?

"Chittim". It was noted by the Jewish historian "Josephus, that 'all islands, and the greatest part of the sea-coast, are called Chethim (=Kittim) by the Hebrews'".[38] Besides, says *The New Unger's Bible Dictionary*, "KITTIM, CHITTIM. A general name (such as our Levant) applied to the islands and coasts of the Mediterranean in a loose way without fixing the particular part..."[39] "Chittim", therefore, can refer to the countries along the northern Mediterranean coasts, many of which are members of the UN and allied with the US.

A coalition of 39 countries, organized mainly by the UN and the US, sent forces to the Persian Gulf region. War broke out between the allied forces and Iraq on January 17, 1991. The coalition forces bombed military targets in Iraq and Kuwait. Iraq responded by firing Scud missiles at populated areas in Israel – to draw the Jewish state into the war and get Arab countries out of the coalition by portraying the war as an Arab-Israeli conflict. However, Israel did not enter the war.[40] The Israel Defense Forces (IDF) neutralized most of the Scud missiles with US-supplied Patriot air-defense missiles.

On February 24, coalition forces began moving into Iraq and Kuwait. They defeated the Iraqi army after 100 hours of fighting.[41] Thus Iraq "was forced out of Kuwait in about six weeks (*'therefore he shall be grieved, and return'*). Tens of thousands of Iraqis were killed, most of the country's armored vehicles and artillery smashed, and some nuclear and chemical weapons facilities destroyed."[42]

Support for terrorists. After the war, Saddam further encouraged and supported terrorist attacks against Israel by giving rewards to the families of suicide bombers ("*shall have indignation against the holy covenant: so shall he do; he shall even return, and have intelligence with them that forsake the holy covenant*" – Dan 11:30b).

Fall of Saddam. Twelve years later, on March 20, 2003, the US led a military campaign to overthrow Saddam Hussein and eliminate Iraq's ability to produce WMDs. On April 9, Baghdad fell, and Saddam fled into hiding. On December 13, US troops captured him in an underground hiding place near Tikrit, his hometown. He went on trial in October 2005 before the Iraqi High Tribunal, which sentenced him to death for crimes against humanity. Saddam Hussein was hanged on December 30, 2006.

"Abomination of desolation". Fast forward to the middle of the last 7 years. "*And arms shall stand on his part, and they shall pollute the sanctuary of strength, and shall take away the daily sacrifice, and they shall place the abomination that maketh desolate*" ("Dan 11:31"). The "vile person" and his men will desecrate "*the sanctuary of strength*" (presumably, Temple Mount in Jerusalem), put a stop to the daily offerings there, and set up the "abomination of desolation".

Wait a minute. Have we not identified Saddam Hussein as the "vile person"? He has been hanged. Didn't he really die, or does the verse refer to one of his successors as ruler of Iraq?

Assyrian invader. Prophecies prefigure a conquest of the Jews by an Assyrian. We read in Isaiah 10:24 – "*Therefore thus saith the Lord GOD of hosts, O my people that dwellest in Zion, be not afraid of the Assyrian: he shall smite thee with a rod, and shall lift up his staff against thee, after the manner of Egypt*"; and in Micah 5:5b – "*...the Assyrian shall come into our land... he shall tread in our palaces...*"

(Assyrians destroyed the northern kingdom of Israel in 721 B.C. In 701 B.C., Assyria was poised to attack Jerusalem when the Assyrian army was suddenly struck by *"the angel of the Lord"* (2 Kings 19:35), probably with a plague. 185,000 Assyrian soldiers died, and the survivors turned back. So, the Jews as a nation, historically speaking, have never been subjugated by Assyria... yet.)

Anciently, Assyria occupied the northern part of modern-day Iraq. Saddam Hussein was born in the town of Tikrit in northern Iraq. Abu Bakr al-Baghdadi (a.k.a. Caliph Ibrahim), head of the Islamic State caliphate, was born near Samarra, also in northern Iraq.

Holy place desecrated. *Let no man deceive you by any means: for that day shall not come, except there come a falling away first, and that man of sin be revealed, the son of perdition; Who opposeth and exalteth himself above all that is called God, or that is worshipped; so that he as God sitteth in the temple of God, shewing himself that he is God"* (2 Thess 2:3-4). Will the end-time Antichrist reveal himself at the Temple Mount in Jerusalem?

Two feet of iron and clay

Daniel ch. 2 portrays the last end-time empire. *"His legs of iron, his feet part of iron and part of clay... And whereas thou sawest the feet and toes, part of potters' clay, and part of iron, the kingdom shall be divided; but there shall be in it of the strength of the iron, forasmuch as thou sawest the iron mixed with miry clay. And as the toes of the feet were part of iron, and part of clay, so the kingdom shall be partly strong, and partly broken. And whereas thou sawest iron mixed with miry clay, they shall mingle themselves with the seed of men: but they shall not cleave one to another, even as iron is not mixed with clay"* (Dan 2:33,41-43).

Ten toes.

The great image having two feet suggests that the last empire, just like the Western and Eastern Roman empires, and the earlier Greco-Macedonian and Medo-Persian empires, will also be made up of two groups of people. Moreover, as the two feet have ten toes, we get the notion that the ultimate empire will be made up of ten nations.

It looks like they are also the ten kings of Revelation 17:12-13 – *"And the ten horns which thou sawest are ten kings, which have received no kingdom as yet; but receive power as kings one hour with the beast. These have one mind, and shall give their power and strength unto the beast."*

So, if the "beast" is the EU, the ten kings are ten nations that will be part of it. Let us examine the ten toes of iron and of clay to see who or what they represent.

Iron. The iron component points to the ancient Roman Empire, which was symbolized by the great image's two legs of iron in Daniel ch. 2 and by the terrible beast with iron teeth in Daniel ch. 7. The Romans used iron extensively, specially in their armaments.

The end-time successor of ancient Rome is the EU, whose association with iron came to the fore in 1951 with the formation of the European Coal and Steel Community (ECSC), which was primarily concerned with iron and steel production. After World War II, "German industry, which was reviving rapidly, needed to be monitored in some way. The ECSC provided an appropriate mechanism since coal and steel are central to many modern industries, especially the armaments industry."[43]

Clay. To whom does the clay apply? What group of people is known for making use of clay? Let us try to dig this up. "The Hebrew and Greek words, as well as the English 'clay,' are... used loosely for any sticky mud."[44]

Clay (and mud) has been much used in the Middle East and North Africa since ancient times. Among its many uses, clay was (and in some areas still is) an important building material. Nimrod and the people with him made bricks of clay or mud to build the Tower of Babel (Gen 11:3). Hebrew slaves made bricks for the Pharaohs of Egypt (Ex 5:7-9). King David put the defeated Ammonites to work making bricks (2 Sam 12:31). "Brick was the chief building material of ancient Mesopotamia and Palestine, which had little wood or stone... Sumerian and Babylonian builders constructed ziggurats, palaces, and city walls of sun-dried brick..."[45]

The *World Book* states that, even today, "Most rural Arabs live in one- or two-story houses of brick, mud-brick, or stone. Mud-brick architecture, in particular, takes a wide variety of forms, from simple rectangular structures to the beehive-shaped houses of northern Syria. Mud-brick is cheap and easy to use, and it provides excellent insulation against heat and cold."[46] Arab countries like Saudi Arabia, Egypt, Iraq, Syria, Yemen and Oman; as well as other non-Arab countries in the Middle East, such as Iran and Afghanistan, use sun-dried mud-bricks to build dwelling places.[47,48,49]

Note that the countries mentioned have predominantly Arab and/or Muslim populations. Does the clay in the great image's feet denote the Muslims from the Middle East and North Africa, many of whom are today immigrants and refugees in EU?

Largest EU minority. The European Union's largest minority group today is made up of Muslims. In the late 20th and early 21st centuries, substantial numbers of non-native Muslims immigrated to Western

Europe. By 2010, an estimated 44 million Muslims were living in all of Europe (6% of the population), including an estimated 19 million in the European Union (3.8% of the population).

Muslim migrant crisis. As an offshoot of the many-sided wars in the Middle East, the number of displaced people inside war-ravaged Syria and Iraq has been estimated at 3 million refugees. As of early December 2015, "Turkey says it has taken in a total of 2.2 million refugees from Syria's four-year civil war and still maintains an 'open door' policy while warning its capacity to take more is limited."[50]

By December 24, 2015, on the Greek island of Byblos alone, some 800,000 refugees, mostly Syrians, had arrived from their war-torn countries of origin. By the end of 2015, more than one million migrants had entered the European Union.

Moreover, "tens of thousands of the 1.1 billion people in Africa are walking towards the Mediterranean Sea in hope of finding a smuggler's boat and a better life... almost all of them are Muslims. Thanks to mass migration from North Africa, France's Muslim population has swelled to 6.5 million, or 10% of its population."[51]

Thus, in the Mediterranean port city of Marseilles in France, guess what is the second most widely spoken language. Arabic? Wrong. It is French. Arabic is Number One.

Islamic invasion. Shira Sorko Ram, a Fox News reporter visiting Austria, reported that what she saw was not a migration. It was an invasion. She confirmed what European sources say: 80% of the migrants are men 18-45 years old.[52] "An army is invading Europe, an army of intensely religious men whose lives are first and foremost dedicated to their god – a god different from the One in the Bible."[53]

Seemingly oblivious to the quietly brewing problem, Germany's Chancellor, Angela Merkel, opened her arms and her nation's borders without limits to asylum seekers. She said Germany could take on half a million asylum seekers per year.[54]

European consent. Idealistic European leaders and elites have opened their doors, even providing mosques and other religious "encouragement" to migrants on the taxpayers' euro.[55] Part of the attraction has been very generous monthly pocket money and benefits for those who arrive.[56] In Sweden, "60% of welfare benefits are going to immigrants who make up about 15% of Sweden's 10,000,000 citizens! Even illegal immigrants now get free health and dental care... there isn't enough housing for Swedes, but 'as soon as an older person moves out, eight foreigners immediately move in'."[57]

Fundamentalist Muslims. All the main Muslim groups in Germany are known to adhere to fundamentalist interpretations of Islam and are anti-Western in outlook.[58] They have no intention of assimilating into the European culture at all. Most immigrants from Muslim countries have been raised with hatred for Western values and contempt for democracy. They demand to recreate in Europe in the image of their own culture wherein Sharia law reigns.

Jihadist terror threat. The British press reported that Islamic State has threatened to release a huge wave of migrants from Libya across the Mediterranean disguised as refugees to sow chaos in Europe. "More than 1,000 French Muslims have joined Islamic State. A recent poll found that 27% of French Muslims ages 18-24 support the Islamic State… Authorities say that they've lost control of the situation. Muslim attacks on police and synagogues are now regular events… Similar problems are cropping up in Germany. After an influx of Syrian and other Muslim immigrants, a recent poll found that 40% of Germans say they don't feel at home in their own country, thanks to "Islamization".[59] Islamic State claims they have already smuggled 4,000 of their jihadists into the continent.

The ten kings ?

In the years following the breakup of the Soviet Union in 1991, former communist countries of eastern and central Europe applied for membership in the European Union. Ten were admitted over the next sixteen years: the Czech Republic, Estonia, Hungary, Latvia, Lithuania, Poland, Slovakia, and Slovenia (2004); Bulgaria and Romania (2007).

If Revelation 16:3 (*"And the second angel poured out his vial upon the sea; and it became as the blood of a dead man: and every living soul died in the sea."*) proves literally true and the original EU members located in Western Europe (*"the sea"*) are wiped out, will these 10 former communist countries from eastern and central Europe, with sizable admixtures of Muslim immigrants, serve as the main force of the European Union (the "beast")?

Desolation of the "whore".

The ten kings will destroy the Roman Catholic Church and the Vatican. *"And the ten horns which thou sawest upon the beast, these shall hate the whore, and shall make her desolate and naked, and shall eat her flesh, and burn her with fire. For God hath put in their hearts to fulfil his will, and to agree, and give their kingdom unto the beast, until the words of God shall be fulfilled"* (Rev 17:16-17).

It is useful to remember that one of the first declarations of the Islamic State caliphate after its establishment was that they would destroy the Vatican in Rome, seat of the Roman Catholic Church.

"Babylon" will burn. *"Therefore shall her plagues come in one day, death, and mourning, and famine; and she shall be utterly burned with fire: for strong is the Lord God who judgeth her.*

"And the kings of the earth, who have committed fornication and lived deliciously with her, shall bewail her, and lament for her, when they shall see the smoke of her burning, Standing afar off for the fear of her torment, saying, Alas, alas, that great city Babylon, that mighty city! for in one hour is thy judgment come" (Rev 18:8-10).

"The merchants of these things, which were made rich by her, shall stand afar off for the fear of her torment, weeping and wailing, And saying, Alas, alas, that great city, that was clothed in fine linen, and purple, and scarlet, and decked with gold, and precious stones, and pearls! For in one hour so great riches is come to nought" (Rev 18:15-17a).

"And in her was found the blood of prophets, and of saints, and of all that were slain upon the earth" (Rev 18:24).

7

The Road to Armageddon

For they are the spirits of devils, working miracles, which go forth unto the kings of the earth and of the whole world, to gather them to the battle of that great day of God Almighty.

- Revelation 16:14

Everything we have read so far in this book leads to the climax of humankind's history – Armageddon, the last and greatest battle on earth, which will coincide with the Day of the LORD, the final cleansing of this corrupted planet that will make way for a new world that the Second Coming of Christ will usher in.

Let us go through a blow-by-blow narrative, albeit in cryptic terms, of the horrifying preliminary events that will transpire up to the very beginning of the grand culmination of this age. These events are enumerated in the book of the Revelation in the veiled prophecies of the seven seals, seven trumpets, and seven vials or bowls.

Sequence of prophecies.

The prophecies of the seals, trumpets, and vials or bowls, contrary to the belief held by most people, are not exactly linear in sequence, that is, all events prophesied in the seven seals would first take place, followed by the events under the seven trumpets, and finally succeeded by the events under the seven vials or bowls.

Clues to sequence.

As we have seen in Chapter 3 of this book, the first four seals started normally, in regular order, presenting the Four Horsemen of the Apocalypse one after another. On scrutiny, though, some events prophesied separately in the three groups appear to be accounts of the same things, not different incidents.

The most telling clue is found in the 6th seal (*"every mountain and island were moved out of their places"*) and in the 7th vial (*"every island fled away, and the mountains were not found"*). The two prophecies speak of apparently the same topic – displacement of mountains and islands. It does not seem logical, or even plausible, for the mountains and islands to be moved out of their places, then return to their former positions, and later be removed again. Hence, the two prophecies must refer to just one event and not two separate happenings.

Contiguous events.

With that insight as a guide, other prophecies found separately under the seals, trumpets, and vials have now been determined to be contiguous or chronologically very close together despite being listed in different groups. Let us cite the examples:

The 1st trumpet and 1st vial both talk about the "earth".
The 2nd trumpet and 2nd vial similarly speak of the "sea".
The 3rd trumpet and 3rd vial both discuss "rivers and fountains".
The 4th trumpet and 4th vial prophesy about the "sun" alike.
The 6th seal and 5th vial similarly foretell "darkness on earth".
The 6th trumpet and 6th vial both touch on the Euphrates River.
The 7th trumpet and 7th vial both mention great voices in heaven.

With the above in mind, let us proceed to analyze and decipher the prophecies enumerated under the seven seals, seven trumpets and seven vials or bowls.

Probable sequence. For the reader's clearer understanding and quick reference, a table has been prepared in the next page showing the perceived probable sequence of the seals, trumpets, and vials prophecies.

Seals, Trumpets, and Bowls Prophecies

Seals	Trumpets	Vials/Bowls
(**1**) White horse		
(**2**)Red horse		
(**3**)Black horse		
(**4**)Pale/green horse		
	(**1**)Earth: hail, fire, blood; 1/3 trees, all green grass burned	(**1**)Earth: sores on men with the mark of the beast
	(**2**)Sea: burning mountain, 1/3 die	(**2**)Sea: turns bloody, all living souls die
	(**3**)Rivers, fountains: 1/3 into Wormwood	(**3**)Rivers, fountains become blood
	(**4**)Sun. moon, stars: third part darkened	(**4**)Sun scorches men with great heat
(**5**)Souls under altar ask for vindication	(**5**)Locust-horsemen from bottomless pit	
(**6**)Sun becomes black, moon as blood		(**5**)Kingdom of the beast darkened
Stars fall from heaven		
	(**6**)Angels at the Euphrates loosed, 200million horsemen	(**6**)Euphrates dries up to make way for the kings of the east
	(**7**)Great voices in heaven; kingdoms become the Lord's	(**7**)Great voice out of temple in heaven: "It is done."
		Great earthquake, cities fall, Babylon remembered
Heaven rolled like a scroll		
Mountains, islands moved out of place		Islands, mountains not found; great hail
(**7**) Silence in heaven ½ hour; censer with fire cast on earth		

First trumpet.
"*The first angel sounded, and there followed hail and fire mingled with blood, and they were cast upon the earth: and the third part of trees was burnt up, and all green grass was burnt up*" (Rev 8:7). The prophecy is couched in symbols; but as we already know the Bible itself provides the keys and clues to their meanings. Let us once again allow the Bible to interpret itself.

"Hail". We read in Isaiah 28:2,17 – "*...the Lord hath a mighty and strong one, as a tempest of hail and a destroying storm, as a flood of mighty waters overflowing, cast down to the earth... Judgment will I lay to the line, the hail shall sweep away the refuge of lies, waters shall overflow the hiding place.*" In Ezekiel 13:13 – "*Therefore thus saith the Lord GOD; I will even rend it with a stormy wind in my fury; and there shall be an overflowing shower in mine anger, and great hailstones in my fury to consume it.*" In Job 38:22-23 – "*Hast thou entered into the treasures of the snow? or hast thou seen the treasures of the hail, Which I have reserved against the time of trouble, against the day of battle and war?*"

From the foregoing passages, it appears that "hail" signifies destruction, as well as divine anger, vengeance, and punishment on the enemies of God and His people.

"Fire". Using the same hermeneutic principle, in Deuteronomy 4:24 we find – "*For the LORD thy God is a consuming fire, even a jealous God.*" Amos 5:6 – "*Seek the LORD, and ye shall live; lest he break out like fire in the house of Joseph, and devour it, and there be none to quench it in Bethel.*" 2 Thessalonians 1:8 – "*In flaming fire taking vengeance on them that know not God, and that obey not the gospel of our Lord Jesus Christ.*" Accordingly, "fire" is a symbol, as well as God's instrument, of judgment and righteous destruction.

"Blood". Isaiah 34:3 reads, "*Their slain also shall be cast out, and their stink shall come up out of their carcases, and the mountains shall be melted with their blood.*" Ezekiel 14:19 – "*Or if I send a pestilence into that land, and pour out my fury upon it in blood, to cut off from it man and beast.*" Apparently, "blood" prophetically means violent death, even slaughter.

"Earth". As borne out in our studies in previous chapters, "earth" means the New World, in general, and the United States of America, in particular.

US attacked? We can now reduce to simple terms the first half of the prophecy. "*The first angel sounded, and there followed hail and fire mingled with blood, and they were cast upon the earth...*" (Rev 8:7a). The US will be the subject of a particularly vicious attack. Was it the

September 11, 2001, attack (9/11) by Islamic terrorists who crashed three of four hijacked jetliners into the twin towers of the World Trade Center and the Pentagon? Or will it be another, more devastating assault yet to come?

The second part of the prophecy tells of vegetation catching "fire" – *"…and the third part of trees was burnt up, and all green grass was burnt up"* (Rev 8:7b).

"Trees". In Ezekiel 31:3a,18 – *"Behold, the Assyrian was a cedar in Lebanon with fair branches, and with a shadowing shroud, and of an high stature… To whom art thou thus like in glory and in greatness among the trees of Eden? yet shalt thou be brought down with the trees of Eden unto the nether parts of the earth: thou shalt lie in the midst of the uncircumcised with them that be slain by the sword. This is Pharaoh and all his multitude, saith the Lord GOD."* The kings of Assyria and Egypt, which conquered Israel and Judah, respectively, are likened to trees.

In Daniel 4:20-22 – *"The tree that thou sawest, which grew, and was strong, whose height reached unto the heaven, and the sight thereof to all the earth; Whose leaves were fair, and the fruit thereof much, and in it was meat for all; under which the beasts of the field dwelt, and upon whose branches the fowls of the heaven had their habitation: It is thou, O king, that art grown and become strong: for thy greatness is grown, and reacheth unto heaven, and thy dominion to the end of the earth."* Nebuchadnezzar, Babylonian king who enslaved the Jews, is likewise compared to a tree. It seems "trees" signify the enemies and conquerors of Israel. Egypt still exists; Assyria is now part of northern Iraq; Babylon, of southern Iraq.

"Grass". We read in Psalm 37:1-2 – *"Fret not because of evildoers, neither be envious against workers of iniquity. For they shall soon be cut down like the grass, and wither as the green herb."* In Psalm 92:7 – *"When the wicked spring as the grass, and when all the workers of iniquity do flourish; it is that they shall be destroyed for ever."* It looks like "grass" is a Biblical euphemism for evildoers and wicked people. That grass is green points to Muslim terrorists?

US retaliates? Does Revelation 8:7b mean that the US will strike back on a third of the enemies of Israel ("trees") and all evildoers ("green grass"/Muslim terrorists?). Is the prophecy still awaiting a future fulfillment, or do relatively recent geopolitical events apply?

The US accused al-Qa'eda, headed by Saudi-born millionaire Osama bin Laden, of masterminding the 9/11 attacks. They charged Afghanistan's Taliban government of harboring the terrorist group. The US demanded that the Taliban arrest the terrorists. When the Taliban refused, the US and

Great Britain launched a bombing campaign and gave logistical support to Afghanistan's Northern Alliance rebel forces. A ground offensive launched in mid-November 2001 by combined Northern Alliance fighters and US special forces drove the Taliban from power on December 7, 2001.

In March-April 2003, the US led a military campaign to oust Iraq's Saddam Hussein, whom they accused of producing weapons of mass destruction (WMDs) and supporting Muslim terrorists. They quickly toppled the Iraqi dictatorship and later captured Saddam, who was sentenced to death by the Iraqi High Tribunal for crimes against humanity and, subsequently, hanged in December 2006.

As of this writing, the US is involved in the many-sided war in Syria, carrying out air strikes in support of anti-government rebels, who are also struggling against Islamic State jihadists.

First vial or bowl.

"And I heard a great voice out of the temple saying to the seven angels, Go your ways, and pour out the vials of the wrath of God upon the earth. And the first went, and poured out his vial upon the earth; and there fell a noisome and grievous sore upon the men which had the mark of the beast, and upon them which worshipped his image" (Rev 16:2).

(Before proceeding further, a word of clarification. A vial, as we know it, is a small bottle containing a dose of medicine. However, the vial in the KJV is *phiale* in the Greek original text. According to the *International Standard Bible Encyclopaedia*, "The phiale was a flat, shallow bowl [Latin, patera], shaped much like a saucer."[1] Hence, the word is translated "bowl" in the NKJV, NIV, and other newer Bible versions. In that light, we shall use "bowl", although we shall also continue quoting from the older KJV, which has the word "vial".)

"Earth". As we have seen earlier, the "earth" is the United States.

Sores. Americans will be afflicted with skin ulcerations (*"noisome and grievous sore"*), particularly those who make Sunday their day of rest (*"which had the mark of the beast"*) and idolize the democratic, capitalist systems which originated in the Old World or Europe (*"them which worshipped his image"*).

Anthrax? The cause of the sores could be biological weapons. Some countries and terrorist groups are known or suspected to be developing this kind of weapon of mass destruction. One such WMD is anthrax, a cattle disease that is communicable to humans and causes festering sores that do not heal. In 1979, anthrax spores (inactive bacteria) were accidentally released from a military facility in the Soviet Union, causing 68 deaths.

In 2001, after 9/11, anthrax spores were sent by mail to several US business and government offices. People in several states became ill with inhalational anthrax and several died, while others contracted cutaneous anthrax (skin sores). In May 2015, the US Defense Department made public that it had accidentally shipped live anthrax bacteria from Dugway Proving Ground facility in Utah to laboratories in nine US states and a US airbase in South Korea.

Second trumpet.
"And the second angel sounded, and as it were a great mountain burning with fire was cast into the sea: and the third part of the sea became blood; And the third part of the creatures which were in the sea, and had life, died; and the third part of the ships were destroyed" (Rev 8:8).

"Great burning mountain". What could this be representing? Thankfully, we can again find the answer in the Scriptures. *"And I will render unto Babylon and to all the inhabitants of Chaldea all their evil that they have done in Zion in your sight, saith the LORD. Behold, I am against thee, O destroying mountain, saith the LORD, which destroyest all the earth: and I will stretch out mine hand upon thee, and roll thee down from the rocks, and will make thee a burnt mountain"* (Jer 51:24-25).

God, through Jeremiah, called Babylon or Chaldea, formerly in the southern part of modern Iraq, a destroying mountain that will be burned. Hence, the "great burning mountain" is today part of Iraq.

"Sea". We have learned earlier from Revelation 17:15 that the "sea", a place of many nations and languages, is the "Old World," primarily Western Europe, where all the founding member-states of the European Union (EU) are located.

"Blood". We saw in Isaiah 34:3 and Ezekiel 14:19 in our analysis of the first trumpet that "blood" signifies violent death and slaughter. It looks like the explanation for the second trumpet prophecy is awfully dreadful. Iraq [the *"great mountain burning with fire"*] will attack the European Union (the *"sea"*), and about 33% of all people and animals will perish (*"third part of the creatures which were in the sea, and had life, died"*). Even those on board 33% of all EU ships, whether military or commercial, will presumably suffer the same fate (*"and the third part of the ships were destroyed"*).

Biological weapon? The reason for the massive and rapid deaths is uncertain. Could it be a biological attack? Could it be the bubonic plague, or Black Death, which, by 1400, had killed about one-third of Europe's medieval population? Or could it be one of the many virulent modern-day menaces – such as the Ebola virus, Severe Acute Respiratory

Syndrome virus (SARS), Middle East Respiratory Syndrome corona virus (MERScov), and others not yet so deadly or well known?

Second bowl.

"And the second angel poured out his vial upon the sea; and it became as the blood of a dead man: and every living soul died in the sea" (Rev 16:3). With the meanings of the prophetic symbols now openly known to us, the interpretation of the second bowl looms unimaginably horrid: All those living in the European Union, people and animals, will end up dead!

Spiritual death? Does the word "died" indicate physical death, literally, or spiritual death, figuratively? If the latter, then it looks like all the inhabitants of EU would give up worshipping the One True God, which, in this writer's opinion, is much worse – the entire EU population would continue living physically, but would be precluded from spiritual salvation. It seems unlikely, though, considering the phrase "every living soul", which includes animals that have no spirits that can be saved. Sadly, it looks like physical death is the literal meaning.

Third trumpet.

The third trumpet appears to prophesy a nuclear war, followed by the Great Tribulation. However, the cataclysmic visions of John in Revelation do not include preliminary events revealed in Daniel, such as the setting up of the "abomination of desolation" (Dan 9 and 11), a local event that will usher in the global calamities. Let us first see how those episodes will serve as a prelude to the nuclear war.

Last "week" of years

"And he shall confirm the covenant with many for one week: and in the midst of the week he shall cause the sacrifice and the oblation to cease, and for the overspreading of abominations he shall make it desolate, even until the consummation, and that determined shall be poured upon the desolate" (Dan 9:27). The passage begins by telling of a group of people ratifying an agreement for "one week" and closes with what appears to be the time of the end ("until the consummation")! The cessation of sacrifice and desolation of its site are reiterated two chapters later.

"And arms shall stand on his part, and they shall pollute the sanctuary of strength, and shall take away the daily sacrifice, and they shall place the abomination that maketh desolate" (Dan 11:31).

Who is "he"?
The identity of the first, and presumably principal, signatory is shrouded in mystery. Who could "*he*" be?

EU chief? The antecedent of "*he*" was "*the prince that shall come*" who "*shall destroy the city and the sanctuary*" (Dan 9:26). That points to the son of Emperor Vespasian, Titus, who razed Jerusalem and the Holy Temple in 70 A.D. So, "*he*" must be an end-time successor of Titus, who became Roman Emperor after his father died. His power over Europe is now in the hands of the European Union. Is "*he*" the present or a future chief of EU?

US president? However, "*he*" may alternatively refer to the modern-day ruler of the empire that has replaced Rome as "*king of the north*". In that case, he could the president of the United States. We are trying to solve a riddle with ambiguous clues.

Iraqi ruler? To further muddle the matter, the antecedent of "*he*" in Daniel 11:21-30 was the "*vile person*", who, as we have seen, was Saddam Hussein. He was hanged in December 2006; yet, starting Daniel 11:31, we see the "*vile person*" carrying out even more misdeeds. Either Saddam did not really die, or the person spoken about is one of his successors as ruler of Iraq.

Iraqi EU chief? Or two of the leaders might be the same person. An Iraqi ruler could become the chief of the EU! That would fulfill the prophecy of the last end-time empire symbolized by the "*two feet of iron and clay*" (Dan 2). With the Muslim immigrant "invasion" of Europe, the Islamic State "caliphate" could take over EU!

We saw in the second bowl prophecy that "*every living soul... in the sea*" (EU) might die in a biological attack . In such a scenario, the Iraqi ruler could come in after the pestilence shall have died out. Or the EU government might relocate outside Western Europe – much like the Eastern Roman Empire, which set up its new capital in Byzantium and lasted nearly 1,000 years longer than the original Western Roman Empire based in Rome.

The "*covenant*".
"*And he shall confirm the covenant...*" (Dan 9:27a). Many eschatologists and prophecy teachers believe it will be some kind of an international treaty. But do we need to watch for any such future compact? There are already several very important covenants in Scriptures, including the Noahic covenant, Abrahamic covenant, Mosaic covenant, Davidic covenant, New Covenant with Christ.

Abrahamic covenant? The covenant that is very much behind the now-smoldering, now-blazing conflict between Israel and its Muslim Arab neighbors and Palestinians is the covenant between God and Abraham which gave his descendants ownership of the Promised Land. *"In the same day the LORD made a covenant with Abram, saying, Unto thy seed have I given this land, from the river of Egypt unto the great river, the river Euphrates..."* (Gen 15:18).

"One week".

"...he shall confirm the covenant with many for one week:..." (Dan 9:27b). The Hebrew word translated "week" is *shabua*, which means "sevened" or a unit with 7 parts – such as 7 days (one week), or 7 years (one sabbatical period). In context, it is generally understood that *shabua* in the verse means a period of 7 years.

"Midst of the week".

"...in the midst of the week..." (Dan 9:27c) simply means in the middle of the 7 years, or 3 ½ years (42 Biblical months of 30 days each) after the covenant is confirmed.

Offerings stopped.

The phrases *"he shall cause the sacrifice and the oblation to cease"* (Dan 9:27d) and *"shall take away the daily sacrifice"* (Dan 11:31b) plainly denote that *"he"* will stop offerings – presumably on Temple Mount, former site of the Jewish Temple in Jerusalem and traditional place of sacrificial offerings to the God of Israel.

Since the last offerings were made before the Temple was destroyed by the Romans in 70 A.D. almost 2,000 years ago, no new offerings have been made at Temple Mount. The Dome of the Rock was built in 691-692 by Caliph Abd al-Malik on the site of the Jewish Temple. According to Islamic legend, the prophet Muhammad ascended to heaven from there, which is why Jerusalem is deemed to be Islam's third holiest city (after Mecca and Medina).

Logically, for offerings to be stopped, they must first be resumed – something that seems uncertain at the present time.

Jewish Temple rebuilt?

Many pious Jews and Gentile watchmen believe that the Temple will have to be rebuilt for offerings to resume. In anticipation, Jewish priests are being trained and ceremonial utensils are being made for use in a rebuilt temple by groups like the Temple Mount Faithful. Also, the search for a perfect red heifer without a single hair of any other color is continually being done (its ashes will be needed for ceremonial purification in a rebuilt Temple).

As proof-text that the holy Temple will be rebuilt, prophecy teachers usually cite 2 Thessalonians 2:3-4 – *"Let no man deceive you by any means: for that day shall not come, except there come a falling away first, and that man of sin be revealed, the son of perdition; Who opposeth and exalteth himself above all that is called God, or that is worshipped; so that he as God sitteth in the temple of God, shewing himself that he is God."* According to the widely accepted interpretation, the Antichrist will enthrone himself as the supreme god in a yet to be rebuilt Temple.

No temple needed?

On the other hand, a growing number of prophecy analysts are beginning to think that offerings on Temple Mount may be made even without a temple. The Greek word translated "temple" (2 Thess 2:3-4) is *naon (naos)*, which can simply mean a "shrine" or "holy place" without any physical structure. Besides, the offerings may just consist of prayers, which do not have to be made in a temple.

Rabbi Akiva's teaching. In the 2nd century, "rabbis under Akiva started to bring in many new rulings and theology. This was in part necessary so you could have Judaism without a Temple and blood sacrifices… Prayer and acts of piety replaced sacrifice."[2]

Christian doctrines. Furthermore, as far as Christians are concerned, there is no longer any need for a temple, because the saints are now God's temple on earth: *"Know ye not that ye are the temple of God, and that the Spirit of God dwelleth in you?"* (1 Cor 3:16); *"And what agreement hath the temple of God with idols? for ye are the temple of the living God…"* (2 Cor 6:16a).

As regards priests officiating at offerings, Christ is now our high priest in heaven: *"Now of the things which we have spoken this is the sum: We have such an high priest, who is set on the right hand of the throne of the Majesty in the heavens"* (Heb 8:1); *"Seeing then that we have a great high priest, that is passed into the heavens, Jesus the Son of God, let us hold fast our profession"* (Heb 4:14).

Christ has also become our sacrificial lamb: *"The next day John seeth Jesus coming unto him, and saith, Behold the Lamb of God, which taketh away the sin of the world"* (John 1:29). His blood has replaced that of sacrificial animals for the atonement of sin: *"Neither by the blood of goats and calves, but by his own blood he entered in once into the holy place, having obtained eternal redemption for us. For if the blood of bulls and* of goats, and the ashes of an heifer sprinkling the unclean, sanctifieth to the purifying of the flesh: How much more shall the blood of Christ, who through the eternal Spirit offered himself without spot to God, purge your conscience from dead works to serve the living God?" (Heb 9:12-14).

Temple rebuilding frustrated.

Dale Parkes, editor-publisher of *The Proclaimer* newsletter, wrote that Julian, the last anti-Christian Roman emperor (361-363), authorized the rebuilding of the Jewish Temple: "Attempts to rebuild the Jewish Temple have been made since the destruction of the last Temple by the Romans in 70 A.D... There was an attempt to rebuild the Temple sometime during the time frame of 361-363 A.D. The following extract is taken from *Mosheim's Institutes of Ecclesiastical History* by James Murdock, D.D. (London, William, 1861, p. 121). The actual extract quoted is in *italics*. *As Julian affected to appear unwilling to trouble any of his subjects on account of their religion and opposed to no sect whatever, he showed so much indulgence to the Jews as to give them liberty to rebuild the Temple of Jerusalem. The Jews commenced the work, but were obliged to desist before even the foundations were laid. For balls of fire issued from the ground, accompanied with a great explosion and a tremendous earthquake, which dispersed both the materials which were collected and the workmen.'"[3] Was it an act of God?

Recent attempts. Since the Muslims recaptured Jerusalem from the Crusaders in 1187, an Islamic *Waqf* (religious trust) has been administering the Temple Mount. During the Six-Day War in 1967 (June 5-10), the site fell under the control of Israel, but its administration was shortly returned to the Jerusalem Islamic Waqf.

In 1974, 1977, and 1983, groups led by one Yoel Lerner conspired to blow up the Dome of the Rock and the adjoining Al-Aqsa Mosque. On January 26, 1984, Waqf guards uncovered a plot by the Messianic group B'nei Yehuda to plant explosives in the area. On October 12, 1990, some Jews tried to lay a cornerstone for a new temple, but were stopped by Israeli authorities when Palestinian Muslims protested violently.

Prayers forbidden. Jews are forbidden to pray on Temple Mount. Several Israeli prime ministers tried to change the policy, but failed. During the 1990s, more attempts were made by Jews to pray on the site, but were prevented by the Israeli police. In the 2010s, out of fears that Jewish prayers would be made or the Muslim shrines destroyed, Palestinians attacked Temple Mount visitors, as well as the police, with stones, firebombs, and fireworks.[4]

The "abomination of desolation"

"...and for the overspreading of abominations he shall make it desolate..." (Dan 9:27e). *"...and they shall place the abomination that maketh desolate"* (Dan 11:31c). *"He"* and his men will enter the Temple Mount compound and set up the dreaded "abomination of desolation".

Assyrian invader.

Isaiah foretold the invasion of Israel by a conqueror from Assyria, today the northern part of Iraq. *"O Assyrian, the rod of mine anger, and the staff in their hand is mine indignation. I will send him against an hypocritical nation, and against the people of my wrath will I give him a charge, to take the spoil, and to take the prey, and to tread them down like the mire of the streets... Therefore thus saith the Lord GOD of hosts, O my people that dwellest in Zion, be not afraid of the Assyrian: he shall smite thee with a rod, and shall lift up his staff against thee, after the manner of Egypt"* (Isa 10:5-6,24).

The prophet Micah foresaw the same thing: *"...the Assyrian shall come into our land: and when he shall tread in our palaces, then shall we raise against him seven shepherds, and eight principal men. And they shall waste the land of Assyria with the sword, and the land of Nimrod in the entrances thereof: thus shall he deliver us from the Assyrian, when he cometh into our land, and when he treadeth within our borders"* (Mic 5:5b-6). The Assyrian invader will ultimately be defeated.

Abomination set up.

Translated differently in the NIV, Daniel 9:27c reads – *"And on a wing [of the temple] he will set up an abomination that causes desolation..."* (the "wing" may also refer to that of an aircraft; the "abomination" could be delivered by an airplane or a helicopter).

What is the "abomination of desolation"? For many years, book authors and eschatologists have taught that it would be a statue of Antichrist installed inside the Temple in Jerusalem. Will it be that, really? Let us analyze the term with the help of a dictionary.

"Abomination" – anything that arouses strong disgust or loathing; hence, a revolting object.

"Desolation" – a ruined or deserted condition; thus, devastation, destruction, or barrenness.

"Abomination of desolation", therefore, signifies something so disgusting because it causes so much destruction!

Instant destruction.

In the words of Christ, the abomination of desolation will cause instantaneous, far-reaching destruction. *"When ye therefore shall see the abomination of desolation, spoken of by Daniel the prophet, stand in the holy place, (whoso readeth, let him understand: Then let them which be in Judaea flee into the mountains: Let him which is on the housetop not come down to take any thing out of his house: Neither let him which is in the field return back to take his clothes. And woe unto them that are with child, and to them that give suck in those days! But pray ye that your flight be not in the winter, neither on the sabbath day"* (Matt 24:15-20).

People in Judea will have to escape to high grounds without a moment to spare. Those coming down from the flat roofs of their houses will have no time to get anything from the ground floor, much less those away from home. Pregnant women and breastfeeding mothers will be disadvantaged, because they will not be able to run fast enough. If it happens in wintertime, the hills will be cold and slippery; if on the Sabbath, pious Jews cannot escape far enough as they may travel only 2,000 paces on the weekly day of rest.

Total and final destruction.

It looks like the abomination of desolation will be the instrument of the Temple Mount's total and final destruction. Christ has voiced a prophecy: *"And Jesus went out, and departed from the temple: and his disciples came to him for to shew him the buildings of the temple. And Jesus said unto them, See ye not all these things? verily I say unto you, There shall not be left here one stone upon another, that shall not be thrown down"* (Matt 24:1-2).

The prophecy has not been fully fulfilled yet, because the Temple Mount's Western Wall is still standing, with its massive stones on top of one another. When the Roman legions destroyed the Holy Temple in 70 A.D., they did not to demolish the Western Wall inasmuch as it served as the retaining wall that kept the steep western hillside from collapsing.

Did God play on words?

Do you now have an idea of what the abomination of desolation could be? Let us assume that the term is an anagram, whose letters we can play with and rearrange to form new words. The results we find are quite surprising.

ABOM. The first four letters of "abomination" give us ABOM. Now, say it aloud – "A BOM". Do you hear "a bomb"? Will the abomination of desolation be a bomb?

MOAB. Juggle the letters a bit more, and one result spells MOAB, the name of the elder incestuous son of Lot, Abraham's nephew. Moab became the ancestor of the Moabite nation, who did not allow the Israelites to pass through their territory in the latter's Exodus from Egypt to Canaan. Later, as vassals, the Moabites rose in rebellion against the northern kingdom of divided Israel.

MOAB is also the acronym for Massive Ordnance Air Blast, the US Air Force's 9,840-kg (21,700-lb) bomb built for the Second Persian Gulf War in 2003 but used only once (in Afghanistan, 2017). It is the largest guided air-dropped weapon in history. The bomb can spread a flammable mist over its target area and then ignite it, creating a massive blast and fireball 40% more powerful than any other conventional weapon in the U.S. arsenal.[5,6]

Also nicknamed "Mother Of All Bombs", MOAB sounds like a rejoinder to Saddam Hussein's boast in 1991 that the impending First Persian Gulf War was going to be the "mother of all battles" (MOAB, too, for short)!

OBAM. Curiously, ABOM further mixed up also produces OBAM, the first four letters of former US President Barack Obama's surname. Will he in one way or another be involved in setting up the abomination of desolation in the holy place? Bear in mind that, in 2017, although Obama had finished his two-term, eight-year US presidency, a group of Frenchmen collected over 300,000 signatures in a campaign for him to run for president of France. Will Obama again become a key player on the world's geopolitical stage?

Preliminary episodes complete.

The foregoing discussion on the cessation of sacrifice and setting up of the abomination of desolation supplies the missing episodes which John did not see in his visions of global cataclysms.

Let us now resume our study of the seals, trumpets, and bowls prophecies. We last saw that, after the contents of the second bowl were poured down, *"every living soul died in the sea"* (Rev 16:3b).

Nuclear war?

The next episode takes us to the blowing of the third trumpet. The prophecy appears to augur the outbreak of nuclear war.

Third trumpet.

"And the third angel sounded, and there fell a great star from heaven, burning as it were a lamp, and it fell upon the third part of the rivers, and upon the fountains of waters" (Rev 8:10). Let us again find out the meanings of the prophetic metaphors.

"Rivers". As we have discovered in an earlier chapter, "rivers" represent attacking enemies and invaders in general. We see this in Isaiah 8:7 – *"Now therefore, behold, the Lord bringeth up upon them the waters of the river, strong and many, even the king of Assyria, and all his glory: and he shall come up over all his channels, and go over all his banks"*; as well as in Jeremiah 46:8 – *"Egypt riseth up like a flood, and his waters are moved like the rivers; and he saith, I will go up, and will cover the earth; I will destroy the city and the inhabitants thereof."*

"Fountains". These have a somewhat more elusive symbolism. *"For the LORD thy God bringeth thee into a good land, a land of brooks of water, of fountains and depths that spring out of valleys and hills"* (Deut 8:7). Also, *"He sendeth the springs into the valleys, which run among the hills"* (Ps 104:10). "Fountains" or springs are the sources of rivers; so if "rivers" are invading armies, "fountains" must be their homelands from where the invaders come.

"Wormwood".

"And the name of the star is called Wormwood: and the third part of the waters became wormwood; and many men died of the waters, because they were made bitter" (Rev 8:11). For over 1,900 years since the time it was written, the meaning of *"Wormwood"* in prophecy had remained a riddle no reader could unravel.

Botanically, wormwood is an aromatic, bitter plant used as a medicine and whose leaves and flowers add flavor to absinthe, an old-time liqueur now considered harmful to health. In the Ukrainian language, wormwood is *chernobyl*, also the name of a city in the Ukraine near where a Soviet nuclear power plant was built and became operational in 1977-1983.

Chernobyl accident. On April 26, 1986, one of the nuclear reactors at the Chernobyl nuclear power plant exploded, releasing an estimated 100-150 million curies of radiation into the atmosphere. Radioactivity from Chernobyl contaminated the atmosphere above the Ukraine, Belarus and Russia, reaching as far as Italy and France in Western Europe. Some 200,000 people near the site had to be relocated. Around 6,000-8,000 victims have died since the accident.

Was it God's end-time inkling to us that "Wormwood" means "radioactive" or "nuclear"? In the primitive world of the first century Middle East, there was no way John, author of the Revelation, could have used the words "radioactive" and "nuclear". So now, having learned the hidden meaning of "Wormwood", we can perhaps more intelligibly paraphrase Revelation 8:10-11.

Attackers nuked? One-third of the various attacking forces ("*third part of the rivers*") and their homelands ("*the fountains of waters*") will be bombed ("*there fell a great star from heaven*") with nuclear weapons ("*the name of the star is called Wormwood*"). One-third of the people there ("*the third part of the waters*") will be afflicted with radioactivity ("*became wormwood*") and there will be numerous casualties ("*many men died*") due to radiation ("*the waters were made bitter*").

Third bowl.
"*And the third angel poured out his vial upon the rivers and fountains of waters; and they became blood*" (Rev 16:4). The third bowl is simply a progression (or deterioration) from the third trumpet – with the situation worsening gravely. Many more fighters among the invading forces ("*rivers*") and the people ("*waters*") in their homelands will lose their lives ("*became blood*").

Damascus obliterated. It seems Damascus, the capital of Syria, will be erased from the map. "*The burden of Damascus. Behold, Damascus is taken away from being a city, and it shall be a ruinous heap*" (Isa 17:1). As a bone of contention, Damascus, the world's oldest continuously inhabited city, could be obliterated by the nuclear powers if it is taken over by jihadist forces. On the other hand, the jihadists, if they fail to capture the city, might decide to wipe it out with a "dirty bomb" or crude nuclear device that might come into their possession.

Nuclear war estimates.
Discover magazine, in its February 1984 issue, reported that "four American scientists... at the invitation of Senators Edward Kennedy and Mark Hatfield, met in Washington in December (1983) for a three-hour open discussion with four Soviet counterparts. The subject of their discussion: the nuclear winter (*Discover*, January).

"Two scientific reports have recently been published, dealing with the probable effects of nuclear war upon the earth's climate and the life of the planet. The first discovery is already widely known within the scientific community of climatologists, geophysicists, and biologists here and abroad, and had been confirmed in detail by scientists in the Soviet Union... the already taken for granted estimate that in an all-out exchange of say, 5,000 megatons, something like a billion people would be killed outright by blast, heat and radiation... more than another billion would die later on, from the delayed effects of the climate and radioactive fallout.

"In the same research, new calculations of the extent and intensity of radioactive fallout predict the exposure of large land areas to much more intense levels of radiation than expected. The report is referred to as TTAPS, an acronym derived from the investigators names: Turco, Toon, Ackerman, Pollack, and Sagan...

"There is no nation on earth free of the jeopardy of destruction if any two countries or groups of countries embark upon a nuclear exchange."

"Extinction of the biosphere". The article continued: "The second piece of work, by Paul Ehrlich and 19 other distinguished biologists, demonstrates that the predictions of TTAPS mean nothing less than the extinction of much of the earth's biosphere, very possibly involving the Southern Hemisphere as well as the Northern... The 20 biologists' paper, summarized by Professor Ehrlich, represents the consensus arrived at by 40 biological scientists at a meeting in Woods Hole, Massachusetts, last spring."

The "Great Tribulation"

The nuclear war, triggered by the abomination of desolation, will be quickly followed in its wake by the "Great Tribulation". Christ's warning to His disciples is worth repeating here. *"When ye therefore shall see the abomination of desolation, spoken of by Daniel the prophet, stand in the holy place... then shall be great tribulation, such as was not since the beginning of the world to this time, no, nor ever shall be"* (Matt 24:15a,21).

God, speaking through the prophet Ezekiel, had much earlier foretold the same thing: *"And I will do in thee that which I have not done, and whereunto I will not do any more the like, because of all thine abominations"* (Ezek 5:9).

So did the angel Gabriel in his prophecy to Daniel: *"And at that time shall Michael stand up, the great prince which standeth for the children of thy people: and there shall be a time of trouble, such as never was since there was a nation even to that same time: and at that time thy people shall be delivered, every one that shall be found written in the book"* (Dan 12:1).

The Great Tribulation will be an unprecedented period of horrific human suffering on earth.

Fourth trumpet.

The fourth trumpet will signal the unfolding Great Tribulation. *"And the fourth angel sounded, and the third part of the sun was smitten, and the third part of the moon, and the third part of the stars; so as the third part of them was darkened, and the day shone not for a third part of it, and the night likewise"* (Rev 8:12).

Scientific studies closely parallel the prophetic picture. According to the magazine article in *Discover* February 1984, "Computer models demonstrate that a nuclear war involving the exchange of less than one-third of the total American and Soviet arsenal will change the climate of the entire Northern Hemisphere, shifting it abruptly from its present seasonal state to a long, sunless, frozen night."

Nuclear winter. Revelation 8:12 presages that the brightness of the heavenly bodies will be reduced by 33%. This would be the effect of the nuclear soot and dust from the explosions, as well as smoke from burning cities and fuel stockpiles suspended in the atmosphere, which would screen light from the celestial sources. The particulates would be wafted around the world by the wind, creating a high-altitude smog-like layer. It would act like a dense sunscreen that would cut down the amount of sunlight reaching the ground.

Consequently, the surface of the earth would cool down – by some estimates to as low as 13°F – remaining at that level for many months before slowly warming up again. Needless to say, agricultural food production would nosedive. More millions of people could die as a result of severe global food shortages.

Fourth bowl.

"And the fourth angel poured out his vial upon the sun; and power was given unto him to scorch men with fire. And men were scorched with great heat, and blasphemed the name of God, which hath power over these plagues: and they repented not to give him glory" (Rev 16:8-9).

Ozone layer destroyed. The *Discover* February 1984 article went on: "This (nuclear winter) will be followed after some months by a settling of nuclear soot and dust, then by a new malignant kind of sunlight, with all of its ultraviolet band, capable of blinding most terrestrial animals, no longer shielded from the sun by the ozonosphere."

When the sky eventually clears up, the ozone layer will have been destroyed – Earth's protection from deadly ultraviolet radiation from the sun gone. The planet will be bathed with intense heat.

700% hotter sun? *"Moreover the light of the moon shall be as the light of the sun, and the light of the sun shall be sevenfold, as the light of seven days"* (Isa 30:26a). Heat waves in the past have registered over 100°F temperatures, but the heat, according to the prophecy, if literally fulfilled, could rise to as high as 700°F!

"I will make waste mountains and hills, and dry up all their herbs; and I will make the rivers islands, and I will dry up the pools" (Isa 42:15). Springs and rivers will dry up. There will be forest fires, brushfires, and

grassfires practically everywhere – much worse and widespread than those happening before the nuclear war: *"...the fire: it shall devour the briers and thorns, and shall kindle in the thickets of the forest, and they shall mount up like the lifting up of smoke"* (Isa 9:18b). Towns and cities spared from the nuclear explosions will burn just the same later in the intense heat.

Back to the Dark Ages. The ferocious heat will destroy most power, utility, transport, communications and military systems on earth. Fuel tanks of vehicles will explode. Insulation materials covering power lines, whether rubber or plastic, will melt. Overheated electronic circuits will stop working. Ammunitions exposed to the extreme heat will blow up. In short – no electricity, no water supply, no computers, no phones, no TV, no cars, no buses, no planes, etcetera. The modern world whose comforts people are presently enjoying will suddenly be thrown back to the Dark Ages.

Survivors in caves. Many people will find places of refuge in the mountains. *"Behold, I will send for many fishers, saith the LORD, and they shall fish them; and after will I send for many hunters, and they shall hunt them from every mountain, and from every hill, and out of the holes of the rocks"* (Jer 16:16). God, by Jeremiah, had prophesied how Christ's apostles would be "fishers of men" (Matt 4:19; Mark 1:17); and then how, later at the end-time, Bible teachers will search for refugees to teach in the mountains and caves.

No safe place. *"Say thou thus unto them, Thus saith the Lord GOD; As I live, surely they that are in the wastes shall fall by the sword, and him that is in the open field will I give to the beasts to be devoured, and they that be in the forts and in the caves shall die of the pestilence"* (Ezek 33:27). Deathly dangers will be everywhere – murderous men foraging in city ruins, roving hunger-crazed animals everywhere, unseen air- and insect-borne viruses and pestilent microbes from millions of unburied, decomposing corpses drifting into even fortified shelters and secluded caverns.

Worldwide famine.

With trees and plants withered or burnt to cinders, livestock and even wild game will die off. *"O LORD, to thee will I cry: for the fire hath devoured the pastures of the wilderness, and the flame hath burned all the trees of the field. The beasts of the field cry also unto thee: for the rivers of waters are dried up, and the fire hath devoured the pastures of the wilderness.* (Joel 1:19-2:1). The inexorable result: global famine.

Pity the infants and young children who will thirst and starve. *"The tongue of the sucking child cleaveth to the roof of his mouth for thirst: the young children ask bread, and no man breaketh it unto them. They that did feed delicately are desolate in the streets: they that were brought up in scarlet embrace dunghills"* (Lam 4:4-5). Members of the moneyed class who are accustomed to fine dining, gourmet dishes, and pricey delicacies will grab even heaps of animal manure to eat.

Roots for food. *"Haggard from want and hunger, they roamed the parched land in desolate wastelands at night. In the brush they gathered salt herbs, and their food was the root of the broom tree"* (Job 30:3-4, NIV). Due to unbearable heat during the day, people will forage for things to eat at night. Those in the boondocks will eat whatever weeds and roots they can find to survive.

Cannibalism! Driven by maddening hunger pangs, some people will resort to the unthinkable. *"And ye shall eat the flesh of your sons, and the flesh of your daughters shall ye eat"* (Lev 26:29). *"Therefore the fathers shall eat the sons in the midst of thee, and the sons shall eat their fathers…"* (Ezek 5:9-10a). During extreme conditions and dire circumstances, some people have done the unthinkable. It is thus not too far-fetched to imagine that it can happen again.

A hint from Christ. *"For if they do these things in a green tree, what shall be done in the dry?"* (Luke 23:31). As He carried the cross to Golgotha, Christ, to console the weeping women accompanying Him, gave them a hint that if men could be cruel in their time, people will become even more inhumane to one another when the trees shall have dried up.

Prophecies confirmed. A future account of Tribulation saints who will be in the kingdom of heaven confirms the prophecies. *"These are they which came out of great tribulation, and have washed their robes, and made them white in the blood of the Lamb. Therefore are they before the throne of God, and serve him day and night in his temple: and he that sitteth on the throne shall dwell among them. They shall hunger no more, neither thirst any more; neither shall the sun light on them, nor any heat"* (Rev 7:14b-16).

In the presence of God, the saints will no longer experience starvation, burning thirst, and unbearable heat from the sun.

Provisions for the righteous. Believers who will have faithfully kept the word of God will find safe havens, as well as adequate nourishment in their highland hideaways. *"He who walks righteously and speaks what is right, who rejects gain from extortion and keeps his hand from accepting bribes, who stops his ears against plots of murder and shuts his eyes* *against contemplating evil -- this is the man who will dwell on the heights, whose refuge will be the mountain fortress. His bread will be supplied, and water will not fail him"* (Isa 33:15-16, NIV).

Rise of "Antichrist".
The "Antichrist" will rise to prominence at this trying time – events possibly conspiring for the "beast" (EU) and the "vile person" (ruler of Iraq) to come together. If, as we have speculated, an Iraqi leader (the "Assyrian" – Saddam Hussein, or one of his successors, such as the Islamic State caliph) becomes the head of the EU, he would be the ruler of the last empire ("the two feet and ten toes of mixed iron and clay"). Like a "horn" in prophecy which can refer to either the king or his kingdom, the "beast" may also refer to either the empire (EU) or its ruler – the end-time "Antichrist"!

Deadly wound. The "beast" would sustain a lethal injury. *"And I saw one of his heads as it were wounded to death; and his deadly wound was healed: and all the world wondered after the beast. And they worshipped the dragon which gave power unto the beast: and they worshipped the beast, saying, Who is like unto the beast? who is able to make war with him?"* (Rev 13:3-4).

Miraculously recovering from his near-fatal wound, the "beast" will seem even more invincible to the world at large.

42-month extension. His term as head of government will be extended. *"And there was given unto him a mouth speaking great things and blasphemies; and power was given unto him to continue forty and two months"* (Rev 13:5). (The extension may or may not be specified as 42 months, but, as the second part of the prophesied last 7 years, it will end on the fateful Day of the LORD.)

Headquarters: Jerusalem. It seems the "beast" will establish his base in Israel, and the Temple Mount will once again be in the hands of non-Jews for the duration of the 42-month period. *"And there was given me a reed like unto a rod: and the angel stood, saying, Rise, and measure the temple of God, and the altar, and them that worship therein. But the court which is without the temple leave out, and measure it not; for it is given unto the Gentiles: and the holy city shall they tread under foot forty and two months"* (Rev 11:1-2).

War on God, angels, and saints. *"And he opened his mouth in blasphemy against God, to blaspheme his name, and his tabernacle, and them that dwell in heaven"* (Rev 13:6). With fiery diabolical oratory, the Antichrist will disparage the Creator and the angels, and persecute faithful believers. *"And it was given unto him to make war with the saints, and to overcome them..."* (Rev 13:7a).

Ruler of the world. The beast will reign over the world: *"…and power was given him over all kindreds, and tongues, and nations. And all that dwell upon the earth shall worship him, whose names are not written in the book of life of the Lamb slain from the foundation of the world"* (Rev 13:7b-8).

"And such as do wickedly against the covenant shall he corrupt by flatteries…" (Dan 11:32a). He will highly praise and encourage all those who reject Israel's claims and rights to the Holy Land.

Fearless preachers.

Undaunted, courageous men of God will carry on with their work and defy the Antichrist: *"…but the people that do know their God shall be strong, and do exploits. And they that understand among the people shall instruct many: yet they shall fall by the sword, and by flame, by captivity, and by spoil, many days"* (Dan 11:-32b-33). The beast will imprison and put to death the God-fearing men who will dare to defy him and teach others to do likewise.

"When they fall, they will receive a little help, and many who are not sincere will join them. Some of the wise will stumble, so that they may be refined, purified and made spotless until the time of the end, for it will still come at the appointed time" (Dan 11:34-35, NIV). Some preachers will be misled by impostors, but their mistakes will serve as lessons that will prepare them to meet the Redeemer.

The two witnesses.

God's two great end-time preachers will carry out their 42-month (1,260-day) ministries. *"And I will give power unto my two witnesses, and they shall prophesy a thousand two hundred and threescore days, clothed in sackcloth. These are the two olive trees, and the two candlesticks standing before the God of the earth"* (Rev 11:3-4).

The identities of these two end-time witnesses are a mystery. Some Bible teachers believe they are the Old and New Testaments; others argue they will be Enoch (Gen 5:24; Heb 11:5) and Elijah (2 Kings 2:11), the only two persons who did not die but were translated alive to heaven; still others assert that they will be Moses and Elijah, who came back to life to converse with Christ at the Transfiguration (Matt 17:1-8; Mark 9:2-8; Luke 9:28-36). If they are persons living at present, we get some clues from the Scriptures.

One might come from the north. *"I have raised up one from the north, and he shall come: from the rising of the sun shall he call upon my name: and he shall come upon princes as upon morter, and as the potter treadeth clay"* (Isa 41:25).

Another could be from the east. *"Calling a ravenous bird from the east, the man that executeth my counsel from a far country: yea, I have spoken it, I will also bring it to pass; I have purposed it, I will also do it"* (Isa 46:11).

"Fire from their mouth". The two witnesses will be supernaturally endowed. *"And if any man will hurt them, fire proceedeth out of their mouth, and devoureth their enemies: and if any man will hurt them, he must in this manner be killed"* (Rev 11:5). It sounds metaphoric. Let us look for the Biblical interpretation.

God told the prophet Jeremiah (Jer 5:14), *"Wherefore thus saith the LORD God of hosts, Because ye speak this word, behold, I will make my words in thy mouth fire, and this people wood, and it shall devour them."* The word of God is the Scripture; and, as we know now, to "devour, eat or swallow" means to defeat or conquer. Thus, the two witnesses will defeat or silence their persecutors with the words of God from the Bible (*"fire out of their mouth"*).

3-1/2-year drought. On top of the unbearable heat from the sun, it will not rain for the next 3 ½ years. Revelation 11:6a says – *"These (two witnesses) have power to shut heaven, that it rain not in the days of their prophecy..."* Elijah performed a similar miracle some 2,900 years ago. *"And Elijah the Tishbite, who was of the inhabitants of Gilead, said unto Ahab, As the LORD God of Israel liveth, before whom I stand, there shall not be dew nor rain these years, but according to my word"* (1 Kings 17:1).

What is more, the two witnesses will *"have power over waters to turn them to blood, and to smite the earth with all plagues, as often as they will"* (Rev 11:6b). In the third bowl prophecy, *"waters"* mean people, while *"blood"* signifies *"death"*. Many people will perish.

The ID of the beast?

"And he causeth all, both small and great, rich and poor, free and bond, to receive a mark in their right hand, or in their foreheads: And that no man might buy or sell, save he that had the mark, or the name of the beast, or the number of his name" (Rev 13:16-17).

Quite predictably, the "beast" will commandeer all remaining food stocks in the world. Only his followers with a special ID bearing his or the government's name, or its corresponding number, printed on the right hand or forehead will be permitted to buy from the supplies under the beast government's control.

Betrayals for food. *"Now the brother shall betray the brother to death, and the father the son; and children shall rise up against their parents, and shall cause them to be put to death"* (Mark 13:12).

Family members, to alleviate their agonizing hunger, will inform on each other in order to obtain for oneself food which will otherwise be next to impossible to find.

End-time god-king.
"And the king shall do according to his will; and he shall exalt himself, and magnify himself above every god, and shall speak marvellous things against the God of gods, and shall prosper till the indignation be accomplished: for that that is determined shall be done. Neither shall he regard the God of his fathers, nor the desire of women, nor regard any god: for he shall magnify himself above all" (Dan 11:36-37). The Antichrist will think of himself as a god greater than even the Creator. He will abandon his people's religion.

"Desire of women". Eschatologists teach the Antichrist will shun sexual relations with the opposite sex. Yet, in Daniel's time the desire of every Jewish woman must have been to be the mother of the prophesied Messiah, that is, Christ. In short, the Antichrist will have no respect whatsoever for Christ, Christianity, and Christians.

A patron of war. "But in his estate shall he honour the God of forces: and a god whom his fathers knew not shall he honour with gold, and silver, and with precious stones, and pleasant things" (Dan 11:38). The Antichrist will pay homage to a new god of war with treasures, no doubt consisting of spoils of war.

"He will attack the mightiest fortresses with the help of a foreign god and will greatly honor those who acknowledge him. He will make them rulers over many people and will distribute the land at a price" (Dan 11:39, NIV). The Antichrist will attribute his military victories to his god, and will promote those who do the same as his deputies over conquered territories, including the Holy Land, which he will partition for money.

Fifth seal.
The spirits of martyred saints who will have proceeded to the third heaven or Paradise (2 Cor 12:2-4) under the altar of God, also referred to in Jewish tradition as "Abraham's bosom" (Luke 16:22), ask for justice. "And when he had opened the fifth seal, I saw under the altar the souls of them that were slain for the word of God, and for the testimony which they held: And they cried with a loud voice, saying, How long, O Lord, holy and true, dost thou not judge and avenge our blood on them that dwell on the earth? And white robes were given unto every one of them; and it was said unto them, that they should rest yet for a little season, until their fellowservants also and their brethren, that should be killed as they were, should be fulfilled" (Rev 6:9-11).

They were told to bide their time and wait for the rest of their fellow-martyrs to suffer the same fate they had met.

Saints beheaded. *"And I saw thrones, and they sat upon them, and judgment was given unto them: and I saw the souls of them that were beheaded for the witness of Jesus, and for the word of God, and which had not worshipped the beast, neither his image, neither had received his mark upon their foreheads, or in their hands"* (Rev 20:4a). Many of the saints will be beheaded by the "beast" for their unwavering faith during the Great Tribulation.

Annihilation of mankind

A half-veiled prophecy in the book of Ezekiel foreshadows the annihilation of mankind in three stages. *"And thou, son of man, take thee a sharp knife, take thee a barber's razor, and cause it to pass upon thine head and upon thy beard: then take thee balances to weight, and divide the hair. Thou shalt burn with fire a third part in the midst of the city, when the days of the siege are fulfilled: and thou shalt take a third part, and smite about it with a knife: and a third part thou shalt scatter in the wind; and I will draw out a sword after them"* (Ezek 5:1-2).

God instructed Ezekiel to shave his head and beard and divide the hair into three parts, adding what to do symbolically with each part. He then explained in plain language: *"A third part of thee shall die with the pestilence, and with famine shall they be consumed in the midst of thee: and a third part shall fall by the sword round about thee and I will scatter a third part into all the winds, and I will draw out a sword after them"* (Ezek 5:12).

Three stages. Let us now try to understand and explain the three stages of the apocalyptic prophecy.

First, 1/3 of the world population will perish in the nuclear war (*"burn with fire a third part in the midst of the city, when the days of the siege are fulfilled"*) and the Great Tribulation that follows (*"A third part of thee shall die with the pestilence, and with famine shall they be consumed in the midst of thee"*).

Next, the second 1/3 will be decimated at Armageddon (*"and thou shalt take a third part, and smite about it with a knife"*, that is, *"a third part shall fall by the sword round about thee"*).

Finally, the last 1/3 will be wiped out on the Day of the LORD (*"and a third part thou shalt scatter in the wind; and I will draw out a sword after them"*, repeated in *"I will scatter a third part into all the winds, and I will draw out a sword after them"*). The last two stages will be explained in detail in the next chapter.

A few will survive. Take heart, though. A blessed few will survive the cataclysms. *"Thou shalt also take thereof a few in number, and bind them in thy skirts"* (Ezek 5:3). Many other Biblical passages confirm this: *"For in the time of trouble he shall hide me in his pavilion: in the secret of his tabernacle shall he hide me…"* (Ps 27:5; see also Ps 32:7; 49:2; 91:1-16; Isa 26:20-21; 49:2; Joel 2:32; Zeph 2:3; Zech 13:9; Luke 21:35-36; Acts 2:21; 1 Thess 5:9; Rev 3:10).

Skeptics may say that the prophecy concerns Israel only, but John (Rev 9:18) and Zechariah (Zech 13:8-9) seem to corroborate that the prophesied events will be global in scope.

Fifth trumpet

Hybrid, chimeric creatures will emerge from underground to torment sinners. *"And the fifth angel sounded, and I saw a star fall from heaven unto the earth: and to him was given the key of the bottomless pit. And he opened the bottomless pit; and there arose a smoke out of the pit, as the smoke of a great furnace; and the sun and the air were darkened by reason of the smoke of the pit. And there came out of the smoke locusts upon the earth: and unto them was given power, as the scorpions of the earth have power. And it was commanded them that they should not hurt the grass of the earth, neither any green thing, neither any tree; but only those men which have not the seal of God in their foreheads. And to them it was given that they should not kill them, but that they should be tormented five months: and their torment was as the torment of a scorpion, when he striketh a man. And in those days shall men seek death, and shall not find it; and shall desire to die, and death shall flee from them. And the shapes of the locusts were like unto horses prepared unto battle; and on their heads were as it were crowns like gold, and their faces were as the faces of men… And they had tails like unto scorpions, and there were stings in their tails: and their power was to hurt men five months. And they had a king over them, which is the angel of the bottomless pit, whose name in the Hebrew tongue is Abaddon, but in the Greek tongue hath his name Apollyon"* (Rev 9:1-7,10-11).

Because of their great number, from afar the multitude of flying monsters will be mistaken for thick smoke. As they get nearer, they will be taken for a swarm of innumerable locusts. Coming even closer, their actual forms will be seen – winged horses with human faces and tails like those of scorpions.

Buraq look-alikes. Their appearance closely resembles that of Buraq, which, according to the *Encylopaedia Britannica*, is "a creature said to have transported the Prophet Muhammad to heaven. Described as 'a white animal, half-mule, half-donkey, with wings on its sides'", it carried him in his "night journey from Mecca to Jerusalem and back, thus explaining how the journey between the cities could have been completed in a single night. In some traditions he became a steed with the head of a woman and the tail of a peacock... From at least the 14th century, the Buraq myth, visualized on the basis of ancient depictions of griffins, sphinxes, and centaurs, became a favourite subject of Persian miniature painting."[7]

The strange creatures are told not to harm *"the grass of the earth, neither any green thing, neither any tree"*. As we have seen in our analysis of the first trumpet prophecy, the "grass" represents evildoers and wicked men (Ps 37:1-2; 92:7), while "trees" stand for the oppressors and conquerors of Israel, such as Assyria and Egypt (Ezek 31:3,18). "Green things", as we have learned in Chapter 2, probably refer to Arab Muslims, inasmuch as green is the traditional color of Islam and the Arabs.

The winged human-headed horses are told to attack *"only those men which have not the seal of God in their foreheads"*. Their targets, therefore, will specifically be those people who refuse to rest on the seventh-day Sabbath, which, as we learned in Chapter 5, is the seal of God. The victims will not die, but will suffer excruciating pains for five months, so much so that they will wish they should have died instead.

The chimeras have a king, whose name is Abaddon (in Hebrew) and Apollyon (in Greek), which both mean "destruction". We get an insight from *Fausset's Bible Dictionary*. As in the case of Job wherein Satan was "permitted to afflict but not to touch life" (Job 1-2), the "king of the locusts... had power to torment not kill... The giving of both the Hebrew and the Greek name implies that he is the destroyer of both Hebrews and Gentiles alike", while "in a beautiful contrast", the Messiah "unites Hebrews and Gentiles in a common salvation".[8] It therefore looks like Abaddon is none other than Satan himself, and the locusts are his demons.

Great Tribulation shortened.

"And except those days should be shortened, there should no flesh be saved: but for the elect's sake those days shall be shortened" (Matt 24:22). With mankind teetering on the brink of extinction, God will cut short the Great Tribulation in order to save the lives of the elect –His chosen few.

Ecology recovers? We get hints from Scriptures that the ecology will gradually return to normal before the end of the last 1,260 days. *"I tell you, in that night there shall be two men in one bed; the one shall be taken, and the other shall be left. Two women shall be grinding together; the one shall be taken, and the other left. Two men shall be in the field; the one shall be taken, and the other shall be left"* (Luke 17:34-36). It will still be too hot to go outdoors during the day, so people will continue to look for food at night, but it looks like they will be able to plant crops in the fields and harvest them for the women to grind.

Back to normal? *"But as the days of Noe were, so shall also the coming of the Son of man be. For as in the days that were before the flood they were eating and drinking, marrying and giving in marriage, until the day that Noe entered into the ark"* (Matt 24:37-38). It seems food, including alcoholic beverages, will once again be in adequate supply for people to enjoy. With the basic problem of survival fading behind them, many men and women will entertain thoughts of having partners and procreating.

Moreover, it appears modern appliances will return to widespread use. *"And they of the people and kindreds and tongues and nations shall see their dead bodies three days and an half, and shall not suffer their dead bodies to be put in graves"* (Rev 11:9). From the looks of it, the dead bodies of the two witnesses will be shown on worldwide television!

Food and other goods will be ample, and people will be able to share their excess with others. *"And they that dwell upon the earth shall rejoice over them, and make merry, and shall send gifts one to another; because these two prophets tormented them that dwelt on the earth"* (Rev 11:10).

Armageddon underway.

"And at the time of the end shall the king of the south push at him: and the king of the north shall come against him like a whirlwind, with chariots, and with horsemen, and with many ships; and he shall enter into the countries, and shall overflow and pass over" (Dan 11:40).

Armageddon will commence with *"the king of the south"* (Iran) advancing on the *"vile person"* (the Assyrian) and his empire (European Union?) and the *"the king of the north"* (United States) attacking with his formidable forces.

The story of moribund mankind continues, or rather ends, in the next chapter.

8

The Day of the LORD

*Blow ye the trumpet in Zion,
and sound an alarm in my holy mountain:
let all the inhabitants of the land tremble:
for the day of the LORD cometh, for it is nigh at hand;*

- Joel 2:1

Armageddon will take place on the Day of the LORD, which will also witness the much-awaited Second Coming of Christ and the catching up of the elect – God's chosen few – in the first resurrection of the dead and "rapture" of the living saints.

Armageddon underway

The soon-to-be protagonists at Armageddon will have recovered much from the grueling ordeals of the Great Tribulation and will again muster armies for invasion and war.

The "vile person" attacked.

"And at the time of the end shall the king of the south push at him: and the king of the north shall come against him like a whirlwind, with chariots, and with horsemen, and with many ships; and he shall enter into the countries, and shall overflow and pass over" (Dan 11:40).

Iran (the *"king of the south"*) will launch aggressive forays on the "vile person" (the Assyrian/Antichrist). The United States (the *"king of the north"*) will enter the fray with a much stronger force.

Neighboring countries will be involved. *"He shall enter also into the glorious land, and many countries shall be overthrown: but these shall escape out of his hand, even Edom, and Moab, and the chief of the children of Ammon"* (Dan 11:41). The war will spill over into Israel (*"the glorious land"*), but will bypass Jordan, a long-time US ally. (The ancient land of Edom is now in southern Jordan; Moab was also in Jordan, east of the Dead Sea; Ammon was located northeast of Moab. Amman, the capital of the kingdom of Jordan today, uses a slightly modified version of the ancient name.)

"He shall stretch forth his hand also upon the countries: and the land of Egypt shall not escape. But he shall have power over the treasures of gold and of silver, and over all the precious things of Egypt: and the Libyans and the Ethiopians shall be at his steps" (Dan 11:42-43). Egypt, Libya, and Ethiopia will be invaded.

Eastern and northern aggressors. *"But tidings out of the east and out of the north shall trouble him: therefore he shall go forth with great fury to destroy, and utterly to make away many"* (Dan 11:44).

Field reports will reach the vile person about two other forces – one from the east and the other from the north – coming to attack him. He will immediately set out to meet the aggressors.

The Wycliffe Bible Commentary notes that author "G. H. Lang (*Histories and Prophecies of Daniel*) applies Ezek 38; 39 at this point."[1]

Northern aggressor.

"Now the word of the LORD came to me, saying, "Son of man, set your face against Gog, of the land of Magog, the prince of Rosh, Meshech, and Tubal, and prophesy against him, and say, 'Thus says the Lord GOD: "Behold, I am against you, O Gog, the prince of Rosh, Meshech, and Tubal. I will turn you around, put hooks into your jaws, and lead you out, with all your army, horses, and horsemen, all splendidly clothed, a great company with bucklers and shields, all of them handling swords. Persia, Ethiopia, and Libya are with them, all of them with shield and helmet; Gomer and all its troops; the house of Togarmah from the far north and all its troops--many people are with you" (Ezek 38:1-6, NKJV). "Gog" will assemble a huge invasion army with many of his allies.

"Gog and Magog". Editor Richard Chaimberlin of *Petah Tikvah* ("Door of Hope") magazine writes: "There are debates as to who Gog and Magog are. Ezekiel 38:6 tells us that Gog and Magog are from 'the remote parts of the north' or the 'uttermost north,' as it is described in some other translations. If you draw a line directly north from Jerusalem, that… line will eventually go right through Moscow. Therefore, it seems apparent that

Russia will one day enter into a conspiracy with other nations to attack Israel."[2]

We get an additional clue from *Fausset's Bible Dictionary*. In the Caucasus Mountains in southern Russia, "Ghogh and Moghef are names still applied to its heights".[3]

"Rosh". Bible scholars have suggested that *Rosh* is none other than Russia. "Rosh is the tribe N. of the Taurus range and near Rha or Volga which gives them their name; the earliest trace of the Russ nation."[4] "Gesenius regarded it as indicating the Russians, who are mentioned in Byzantine writers of the 10th century under the name of Rhos. He adds that they are also noticed by Ibn Fosslan (same period), under the name of Rus, as a people dwelling on the river Rha (Volga)."[5]

"Meschech and Tubal". "Moscow and Tobolsk may derive their names from Mesech and Tubal. Magog was Gog's original kingdom; he acquired also Mesech and Tubal, becoming their 'chief prince'".[6] Moscow is the capital of Russia; Tobolsk was the first and is today the largest city in Siberia.

"Persia, Ethiopia, Put". "Some other nations in this unholy End-Time alliance are 'Persia, Ethiopia, and Put'… Persia is identifiable today as Iran… Regarding Ethiopia, the Hebrew uses the word 'Cush' to describe this country… The ancient queen of Sheba ruled over areas on both sides of the Red Sea, including much of modern-day Yemen as well as Ethiopia. Put is usually described as 'Libya.'"[7]

"Gomer". According to some Bible commentaries, these are the "people descended from Gomer, son of Japheth. Apparently they lived to the far north, beyond the Black Sea (Ezek 38:6). They were probably the Cimmerians of classical history."[8] "The Cimmerians warred in northwestern Asia from 670 to 570 B.C. Originally dwelling in what is now southern Russia, the Ukraine (the Crimea betrays their name, the Cimmerian Bosphorus); then being dispossessed by the Scythians, they fled across the Caucasus into Armenia and Asia Minor."[9] Hence, Gomer alludes to the modern-day nations of the Ukraine, Georgia, Armenia, Azerbaijan.

"Togarmah". This refers to the name of a "son of Gomer… The descendants of Togarmah (Beth Togarmah, NIV) are mentioned among the merchants who trafficked with Tyre in 'horses and war horses and mules' (Ezek 27:14)… The name may be preserved in the E. Cappadocian city of Til-garimmu, listed in the Assyrian records."[10] Cappadocia was an ancient kingdom of eastern Asia Minor (modern Turkey). More specifically, "(t)he Imperial Dictionary makes Togarmah to mean the Turkomans who have always joined the Turks…"[11] Togarmah, therefore, means Turkey and other Turkic peoples in countries around the Aral Sea in Central Asia, such as Kazakhstan and Uzbekistan, including adjacent Turkmenistan and Kyrgyzstan, and parts of Iran and Afghanistan.

Russian allies. The Ukraine, Armenia, Georgia, Azerbaijan, Kazakhstan, Uzbekistan, Turkmenistan, and Kyrgyzstan were former Soviet republics of the USSR under Russia; while Iran, Ethiopia, Libya, and Afghanistan have or had close relations with Russia.

Advance on Israel.

"After many days thou shalt be visited: in the latter years thou shalt come into the land that is brought back from the sword, and is gathered out of many people, against the mountains of Israel, which have been always waste: but it is brought forth out of the nations, and they shall dwell safely all of them. Thou shalt ascend and come like a storm, thou shalt be like a cloud to cover the land, thou, and all thy bands, and many people with thee" (Ezek 38:8-9).

The passage leaves little doubt that the object of the invasion is Israel – which has been *"brought back from the sword, and is gathered out of many people"*.

Chaimberlin notes, "We have seen much of this prophecy already fulfilled. Jews have returned to Israel from over 100 nations. And Israel was basically a wasteland until the return of her people. Israel won her place in the land with the sword (warfare) because of all the nations (primarily Arabs) who sought to prevent the rebirth of the Jewish nation."[12]

A land of plenty. *"Thus saith the Lord GOD; It shall also come to pass, that at the same time shall things come into thy mind, and thou shalt think an evil thought: And thou shalt say, I will go up to the land of unwalled villages; I will go to them that are at rest, that dwell safely, all of them dwelling without walls, and having neither bars nor gates, To take a spoil, and to take a prey; to turn thine hand upon the desolate places that are now inhabited, and upon the people that are gathered out of the nations, which have gotten cattle and goods, that dwell in the midst of the land"* (Ezek 38:10-12). One of Gog's main objectives could be Israel's abundant natural resources.

Minerals. Messianic leader Roger Walkwitz reported that there is great wealth locked up in the Salt Sea – also called the Dead Sea – with its many minerals, such as sodium chloride, calcium chloride, and potassium chloride, as well as bromine. These are extracted from the water for use in making table salt, fertilizers, and drugs. Huge gas and oil fields have been reportedly discovered recently.

"**Gas**. Israel's recent discovery of mega gas fields titled Tamar and Leviathan are located off the Israeli coast from Haifa. These massive discoveries will soon transform Israel as they will adequately look after Israel's domestic needs and thereafter to supply foreign markets. A number of countries are pursuing involvement in these finds. Among them are Russia, China, Europe and South Korea. Putin was in Israel (recently) pursuing a contractual relationship with Israel on its gas development projects…

"**Oil**. Geologists have recently completed a large mapping of most of southern Israel and preliminary findings indicate there are vast amounts of oil trapped in rock layers under about 15% of the State of Israel… The World Energy Council and Israel Energy Initiatives have completed a detailed study… They estimate that Israel's shale reserves could contain as much as 250 billion barrels of potentially recoverable oil. This would be putting Israel on a par with Saudi Arabia in terms of its oil reserves!"[13]

Western powers intervene?

It looks like Gog and his allies will be confronted by Western nations. *"Sheba, and Dedan, and the merchants of Tarshish, with all the young lions thereof, shall say unto thee, Art thou come to take a spoil? hast thou gathered thy company to take a prey? to carry away silver and gold, to take away cattle and goods, to take a great spoil?"* (Ezek 38:13). New protagonists enter the brewing war scene.

"Sheba". From what we have read above about Ethiopia, Sheba could mean countries on both sides of the Red Sea, such as Somalia and Yemen.

"Dedan". *The New Unger's Bible Dictionary* states: "Dedan, son of Raamah, settled on the shores of the Persian Gulf, and his descendants became caravan merchants between that coast and Palestine".[14] Hence, "Dedan" could be the Persian Gulf states of Saudi Arabia, Kuwait, Qatar, Bahrain, United Arab Emirates, and Oman, which have been allies of the West.

"Tarshish". *Nelson's Illustrated Bible Dictionary* describes it as a "territory in the western portion of the Mediterranean Sea with which the Phoenicians traded".[15] *Fausset's Bible Dictionary* adds that "Tarshish was famed for various metals exported to Tyre; most of them were drawn from Spain and Portugal, tin possibly from Cornwall or from Lusitania or Portugal".[16]

Spain, Portugal, and England (Cornwall) established colonies in the New World, from which they brought back much merchandise to Europe. They must be the "merchants of Tarshish".

"Young lions". The lion has been a symbol of England since the Middle Ages; so the "young lions" must refer to former British colonies that have become independent and powerful nations on their own, such as the USA, Canada, Australia, New Zealand.

Accompanying phenomena.
Armageddon will coincide with various mind-blowing geophysical phenomena. In fact, the skirmishes will take place at the unfolding of the Day of the LORD. *"And there shall be signs in the sun, and in the moon, and in the stars; and upon the earth distress of nations, with perplexity; the sea and the waves roaring; Men's hearts failing them for fear, and for looking after those things which are coming on the earth: for the powers of heaven shall be shaken"* (Luke 21:25-26).

Sixth seal

"And I beheld when he had opened the sixth seal, and, lo, there was a great earthquake; and the sun became black as sackcloth of hair, and the moon became as blood. And the stars of heaven fell unto the earth, even as a fig tree casteth her untimely figs, when she is shaken of a mighty wind" (Rev 6:12-13).

Day of darkness. The prophecy matches the one Christ uttered about 60 years earlier: *"Immediately after the tribulation of those days shall the sun be darkened, and the moon shall not give her light, and the stars shall fall from heaven, and the powers of the heavens shall be shaken"* (Matt 24:29; cf. Mark 13:24-24; Luke 21:25-26); as well as those voiced by ancient prophets some 700-800 years before:

"Behold, the day of the LORD cometh, cruel both with wrath and fierce anger, to lay the land desolate: and he shall destroy the sinners thereof out of it. For the stars of heaven and the constellations thereof shall not give their light: the sun shall be darkened in his going forth, and the moon shall not cause her light to shine" (Isa 13:9-10); *"The sun shall be turned into darkness, and the moon into blood, before the great and the terrible day of the LORD come"* (Joel 2:31). Judging from the contexts and tone of the prophecies, the darkness will be global, not just local, in scope.

Fifth bowl

"And the fifth angel poured out his vial upon the seat of the beast; and his kingdom was full of darkness; and they gnawed their tongues for pain" (Rev 16:10). As the beast will be the ruler of the world, the whole earth will be darkened should his kingdom be covered with darkness. *"And (they)*

blasphemed the God of heaven because of their pains and their sores, and repented not of their deeds" (Rev 16:11). The physical afflictions suffered by the followers of the beast will be greatly compounded by the gloom, yet they will not see the hand of the Almighty in the supernatural occurrences and will fail to ask for His mercy and forgiveness for their sins.

Biblical days of darkness.

There are three mystifying days of darkness in the Bible. Two have already taken place, one each in Old Testament and New Testament times.

In the 9th plague of Egypt. *"And the LORD said unto Moses, Stretch out thine hand toward heaven, that there may be darkness over the land of Egypt, even darkness which may be felt. And Moses stretched forth his hand toward heaven; and there was a thick darkness in all the land of Egypt three days"* (Ex 10:21-22).

Most scholars agree that the darkness was probably caused by the *chamsin*, the much-dreaded sandstorm. After the vernal equinox the southwest wind from the desert blew some 50 days, not continuously but at intervals, lasting generally some two or three days. It filled the atmosphere with dense masses of fine sand.[17]

The heat, the dust, and the static electricity made conditions almost unbearable physically[18,19] (*"darkness which may be felt"*).

At the Crucifixion. *"Now from the sixth hour there was darkness over all the land unto the ninth hour"* (Matt 27:45; cf. Luke 23:44). Christ was nailed to the cross at 9:00 A.M. (*"third hour,"* Mark 15:25). After three hours had passed, a supernatural darkness enveloped the land from the sixth to the ninth hour (12:00 noon to 3:00 P.M.).

Some writers in the past favored *"upon all the earth"* instead of *"over all the land"* and accounted for it by an eclipse of the sun. But this was not possible, because the Passover is celebrated at the time of the full moon, when the moon is behind the earth opposite the sun and could not come between the sun and the earth. The darkness, therefore, seems to have been confined to Judea. According to *The New Unger's Bible Dictionary*, the darkness "may have been caused by an extraordinary and preternatural obstruction of the light of the sun by the sulphurous vapors accompanying the earthquake that then occurred"[20] (Matt 27:54).

Matthew Henry's Commentary notes that "it was proper that an extraordinary darkness should notify his death, for he is the Light of the world."[21] There seems to be a distinct prophecy that foretold the darkness during the Crucifixion in Amos 8:9 – *"And it shall come to pass in that day, saith the Lord GOD, that I will cause the sun to go down at noon, and I will darken the earth in the clear day."*

On the Day of the LORD. What will cause of the darkness on the Day of the LORD? God had said through the prophet Ezekiel: *"And when I shall put thee out, I will cover the heaven, and make the stars thereof dark; I will cover the sun with a cloud, and the moon shall not give her light. All the bright lights of heaven will I make dark over thee, and set darkness upon thy land, saith the Lord GOD"* (Ezek 32:7-8). A cloud will come between the sun and the earth, casting a dark pall over the land. The whole planet? Ezekiel said *"All the bright lights of heaven"*, so it must be global.

One cosmic phenomenon, realized only in these modern times, can account for the global darkness and all the other heart-stopping geophysical events that will take place on the Day of the LORD.

Comets

Science writers John and Mary Gribbin wrote that "comets are like dirty snowballs, made out of a mixture of ice and dust. When the ice thaws during a close approach to the Sun, large amounts of dust can be released to form a belt girdling the solar system – and if the Earth passes through such a dust belt, the dust acts as sunshield... This argument has been around for some time, but has lately been revived by Richard Muller and Gordon MacDonald of the University of California."[22]

Clouds of comet tailings.

Most comets are made up of compounds of hydrogen, carbon, nitrogen, and oxygen (e.g., ammonia, methane, cyanogen), plus heavy elements like sodium, calcium, iron, nickel, sulfur.

Way out in space, the frozen comets have no tails, but as they approach the sun, the solar wind begins to thaw and blow away their components, forming the comets' "tails." The tails are usually well-formed by the time comets reach the vicinity of the orbit of Mars. After perihelion (point of orbit nearest the sun), the tails begin to disintegrate on the comets' way out of the solar system, leaving behind trails of dust, gases, and debris.

Over the billions of years that countless comets have circled the sun, clouds of comet tailings – some thick, some thin – have formed in various parts of the solar system.

Meteor showers. Whenever Earth passes by the remains of comet tails, a meteor shower occurs. "(B)y the 1860s the Leonid shower had been shown to be due to debris from Comet Swift-Tuttle. Similarly, astronomers realized that the Perseid meteors that appear every August are rubble from Comet Tempel-Tuttle."[23] Astronomers in 1845 and 1846 saw Comet Biela split into two pieces. In 1856 these were observed as various fragments extending over 1 million miles. In 1872 and 1885, Earth crossed its orbit, experiencing meteor showers of unusual volume.[24] What are the odds that Planet Earth might pass through a voluminous cloud of comet tailings?

Variations in the Earth's orbit.
Planet Earth does not always orbit the Sun on the same plane and at the same distance. In the 1940s, Milutin Milankovitch, a Serbian mathematician, discovered three cyclical variations in the Earth's orbit (now called the Milankovitch Cycles). These are:
1. 23,000-year cycle: Precession (caused by the wobble of the planet's axis) alters the times of the year when the Earth is closest and farthest from the Sun.
2. 41,000-year cycle: The changing tilt of the Earth's axis toward the Sun (from 22.1° to 24.5°) affects the contrast between winter and summer temperatures.
3. 100,000-year cycle: The Earth's orbit gradually changes its shape from elliptical to circular and back, varying the distance between the Earth and the Sun.

Cycle of ice ages?
The Gribbins relate: "Richard Muller and Gordon MacDonald… got on the trail of… cometary influences on climate through studies of the way the world's weather has changed over the past six hundred thousand years or so. During that time, geological evidences show, the planet has been plunged into a succession of ice ages, roughly once every 100,000 years. Muller and MacDonald agree that this is because the tilt of the Earth's orbit around the Sun changes over exactly that timetable, making it wobble up and down slightly.

"They calculated the effect of this wobble, and found that the cycle exactly matches the climate cycle. As the Earth's orbit moves up and down, every 100,000 years it will happen to lie in exactly the same plane as streams of dust produced by countless comets that have broken up in orbit around the Sun in the past."[25]

The presumed cycle of ice ages is based on observations that, every 100,000 years, there are layers in the earth's crust with much decreased fossilized flora and fauna. Geologists ascribe these to ice ages. A sudden ice age is thought by some to have been responsible for the extinction of the dinosaurs and the quick-frozen mammoths being found in the arctic tundra.

From the title of the Gribbins' article ("'97 Comet May Spread Chill to Planet Earth in 2000"), it looks like they believed that the next cycle would begin sometime around the year 2000.

Comet Hale-Bopp.
In mid-1995, a giant comet was spotted in distant outer space. The Gribbins were awed, "Hale-Bopp... is a maverick that brings a cooling effect regardless of the rhythm of this long-term cycle. To be seen as it is now, still far out from the Sun, it must be a very large object indeed, carrying a large burden of dust to scatter in the inner Solar System."[26]

Comet Hale-Bopp, a gargantuan cosmic prodigy, was first seen by telescope on July 26, 1995, from a distance at which most comets are still invisible – 7 AUs (AU = astronomical unit/Earth-Sun distance = 93 million miles or 150 million kilometers), more than a billion kilometers away.

Bigger than the sun. Comet Hale-Bopp's nucleus lay buried in a vast cloud that stretched 2.5 million kilometers across. The shell of material it carried into the inner solar system filled a volume of space larger than the sun! It became more ominous when, in late August 1995, a large jet emerged from the core of Hale-Bopp. A crack in the comet's frozen nucleus began spewing a stream of material, much like a fire hose or the smokestack of an old-fashioned steam locomotive.[27]

"A huge cloud of hydrogen surrounded Comet Hale-Bopp when it neared the Sun in the spring of 1997. Ultraviolet light revealed a cloud 100 million kilometers (60 million miles) wide... It far exceeded the great comet's visible tail... Although generated by a comet nucleus perhaps only 40 kilometers (24 miles) in diameter, the hydrogen cloud was 70 times wider than the Sun itself."[28]

6,000th year from Adam. Comet Hale-Bopp became visible to the naked eye in March 1997. To Bible prophecy watchers, the year 1997 was highly significant: it marked the 6,000th year from the creation of Adam in 4004 B.C., according to the Biblical chronology of the *Annals of the World*, which Archbishop James Ussher of Armagh, Ireland, worked out in 1650-1654.[29]

Sign of the Flood? *The Open Scroll* newsletter writer-editor Bob Schlenker reported: "According to recent orbital calculations by astronomers... Hale-Bopp passed through the inner solar system once before – about 4210 years ago."[30] Other estimates put it at 4,200-4,400 years in the past. Based on that very long period, the comet was last seen on earth around the time of Noah's Flood, which destroyed the world in 2348 B.C.[31], roughly 4,350 years ago.

Omen of destruction? Schlenker further wrote: "According to what is recorded in the *Seder Olam Rabah*, an ancient Jewish text... a comet appeared at about the time Noah began building the ark. It was probably the comet we know now as Hale-Bopp! ...this comet may have been a sign of the impending destruction of the world by water."[32]

The Jewish sages taught that no comet had ever entered the constellation of Orion. "The Talmud records the oral tradition of the Jews (Berachoth 58b) which tells us that when a comet passes through the constellation Orion, the world would be destroyed."[33]

Comet Hale-Bopp entered the section of the sky occupied by Orion on April 22, 1997, and exited on June 11, 1997. Was Comet Hale-Bopp a celestial sign of the end of the world and the Second Coming of Christ? This brings to mind the words of Christ in Matthew 24:37, NIV: *"As it was in the days of Noah, so it will be at the coming of the Son of Man."*

Prophetic psalms.

In the 1986 book *Hidden Prophecies in the Psalms*, author J.R. Church revealed his insight that each psalm was a prophecy for each year in the twentieth century, starting with 1901 (i.e., Psalm 1 = 1901; Psalm 2 = 1902; Psalm 3 = 1903; and so on). Was Psalm 97 a prophecy of the coming of Comet Hale-Bopp in 1997? Let us read a pertinent portion of the psalm:

"Clouds and darkness are round about him: righteousness and judgment are the habitation of his throne. A fire goeth before him, and burneth up his enemies round about. His lightnings enlightened the world: the earth saw, and trembled. The hills melted like wax at the presence of the LORD, at the presence of the Lord of the whole earth" (Ps 97:2-5). Though not word-for-word, it sounds ominously similar to an account of the Day of the LORD in Psalm 18:7-9,11-12 – *"Then the earth shook and trembled; the foundations also of the hills moved and were shaken, because he was wroth. There went up a smoke out of his nostrils, and fire out of his mouth devoured: coals were kindled by it. He bowed the heavens also, and came down: and darkness was under his feet... He made darkness his secret place; his pavilion round about him were dark waters and thick clouds of the skies. At the brightness that was before him his thick clouds passed, hail stones and coals of fire."*

The similarity between the passages sounds like a hint to us that Comet Hale-Bopp (or some things it left behind) would be God's instrument of judgment on the world on the Day of the LORD!

Comet ISON.

Another spectacular cosmic visitor, Comet ISON, was a sun-grazing comet discovered on September 21, 2012. Named "ISON" after the organization through which it was discovered (the Russia-based International Scientific Optical Network), it was found to be a first-time visitor traveling straight into a near-miss with the sun.

"Comet of the Century". A Lowell Observatory astronomer, Matthew Knight, a member of NASA's Comet ISON Observing Campaign (CIOC), reported that "some media sources… speculated that it might outshine the full moon. An *Astronomy Now* columnist wrote in September 2012 that 'if predictions hold true then Comet ISON will certainly be one of the greatest comets in human history.' As recently as October 2013, a *Daily Mail* columnist described Comet ISON as 'the Comet of the Century' and said it was 'hoped to be 15 times brighter than the Moon'."

An observation in January 2013 by NASA's Swift spacecraft, when ISON was still near the orbit of Jupiter, showed that it was already very active. The comet was ejecting more than 112,000 pounds of dust from its nucleus every minute.[34]

Cloud of dust. However, Comet ISON broke apart as it passed close to the Sun. Reports on Nov. 28, 2013, (the day of perihelion passage) indicated that Comet ISON had partially or completely disintegrated due to the Sun's heat and tidal forces. Karl Battams posted online: "As we all know, comet ISON is no more. It clearly fell apart in the hours surrounding its close brush with the Sun and now exists simply as a dusty cloud and some warm fuzzy memories. But what of that dusty cloud? What if there are chunks remaining? Where are they going? Will they change course and hit Earth? Is Earth going to pass through ISON's remains? *Are we doomed?!!*"[35] He nonetheless proceeded to allay the fears of his readers.

Interestingly, the name "Comet ISON" may be modified as: "Cometh… I, Son." Was Comet ISON, perhaps, another end-time portent of the impending Second Coming of the Son of God?

The Day of the LORD

Several other ancient prophets painted perturbing pictures of the terrifying sights and sounds and other phenomena in heaven and earth that will characterize the fateful Day of the LORD.

Sun darkened.

"*Give glory to the LORD your God, before he cause darkness, and before your feet stumble upon the dark mountains, and, while ye look for light, he turn it into the shadow of death, and make it gross darkness*" (Jer 13:16); "*Woe unto you that desire the day of the LORD! to what end is it for you? the day of the LORD is darkness, and not light*" (Amos 5:18).

"Moon into blood".

"*The sun shall be turned into darkness, and the moon into blood, before the great and the terrible day of the LORD come*" (Joel 2:31).

If the Earth truly happens to pass through a cometary cloud containing particulates of hydrated ferric oxide [rust], a brownish-red substance that forms on the surface of iron, the moon would be seen through the haze as a fuzzy red orb with blurred edges, much like a bloodstain on a piece of cloth. There were some "comets that passed very close to the Sun in 1882 and displayed evidence of sodium and even iron vapor."[36]

Stars rain down.
"And the stars of heaven fell unto the earth, even as a fig tree casteth her untimely figs, when she is shaken of a mighty wind" (Rev 6:13). Christ was quoted by two gospel writers as saying the same thing – *"...and the stars shall fall from heaven..."* (Matt 24:29b); *"And the stars of heaven shall fall..."* (Mark 13:25a).

The debris in the clouds of comet tailings – from as small as specks of dust and grains of sand to as big as rock fragments, boulders and mountains – will be pulled in by the earth's gravity. A global rain of meteors will result. In the pitch darkness, it would look as though the stars are indeed falling from heaven.

The earth shaken. *"...and the powers of the heavens shall be shaken:"* (Matt 24:29d). The impact of huge meteors crashing on earth will cause the planet to shudder and shake. From the ground, it would look like the sky is shaking, not vice-versa.

"For thus saith the LORD of hosts; Yet once, it is a little while, and I will shake the heavens, and the earth, and the sea, and the dry land; And I will shake all nations, and the desire of all nations shall come: and I will fill this house with glory, saith the LORD of hosts" (Hag 2:6-7).

The shaking will coincide with the invasion of Israel. *"And it shall come to pass at the same time when Gog shall come against the land of Israel, saith the Lord GOD, that my fury shall come up in my face. For in my jealousy and in the fire of my wrath have I spoken, Surely in that day there shall be a great shaking in the land of Israel; So that the fishes of the sea, and the fowls of the heaven, and the beasts of the field, and all creeping things that creep upon the earth, and all the men that are upon the face of the earth, shall shake at my presence, and the mountains shall be thrown down, and the steep places shall fall, and every wall shall fall to the ground"* (Ezek 38:18-20).

Monster tsunamis. *"...and upon the earth distress of nations, with perplexity; the sea and the waves roaring"* (Luke 21:25d).

The oceans, like water shaken in a basin, will spawn monster tsunamis. Asteroids and other large comet debris crashing in the oceans would produce enormous waves that would sweep out in all directions from the crash sites. "Calculations by Jack Hills of the Los Alamos National Laboratory in New Mexico predict that if an asteroid about 1-km (about 0.6-mi) wide fell in the Atlantic Ocean a wall of water as tall as a 30-story building would rush across New York City, Boston, Massachusetts, and other Atlantic coast cities."[37]

Sixth trumpet

"And the sixth angel sounded, and I heard a voice from the four horns of the golden altar which is before God, Saying to the sixth angel which had the trumpet, Loose the four angels which are bound in the great river Euphrates. And the four angels were loosed, which were prepared for an hour, and a day, and a month, and a year, for to slay the third part of men.

"And the number of the army of the horsemen were two hundred thousand thousand: and I heard the number of them. And thus I saw the horses in the vision, and them that sat on them, having breastplates of fire, and of jacinth, and brimstone: and the heads of the horses were as the heads of lions; and out of their mouths issued fire and smoke and brimstone. By these three was the third part of men killed, by the fire, and by the smoke, and by the brimstone, which issued out of their mouths" (Rev 9:13-18).

Who are these 200 million (*"two hundred thousand thousand"*) horsemen? Some Bible teachers and prophecy watchers teach that these will be armies of the *"kings of the east"*. But the 200 million will come at the sound of the sixth trumpet, whereas the kings of the east will not make their appearance until the contents of the sixth bowl are poured out later (Rev 16:12).

Destroying angels. The prophet Isaiah gives us some hints on the identity of these 200 million horsemen. *"I have commanded my sanctified ones, I have also called my mighty ones for mine anger, even them that rejoice in my highness. The noise of a multitude in the mountains, like as of a great people; a tumultuous noise of the kingdoms of nations gathered together: the LORD of hosts mustereth the host of the battle. They come from a far country, from the end of heaven, even the LORD, and the weapons of his indignation, to destroy the whole land. Howl ye; for the day of the LORD is at hand; it shall come as a destruction from the Almighty"* (Isa 13:3-6).

God will send his *"sanctified ones"* *"from the end of heaven"* *"to destroy the whole land"*. Therefore, the 200 million horsemen must be destroying angels who will be sent forth from heaven!

Horse-men. The prophet Joel confirms the thought. *"A fire devoureth before them; and behind them a flame burneth: the land is as the garden* *of Eden before them, and behind them a desolate wilderness; yea, and nothing shall escape them. The appearance of them is as the appearance of horses; and as horsemen, so shall they run. Like the noise of chariots on the tops of mountains shall they leap, like the noise of a flame of fire that devoureth the stubble, as a strong people set in battle array. Before their face the people shall be much pained: all faces shall gather blackness"* (Joel 2:3-6).

No place to hide. *"They shall run like mighty men; they shall climb the wall like men of war; and they shall march every one on his ways, and they shall not break their ranks: Neither shall one thrust another; they shall walk every one in his path: and when they fall upon the sword, they shall not be wounded. They shall run to and fro in the city; they shall run upon the wall, they shall climb up upon the houses; they shall enter in at the windows like a thief"* (Joel 2:7-9).

The wicked first. A parable of Christ marks out the target of the angelic army. *"Gather ye together first the tares, and bind them in bundles to burn them: but gather the wheat into my barn... As therefore the tares are gathered and burned in the fire; so shall it be in the end of this world. The Son of man shall send forth his angels, and they shall gather out of his kingdom all things that offend, and them which do iniquity; And shall cast them into a furnace of fire: there shall be wailing and gnashing of teeth"* (Matt 13:30b,40-42).

Sixth bowl

"And the sixth angel poured out his vial upon the great river Euphrates; and the water thereof was dried up, that the way of the kings of the east might be prepared. And I saw three unclean spirits like frogs come out of the mouth of the dragon, and out of the mouth of the beast, and out of the mouth of the false prophet. For they are the spirits of devils, working miracles, which go forth unto the kings of the earth and of the whole world, to gather them to the battle of that great day of God Almighty... And he gathered them together into a place called in the Hebrew tongue Armageddon" (Rev 16:12-14,16).

The kings of the east (China?, India?, Japan?, North Korea?, Pakistan?, et al.), and the other forces mentioned earlier: from the south (Iran), west (US), north (Gog), and their allies will converge at Armageddon. *The New Unger's Bible Dictionary* notes: "Ezek 38-39, which deal with Gog, the prince, and Magog, his land... The entire prophecy belongs to the "Day of the Lord" (cf. Isa 2:10-22; Rev 19:11-21)..."[38]

Har Megiddo.

Armageddon is Greek transliteration of the Hebrew *har Megiddo* ("hill or mountain of Megiddo"). Scholars disagree on the exact location of this place, but the most likely area is the valley between Mount Carmel and the city of Jezreel. This valley (known as the Valley of Jezreel and sometimes referred to as the Plain of Esdraelon) was the crossroads of two ancient trade routes and, thus, was a strategic military site.[39] Called the great battlefield of Palestine, Megiddo was famous for two great victories – Barak over the Canaanites (Judg 4:15) and Gideon over the Midianites (chap. 7) – and for two great disasters – the deaths of Saul (1 Sam 31:8) and Josiah (2 Kings 23:29-30; 2 Chron 35:22).[40]

Vile person's base.

The vile person, a.k.a. Antichrist, will have deployed his forces on high ground. *"And he shall plant the tabernacles of his palace between the seas in the glorious holy mountain; yet he shall come to his end, and none shall help him"* (Dan 11:45).

"Theodoret takes it for a place near Jerusalem; Jerome says it was near Nicopolis, which was formerly called Emmaus, where the mountainous parts of Judea began to rise, and that it lay between the Dead Sea on the east, and the Mediterranean on the west, where he supposes that Antichrist will pitch his tent… The most obvious application of this phrase, it cannot be doubted, would be Jerusalem, as being the 'holy mountain,' or 'the mountain of holiness'."[41]

Two witnesses killed.

"And when they shall have finished their testimony, the beast that ascendeth out of the bottomless pit shall make war against them, and shall overcome them, and kill them. And their dead bodies shall lie in the street of the great city, which spiritually is called Sodom and Egypt, where also our Lord was crucified.

"And they of the people and kindreds and tongues and nations shall see their dead bodies three days and an half, and shall not suffer their dead bodies to be put in graves. And they that dwell upon the earth shall rejoice over them, and make merry, and shall send gifts one to another; because these two prophets tormented them that dwelt on the earth" (Rev 11:7-10).

Based on the prophetic timetable, 1,260 days after beginning their ministry, the two witnesses will have been killed in Jerusalem 3 ½ days before the returning Messiah appears in the sky.

Jerusalem ravaged.
"For I will gather all nations against Jerusalem to battle; and the city shall be taken, and the houses rifled, and the women ravished; and half of the city shall go forth into captivity, and the residue of the people shall not be cut off from the city" (Zech 14:2).

The Second Coming

At precisely the right moment, in God's perfect timing, Christ will return to save the day for the Jews, Jerusalem and Israel.

Flash of lightning.
"For as the lightning cometh out of the east, and shineth even unto the west; so shall also the coming of the Son of man be" (Matt 24:27). The returning Messiah, still unseen below the horizon, will approach earth from heaven like the sun, shining with blinding light ("…*the Lord shall consume with the spirit of his mouth, and shall destroy with the brightness of his coming*" - 2 Thess 2:8b).

As huge meteors pound the surface of the planet, the earth will continue to shake, jerking this way and that. At some point, when the earth happens to lurch forward to the east, the brightness of Christ's coming will be seen over the eastern horizon momentarily, like a flash of lightning illuminating the dark, cloudy sky westward.

Sign of the Son.
"And then shall appear the sign of the Son of man in heaven…" (Matt 24:30a). What is the sign of the Son of man?

Many will say it is the cross. Some churches, though, refuse to accept the idea that it is the cross, arguing that it was an ancient pagan symbol for the sun long before the crucifixion of Christ.

If not the cross, is it the fish? Can you imagine a gigantic fish or even a fish-like icon appearing in the sky? Besides, ancient pagans also worshipped the fish (Dag-on, the sun-fish) as a god of fertility.

The author may have been blessed with the answer. He used to live in a house with textured smoked glass windows. Curiously, outside lights came through in the form of a Latin cross (top vertical section shorter than the lower), not a Greek cross with four arms of equal length. In some window panes wherein the glass was inverted, the Latin cross was also inverted! It looks like the phenomenon showed that, just like certain textured smoked glass, dark clouds of dust and gases can also produce the same effect – showing the brightness of Christ's Second Coming in the form of a Latin cross!

Heaven opens.

The clouds will part to reveal Christ. *"And I saw heaven opened, and behold a white horse; and he that sat upon him was called Faithful and True, and in righteousness he doth judge and make war. His eyes were as a flame of fire, and on his head were many crowns; and he had a name written, that no man knew, but he himself. And he was clothed with a vesture dipped in blood: and his name is called The Word of God. And the armies which were in heaven followed him upon white horses, clothed in fine linen, white and clean... And he hath on his vesture and on his thigh a name written, KING OF KINGS, AND LORD OF LORDS"* (Rev 19:11-14,16).

Christ will descend to earth. *"And then shall they see the Son of man coming in the clouds with great power and glory"* (Mark 13:26).

Remorseful unbelievers. All the people who denied or ignored Christ as the Savior of mankind will be filled with remorse upon seeing Him in the sky; *"...and then shall all the tribes of the earth mourn, and they shall see the Son of man coming in the clouds of heaven with power and great glory"* (Matt 24:30b).

"Behold, he cometh with clouds; and every eye shall see him, and they also which pierced him: and all kindreds of the earth shall wail because of him" (Rev 1:7a). Many Jews will sorely repent of having rejected or not even recognizing their much-awaited Messiah.

Yet, He will be merciful to those who will finally accept Him. *"And I will pour upon the house of David, and upon the inhabitants of Jerusalem, the spirit of grace and of supplications: and they shall look upon me whom they have pierced, and they shall mourn for him, as one mourneth for his only son, and shall be in bitterness for him, as one that is in bitterness for his firstborn"* (Zech 12:10).

First resurrection and "rapture".

"And I looked, and behold a white cloud, and upon the cloud one sat like unto the Son of man, having on his head a golden crown, and in his hand a sharp sickle. And another angel came out of the temple, crying with a loud voice to him that sat on the cloud, Thrust in thy sickle, and reap: for the time is come for thee to reap; for the harvest of the earth is ripe. And he that sat on the cloud thrust in his sickle on the earth; and the earth was reaped" (Rev 14:14-16).

The veiled metaphorical prophecy prefigures the first resurrection of the righteous dead and "rapture" of the living saints. *"And he shall send his angels with a great sound of a trumpet, and they shall gather together his elect from the four winds, from one end of heaven to the other"* (Matt 24:31; cf. Mark 13:27).

Two witnesses resurrected. *"And after three days and an half the Spirit of life from God entered into them, and they stood upon their feet; and great fear fell upon them which saw them. And they heard a great voice from heaven saying unto them, Come up hither. And they ascended up to heaven in a cloud; and their enemies beheld them"* (Rev 11:11-12).

First the dead, then the living. *"In a moment, in the twinkling of an eye, at the last trump: for the trumpet shall sound, and the dead shall be raised incorruptible, and we shall be changed. For this corruptible must put on incorruption, and this mortal must put on immortality"* (1 Cor 15:52-53). *"For this we say unto you by the word of the Lord, that we which are alive and remain unto the coming of the Lord shall not prevent them which are asleep. For the Lord himself shall descend from heaven with a shout, with the voice of the archangel, and with the trump of God: and the dead in Christ shall rise first: Then we which are alive and remain shall be caught up together with them in the clouds, to meet the Lord in the air: and so shall we ever be with the Lord"* (1 Thess 4:15-17).

One-half left behind. Just half of the saints destined for salvation will be taken up. *"I tell you, in that night there shall be two men in one bed; the one shall be taken, and the other shall be left. Two women shall be grinding together; the one shall be taken, and the other left. Two men shall be in the field; the one shall be taken, and the other left"* (Luke 17:34-36; cf. Matt 24:40-41).

The *"foolish virgins"*. Christ hinted at this separation in a parable. *"Then shall the kingdom of heaven be likened unto ten virgins, which took their lamps, and went forth to meet the bridegroom. And five of them were wise, and five were foolish. They that were foolish took their lamps, and took no oil with them: But the wise took oil in their vessels with their lamps... And while they went to buy, the bridegroom came; and they that were ready went in with him to the marriage: and the door was shut. Afterward came also the other virgins, saying, Lord, Lord, open to us. But he answered and said, Verily I say unto you, I know you not"* (Matt 25:1-4,10-12).

The "virgins" personify churches and spiritually saved believers (all of them saints); the "oil" is a metaphor for the: Name of God (Song 1:3) and the Holy Spirit (Isa 61:1). About half of the saints will not be taken up in the first resurrection for not knowing or calling on the true Name of God and not leading Spirit-filled lives..

The 144,000. *"And I looked, and, lo, a Lamb stood on the mount Sion, and with him an hundred forty and four thousand, having his Father's name written in their foreheads... These are they which were not defiled with women; for they are virgins. These are they which follow the*

Lamb whithersoever he goeth. These were redeemed from among men, being the firstfruits unto God and to the Lamb" (Rev 14:1,4). The elect comprises the 12 tribes of "spiritual" Israel, composed of righteous men and women from various nations.

As *"firstfruits unto God and to the Lamb"*, the 144,000 (both Israelites and Gentiles – Gal 6:15-16) will be the harvest of the first resurrection. That they are *"not defiled"* connotes that they are not tainted with the wrong teachings of erring churches (*"women"*); that they are *"virgins"* means they are born-again individuals through baptism in Christ.

Angelic armies. *"And the armies which were in heaven followed him upon white horses, clothed in fine linen, white and clean"* (Rev 19:14). Fine linen is a special cloth worn by the wealthy and nobility (Gen 41:42), just like the Temple priests (Ex 39:27) and the angels (Ezek 9:3). The body of the crucified Christ was wrapped in linen (Mark 15:46). The bride of the Lamb (the Church) will be dressed in fine linen: *"And to her was granted that she should be arrayed in fine linen, clean and white: for the fine linen is the righteousness of saints"* (Rev 19:8). The angelic armies will include the resurrected saints who will have become like the angels of heaven (Luke 20:36). They will follow the Messiah into battle.

The final confrontation

"And I saw the beast, and the kings of the earth, and their armies, gathered together to make war against him that sat on the horse, and against his army" (Rev 19:19). The armies of mere mortals will be emboldened by the demons from the bottomless pit reinforcing them.

Sword of His mouth. *"And out of his mouth goeth a sharp sword, that with it he should smite the nations: and he shall rule them with a rod of iron: and he treadeth the winepress of the fierceness and wrath of Almighty God"* (Rev 19:11-15). A sword from His mouth?

Hebrews 4:12 makes it plain for us: *"For the word of God is quick, and powerful, and sharper than any twoedged sword, piercing even to the dividing asunder of soul and spirit, and of the joints and marrow, and is a discerner of the thoughts and intents of the heart."* The "sword" is the word of God!

Hazy day. *"And it shall come to pass in that day, that the light shall not be clear, nor dark: But it shall be one day which shall be known to the LORD, not day, nor night: but it shall come to pass, that at evening time it shall be light"* (Zech 14:6-7).

Last and greatest battle.
"*Then shall the LORD go forth, and fight against those nations, as when he fought in the day of battle. And his feet shall stand in that day upon the mount of Olives, which is before Jerusalem on the east...*" (Zech 14:3-4a). "*These shall make war with the Lamb, and the Lamb shall overcome them: for he is Lord of lords, and King of kings: and they that are with him are called, and chosen, and faithful*" (Rev 17:14; cf. Matt 22:14).

Invaders kill each other.
In a bizarre turn of events, Gog and the other invaders, probably rattled by the tumultuous goings-on and hampered by the half-light, will turn on one another. "*And I will call for a sword against him throughout all my mountains, saith the Lord GOD: every man's sword shall be against his brother. And I will plead against him with pestilence and with blood; and I will rain upon him, and upon his bands, and upon the many people that are with him, an overflowing rain, and great hailstones, fire, and brimstone*" (Ezek 38:21-22).

Zechariah foresaw the same thing: "*And it shall come to pass in that day, that a great tumult from the LORD shall be among them; and they shall lay hold every one on the hand of his neighbour, and his hand shall rise up against the hand of his neighbour*" (Zech 14:13).The invaders, unable to distinguish between their comrades and their adversaries in the haze, will kill one another. Yet, it will not be the first time for this strange thing to happen. There were similar incidents in ancient and even recent times when the enemies of Israel fought one another.

Midianites, Amalekites, et al. Against a great army of Midianites, Amalekites, and other eastern peoples, Gideon and his 300 men, each one carrying a trumpet, surrounded the enemy camp at night. "*When the three hundred trumpets sounded, the LORD caused the men throughout the camp to turn on each other with their swords*" (Judg 7:22, NIV). Israel won a miraculous victory over the enemies.

Philistines. At war with their long-time enemies, "*Saul and all his men assembled and went to the battle. They found the Philistines in total confusion, striking each other with their swords*" (1 Sam 14:20-21, NIV). God caused panic among the Philistines, making them fight among themselves, with the Israelites easily putting them to flight.

Ammonites, Moabites, et al. To repulse an invasion, "*the LORD set ambushes against the men of Ammon and Moab and Mount Seir who were invading Judah, and they were defeated. The men of Ammon and Moab rose up against the men from Mount Seir to destroy and annihilate* them. *After they finished slaughtering the men from Seir, they helped to destroy one another. When the men of Judah came... they saw only dead bodies lying on the ground; no one had escaped"* (2 Chron 20:22-24, NIV).

Terrorists and Ugandan soldiers. In 1976, German and Arab terrorists hijacked an Air France jetliner with Jewish passengers to Entebbe, Uganda. 100 Israeli commandos led by Major Jonathan Netanyahu (brother of future Prime Minister Benjamin Netanyahu) launched a rescue operation by night. 102 hostages were rescued alive; only 3 hostages and 1 commando died (Netanyahu); 45 Ugandan soldiers were killed, mostly by fellow Ugandan soldiers who could not recognize them in the dark. The shooting went on for hours *after* the Israelis had left Uganda.

Islamic jihadists. Chaimberlin observes: "Israel's enemies continue to fight against each other. ISIS is an evil terrorist organization, killing many Christians and Yazidis. However, they kill more Muslims than non-Muslims. They kill Sunni Muslims, and any Muslims that they consider to be their enemies, including Iraqi and Syrian soldiers, often with barbaric public executions, being beheaded or even burned alive in cages. We see Sunnis and Shi'ites killing each other. It seems that the entire Arab world has erupted into a flood of violence, with Arab against Arab... The good news, however, is that Israel's enemies are so busy killing each other that they have no time to kill Jews!"[42]

Breath of the LORD.

"And the LORD shall cause his glorious voice to be heard, and shall shew the lighting down of his arm, with the indignation of his anger, and with the flame of a devouring fire, with scattering, and tempest, and hailstones. For through the voice of the LORD shall the Assyrian be beaten down, which smote with a rod... For Tophet is ordained of old; yea, for the king it is prepared; he hath made it deep and large: the pile thereof is fire and much wood; the breath of the LORD, like a stream of brimstone, doth kindle it" (Isa 30:30-31,33).

("Tophet" is a place southeast of Jerusalem, in the Valley of Hinnom, where child sacrifices used to be offered and dead bodies were buried or burned – Isa 30:33; Jer 7:31-32; 19:6,11-14).[43]

Disintegrating flesh. *"And this shall be the plague wherewith the LORD will smite all the people that have fought against Jerusalem; Their flesh shall consume away while they stand upon their feet, and their eyes shall consume away in their holes, and their tongue shall consume away in their mouth"* (Zech 14:12). "That sounds identical to the damage inflicted by a neutron bomb, which explodes the protein cells in the body. It destroys people, not buildings!"[44]

Stragglers hide.
Remnants of the invading armies will run and hide. *"And ye shall flee to the valley of the mountains; for the valley of the mountains shall reach unto Azal: yea, ye shall flee, like as ye fled from before the earthquake in the days of Uzziah king of Judah: and the LORD my God shall come, and all the saints with thee"* (Zech 14:5).

"Enter into the rock, and hide thee in the dust, for fear of the LORD, and for the glory of his majesty... For the day of the LORD of hosts shall be upon every one that is proud and lofty, and upon every one that is lifted up; and he shall be brought low... And they shall go into the holes of the rocks, and into the caves of the earth, for fear of the LORD, and for the glory of his majesty, when he ariseth to shake terribly the earth" (Isa 2:10, 12, 19).

"Then shall they begin to say to the mountains, Fall on us; and to the hills, Cover us" (Luke 23:30). *"And said to the mountains and rocks, Fall on us, and hide us from the face of him that sitteth on the throne, and from the wrath of the Lamb: For the great day of his wrath is come; and who shall be able to stand?"* (Rev 6:16-17).

Enemies wiped out.
The invaders will be thoroughly defeated and annihilated.

Gog falls. *"Behold, I am against thee, O Gog, the chief prince of Meshech and Tubal: And I will turn thee back, and leave but the sixth part of thee... And I will smite thy bow out of thy left hand, and will cause thine arrows to fall out of thy right hand. Thou shalt fall upon the mountains of Israel, thou, and all thy bands, and the people that is with thee: I will give thee unto the ravenous birds of every sort, and to the beasts of the field to be devoured"* (Ezek 39:1b-2a, 3-4).

Assyrian defeated. The man who will have subjugated Israel will finally meet his end. *"That I will break the Assyrian in my land, and upon my mountains tread him under foot: then shall his yoke depart from off them, and his burden depart from off their shoulders"* (Isa 14:25). *"Then shall the Assyrian fall with the sword, not of a mighty man; and the sword, not of a mean man, shall devour him: but he shall flee from the sword, and his young men shall be discomfited. And he shall pass over to his strong hold for fear, and his princes shall be afraid of the ensign, saith the LORD, whose fire is in Zion, and his furnace in Jerusalem"* (Isa 31:8-9).

"Thou sawest till that a stone was cut out without hands, which smote the image upon his feet that were of iron and clay, and brake them to pieces" (Dan 2:34). Christ (the *"stone cut without hands"*) will destroy the ten kings (*"ten toes of iron and clay"*) who *"shall give their power and strength unto the beast"*, the end-time ruler of the world (Rev 17:12-13).

Beast and false prophet fired. *"And the beast was taken, and with him the false prophet that wrought miracles before him, with which he deceived them that had received the mark of the beast, and them that worshipped his image. These both were cast alive into a lake of fire burning with brimstone"* (Rev 19:20).

Here, the "beast" refers only to the end-time empire, not to its ruler, the Antichrist ("man of sin", "son of perdition" – 2 Thess 2:3). No human being will be thrown into the lake of fire until after the Last Judgment, when *"the books were opened: and another book was opened, which is the book of life: and the dead were judged out of those things which were written in the books... and they were judged every man according to their works"* (Rev 20:11-15).

The "false prophet" may not be the "second beast" (America) as some eschatologists think. Could it be Islam? Its founder Muhammad is called "the last prophet of God" by Muslims (whose God is Allah, from *al-illah*, "the God", the moon-god and supreme deity of Muhammad's formerly polytheistic Quraysh tribe). Or is it the Vatican (the "little horn" or Papacy)? It sits on Rome's Vatican Hill (Latin *Vaticanus*, whose root-word is *vates*, meaning "prophet".)[45]

Fowl feast on flesh.

"And, thou son of man, thus saith the Lord GOD; Speak unto every feathered fowl, and to every beast of the field, Assemble yourselves, and come; gather yourselves on every side to my sacrifice that I do sacrifice for you, even a great sacrifice upon the mountains of Israel, that ye may eat flesh, and drink blood. Ye shall eat the flesh of the mighty, and drink the blood of the princes of the earth, of rams, of lambs, and of goats, of bullocks, all of them fatlings of Bashan. And ye shall eat fat till ye be full, and drink blood till ye be drunken, of my sacrifice which I have sacrificed for you. Thus ye shall be filled at my table with horses and chariots, with mighty men, and with all men of war, saith the Lord GOD" (Ezek 39:17-20).

"And I saw an angel standing in the sun; and he cried with a loud voice, saying to all the fowls that fly in the midst of heaven, Come and gather yourselves together unto the supper of the great God; That ye may eat the flesh of kings, and the flesh of captains, and the flesh of mighty men, and the flesh of horses, and of them that sit on them, and the flesh of all men, both free and bond, both small and great... And the remnant were slain with the sword of him that sat upon the horse, which sword proceeded out of his mouth: and all the fowls were filled with their flesh" (Rev 19:17-18,21).

Second third of men gone.
The second part of Ezekiel's apocalyptic prophecy shall have been fulfilled. *"…and thou shalt take a third part, and smite about it with a knife…"* (Ezek 5:2b). The second 33% percent of the world population will have perished in Armageddon. Zechariah explicitly summarizes the tally: *"And it shall come to pass, that in all the land, saith the LORD, two parts therein shall be cut off and die; but the third shall be left therein"* (Zech 13:8). The last 33% of mankind will still be alive after the nuclear war and Great Tribulation (first 33% die), and Armageddon (second 33% die).

Seven-year cleanup?
It looks like it will take a tediously long time to dispose of the remains of war at Armageddon.
Burning of weapons. *"And they that dwell in the cities of Israel shall go forth, and shall set on fire and burn the weapons, both the shields and the bucklers, the bows and the arrows, and the handstaves, and the spears, and they shall burn them with fire seven years: So that they shall take no wood out of the field, neither cut down any out of the forests; for they shall burn the weapons with fire: and they shall spoil those that spoiled them, and rob those that robbed them, saith the Lord GOD"* (Ezek 39:9-10).
Lignostone. Some end-time watchers think the weapons of Gog and Magog could be made of a tightly compressed wood-based material called "lignostone", which the Dutch have developed and which the Russians are said to be adapting for military use. Lignostone is reportedly stronger than steel, relatively lightweight, virtually invisible to radar, and resistant to nuclear radiation.[46] Due to its extremely compact characteristic, lignostone, even if ignited, would take a long, long time to burn.
Burial of corpses. *"And it shall come to pass in that day, that I will give unto Gog a place there of graves in Israel, the valley of the passengers on the east of the sea: and it shall stop the noses of the passengers: and there shall they bury Gog and all his multitude: and they shall call it The valley of Hamon-gog. And seven months shall the house of Israel be burying of them, that they may cleanse the land"* (Ezek 39:11-12). Seven months are an exhaustingly long time for the bodies of the dead invaders to be buried in mass graves!
Figures of speech? "Seven years" and "seven months", however, could be mere figures of speech. "Many times in the Bible, 'seven' is used as a symbol rather than a number. It often expresses the idea of 'completeness or perfection'."[47] "The Sumerians, from whom the Semitic

Babylonians borrowed the idea, equated 7 and 'all.' The 7-storied towers of Babylonia represented the universe... 'Seven gods' at the end of an enumeration meant 'all the gods'."[48] In Psalm 12:6 (*"The words of the LORD are pure words: as silver tried in a furnace of earth, purified seven times."*), "seven times" means very often. The process was repeated until the silver became entirely pure.[49] In Psalm 119:164 (*"Seven times a day do I praise thee because of thy righteous judgments."*), "seven" is used to denote many, or often.[50]

Hence, "seven years" and "seven months" may simply mean that it would take an indefinitely long period for the invaders' weapons to be burned and their corpses buried.

Satan and demons chained.
"And I saw an angel come down from heaven, having the key of the bottomless pit and a great chain in his hand. And he laid hold on the dragon, that old serpent, which is the Devil, and Satan, and bound him a thousand years, And cast him into the bottomless pit, and shut him up, and set a seal upon him, that he should deceive the nations no more, till the thousand years should be fulfilled: and after that he must be loosed a little season" (Rev 20:1-3).

The devil's demonic hordes will be imprisoned with him. *"In that day the LORD will punish the powers in the heavens above and the kings on the earth below. They will be herded together like prisoners bound in a dungeon; they will be shut up in prison and be punished after many days"* (Isa 24:21-22, NIV). They will get their final due after 1,000 years – at the end of Christ's Millennial Kingdom – for the Last Judgment.

Seventh trumpet

"And the seventh angel sounded; and there were great voices in heaven, saying, The kingdoms of this world are become the kingdoms of our Lord, and of his Christ; and he shall reign for ever and ever. Amen!" (Rev 11:15).

Zechariah saw it some 610 years before John. *"And the LORD shall be king over all the earth: in that day shall there be one LORD, and his name one"* (Zech 14:9).

Seventh bowl

"And the seventh angel poured out his vial into the air; and there came a great voice out of the temple of heaven, from the throne, saying, It is done" (Rev 16:17). Ezekiel also heard similar words some 680 years before. *"Behold, it is come, and it is done, saith the Lord GOD; this is the day whereof I have spoken"* (Ezek 39:8).

Mountain-size meteors.

In an astounding instance of multiple fulfillment of prophecy, the figurative crashing of a mountain on earth will literally take place: *"...a great mountain burning with fire was cast into the sea"* (Rev 8:8b). Pieces of comet debris as big as mountains will fall on earth!

Solid nuclei. Some comets are not simply made up of frozen dust and gases; astronomer Mark V. Sykes of the University of Arizona has argued that in at least some comets the proportion of the nucleus made up of rock (as opposed to ice) may be greater than once thought, and that comets may be more like frozen mud balls than dirty snowballs. "Close-up images of the heretofore unseen nucleus of Comet Halley showed a solid, potato-shaped body mostly covered with a coal-black crust, with jets of gas and dust erupting from a few active areas of exposed ices. This comet, at least, has a solid nucleus... Closer to Earth there are a number of 'asteroids' that may be the nonvolatile remains (what is left after the ices evaporate) of short-period comets."[51]

Explosive impacts. In July 1994, Comet Shoemaker-Levy 9 broke up and pelted Jupiter in a week-long barrage of truly astronomical proportions. "The average size of the fragments was about 0.5 km (about 0.30 mi)... some of the impacts produced huge plumes of hot gas that rose some 3000 km (2000 mi) above the Jovian cloud tops and spread dark particulate debris over regions more than 10,000-km (6000-mi) across. By comparison, the diameter of Earth is 12,756 km (7926 mi)."[52]

"According to Spaceguard's Duncan Steel, an asteroid with a diameter of about 1 to 2 km (about 0.6 to 1.2 mi) could strike Earth with the force of 100,000 to 1 million megatons—many times more powerful than the atomic bombs dropped on Japan at the end of World War II in 1945. A megaton is a unit of explosive force equal to that of 1 million metric tons of TNT... the explosive force of the impact would generate a blast wave (a wave of compressed air thrown outward by the explosion) that could travel hundreds, even thousands of kilometers, leveling trees, houses, and other buildings in its path. The impact might also set off a huge firestorm that would consume anything flammable. Depending on the location of the impact site, hundreds of millions of people could be killed by the blast and firestorm."[53]

Greatest earthquake ever.

A monstrous meteor crashing on earth could also produce effects like those of a super-quake. *"And there were voices, and thunders, and lightnings; and there was a great earthquake, such as was not since men were upon the earth, so mighty an earthquake, and so great. And the great city was divided into three parts, and the cities of the nations fell"* (Rev 16:18-19a). The earthquake will change the topography of Jerusalem: *"and the mount of Olives shall cleave in the midst thereof toward the east and toward the west, and there shall be a very great valley; and half of the mountain shall remove toward the north, and half of it toward the south"* (Zech 14:4b).

"Babylon" remembered.
The much-delayed destruction of "Babylon" will take place: *"and great Babylon came in remembrance before God, to give unto her the cup of the wine of the fierceness of his wrath"* (Rev 16:19b). The destruction could be both literal and figurative.

Apostate religion. *The New Unger's Bible Dictionary* notes: "In the prophetical writings, when the actual city is not meant, the illustration is to the 'confusion' into which the whole social order of the world has fallen under Gentile world domination (Luke 21:24; Rev 6:16)... In the NT Babylon prefigures apostate Christendom, that is, ecclesiastical Babylon, the great harlot (Rev 17:5-18)."[54]

In Revelation 17, we saw that "Babylon" is not the ancient city of history, but a sinful "woman" representing an apostate church or religion. The ten kings with the beast will accomplish her destruction. *"And the ten horns which thou sawest upon the beast, these shall hate the whore, and shall make her desolate and naked, and shall eat her flesh, and burn her with fire"* (Rev 17:16). (The Islamic State caliphate has vowed to destroy the Vatican, remember?)

"Therefore shall her plagues come in one day, death, and mourning, and famine; and she shall be utterly burned with fire: for strong is the Lord God who judgeth her" (Rev 18:8).

Earth derailed from orbit.
Massive meteoric impacts could derail Earth from its orbit. *"Therefore I will shake the heavens, and the earth shall remove out of her place, in the wrath of the LORD of hosts, and in the day of his fierce anger"* (Isa 13:13). The situation will further worsen.

"The earth shall reel to and fro like a drunkard, and shall be removed like a cottage; and the transgression thereof shall be heavy upon it; and it shall fall, and not rise again" (Isa 24:20).

Author Immanuel Velikovsky (*Worlds in Collision*, 1950), noted that the force holding Earth in its orbit around the sun is so delicate that even the faint gravitation of a smaller celestial body, such as a comet or asteroid passing close to the planet, could alter its orbit.

Earth overturns!

An unthinkable thing will next happen. *"Behold, the LORD maketh the earth empty, and maketh it waste, and turneth it upside down, and scattereth abroad the inhabitants thereof"* (Isa 24:1). The planet will flip, bottom up! The poles will exchange places – the north will become south, and vice-versa.

Author Peter Lorie wrote: "The concept of the Earth's axis shifting… is something that has been considered a possibility for many years. Evidence indicates that the polar ice-caps have moved from their present position at least two hundred times in the past billion years. These shifts are considered by many scientists to have been responsible for various prehistoric mass extinctions."[55]

In a study done in the early 1980s, Peter Warlow demonstrated that a rotating sphere was quite unstable and easy to overturn. More so with Earth, as it is not perfectly spherical, but slightly pear-shaped; a force applied to its heavier end could tip it over.[56]

Heaven rolled together. *"And the heaven departed as a scroll when it is rolled together…"* (Rev 6:14a). If the Earth overturns, air resistance would push the planet's cloud cover back, creating the appearance that the sky is being rolled like a scroll or a carpet.

People scattered. Ezekiel had prophesied: *"…and a third part thou shalt scatter in the wind; and I will draw out a sword after them"* (Ezek 5:2b). If the Earth overturns, inertia will fling people far and wide in the air, together with all things not affixed to the surface. Thus will the last 33% of mankind begin to pass away.

Earthly kingdoms fall. All the kingdoms of the world will crumble to dust. *"Then was the iron, the clay, the brass, the silver, and the gold, broken to pieces together, and became like the chaff of the summer threshingfloors; and the wind carried them away, that no place was found for them…"* (Dan 2:35a).

Mountains, islands vanish! The prophecy is first told in the sixth seal: *"…and every mountain and island were moved out of their places"* (Rev 6:14b) and repeated in the seventh bowl: *"And every island fled away, and the mountains were not found"* (Rev 16:20).

Inertia will also cause the oceans to wash over the continents, emptying many seas and most other bodies of water. Result: what used to be mountain peaks will become islands. On the other hand, islands will be left high and dry, becoming mountain-tops.

New heaven and earth. *"And I saw a new heaven and a new earth: for the first heaven and the first earth were passed away"* (Rev 21:1). God has said: *"For, behold, I create new heavens and a new earth: and* *the former shall not be remembered, nor come into mind"* (Isa 65:17). Barnabas had also written: *"His Son shall come, and abolish the season of the wicked one (Satan), and judge the ungodly; and shall change the sun and the moon, and the stars..."*[57]

Indeed, if the Earth overturns, the positions of the sun, moon, and stars will be changed. The sun and the moon will rise in the west and set in the east; Polaris will no longer be the polestar.

Greatest hailstorm ever. *"And there fell upon men a great hail out of heaven, every stone about the weight of a talent: and men blasphemed God because of the plague of the hail; for the plague thereof was exceeding great"* (Rev 16:21). A talent weighed about as much as the full weight that a man could carry (2 Kings 5:23).[58]

God foretold the hailstorm through Job about 4,100 years ago. *"Hast thou entered into the treasures of the snow? or hast thou seen the treasures of the hail, Which I have reserved against the time of trouble, against the day of battle and war?"* (Job 38:22-23). The prophecy in the Bible's oldest book, written about 2100 B.C., dovetails with that in Revelation (circa 95 A.D.).

With the abundant presence of refrigerant gases, like nitrogen and ammonia in the cometary cloud, moisture in the upper layers of gases above the earth will condense and solidify, bringing about a hailstorm of unprecedented magnitude.

Cleansing and renewal

"And when he had opened the seventh seal, there was silence in heaven about the space of half an hour" (Rev 8:1).

The silence in heaven will be ominous – as if the scourges that the earth will have so far gone through were not yet enough, an even more horrendous blow will still come.

Divine protection.

God has promised to protect a blessed few. *"Thou shalt also take thereof a few in number, and bind them in thy skirts"* (Ezek 5:3). They will be divinely protected through the nuclear war, the Great Tribulation, Armageddon, and the overturning of planet Earth.

Many of them will be taken up in the nick of time. *"Likewise also as it was in the days of Lot; they did eat, they drank, they bought, they sold, they planted, they builded; But the same day that Lot went out of Sodom it rained fire and brimstone from heaven, and destroyed them all"* (Luke 17:28-29).

In this veiled prophecy, Lot is a type of the elect, both dead and living elect saints, who, before fire pours down from heaven on the Day of the LORD, will have been caught up to Christ in the first resurrection and "rapture".

Sadly, not all of those who will have been protected earlier will be taken up. Some of them will be left behind and go through the final and fieriest affliction – the trial and refining by fire! *"Then take of them again, and cast them into the midst of the fire, and burn them in the fire; for thereof shall a fire come forth into all the house of Israel"* (Ezek 5:4).

Blanket of fire.

"And another angel came out from the altar, which had power over fire; and cried with a loud cry to him that had the sharp sickle, saying, Thrust in thy sharp sickle, and gather the clusters of the vine of the earth; for her grapes are fully ripe" (Rev 14:18). Whereas in the time of Noah the earth was cleansed with water, this time the sinful world will be sanitized by fire.

"And the angel took the censer, and filled it with fire of the altar, and cast it into the earth: and there were voices, and thunderings, and lightnings, and an earthquake" (Rev 8:5).

Flammable gases. The clouds of gases and dust left behind by comets contain many flammable elements and compounds, such as hydrogen, carbon, oxygen, methane, sulfur.

As the cometary meteors that will be plummeting through the earth's atmosphere are heated and fired up by friction, the flammable gases they will pass through can suddenly burst into flames, turning planet Earth into one gargantuan fireball.

Firestorm. It will be a worldwide blanket of fire. *"The mountains quake at him, and the hills melt, and the earth is burned at his presence, yea, the world, and all that dwell therein. Who can stand before his indignation? and who can abide in the fierceness of his anger? his fury is poured out like fire, and the rocks are thrown down by him"* (Nah 1:5-6).

Peter depicts a most horrifying picture. *"But the day of the Lord will come as a thief in the night; in the which the heavens shall pass away with a great noise, and the elements shall melt with fervent heat, the earth also and the works that are therein shall be burned up"* (2 Pet 3:10).

God's Name saves.

"And I will bring the third part through the fire, and will refine them as silver is refined, and will try them as gold is tried: they shall call on my name, and I will hear them: I will say, It is my people: and they shall say, The LORD is my God" (Zech 13:8-9).

The spiritually saved but left behind believers who will know and call on the true name of God will be physically delivered.

Few men left. *"Therefore hath the curse devoured the earth, and they that dwell therein are desolate: therefore the inhabitants of the earth are burned, and few men left"* (Isa 24:6).

"I will make a man more precious than fine gold; even a man than the golden wedge of Ophir" (Isa 13:12). The people left alive will be so few, it will be easier to find gold than a living human being.

The kingdom of heaven

"And in the days of these kings shall the God of heaven set up a kingdom, which shall never be destroyed: and the kingdom shall not be left to other people, but it shall break in pieces and consume all these kingdoms, and it shall stand for ever" (Dan 2:44); *"...and the stone that smote the image became a great mountain, and filled the whole earth"* (Dan 2:35b).

Millennial Kingdom. Christ will reign as King of kings, and the elect saints will reign as kings under Him. *"And I saw thrones, and they sat upon them, and judgment was given unto them: and I saw the souls of them that were beheaded for the witness of Jesus, and for the word of God, and which had not worshipped the beast, neither his image, neither had received his mark upon their foreheads, or in their hands; and they lived and reigned with Christ a thousand years"* (Rev 20:4).

The elect saints will each receive a crown. *"Blessed is the man that endureth temptation: for when he is tried, he shall receive the crown of life, which the Lord hath promised to them that love him"* (James 1:12; see also 1 Cor 9:25). (Earth will be repopulated by the descendants of the few physical survivors after the cleansing of the planet by fire.)

Peace and bliss. Indescribable happiness and untold pleasures are in store for the elect in the Millennial Kingdom. *"But as it is written, Eye hath not seen, nor ear heard, neither have entered into the heart of man, the things which God hath prepared for them that love him"* (1 Cor 2:9).

With the Prince of Peace (Isa 9:6) as supreme sovereign, the renewed world will be a realm of bliss and serenity.

"And there was given him dominion, and glory, and a kingdom, that all people, nations, and languages, should serve him: his dominion is an everlasting dominion, which shall not pass away, and his kingdom that which shall not be destroyed" (Dan 7:14).

HalleluYah!

9

The Time of the End

*And he said, Go thy way, Daniel:
for the words are closed up and sealed till the time of the end.*

- Daniel 12:9

This is it – a Biblical study of the timeline that will culminate in the "end of the world" – the event much dreaded by many, laughed at by some, yet eagerly awaited by a very, very few. Christ gave a conclusive, yet open-ended prediction as to when that cataclysmic climax of humankind's history will take place. *"And this gospel of the kingdom shall be preached in all the world for a witness unto all nations; and then shall the end come"* (Matt 24:14).

In 1999, the world population hit the 6 billion mark. Interestingly, since the first complete Bible was published in Latin (the Vulgate) some 1,600 years ago, more than 6 billion copies of the Bible have been printed.[1] Complete versions with both the Old and New Testaments are in 363 languages, while partial translations come in 2,197 languages.[2]

In 2011, the number of people in the world swelled to 7 billion. Yet, many times outpacing the population growth, in the early 1990s alone, Christian organizations like the American Bible Society and the British and Foreign Bible Society distributed some 630 million Bibles annually.[3]

In the meantime, Christian evangelists and missionaries from various churches and denominations preach the gospel everywhere, even in the most remote nooks and corners of the globe.

Thus, we seem to have reached the time of the end – with the very last day fast approaching. Sadly, watchmen who attempt to discern the time as we walk in the uncertainty of these last days are quickly accused of date-setting. Nonetheless, in this last chapter we shall proceed with our study. After all, the hints and clues regarding the time of the end are in the Bible itself!

Armageddon and Christ's return

The last and greatest battle ever on earth, Armageddon, wherein the armies of the kings of the earth and demons from the bottomless pit will fight against Israel and the army of angels from heaven, will coincide with the Second Coming of Christ on the Day of the LORD. We have seen this in the preceding chapter. But, always, the nagging question is… when?

Only the Father knows.

The apostles, to whom Christ had revealed many secrets of heaven and earth, asked when that fateful time would come. *"And as he sat upon the mount of Olives over against the temple, Peter and James and John and Andrew asked him privately, Tell us, when shall these things be?"* (Mark 13:3-4a, NKJV). Christ said to them. *"But of that day and hour no one knows, not even the angels in heaven, nor the Son, but only the Father. Take heed, watch and pray; for you do not know when the time is"* (Mark 13:32-33, NKJV).

His reply must have been quite disappointing, but what He said was true. In the ancient Hebrew calendar system, it was truly not possible to precisely pinpoint any future day and hour beyond the present time.

The hours of the day.

In Israel, the day is reckoned from sunset to sunset, based on Genesis 1:5 (*"and the evening and the morning were the first day"*). The old day ends and a new day begins when the sun disappears from sight below the horizon at sundown. Since the sun does not set at the same time every day, before the development of modern astronomical science the beginning of a new day and its first hour could not be foretold exactly to the minute.

The evening hours therefore also vary from day to day; and the night can be longer or shorter, depending on the season of the year. In view of this, the Hebrews traditionally made use of at least two ways to tell if night had fallen:
1. When one could no longer distinguish between two dark-colored threads, say, blue and violet; and
2. When three stars could already be seen in the evening sky.

The days of the month.

The Hebrew Talmudic calendar is luni-solar, that is, based on both the lunar and solar cycles, unlike the modern Gregorian calendar, which is solely solar, calculated according to the earth's regular revolution around the sun (365.242189 days), allowing precise astronomical forecasting of the days of the month.

This is not the case with the Hebrew calendar, wherein the first naked-eye sighting of the new moon's crescent after sunset signals the beginning of a new month. As it is not forecast astronomically, the first day of the month, as well as all succeeding days, cannot be known beforehand by anyone, except by the Father in heaven.

The hour of His coming

Yet, despite Christ's statement that the day and hour of His Second Coming are unknowable to all except the Father, He provided a hint that we will not be entirely clueless. He gives us a seemingly simple advice in Revelation 3:3 – *"Remember therefore how thou hast received and heard, and hold fast, and repent. If therefore thou shalt not watch, I will come on thee as a thief, and thou shalt not know what hour I will come upon thee."*

However, the admonition is loaded. Let us turn the wording around – what if we watch, will we know the hour?

The hour is hinted at?

It looks like faithful believers who will be watching will not be completely in the dark. Christ tells us in Mark 13:35 – *"Watch ye therefore: for ye know not when the master of the house cometh, at even, or at midnight, or at the cockcrowing, or in the morning."*

In a thinly veiled illustration wherein He personifies the *"master of the house"*, He is asking us to guess from multiple choices. Christ is suggesting He might return at a nighttime hour!

Under Roman rule, four night watches were kept in Judea. These were: "even" [about 6:00-9:00 p.m.]; "midnight" [about 9:00 p.m.-12:00 midnight); "cockcrowing" [about 12:00 midnight-3:00 a.m.); and "morning" [dawn, about 3:00-6:00 a.m.).

At midnight? We get a more specific lead from a hidden prophecy in the parable of the "Ten Virgins," wherein ten young women were waiting to accompany the bridegroom to the wedding. In this prophecy of types, the "virgins" are a type of the righteous churches and their faithful followers; the "bridegroom" is obviously Christ; and the "wedding" is the Second Coming and first resurrection, when Christ will be met in the air by the elect who will be caught up to Him. What happens next is eye-opening.

"And at midnight there was a cry made, Behold, the bridegroom cometh; go ye out to meet him" (Matt 25:6). The "bridegroom" arrived at midnight! Does that mean Christ will return at midnight?

Trumpet sounds. Trumpet blasts will herald Christ's return. *"Behold, I shew you a mystery; We shall not all sleep, but we shall all be changed, In a moment, in the twinkling of an eye, at the last trump: for the trumpet shall sound, and the dead shall be raised incorruptible, and we shall be changed"* (1 Cor 15:51-53). The phrase *"last trump"* tells us there will not be just one trumpet blast, but several. How many trumpet blasts do you suppose there will be?

What number is most often associated with God? That ought to be easy. Did you say "seven"? God often takes action or ordains activities in periods with 7 parts (7 days, 7 weeks, 7 months, 7 years) or multiples thereof. Author Ed. F. Vallowe (*Biblical Mathematics*, 1998) notes: "SEVEN, the most sacred number to the Hebrews... This number is used more than all other numbers in the Word of God, save the number ONE... The whole Word of God is founded upon the number SEVEN... SEVEN is found 735 times in the Bible."[4] (Incidentally, 735 is also a multiple of 7: 105 x 7.)

We can thus presume there will be seven trumpet blasts, starting at midnight. A possible sequence may be approximately as follows:

1) 12:00 midnight - First trumpet
2) 1:00 a.m. - Second trumpet
3) 2:00 a.m. - Third trumpet
4) 3:00 a.m. - Fourth trumpet
5) 4:00 a.m. - Fifth trumpet
6) 5:00 a.m. - Sixth trumpet
7) 6:00 a.m. - Seventh trumpet

Landing in the morning? It appears Christ's feet will touch the ground at the *"last trump"* in the morning. *"And his feet shall stand in that day upon the mount of Olives, which is before Jerusalem on the east"* (Zech 14:4a). Will Christ alight on Mount Olivet at the first light of day at His Second Coming?

Mount of Olives. Christ will return exactly as prophesied. *"And when he had spoken these things, while they beheld, he was taken up; and a cloud received him out of their sight. And while they looked stedfastly toward heaven as he went up, behold, two men stood by them in white apparel; Which also said, Ye men of Galilee, why stand ye gazing up into heaven? this same Jesus, which is taken up from you into heaven, shall so* *come in like manner as ye have seen him go into heaven. Then returned they unto Jerusalem from the mount called Olivet, which is from Jerusalem a sabbath day's journey"* (Acts 1:9-12). Christ ascended to heaven from the Mount of Olives, or Mount Olivet, and there He will descend on His return.

The day of His coming

If there are clues surrounding the hour of Christ's return, there are probably also inklings as to when the approximate day of the Second Coming will be.

The day is foreshadowed?

God commanded the Israelites to keep a number of feast days. *"The LORD said to Moses, "Speak to the Israelites and say to them: `These are my appointed feasts, the appointed feasts of the LORD, which you are to proclaim as sacred assemblies..."'* (Lev 23:1-2, NIV). Most of the feasts include holy days, also called "sabbath days", when no work must be done, but, more than that, the feasts are also prophecies! *"Let no man therefore judge you in meat, or in drink, or in respect of an holyday, or of the new moon, or of the sabbath days: Which are a shadow of things to come; but the body is of Christ"* (Col 2:16-17). Accordingly, the holy days God ordained are "shadows" or visions of future events!

Seven annual feasts.

God commanded the observance of seven annual feasts. *"These are the feasts of the LORD, even holy convocations, which ye shall proclaim in their seasons"* (Lev 23:4).

1. Passover. *"In the fourteenth day of the first month at even is the LORD's Passover"* (Lev 23:5). The first month (Abib or Nisan today) began with the sighting of the first new moon crescent after the spring equinox in late March or early April. *"Speak ye unto all the congregation of Israel, saying, In the tenth day of this month they shall take to them every man a lamb, according to the house of their fathers, a lamb for an house... Your lamb shall be without blemish, a male of the first year: ye shall take it out from the sheep, or from the goats: And ye shall keep it up until the fourteenth day of the same month: and the whole assembly of the congregation of Israel shall kill it in the evening"* (Ex 12:3,5-6).

Fulfillment: Crucifixion on the 14th day. *"And it was the preparation of the passover, and about the sixth hour: and he saith unto the Jews, Behold your King!"* (John 19:14).

The 14th day was the preparation day on which each Hebrew family killed a lamb for the Passover meal in the evening. (The next day is the first day of the Feast of Unleavened Bread, the 15th day of the month – a holy day wherein no work may be done.)

Christ, the Lamb of God (John 1:29), was crucified on the 14th day of the first month. For that reason, He truly is our Passover Lamb – *"Purge out therefore the old leaven, that ye may be a new lump, as ye are unleavened. For even Christ our passover is sacrificed for us."* (1 Cor 5:7). Just as the blood of the Passover lamb smeared on their lintels and door posts saved the firstborn Israelites from physical death in Egypt, the blood of the Lamb of God saves believers today from spiritual death.

Like the Passover lamb, Christ died in the *"evening"*, but not in the period we know that follows sunset. In the original Hebrew text, the word used was *"ha'arbayim"*, literally *"evenings"* (or *"between the evenings"*). "The Pharisees held to the traditional explanation that it was from the beginning of lengthening shadows to sunset, approximately 3:00 to 5:00 P.M., and with this the Talmud agrees (*Pesahim* 61 a). This was the usual practice, according to Josephus (*Wars of the Jews*, VI. 9,3)."[5] Moreover, "It is clear that they would not wait until sunset, at which time the evening meal would take place. The slaying of the lamb thus coincides exactly with the death of our Saviour, at the ninth hour of the day (Matt 27:46)."[6]

We also find recorded in Luke 23:44-46: *"And it was about the sixth hour, and there was a darkness over all the earth until the ninth hour. And the sun was darkened, and the veil of the temple was rent in the midst. And when Jesus had cried with a loud voice, he said, Father, into thy hands I commend my spirit: and having said thus, he gave up the ghost."* (From sunrise, the first hour at about 6:00 a.m., the sixth hour was 12:00 noon, and the ninth hour was 3:00 p.m.)

2. Feast of Unleavened Bread. *"And on the fifteenth day of the same month is the feast of unleavened bread unto the LORD: seven days ye must eat unleavened bread"* (Lev 23:6). The tradition of eating unleavened bread began at the Exodus, when the Israelites left Egypt in such haste they had no time to leaven their bread. *"And the people took their dough before it was leavened, their kneading-troughs being bound up in their clothes upon their shoulders... And they baked unleavened cakes of the dough which they brought forth out of Egypt, for it was not leavened; because they were thrust out of Egypt, and could not tarry..."* (Ex 12:34,39a).

Fulfillment: Christ in the tomb. On the 15th day of the month, the day after the Crucifixion, Christ lay dead inside the rock tomb, very much like flat unleavened bread. What other basis is there for the comparison? Leaven or yeast causes dough to rise, making bread appear bigger than it really is. So did the "leaven" or doctrine (hypocritical ways and teachings) of the Pharisees and Sadducees which made them seem greater than what they really were. *"Then Jesus said unto them, Take heed and beware of the leaven of the Pharisees and of the Sadducees... Then understood they how that he bade them not beware of the leaven of bread, but of the doctrine of the Pharisees and of the Sadducees"* (Matt 16:6,12).

"Therefore let us keep the feast, not with old leaven, neither with the leaven of malice and wickedness; but with the unleavened bread of sincerity and truth." (1 Cor 5:8). In death, all men are equal, like unleavened bread – no one is richer, wiser, more powerful, or greater in any way than the others.

3. Feast of Firstfruits or Wave-Sheaf. *"When ye be come into the land which I give unto you, and shall reap the harvest thereof, then ye shall bring a sheaf of the firstfruits of your harvest unto the priest: And he shall wave the sheaf before the LORD, to be accepted for you: on the morrow after the sabbath the priest shall wave it"* (Lev 23:10b-11).

The Feast of Firstfruits is celebrated on Sunday, the day after the Sabbath in the week of the Feast of Unleavened Bread.

Fulfilment: Resurrection of Christ. *"Now when Jesus was risen early the first day of the week, he appeared first to Mary Magdalene, out of whom he had cast seven devils"* (Mark 16:9). Christ resurrected from the dead on Sunday, the first day of the week after the Sabbath, exactly on the Feast of Firstfruits.

Christ is God's firstfruits from the dead. *"But now is Christ risen from the dead, and become the firstfruits of them that slept. For since by man came death, by man came also the resurrection of the dead. For as in Adam all die, even so in Christ shall all be made alive. But every man in his own order: Christ the firstfruits; afterward they that are Christ's at his coming"* (1 Cor 15:20-23).

4. Pentecost (Feast of Weeks or Feast of Harvest). *"And ye shall count unto you from the morrow after the sabbath, from the day that ye brought the sheaf of the wave offering; seven sabbaths shall be complete: Even unto the morrow after the seventh sabbath shall ye number fifty days; and ye shall offer a new meat offering unto the LORD"* (Lev 23:15-16). Pentecost (meaning "fiftieth" in Greek) comes seven sabbaths and one day (the 50th day) after the Feast of Firstfruits, marking the end of the grain harvest.

Fulfilment: Birth of the Christian Church. *"And when the day of Pentecost was fully come, they were all with one accord in one* place. And suddenly there came a sound from heaven as of a rushing mighty wind, and it filled all the house where they were sitting. And there appeared unto them cloven tongues like as of fire, and it sat upon each of them. And they were all filled with the Holy Ghost, and began to speak with other tongues, as the Spirit gave them utterance" (Acts 2:1-4).

The assembly or church (*ekklesia* in Greek) of the first Christians made up the harvest of the Holy Spirit on the day of Pentecost or Feast of Harvest. The fourth prophetic feast day was fulfilled precisely on the day of its observance with the baptism of Church members with "tongues of fire" over each of them from the Holy Spirit.

Thus were fulfilled the prophecies of the first four annual feasts God commanded the nation of Israel to observe.

Last three annual feasts.

The fulfillment of the prophecies of three more annual feasts remains to be seen. These are the autumn holy days observed within a span of three weeks in late September to early October.

5. Feast of Trumpets. The fifth annual feast is observed on the first day of the seventh month in autumn (late September or early October). *"And the LORD spake unto Moses, saying, Speak unto the children of Israel, saying, In the seventh month, in the first day of the month, shall ye have a sabbath, a memorial of blowing of trumpets, an holy convocation"* (Lev 23:23-24). The first day of the seventh month begins the Jewish civil new year, marked by trumpet blasts.

Fulfillment: The Day of the LORD? *"Blow ye the trumpet in Zion, and sound an alarm in my holy mountain: let all the inhabitants of the land tremble: for the day of the LORD cometh, for it is nigh at hand; A day of darkness and of gloominess, a day of clouds and of thick darkness, as the morning spread upon the mountains: a great people and a strong; there hath not been ever the like, neither shall be any more after it, even to the years of many generations. A fire devoureth before them; and behind them a flame burneth: the land is as the garden of Eden before them, and behind them a desolate wilderness; yea, and nothing shall escape them"* (Joel 2:1-4).

Will the Feast of Trumpets mark the beginning of the Day of the LORD, when an army of 200 million destroying angels from heaven will proceed before Christ and sweep across the earth to destroy the wicked? *"And the number of the army of the horsemen were two hundred thousand thousand: and I heard the number of them. And thus I saw the horses in the vision, and them that sat on them, having breastplates of fire, and of jacinth, and brimstone: and the heads of the horses were as the heads of* lions; and out of their mouths issued fire and smoke and brimstone. By these three was the third part of men killed, by the fire, and by the smoke, and by the brimstone, which issued out of their mouths" (Rev 9:16-18).

"Ten Days of Awe"? Jews observe a period called "Ten Days of Awe" from the Feast of Trumpets to the Day of Atonement. *"Fear none of those things which thou shalt suffer: behold, the devil shall cast some of you into prison, that ye may be tried; and ye shall have tribulation ten days: be thou faithful unto death, and I will give thee a crown of life"* (Rev 2:10). Do the ten days of tribulation in the prophecy correspond to the "Ten Days of Awe"? "

6. Day of Atonement. The tenth day from the Feast of Trumpets is the Day of Atonement. *"Also on the tenth day of this seventh month there shall be a day of atonement: it shall be an holy convocation unto you; and ye shall afflict your souls, and offer an offering made by fire unto the LORD"* (Lev 23:27).

Fulfillment: Appearance of Christ in the sky? Will Christ appear in the sky on the Day of Atonement on His return? If so, the Jews will have one last chance to accept the Messiah they rejected and thereby reconcile themselves to God. *"And then shall appear the sign of the Son of man in heaven: and then shall all the tribes of the earth mourn, and they shall see the Son of man coming in the clouds of heaven with power and great glory"* (Matt 24:30).

Many Jews will finally recognize the Messiah they had been waiting for. *"And I will pour upon the house of David, and upon the inhabitants of Jerusalem, the spirit of grace and of supplications: and they shall look upon me whom they have pierced, and they shall mourn for him, as one mourneth for his only son, and shall be in bitterness for him, as one that is in bitterness for his firstborn"* (Zech 12:10). Formerly unbelieving Jews will be filled with remorse. *"Behold, he cometh with clouds; and every eye shall see him, and they also which pierced him: and all kindreds of the earth shall wail because of him"* (Rev 1:7).

7. Feast of Tabernacles or Booths (Ingathering). Five days after the Day of Atonement, the seventh and last annual feast commanded by God begins on the fifteenth day. The Feast of Tabernacles is also called the Feast of Ingathering (the last harvests of the year).

"Speak unto the children of Israel, saying, The fifteenth day of this seventh month shall be the feast of tabernacles for seven days unto the LORD" (Lev 23:34). It is *"…the feast of ingathering, which is in the end of the year, when thou hast gathered in thy labours out of the field"* (Ex 23:16).

Fulfillment: First resurrection and "rapture"? Will the first resurrection of the dead and "rapture" of the living elect saints take place during the week-long Feast of Tabernacles or Ingathering?

"And he shall send his angels with a great sound of a trumpet, and they shall gather together his elect from the four winds, from one end of heaven to the other" (Matt 24:31).

God's two witnesses will be among the first to be resurrected. *"And after three days and an half the Spirit of life from God entered into them, and they stood upon their feet; and great fear fell upon them which saw them. And they heard a great voice from heaven saying unto them, Come up hither. And they ascended up to heaven in a cloud; and their enemies beheld them"* (Rev 11:11-12).

The year of His coming

Aside from the seven annual feasts, God has commanded the observance of a weekly holy day – the seventh-day Sabbath of rest.

"Six days shall work be done: but the seventh day is the sabbath of rest, an holy convocation; ye shall do no work therein: it is the sabbath of the LORD in all your dwellings" (Lev 23:1-3).

The "Great Sabbath".

As we have seen in Psalm 90:4 and 2 Peter 3:8, in the eyes of God 1,000 years are just one day, and vice-versa. Some eschatology teachers call the seventh thousand years from the creation of Adam the "Millennium" or the "Great Sabbath". It will shortly follow the cataclysmic cleansing of the earth on the Day of the LORD. A number of early Christian theologians knew this well.

The last 6,000 Years

Barnabas, Paul's missionary companion, preached in his epistle to the first Christians: *"And God made in six days the works of his hands; and he finished them on the sixth day, and he rested the seventh day, and sanctified it. Consider, my children, what that signifies, he finished them in six days. The meaning of it is this; that in six thousand years the Lord God will bring all things to an end. For with him one day is a thousand years; as himself testifieth, saying, Behold this day shall be as a thousand years. Therefore, children, in six days, that is, in six thousand years, shall all things be accomplished.*

"And what is it that He saith, and He rested the seventh day; He meaneth this; that when His Son shall come, and abolish the season of the wicked one (Satan), and judge the ungodly; and shall change the sun and the moon, and the stars, then He shall gloriously rest in that seventh day."[7]

Irenaeus, an early Church father, restated the teaching in his writings. In A.D. 150, he wrote in his book *Against Heresies*: "This is an account of the things formerly created, as also it is a prophecy of what is to come. For the day of the Lord is as a thousand years, and in six days created things were completed; it is evident, therefore, that they will come to an end at the sixth thousand years."[8]

Lactantius, a second century Christian writer, echoed the same belief. "Because all the works of God were finished in six days, it is necessary that the world should remain in this state six ages, that is, six thousand years. Because having finished the works He rested on the seventh day and blessed it; it is necessary that at the end of the six thousandth year all wickedness should be abolished out of the earth and justice should reign for a thousand years."[9]

Six *"thousand years"*.

We find another hint in Revelation 20:2-7, wherein John narrates the chaining and imprisonment of Satan in the bottomless pit for 1,000 years, followed by the reign of the tribulation saints with Christ for 1,000 years, after which Satan will be loosed from his prison.

In six verses, the phrase *"thousand years"* appears six times. Not a few end-time prophecy watchmen think it is a hidden prophecy of the 6,000 years allotted to mankind before Armageddon, the Day of the LORD, and the Second Coming take place.

Three 2,000-year periods.

During the 6,000-year timeline, three eras consisting of two millennia each are predicted to precede the coming "end of the world". Rabbi Elias, who lived some 200 years before Christ, said: "The world endures six thousand years: two thousand before the law, two thousand under the law, and two thousand under Messiah."[10]

Let us examine if there is any modicum of probability in this rabbinical prognosis.

2,000 years before the law. According to the biblical chronology worked out in 1650 by Archbishop James Ussher of Armagh, Ireland, Adam was created in 4004 B.C.[11]

This was some 2,000 years before the birth of Abraham, the forefather of the Hebrew nation, later called Israel.

2,000 years under the law. God gave the first commandments of His law for His chosen people to Abraham (e.g., worship of the one true God, circumcision) under the agreement they entered into – the Abrahamic Covenant (Gen 15:18; cf. 17:2-21).

As recorded in a Biblical timeline calculated by Beecher, another highly esteemed chronologist, Abraham was born in 2003 B.C.[12] (which began in late September or early October of 2004 B.C. in the Hebrew calendar). In line with Rabbi Elias's prediction, the 2,000-year period "under the law" ended when Christ was born.

2,000 years under Messiah. In his timetable, Archbishop Ussher placed the birth of Christ in 4 B.C.[13]

Christ replaced the Old Covenant and its animal sacrifices with the New Covenant through His sacrifice on the cross. His blood, rather than the blood of animals, has since become the atonement for the sins of men.

As inferred in Rabbi Elias's prediction, 2,000 years after the Messiah the world will end and the Great Sabbath of rest will begin. We see this in more specific terms in *"The Chronology of the Old and New Testament,* written by Archbishop Ussher in A.D. 1650. In this Latin volume, Ussher… calculated that the Millennium would begin in A.D. 1997."[14]

Three 2,000-year Periods

Event	Year	Interval	
Creation of Adam	4004 B.C.		
Birth of Abraham	2004 B.C.*	2,000 years	before the law
Birth of Christ	4 B.C.	2,000 years	under the law
End of 6,000 years	1997 A.D.**	2,000 years	under Messiah
Total:		6,000 years	

*2003 B.C. began in autumn of 2004 B.C.
**No 0 B.C./A.D. year, add 1 after subtracting 4 from 2,000

Bible Code. In the book *Bible Code* (1997), author Michael Drosnin showed how secret words and messages can be found in the Hebrew text of the Torah (first 5 books of the Bible) by taking one letter at a time at regular intervals, a technique called Equidistant Letter Sequencing (ELS). It has been known to Jewish sages since the 12th century, leading an 18th century rabbi, the Gaon (genius) of Vilna, to say: "all that was, is, and will be is included in the Torah."

Among the secret words Drosnin found grouped together were "Bible code," "sealed before God," "shut up the words and seal the book until the end," "He sealed the book until the time of the end," and "5757" (Jewish year corresponding to 1997). As the book was published in 1997, it looks like "the time of the end" was 1997!

The year 1997, however, has come and gone, but the Millennium does not seem to have begun yet. At this writing, the world, except for worsening conditions, still appears to be basically the same. There must be some plausible Biblical explanation.

We are much indebted to Brian Allen of the Last Day Ministries of Texas for the following speculation: Is the reason because mankind has not yet fully completed the 6,000 years (6 "days") of labor necessary before we can enter into the Great Sabbath of rest?

Adam's years in Paradise.

Adam did not work for his food immediately after his creation; he simply picked whatever he wanted to eat in the Garden of Eden (Gen 2:9,16). Adam began working only after he and Eve were sent out of the Garden (Gen 3:23). It seems the years that he did not work must be added to 1997 for us to complete the 6,000 years of man's labor before the Millennium can begin! So, when did Adam begin working? Let us do some speculative calculations.

Adam created an infant? Some Bible students speculate that Adam was not created as a grownup man but, rather, as an infant or a baby.[15] The Hebrew word used for "man" in Genesis 2:7 (*"And the LORD God formed man of the dust of the ground..."*) is *adam*, which means "human being", not a grownup male person (as in *geber*, "strong male person").

Animals for company. God saw that Adam needed a companion. *"And the LORD God said, It is not good that the man should be alone; I will make him an help meet for him. And out of the ground the LORD God formed every beast of the field, and every fowl of the air; and brought them unto Adam..."* (Gen 2:18-19a). Now, when did that possibly happen?

Again, let us consider the number most often associated with God – seven ("7"). Did God create the animals 7 years after creating Adam, when the boy was 7 years old?

Eve cloned from Adam. No animal formed by God was deemed suitable as a companion for Adam (*"but for Adam there was not found an help meet for him"* – Gen 2:20b).

Thus God, from Adam's own genetic material, made a female version of the human being. *"And the LORD God caused a deep sleep to fall upon Adam and he slept: and he took one of his ribs, and closed up the flesh instead thereof; And the rib, which the LORD God had taken from man, made he a woman, and brought her unto the man"* (Gen 2:21-22).

Did God clone Eve from the first human after another 7 years, when Adam was a 14-year-old adolescent?

The serpent tempts Eve. As we know, Satan, in the guise of a serpent, came and induced Eve to disobey God by eating of the forbidden fruit.

"And when the woman saw that the tree was good for food, and that it was pleasant to the eyes, and a tree to be desired to make one wise, she took of the fruit thereof, and did eat, and gave also unto her husband with her; and he did eat" (Gen 3:6).

Did the serpent tempt Eve when she was still a gullible 7-year-old girl? Adam would have been 21 years old then.

Adam began working. The LORD was angry. *"Therefore the LORD God sent him forth from the garden of Eden, to till the ground from whence he was taken"* (Gen 3:23).

If Adam was 21 and Eve was 7 when they were sent out of the Garden of Eden, that must be the reason why they did not have intimate relations while in the Garden – Eve was still underage!

They slept together only after they went out of the Garden. *"And Adam knew Eve his wife; and she conceived, and bare Cain, and said, I have gotten a man from the LORD"* (Gen 4:1).

Adam and Eve must have had sex after another 7 years, when Eve attained puberty at the age of 14 and Adam was 28. We may thus summarize the presumed sequence of events as follows:

Early Years of Adam and Eve

Event	Adam	Eve
Adam created	0 y.o.	
Animals created	7 y.o.	
Eve cloned from Adam	14 y.o.	0 y.o.
Adam and Eve sent out of Garden	21 y.o.	7 y.o.
Sexual relations outside the Garden	28 y.o.	14 y.o.

*y.o. (years old)

Let us now add the 21 years that Adam did not work in the Garden to the end of the 6,000 years after his creation (1997 A.D.) for us to arrive at the probable year when the 6,000 years of man's labor presumably ended and when the Millennium would begin.

6000 Years of Man's Labor*

Event		Year
Creation of Adam		4004 B.C.
Plus: 6,000 years	+	6000
End of 6,000 years	=	1997 A.D.*
Years Adam did not work in Eden	+	21
Adjusted end of 6,000 years	=	2018 A.D.
Beginning of the Millennium		2019 A.D.

*No 0 B.C./A.D. year, add 1 after subtracting 4004 from 6000

The last 4,000 Years

Several times in hidden Bible prophecies, the Hebrew nation is metaphorically represented by a fig tree. Here is one example.

Fig tree in a vineyard.

In this prophecy of types, Christ insinuated to His disciples a 4,000-year interval between Abraham's birth and the end of the world. *"He spake also this parable; A certain man had a fig tree planted in his vineyard; and he came and sought fruit thereon, and found none"* (Luke 13:6).

Let us explain the meanings of the metaphors. The *"vineyard"* is symbolically the world; the owner is a type for God; the *"fig tree"*, the Hebrew nation (Israel and the Jews) descended from Abraham; the missing fruit, faithful believers and followers.

"Destroy the fig tree". The vineyard owner, finding no fruit, was irked. *"Then said he unto the dresser of his vineyard, Behold, these three years I come seeking fruit on this fig tree, and find none: cut it down; why cumbereth it the ground?"* (Luke 13:7).

He (God) ordered the fig tree (Hebrew nation) destroyed. The *"dresser"* is a type for the Holy Spirit; *"three years"* signify 3,000 years (from the birth of Abraham in 2004 B.C. to the years following the close of 1000 A.D., when the Jews, becoming the objects of expulsions and massacres, came to the brink of extermination).

In 1010 and 1012, the unwanted Jews were expelled from some of their host countries (Limoges, France; Mainz, Germany). In 1066, they were massacred in Granada, Spain. After Pope Urban II called for the first Crusade in 1096, Crusaders on their way to the Holy Land massacred Jews in England, France, Germany, Austria and all across Europe.

The first pogrom (organized massacre) of the Jews took place in 1113 in Kiev, Russia. In the Second Crusade: (1147-1149), Jews accused of "blood libel" (killing Christian children at Passover to use their blood for unleavened bread) were murdered in Troyes, France; Bohemia; Halle, Germany; Carinthia, Austria. In 1171, similarly accused Jews in Blois, France, were burned alive *en masse*. The persecutions would grow worse through the centuries.

One "year" grace period. The vineyard dresser asked the owner to be a little more patient. *"And he answering said unto him, Lord, let it alone this year also, till I shall dig about it, and dung it: And if it bear fruit, well: and if not, then after that thou shalt cut it down"* (Luke 13:8-9).

The vineyard owner (God) relented and the Jews (*"fig tree"*) were given a "grace period" of one more "year" (another 1,000 years). The Jews are to be either saved or destroyed after the 1,000-year reprieve, depending on whether or not they will bear "fruit" (faithful followers) to God.

The "one-year" (1,000 years) grace period is supposed to have ended around 2000 A.D., or shortly thereafter. More specifically, 4,000 years from 2004 B.C. (birth of Abraham) ended in 1997 A.D. (4,000 - 2004 = 1,996 + 1). As in the 6,000-year countdown, we must add the 21 years that Adam did not work in Eden to 1997, which will take us again to the year 2018.

The last 2,000 Years

Other hidden prophecies in the Old Testament prefigure a 2,000-year-long countdown.

"After two days..."

A veiled prophecy of a 2,000-year waiting period is less obscure. Around 760 B.C., the prophet Hosea had a vision of the first resurrection and "rapture". *"After two days will he revive us: in the third day he will raise us up, and we shall live in his sight"* (Hos 6:2).

Based on the prophetic principle that one day equals a thousand years, *"after two days"* can mean "after two thousand years"; while *"in the third day"* is interpreted as "sometime after the beginning of the third thousand years." (Note that the two phrases can refer to the same point in time.)

2,000 years from Nativity? The question is, two thousand years from when? If after the birth of Christ, the *Encarta Encyclopedia* states: "Historical evidence indicates that Jesus was actually born in 4 bc or earlier. As a result, the 2,000-year anniversary of the birth of Jesus may have occurred sometime in the 1990s"[16] (likely 1997).

This lines up with the reckoning that both the 6,000-year and 4,000-year countdowns ended in 1997. On the other hand, if the count began after the death of Christ, we must use the Crucifixion as the starting point.

2,000 years from Crucifixion? Many believe Christ was crucified in 33 A.D., based on the Church tradition that He was born in 1 A.D. and died at the age of 33 ½ years. But the *Encarta Encyclopedia* notes that the monk who introduced the B.C./A.D. calendar system in 532 A.D., Dionysius Exiguus, made various errors in calculating Christ's birth date and mistakenly pegged His birth in 1 A.D.[17]

Inasmuch as Christ was actually born in the autumn ending 5 B.C. and starting 4 B.C. in the Jewish calendar, His crucifixion at the age of 33 ½ years must have occurred in the spring of 30 A.D.

Therefore, if we count 2,000 years from 30 A.D., the *"two days"* will end in 2030.

"2,000 cubits behind the ark".

The following is an instance of an actual event that is also a hidden prophecy. The Israelites in the Exodus from Egypt, after forty years of wandering in the wilderness, reached the Jordan River around 1551 B.C. (Ussher's chronology). They had to cross the stream to enter Canaan, the Promised Land.

"And they commanded the people, saying, When ye see the ark of the covenant of the LORD your God, and the priests the Levites bearing it, then ye shall remove from your place, and go after it. Yet there shall be a space between you and it, about two thousand cubits by measure: come not near unto it, that ye may know the way by which ye must go: for ye have not passed this way heretofore" (Josh 3:3-4).

Joshua, who led the Israelites after Moses died, said the people must follow the Ark of the Covenant carried by the priests, but they should walk 2,000 cubits behind it.

In this prophecy of types, the Ark is a type for Christ; the priests carrying the Ark, the angels; the people, the elect saints; the 2,000 cubits, 2,000 years after Christ's crucifixion and ascension to heaven (the Promised Land). Prophetically, the elect saints are to follow Christ to heaven after 2,000 years. Hence, if the count started from the year of the Ascension in 30 A.D., the end of the prophesied interval of two millennia will also be in 2030.

The Last 490 Years

An Old Testament prophecy presents a more straightforward timetable, parts of which have already been fulfilled. We refer to the "seventy 'weeks' of years" the angel Gabriel foretold to Daniel in the 6th century B.C., when he was a young Jewish captive in Babylon.

The 70 "weeks" of years.
Gabriel said, *"Seventy weeks are determined upon thy people and upon thy holy city, to finish the transgression, and to make an end of sins, and to make reconciliation for iniquity, and to bring in everlasting righteousness, and to seal up the vision and prophecy, and to anoint the most Holy"* (Dan 9:24). The Hebrew word for "week" is *shabua*, a unit of 7 parts (i.e., 7 days, 7 years, etc.). In the context the prophecy, one "week" means seven years. Thus, seventy "weeks" (70x7) means the Jews were given 490 years to do several things that would restore their relationship with God.

Decree to rebuild Jerusalem. The timetable began with a royal decree. *"Know therefore and understand, that from the going forth of the commandment to restore and to build Jerusalem unto the Messiah the Prince shall be seven weeks, and threescore and two weeks: the street shall be built again, and the wall, even in troublous times"* (Dan 9:25).

In 458 B.C., Persian king Artaxerxes Longimanus issued a decree to the Jewish priest-scribe Ezra for the captive Jews in Babylon to rebuild Jerusalem. (There were previous decrees by earlier kings after Persia conquered Babylon in 539 B.C.) Some 50,000 Jews returned to Jerusalem. As foretold by Gabriel, the walls of the city were rebuilt after *"seven weeks"* or 49 years (7x7) in 409 B.C. The rest of the restoration work would be accomplished within the next 434 years (*"threescore and two weeks"*/ 62x7).

Oddly, the events that would next take place, although part of the prophecy, were not part of the 490-year count. These would transpire in an interim period before the count for the final 7 years (last "week") is to resume.

Advent of Christ. The end of 434 years came in 26 A.D. (*"unto the Messiah"* – advent of Christ). John the Baptist baptized Christ (Messiah and Christ both mean "Anointed") in the autumn of that year in the Jordan River, with the anointing of the Holy Spirit.

(Born during the Feast of Tabernacles in the fall or autumn ending 5 B.C. and starting 4 B.C., Christ turned 30 years old in the autumn of 26 A.D., the age at which a male Jew can start serving as a minister – Num 4:47a). The prophecy was fulfilled precisely at the end of the sixty-ninth "week" (483rd year)!

Crucifixion of Christ. *"And after threescore and two weeks shall Messiah be cut off, but not for himself..."* (Dan 9:26a). Three-and-a-half years after the autumn of 26 A.D., Christ was *"cut off"* (killed) in the spring of 30 A.D. at the age of 33-½ years. He was killed *"not for himself"* – that is, not in punishment for His own personal wrongdoing, but as the atonement for the sins of mankind.

Jerusalem and Temple destroyed. *"…and the people of the prince that shall come shall destroy the city and the sanctuary…"* (Dan 9:26b). Forty years later, in 70 A.D., Roman legions besieging Jerusalem, led by Titus, son of Emperor Vespasian (*"the people of the prince that shall come"*), razed Jerusalem and the Holy Temple (*"shall destroy the city and the sanctuary"*). ("Forty" [40] is the number of trial and testing in the Bible: e.g., the Jews wandered 40 years in the wilderness before reaching the Promised Land [Deut 8:2]; the people of Nineveh were given 40 days to repent or their city would be destroyed [Jonah 3:4]; Christ was tempted 40 days and 40 nights by the devil [Matt 4:2; Mark 1:13; Luke 4:2].)

It looks like God gave the Jews a grace period of 40 years to see if they would still accept the Messiah they rejected and killed in 30 A.D. When they failed to do so, God allowed the destruction of Jerusalem and the Temple to proceed in 70 A.D. The Roman legions completely overran Jerusalem (*"the end thereof shall be with a flood"* – Dan 9:26c). In Bible prophecy, "flood" is a metaphor for invading armies (Isa 8:7; Jer 46:8).

This event in the prophecy would be followed by a long interval before the count is resumed at the start of the seventieth and last "week" (last 7 years), which portends to be the grand beginning of the "end". We shall be discussing this shortly.

The last generation

Once again, in an actual incident that was also a prophecy, the Jewish nation is symbolized by a fruitless fig tree.

The withered fig tree.

About four days before the Crucifixion, *"Now in the morning as he returned into the city, he hungered. And when he saw a fig tree in the way, he came to it, and found nothing thereon, but leaves only, and said unto it, Let no fruit grow on thee henceforward for ever. And presently the fig tree withered away. And when the disciples saw it, they marvelled, saying, How soon is the fig tree withered away!"* (Matt 21:18-20). Just like the fig tree, the Jews, with very few believers in Christ, yielded practically no fruit to God. The "fig tree" (the Jews) *"withered"* initially in 70 A.D. and, finally, in 135 A.D.

Decimation and dispersion. *"And they shall fall by the edge of the sword, and shall be led away captive into all nations: and Jerusalem* shall be trodden down of the Gentiles, until the times of the Gentiles be fulfilled" (Luke 21:24).

Roman legions, putting down a Jewish revolt that began in 66 A.D., destroyed Jerusalem and the Temple in 70 A.D., leaving just parts of the Western Wall on Temple Mount standing. They killed some 1,100,000 Jews during the war and took over 100,000 survivors to the slave markets of the ancient world.

After a little over 60 years, the Jews rose again in 132 A.D. under the warrior Simon Bar Kokhba. When the uprising was crushed in 135 A.D., leaving some 500,000 Jews dead, Rome expelled all remaining Jews and plowed Jerusalem with salt to symbolically erase their memory. Jerusalem was renamed "Aelia Capitolina" (after the clan name "Aelius" of Emperor Hadrian); while Judea was called "Syria Palaestina" (after the Philistines of southwestern Canaan who had ceased to exist as a people shortly after 600 B.C.).[18]

For the next 1,750 years or so the Holy Land was successively governed by the Romans, Byzantines, Persians, Arabs, Crusaders, Mamelukes, Ottoman Turks, and the British.

Revival of the "fig tree". The withered "fig tree" was to revive and flourish once again. God had promised: *"If any of thine be driven out unto the outmost parts of heaven, from thence will the LORD thy God gather thee, and from thence will he fetch thee: And the LORD thy God will bring thee into the land which thy fathers possessed, and thou shalt possess it; and he will do thee good, and multiply thee above thy fathers"* (Deut 30:4-5; etc.). The Jews began returning to the Promised Land from their worldwide *diaspora* (dispersion). In 1878, the first *aliyah* ("ascent") was made by a group of eight young Jews from Russia. From 12,000 in 1845, the number of Jews in Palestine had quickly grown to 670,000 by 1948.

Christ had said, *"Now learn a parable of the fig tree; When his branch is yet tender, and putteth forth leaves, ye know that summer is nigh"* (Matt 24:32). The "fig tree" sprouted new leaves and revived after nearly 1,900 years when the modern state of Israel declared its independence at midnight of May 14, 1948.

Prophecy in the psalms. In the book *Hidden Prophecies in the Psalms* (1986, revised 1990), author and end-time watchman J.R. Church revealed his surprising insight that Psalms 1-100 are year-by-year prophecies for the 20th century. The blurb on the back cover reads: "The Psalms tell the story of the 20th century. Compare Psalm 17 with 1917, when the British liberated Jerusalem; or Psalms 39-45 with 1939-45, when six million Jews died; or Psalm 48 with 1948, the year Israel was born!"[19]

Indeed, the verses of Psalm 48 sound like accounts of the events in Israel that landmark year. Within 24 hours after Israel declared its independence, five neighboring Arab countries attacked (*"lo, the kings were assembled, they passed by together"*); but were repulsed (*"they marvelled; they were troubled, and hasted away"*); *"Fear took hold upon them there, and pain, as of a woman in travail"* (labor pains in the rebirth of Israel); *"Thou breakest the ships* (discourage intervention) *of Tarshish* (western end and beyond of Mediterranean Sea, i.e., U.K., former administrator of Palestine) *with an east wind"* (Mideast war); *"As we have heard, so have we seen in the city of the LORD of hosts, in the city of our God* (Jerusalem): *God will establish it for ever"* (Ps 48:4-8).

Bible book numbers. The Psalms is the 19th book of the Bible from the first (Genesis); but, counted from the last (Revelation), it is the 48th. When 19 and 48 are placed side-by-side, we get 1948! It is as if the Bible is telling us that 1948 was one very important year.

Blood moon tetrads. In the blood moon tetrads (Chapter 1), there were 19 years between the first blood moon of the 1949-1950 tetrad and the last blood moon of the succeeding 1967-1968 tetrad. Then, there were 48 years between the first blood moon of the 1967-1968 tetrad and the last blood moon of the following 2014-2015 tetrad. Together (19+48), they again form 1948.

As nothing happens by chance (Prov 16:33), these coincidences look like they attach truly great significance to the year 1948.

The last 70-80 years.

Christ said: *"So likewise ye, when ye shall see all these things, know that it is near, even at the doors. Verily I say unto you, This generation shall not pass, till all these things be fulfilled"* (Matt 24:33-34). Accordingly, the fulfillment of remaining end-time prophecies will take place within the lifetime of the members (or remnants) of the generation in existence at the rebirth of Israel. The reader must be wondering... until when will that generation live?

Moses answers this for us in Psalm 90:10. *"The days of our years are threescore years and ten; and if by reason of strength they be fourscore years, yet is their strength labour and sorrow; for it is soon cut off, and we fly away."* People, he said, live an average of 70 years, which may extend to 80 if one is strong, but life will then be full of difficulties. In any case, an average generation of 70 years from 1948 will live until 2018; if 80 years, up to 2028. Are these the probable limits God has ordained for the "end"?

End of the "Last Generation"

Revival of the "fig tree"/rebirth of Israel	1948		1948
Lifespan of one generation (no. of years)	+70	or	+80
Fulfillment of end-time prophecies	**2018**	or	**2028**

The last 7 years

Daniel's 70th "week" (last 7 years) was to follow the end of the 69th "week", marked by the advent of the Messiah at His baptism in the Jordan in 26 A.D., but it seems to have been held in abeyance.

The 70th "week" of Daniel.

"And he shall confirm the covenant with many for one week: and in the midst of the week he shall cause the sacrifice and the oblation to cease, and for the overspreading of abominations he shall make it desolate, even until the consummation, and that determined shall be poured upon the desolate" (Dan 9:27). The covenant, as we have seen earlier, may very well be the one wherein God gave Abraham and his descendants ownership of the Promised Land (Gen 15:18).

2011-2018? If 2018 would be the end of the last 7 years in Daniel's prophecy, then the covenant should have been confirmed at the start of the 7 years, that is, in 2011. Did any such thing happen?

One event appears to have fulfilled the prophecy that year, although rather unnoticeably.

Covenant confirmed? On September 23, 2011, the Palestinian Authority (PA) applied for recognition as an independent state to the United Nations Security Council. If their application would be approved, the PA would get large chunks of the Holy Land and the present territory held by Israel would be dismembered.

After several postponements, the Security Council scheduled the voting on November 11, 2011 (11/11/11). Eight of the 15 members of the Security Council (Brazil, China, Gabon, India, Lebanon, Nigeria, Russia, South Africa) indicated they would vote in favor of the PA application; six (Bosnia-Herzegovina, Colombia, France, Germany, Portugal, United Kingdom) would either vote against or abstain; the United States was the only member openly against. However, since a decision by the Council requires 9 votes, it looked like the PA application would not be approved. In any case, a "yes" result would certainly be vetoed by the United States.

Without the prospect of the PA application getting approved, the UN Security Council announced on the scheduled day that they were not proceeding with the vote. The PA application was shelved, and the land of Israel was not partitioned. Bottom line: It was as if the UN Security

Council confirmed God's covenant with Abraham, even if unintentionally, that the Promised Land belongs to Israel.

Prophesied in a psalm? Did the last 7 years really begin on November 11, 2011? Let us verify this by extending to the 21st century the insight of author J.R. Church that every psalm is a prophecy for each year in the end-times. Being a major event in apocalyptic prophecy, the confirmation of the covenant in 2011 should be found in Psalm 111. Is it? *"He hath given meat unto them that fear him: he will ever be mindful of his covenant... He sent redemption unto his people: he hath commanded his covenant for ever: holy and reverend is his name"* (Ps 111:5,9).

The word "covenant" is mentioned two times! Do we not repeat or say something twice in order to confirm a matter? Does Psalm 111 affirm that the covenant was truly confirmed in 2011? If so, then the last 7 years should really end sometime in late 2018.

Mysterious psalm grouping

Three peculiar psalms are strangely grouped together, intriguing Bible scholars for generations: Psalm 117, the shortest chapter in the Bible; Psalm 118:8, the exact middle verse of the Bible; and Psalm 119, the longest chapter in the Bible. How come these three passages are closely clustered right in the heart of the Scriptures, as if attaching great importance and calling attention to them?

The author of *Cheiro's Book of Numbers* mused: "These three psalms were purposely planned to come together for a definite reason – that reason evidently being that the relation of such coincidences would sooner or later strike some searcher of truth, as an illustration of Divine design..."[20] Along the line of J.R. Church's insight, do Psalms 117, 118:8, and 119 correspond to the years 2017, 2018, and 2019?

Psalm 118:8 – middle verse of the Bible.

The verse seems to contain the underlying theme of the entire Scriptures. *"It is better to trust in the LORD than to put confidence in man"* (Ps 118:8). To paraphrase, "Believe only in the word of God – the Bible – not what any person may tell you." If we closely examine Psalm 118, we will find visions of the events on the Day of the LORD.

Armageddon? *"All nations compassed me about: but in the name of the LORD will I destroy them... They compassed me about like bees; they are quenched as the fire of thorns: for in the name of the LORD I will destroy them"* (Ps 118:10,12). ("Two symbols are used in this verse which typify the antichrist – bees and thorns. Midrash Shocher Tov described the bees as typical of that final war when God gathers all the nations of the world and brings them against Jerusalem."[21]) In Micah 7:4, the unrighteous are likened to a *"brier"* and a *"thorn hedge"* in the day of their *"visitation"*. In Psalm 118:16 – *"The right hand of the LORD is exalted: the right hand of the LORD doeth valiantly."* The verses sound like Armageddon!

First resurrection and "rapture"? *"I called upon the LORD in distress: the LORD answered me, and set me in a large place... Open to me the gates of righteousness: I will go into them, and I will praise the LORD: This gate of the LORD, into which the righteous shall enter"* (Ps 118:5,19-20; cf. 2 Cor 12:2-3). The verses present vivid pictures of the "catching-up" of the elect in the first resurrection of the righteous dead and "rapture" of the living elect saints.

The Second Coming? *"The stone which the builders refused is become the head stone of the corner... This is the day which the LORD hath made; we will rejoice and be glad in it. Save now, I beseech thee, O LORD: O LORD, I beseech thee, send now prosperity* (success). *Blessed be he that cometh in the name of the LORD: we have blessed you out of the house of the LORD"* (Ps 118:22-24). The last verse echoes a prophecy of the Second Coming! *"For I say unto you, Ye shall not see me henceforth, till ye shall say, Blessed is he that cometh in the name of the Lord"* (Matt 23:39).

October 2018? J.R. Church saw another extraordinary feature. "There are 1189 chapters in the Bible, making a total of 1188 chapters apart from the middle chapter. It must be more than a coincidence that Psalm 118:8 is the middle verse of the Bible – making the number 1188 compare with uncanny accuracy. This must be a product of Divine inspiration."[22] In other words, if we set apart Psalm 118 from the Bible's total of 1,189 chapters, 1,188 chapters will be left, repeating the mystical numbers of Psalm 118:8!

Now, if chapter 118 denotes the year 2018, could verse 8 be indicative of October (Latin *octo* = 8), the month wherein the autumn holy days of the Feast of Trumpets, Day of Atonement, and Feast of Tabernacles usually fall?

Psalm 117 – shortest chapter in the Bible.

This shortest of Bible chapters has only 2 verses. *"O praise the LORD, all ye nations: praise him, all ye people. For his merciful kindness is great toward us: and the truth of the LORD endureth for ever. Praise ye the LORD"* (Ps 117:1-2). It is a psalm of praise for the mercy and kindness of the LORD.

Tribulation cut short? The Second Coming and first resurrection will follow the Great Tribulation, which Christ said will be cut short. *"For then shall be great tribulation, such as was not since the beginning of the world to this time, no, nor ever shall be. And except those days should be shortened, there should no flesh be saved: but for the elect's sake those days shall be shortened"* (Matt 24:21-22).

Is Psalm 117 a prophecy that God will show His merciful kindness by shortening the Great Tribulation sometime in 2017?

Psalm 119 – longest chapter in the Bible.
Psalm 119 has a total of 176 verses, more than twice as many as any other chapter in the Scriptures. How does Psalm 119 figure in end-time prophecy?

Most sabbaths are observed for just one day – such as the weekly seventh-day Sabbath of rest; the first and seventh days of the Feast of Unleavened Bread; the seventh-week Sabbath (Pentecost); the seventh-month Sabbath (Feast of Trumpets); the Day of Atonement; the first and eighth days of the Feast of Tabernacles.

The seventh-year Sabbath, called the sabbatical year or "year of release," because debts were canceled and Hebrew slaves were freed, is much longer – the land was not planted but allowed to rest for one whole year.

The longest Sabbath, however, is the Great Sabbath (the Millennium) or seventh thousand year Sabbath, when the earth will enjoy 1,000 years of peace under the reign of Christ as King of kings.

Is Psalm 119, the longest chapter in the Holy Bible, a prophecy that the Millennium or longest Sabbath will begin in 2019?

The last 3 ½ years

Three-and-a-half years after the confirmation of the covenant, *"in the midst of the week he shall cause the sacrifice and the oblation to cease, and for the overspreading of abominations he shall make it desolate"* (Dan 9:27b) and *"arms shall stand on his part, and they shall pollute the sanctuary of strength, and shall take away the daily sacrifice, and they shall place the abomination that maketh desolate"* (Dan 11:31).

If the covenant was indeed confirmed on November 11, 2011, then, based on Revelation 12:6,14, wherein 3 ½ years (*"a time, and times, and half a time"*) are equal to *"a thousand two hundred and threescore days"* (1,260 days), the *"midst of the week"* fell in the last week of April 2015, and the following events should have already taken place:

Cessation of offerings. No offerings were stopped, because no offerings had been restored. Watchman Ed Spurlin, editor-publisher of *Voice in the Wilderness* (New Hampshire), pointed out that it could happen sometime later since *"midst of the week"* can mean any point in time within the supposed last 7 years, like 3:00 a.m. can be said to be the middle of the night.

Abomination of desolation. If it was to be "a bomb", as suggested by its abbreviation "A BOM" (also an anagram for "MOAB" [Massive Ordnance Air Blast or "Mother of All Bombs"]), to be set up by the "vile person" (Dan 11:21,31), deduced to be Saddam Hussein or his successor (the Assyrian Antichrist), it did not materialize.

Assyrian invasion. The "Assyrian" should have invaded Israel (Isa 10:5-6,24; Mic 5:5-6). Ancient Assyria lay in northern Iraq, parts of which are now under the Islamic State (ISIS) led by Abu Bakr al-Baghdadi or Caliph Ibrahim, who was born near Samarra in northern Iraq. (Saddam Hussein was born in Tikrit, also in northern Iraq).

The prophesied invader should have already desecrated the holy place and defamed God; *"...and that man of sin be revealed, the son of perdition; Who opposeth and exalteth himself above all that is called God, or that is worshipped; so that he as God sitteth in the temple of God, shewing himself that he is God"* (2 Thess 2:3-4). No such things took place.

Nuclear war. A nuclear conflict (Rev 8:10-11) was supposed to have broken out, brought about a nuclear winter (Rev 8:12), and destroyed the ozone layer, thereafter allowing intense heat (Rev 16:9) to bathe the planet. Those events did not transpire, either.

"Great Tribulation". Most vegetation on earth should have dried up, and an ensuing global famine would have caused unprecedented human sufferings (Matt 24:15-22) for the next 3 ½ years or so. So far, no sign of the Great Tribulation unfolding is evident.

Occupation of Jerusalem. The city should have been held captive at the start of a 42-month period. *"And there was given me a reed like unto a rod: and the angel stood, saying, Rise, and measure the temple of God, and the altar, and them that worship therein. But the court which is without the temple leave out, and measure it not; for it is given unto the Gentiles: and the holy city shall they tread under foot forty and two months"* (Rev 11:1-2). It has not happened.

Extended to 2028?

Perhaps the actual year of the end is 2028, the extended limit of the lifespan of one generation (80 years) from 1948 if some of its members are durably strong. However, other than the one about the average length of a generation (Matt 24:33-34), no other prophetic clue pointing to 2028 had been seen.

Now, if 2028 would be the end of the last seven years, then the confirmation of the covenant in the first year (2021) might be prophesied in Psalm 121 (just like 2011 in Psalm 111). Let us check.

Negative. Not the slightest hint of a covenant in the eight short verses of Psalm 121. Virtually all the signs we have seen point to 2018. It seems we cannot avoid reaching one conclusion.

End of the world postponed?

It looks like mankind has again been given a reprieve. The end of the world has been postponed! Sinners and unbelievers now have one more chance to repent and be saved (2 Pet 3:9).

Biblical grace periods.
True to His merciful character, the Creator gives His wayward creatures ample warning before executing judgment upon them. Remember, *"Surely the Lord GOD will do nothing, but he revealeth his secret unto his servants the prophets"* (Amos 3:7). We find several instances of this act of divine lovingkindness in the Scriptures.

Noah's Flood. *"And the LORD said, My spirit shall not always strive with man, for that he also is flesh: yet his days shall be an hundred and twenty years"* (Gen 6:3). God gave the antediluvians a grace period of 120 years to turn away from their wicked ways before destroying the world by flood in Noah's time.

Nineveh. *"And Jonah began to enter into the city a day's journey, and he cried, and said, Yet forty days, and Nineveh shall be overthrown"* (Jonah 3:4). Jonah warned the people of Nineveh that their city would be destroyed after 40 days if they did not repent.

Israel. As we have seen in Daniel 9, God gave the Jews 490 years *"to finish the transgression, and to make an end of sins, and to make reconciliation for iniquity, and to bring in everlasting righteousness, and to seal up the vision and prophecy, and to anoint the most Holy"* in order to restore their special relationship with Him.

Fourteen-year delay?
Hidden prophecies have been found in both the Old and New Testaments suggesting a 14-year delay.

Invasion of Israel. *"Now it came to pass in the fourteenth year of king Hezekiah, that Sennacherib king of Assyria came up against all the defenced cities of Judah, and took them"* (Isa 36:1; cf. 2 Kings 18:13). In this lately discovered prophecy of types, Sennacherib stands for a king who will invade Israel in the 14th year.

Armageddon. *"And in the fourteenth year came Chedorlaomer, and the kings that were with him, and smote the Rephaims in Ashteroth Karnaim, and the Zuzims in Ham, and the Emims in Shaveh Kiriathaim"* (Gen 14:5). In an allusion to Armageddon, Chedorlaomer is the type for an invader who, with his allies, will war with other nations in the Holy Land at the end of a 14-year period.

First resurrection. *"I will come to visions and revelations of the Lord. I knew a man in Christ above fourteen years ago, (whether in the body, I cannot tell; or whether out of the body, I cannot tell: God knoweth;) such an one caught up to the third heaven... How that he was caught up into paradise..."* (2 Cor 12:1-2,4a). The *"man in Christ"* means the elect; *"fourteen years ago"* must be interpreted as *"fourteen years later"* being a vision of the future; *"caught up to the third heaven"* or *"paradise"* points to the first resurrection of the dead and "rapture" of the living elect saints at the Second Coming.

Jews and Gentiles. *"Then fourteen years after I went up again to Jerusalem with Barnabas, and took Titus with me also"* (Gal 2:1).

Jerusalem typifies the kingdom of heaven; Barnabas (a Jewish name) personifies the Jews; Titus (a Roman name), the Gentiles. Christ (represented by Paul, the writer) will take up with him both the elect Jews and Christians at His Second Coming after 14 years.

Two "daughters". *"And Laban had two daughters: the name of the elder was Leah, and the name of the younger was Rachel... And Jacob loved Rachel; and said, I will serve thee seven years for Rachel thy younger daughter... And Laban said, It must not be so done in our country, to give the younger before the firstborn. Fulfil her week, and we will give thee this also for the service which thou shalt serve with me yet seven other years. And Jacob did so, and fulfilled her week: and he gave him Rachel his daughter to wife also"* (Gen 29:16,18,26-28).

Laban is a type for God; Jacob is Christ (as the Hoy Spirit [2 Cor 3:17]); his two brides, the elder Leah (Jews) and the younger Rachel (Gentile Christians); 7 years would be served for each "woman" (religion or church) for a total of 14 years.

New date: 2032?

If the 14-year grace period discovery is valid, 14 years must be added to 2018 – which take us to 2032. Is this the new date for Armageddon and the Second Coming?

42-year periods.

The new date of 2032 for the end of the world appears to be corroborated by hidden prophecies containing references to at least two 42-year periods.

"42 months" longer in power? In Revelation 13:3-4, we saw that the seven-headed beast from the "sea" (Western Europe) sustained a deadly wound (Germany divided); but the wound was healed (December 1990, when East Germany and West Germany were reunified as one Germany). *"And there was given unto him a mouth speaking great things and blasphemies; and power was given unto him to continue forty and two months"* (Rev 13:5).

Did the "beast" (EU) and one of its "heads" that was wounded (Germany) continue in power since December 1990 for only 42 months? Both have been prospering and growing stronger for nearly 30 years now.

Some veiled prophecies speak of a short unit of time to denote a longer period. For instance, a "day" could mean a "year" (Num 14:34; Ezek 4:6; Dan 7:25); or a "year" may signify a "millennium" (Luke 13:6-9). If the *"forty and two months"* are not literal, but prophetically mean 42 years instead, then the "beast" would remain in power for 42 more years from the time divided Germany was reunified in 1990. That period would end in the year 2032.

One "hour" with the beast? *"And the ten horns which thou sawest are ten kings, which have received no kingdom as yet; but receive power* ***as*** *kings one hour with the beast. These have one mind, and shall give their power and strength unto the beast."* (Rev 17:12-13).

While possible, it is highly improbable that the ten kings will wield power with the beast for just one literal 60-minute hour. The passage likely means a prophetic "hour". Now, if a prophetic "day" is 1,000 years long (Ps 90:4; 2 Pet 3:8), a prophetic "hour" must be 1/24 of a millennium. In that case, let us divide 1,000 years by 24. We get 41.66 years (41 years and 8 months), or nearly 42 years.

The ten kings or nations, as we have discerned previously, correspond to the "ten toes of iron and clay" in Daniel 2:41-43 (descendants of the Roman Empire commingled with Muslim immigrants and refugees from the Middle East and Africa).

Soviet control over Eastern Europe ended in 1989. In 1990, former Communist nations began withdrawing from the USSR and/or the Warsaw Pact, including ten which later joined the EU (the beast).[23] Will the ten end-time kings come from these nations?

In any case, 42 years from 1990 will end sometime in late 2032.

Revised timetable

To find out the new starting point for the last 7 years, we have to count back from 2032. Seven years prior to 2032 is 2025.

Confirmation of the covenant.

Will the covenant be confirmed again in 2025? Or was the "confirmation" by the UN Security Council in 2011 sufficient? If that is the case, the *"midst of the week"* could come without warning.

"Midst of the week".

Whether or not the covenant is confirmed again in 2025, the *"midst of the week"* or halfway point will be sometime in 2029. Here again are the events we have to watch out for –

Cessation of offerings. Will offerings of any kind be stopped at Temple Mount in Jerusalem in 2029?

Abomination of desolation. Will the devastating "abomination of desolation" be set up in the holy place in 2029?

Nuclear war. Will the global conflagration involving the nuclear powers take place shortly thereafter in 2029?

Great Tribulation. After the nuclear winter and destruction of the ozone layer, will the Great Tribulation begin sometime in 2029?

Interestingly, 2029 will be 14 years from the fourth and last blood moon (September 28, 2015) of the eighth and last "blood moon tetrad" in 2014-2015 (Chapter 1).

The last 1,335 days.

When the abomination of desolation is ultimately set up, the final countdown starts. *"And from the time that the daily sacrifice shall be taken away, and the abomination that maketh desolate set up, there shall be a thousand two hundred and ninety days"* (Dan 12:11).

The second half of the last 7 years will be slightly longer than the first: 1,290 days, not just 1,260. In addition, there will be 45 days more. *"Blessed is he that waiteth, and cometh to the thousand three hundred and five and thirty days"* (Dan 12:12). The climactic events of humankind's history will take place on those last days:

> **Armageddon** (late 2032?).
> **Day of the LORD** (late 2032?).
> **The first resurrection and "rapture"** (late 2032?).
> **The Second Coming** (late 2032?).

Passover lamb. Another hidden prophecy (Ex 12:3,5-6) appears to dovetail into our revised timetable. *"Speak ye unto all the congregation of Israel, saying, In the tenth day of this month they shall take to them every man a lamb, according to the house of their fathers, a lamb for an house... And ye shall keep it up until the fourteenth day of the same month: and the whole assembly of the congregation of Israel shall kill it in the evening."* This may be interpreted as follows:

The 10th day stands for the 10th year from late 2018 – that is, 2028. The *"lamb"* symbolizes Israel. To *"keep it"* means the Jews will be held captive (by the Assyrian Antichrist) *"until the fourteenth day"* (2032), when *"the whole assembly of the congregation"* (nations of the world gathered at Armageddon) *"shall kill it* (destroy Israel) *in the evening"* (late 2032).

The angel in Daniel's vision seems to affirm this. *"And I heard the man clothed in linen, which was upon the waters of the river, when he held up his right hand and his left hand unto heaven, and sware by him that liveth for ever that it shall be for a time, times, and an half; and when he shall have accomplished to scatter the power of the holy people, all these things shall be finished"* (Dan 12:7).

"The wise shall understand."

Daniel, though, was not told everything. *"And I heard, but I understood not: then said I, O my Lord, what shall be the end of these things? And he said, Go thy way, Daniel: for the words are closed up and sealed till the time of the end"* (Dan 12:8-9).

But the angel Gabriel gave his posterity hope. *"But thou, O Daniel, shut up the words, and seal the book, even to the time of the end: many shall run to and fro, and knowledge shall be increased"* (Dan 12:4). We are blessed, for knowledge of the end time has truly increased in our generation.

Moreover, not a few among us will be given much understanding – *"Many shall be purified, and made white, and tried; but the wicked shall do wickedly: and none of the wicked shall understand; but the wise shall understand"* (Dan 12:10).

"Thy kingdom come." Amen!

Timeline of the End

Prophecy	4004BC	2004BC	4 BC	30 AD	1948	1990	1997	2011	2015	2017	2018	2028	2029	2030	2032	2033
6,000 years	Adam created						End									
4,000 years		Abraham born					End									
2,000 years			Christ born				End									
Bible Code (time of end)			¹Christ born	²Christ crucified			¹End							²End		
After 2 'days' (2,000 years)																
Adam's 21 idle years							Start			End	End of 70 years	End of 80 years				
Last generation					Israel/fig tree revives											
Daniel's 70th "week" (last 7 years)								Start; covenant confirmed	~~Abomi-nation; nuclear war; great tribulation~~	Great tribulation cut-short	~~End; Armageddon; 2nd Coming; 1st resurrection~~					
Continue 42 "months" (42 years)														End		
Last "hour" (42 years)						Beast's wound healed; 10 kings w/beast									End	
14-year grace period											Start		Abomi-nation; nuclear war; great tribulation		End; Armageddon; 2nd Coming; 1st resurrection	Millennial kingdom/ "Great Sabbath" begins

Addendum: *END TIME Decoded*, by M.M. Tauson

Appendix "A"

False Christs and Prophets (1st-19th Centuries)

Dositheos the Samaritan (mid-1st century), one of the supposed founders of Manichaeism (conflict between good and evil, spirit and matter), tried to persuade the Samaritans that he was the Messiah, applying Deuteronomy 18:15 (rise of a new prophet) to himself and comparing himself to Theudas and Judas the Galilean (both Jewish rebel leaders).

Simon bar Kokhba (died 135) founded a short-lived Jewish state, but was defeated in the Second Jewish-Roman War.

Moses of Crete (circa 440-470) persuaded the Jews of Crete to walk into the sea, as Moses had done, to return to Israel; vanished after the disastrous results.

Ishak ben Ya'kub Obadiah Abu 'Isa al-Isfahani (684-705) led a revolt in Persia against the Umayyad Caliph 'Abd al-Malik ibn Marwan.

Yudghan was a disciple of Abu 'Isa who continued the faith after Isa was killed.

Tanchelm of Antwerp (c. 1110) violently opposed the Catholic sacraments and the Eucharist.

David Alroy of Kurdistan (c. 1160) agitated against the caliph and was assassinated.

Nissim ben Abraham (c. 1295).

Moses Botarel of Cisneros (c. 1413) claimed to be a sorcerer able to combine the names of God.

Asher Lammlein (c.1502), a German who lived near Venice, proclaimed himself a forerunner of the Messiah.

Solomon Molcho (1500-1532), a messianic adventurer in Portugal, Italy and Turkey, and a baptized Catholic, was tried by the Inquisition, convicted of apostasy, and burned at the stake.

David Reubeni (1490-1541) was the companion of Molcho.

An unnamed Czech Jew (1650s).

Sabbatai Zevi (1626-1676), an Ottoman Jew, claimed to be the Messiah, but converted to Islam; still has followers today in the Donmeh (Turkish sect of Jewish converts to Islam he founded in Salonika).

Jacob Querido (d. 1690) claimed to be the incarnation of Sabbatai, but later also converted to Islam and led the Donmeh.

Miguel Cardoso (1630-1706), another successor of Sabbatai, claimed to be the "Messiah ben Ephraim".

Lobele Prossnitz (d. 1750) attracted some following from the disciples of Sabbatai; called himself the "Messiah ben Joseph."

Ann Lee (1736-1784), a central figure among the Shakers, thought she "embodied all the perfections of God" in female form; claimed to be Christ's female counterpart in 1772.

Jacob Joseph Frank (1726-1791) said he was the reincarnation of King David; preached a synthesis of Christianity and Judaism.

Bernhard Muller (1799-1834) claimed to be the "Lion of Judah" and a prophet in possession of the Philosopher's Stone. .

John Nichols Thom (1799-1838) was a Cornish tax rebel.

Hong Xiuquan (1814-1864) was a Hakka Chinese who said he was the younger brother of Jesus Christ; he started the Taiping Rebellion and founded the Heavenly Kingdom of Great Peace; committed suicide before the fall of Tianjing (Nanjing) in 1864.

Mirza Husayn Ali Nuri, Baha'u'llah (1817-1864) was born a Shiite, but adopted Babism later in life; claimed to be the promised one of all religions and founded the Baha'i Faith.

Arnold Potter (1804-1872) was a Latter-Day Saints schismatic leader who called himself "Potter Christ".

Jacobina Mentz Maurer (1842-1874), was a German-Brazilian woman in Rio Grande do Sul who emerged as a messianic prophetess and a representation of God; declared the reincarnation of Jesus Christ by her German-speaking community; shot to death with many of her followers by the Brazilian Imperial Army.

Appendix "B"

Famous Wars (since A.D. 43)

A.D. 1 – 1000

43 - 96	Roman conquest of Britain
60 - 61	Boudica's Uprising
66 - 70	Jewish Uprising
132 - 135	Bar Kokhba Rebellion
184 - 205	Yellow Turban Rebellion
533 - 534	Vandal War
772 - 804	Saxon Wars

1001 - 1200

1066 -1088	Norman conquest of England
1096 - 1099	First Crusade
1145 - 1149	Second Crusade
1189 - 1192	Third Crusade

1201 - 1300

1202 - 1204	Fourth Crusade
1206 - 1324	Mongol wars and conquests
1213 - 1221	Fifth Crusade
1215 - 1217	First Barons' War (England)
1248 - 1254	Seventh Crusade
1270	Eighth Crusade
1271 - 1272	Ninth Crusade
1296 - 1328	First War of Scottish Independence

1301 – 1400

1323 - 1328	Peasant revolt in Flanders
1326 - 1332	Polish-Teutonic War
1337 - 1453	Hundred Years' War

1401 - 1500

1419 - 1434	Hussite Wars
1425 - 1454	Wars in Lombardy
1454 - 1466	Thirteen Years' War
1455 - 1485	Wars of the Roses

1501 - 1600

1509 - 1512	Ottoman Civil War
1519 - 1521	Spanish conquest of the Aztec Empire
1529 - 1532	Inca Civil War
1531 - 1532	Spanish conquest of the Inca Empire
1537 - 1548	Conquistador Civil War in Peru

1563 - 1564	Russo-Swedish War
1568 - 1648	Burmese-Siamese War
1570 - 1573	Eighty Years' War
1571	Ottoman-Venetian War
1554 - 1557	Russo-Crimean War

1601 - 1700

1600 - 1611	Polish-Swedish War
1602 - 1661	Dutch-Portuguese War
1618 - 1648	Thirty Years' War
1634 - 1638	Pequot War
1635 - 1659	Franco-Spanish War
1640 - 1701	Beaver Wars (Iroquois)
1642 - 1646	First English Civil War
1648 - 1649	Second English Civil War
1649 - 1651	Third English Civil War
1652 - 1654	First Anglo-Dutch War
1654 - 1660	Anglo-Spanish War
1655	Peach Tree War (Susquehannock)
1675 - 1676	King Philip's War
1683 - 1699	Great Turkish War
1688 - 1697	Nine Years' War, incl. King William's War
1689 - 1692	Jacobean Rising in Scotland
1700 - 1721	Great Northern War

1701 - 1800

1711 - 1715	Tuscarora War
1712 - 1716	First Fox War
1715 - 1717	Yamasee War
1721 - 1763	Chickasaw Wars
1728 - 1733	Second Fox War
1739 - 1748	War of Jenkins' Ear
1744 - 1748	King George's War
1754 - 1763	French and Indian War (Seven Years War)
1756 - 1763	Seven Years' War
1758 - 1761	Anglo-Cherokee War
1763 - 1766	Pontiac's War
1775 - 1783	American Revolutionary War
1776 - 1794	Chickamauga Wars
1779 - 1783	Anglo-Spanish War
1785 - 1795	Northwest Indian War
1789 - 1799	The French Revolution
1791 - 1804	Haitian Revolution

1801 - 1900

1803 - 1815	Napoleonic Wars
1804 - 1813	Russo-Persian War
1808 - 1810	Rum Rebellion
1808 - 1833	Spanish American wars of independence
1810 - 1821	Mexican War of Independence
1812 - 1815	War of 1812
1813 - 1814	Creek War
1817 - 1858	Seminole Wars
1818 - 1828	Zulu Wars of Conquest
1820 - 1875	Texas-Indian wars
1821 - 1832	Greek War of Independence
1821 - 1848	Comanche-Mexico War
1825 - 1830	Java War
1827	Winnebago War
1832	Black Hawk War
1835 - 1836	Texas Revolution
1839 - 1842	First Opium War
1846 - 1864	Navajo Wars
1846 - 1848	Mexican-American War
1849 - 1924	Apache Wars
1850 - 1865	California Indian Wars
1853 - 1856	Crimean War
1861 - 1865	American Civil War
1864 - 1868	Snake War
1866 - 1868	Red Cloud's War
1867 - 1875	Comanche Campaign
1876 - 1877	Great Sioux War (Black Hills War)
1877	Nez Perce War
1878 - 1879	Cheyenne War
1879	Sheepeater Indian War
1879 - 1880	Victorio's War
1896-- 1899	Philippine Revolution
1898	Spanish-American War
1899 - 1901	Boxer Rebellion
1899 - 1902	Filipino-American War
1899 - 1902	Second Boer War

1901 - 2000

1905	Russian Revolution
1910 - 1921	Mexican Revolution
1914 - 1918	World War I
1917 - 1923	Russian Civil War

1919 - 1923	Turkish War of Independence
1919 - 1921	Irish War of Independence
1927 - 1949	Chinese Civil War
1936 - 1939	Spanish Civil War
1939 - 1945	World War II
1946 - 1949	Greek Civil War
1948 - 1949	Arab-Israeli War
1950 - 1953	Korean War
1952 - 1960	Mau Mau Uprising
1953 - 1959	Cuban Revolution
1954 - 1962	Algerian War
1955 - 1975	Vietnam War
1961	Bay of Pigs Invasion
1979 - 1989	Soviet war in Afghanistan
1980 - 1988	Iran-Iraq War
1982	Falklands War
1990 - 1991	Gulf War
1991 - 1995	Croatian War of Independence
1992 - 1995	Bosnian War
1998 - 1999	Kosovo War
1998 - 2003	Second Congo War

2001 - to date

2001 - to date	War in Afghanistan
2003 - 2008	Sudan, Darfur conflict
2003 - 2011	Iraq War
2006 - 2009	War in Somalia
2008 - 2009	Gaza War
2009 - to date	War in Somalia
2009 - to date	Nigeria, Boko Haram insurgency
2011 - to date	South Sudanese Civil War
2011 - to date	Yemeni Civil War
2012 - to date	Central African Republic conflict
2013 - to date	Syrian Civil War, ISIS conflict
2013 - to date	Iraq-ISIS conflict
2014	Israel–Gaza conflict
2014 - to date	Ukraine conflict
2014 - to date	Iraq War
2014 - to date	Turkey–ISIS conflict
2014 - to date	Libyan Civil War
2014 - to date	Boko Haram insurgency in Cameroon
2015 - to date	Tunisia: ISIS insurgency
2015 - to date	Kurdish-Turkish conflict
2017 - to date	Third Iraqi-Kurdish War
2017	Philippines, Maute Group-ISIS insurgency

Appendix "C"

Famines in History (since A.D. 400)

400-800 A.D., Western Europe. Various famines related to the Fall of the Western Roman Empire and its sack by Alaric I; population of Rome fell by over 90%, mainly because of famine and the plague.
639, Arabia. Famine during the caliphate of Umar ibn al-Khattab.
750s, Spain. Food shortages.
800-1000, Central America. Severe droughts killed millions of Mayans by hunger and thirst; led to a series of internal collapses that destroyed their civilization.
809, Frankish Empire. Food shortages.
875-884, China. Famine sparked peasant rebellion; capture of the capital by Huang Chao.
927-928, Byzantine Empire. Famine caused by four months of frost.
1005, England. Food shortages.
1016, Europe. Continent-wide food shortages.
1051, Mexico. Famine forced the Toltecs to migrate from stricken region in what is now central Mexico.
1064-1072, Egypt. Seven-year famine killed around 40,000 people.
1097, France. Famine and plague caused death of about 100,000.
1229-1232, Japan. Kangi Famine, possibly the worst famine in Japan's history, was caused by volcanic eruptions.
1230, Russia. Famine in the state of Velikiy, Novgorod.
1235, England. Famine killed 20,000 people in London alone.
1255, Portugal. Food shortages.
1275-1299, North America. Famine caused the collapse of the Anasazi civilization.
1315-1317, Europe. Called the Great Famine of 1315-1317.
1333-1337, China. Food shortages.
1344-1345, India. Famine under the regime of Muhammad bin Tughluq.
1387, Anatolia. Severe famine afflicted the region after Timur the Lame left Asia Minor.
1396-1407, India. Calamity was called the Durga Devi Famine.
1441, Mexico. Famine in Mayapan.
1450-1454, Mexico. Famine in the Aztec Empire; interpreted as a call by the gods for sacrifices.
1460-1461, Japan. Disaster was known as the Kansho Famine.
1504, Spain. Food shortages.

1518, Italy. Famine took place in and around Venice.
1528, France. The famine occurred mainly in Languedoc.
1535, Ethiopia. Widespread food shortages.
1567-1570, Ethiopia. Famine in Harar, accompanied by plague, killed even the Emir of Harar himself.
1586, England. Famine gave rise to the Poor Law system.
1601-1603, Russia. One of the worst famines in Russian history; killed as many as 100,000 in Moscow and up to one-third of Tsar Godunov's subjects; also killed about half of the Estonian population; total of about 2 million people died.
1618-1648, Europe. Famine was an offshoot of the protracted Thirty Years' War.
1619, Japan. Of 154 famines during the Tokugawa period, 21 were widespread and serious; the worst was in 1619.
1630-1632, India. Called the Deccan Famine of 1630-1632.
1630-1632, northwestern China. Famine eventually caused the Ming dynasty to collapse in 1644.
1648-1660, Poland. Country lost an estimated one-third of its population due to wars, famine, and plague.
1649, England. Famine in northern England.
1650-1652, France. Famine in the east of France.
1651-1653, Ireland. Famine afflicted much of Ireland during Cromwell's conquest of Ireland.
1661, India. Famine was caused by lack of rainfall for two years.
1670s-1680s, Spain. Plague and famines struck the country.
1680, Italy. Famine in Sardinia killed 80,000 people.
1680s, Sahel, Africa. Food shortages.
1690s, Scotland. Famine throughout the country killed 5-15% of the population.
1693-1694, France. Some two million people died in the famine.
1695-1697, Swedish Empire, dominions of Estonia and Livonia. Called the Great Famine of Estonia; killed about a fifth of the Estonian and Livonian population (70,000–75,000 people); also hit Sweden, where 150,000-175,000 people died.
1696-1697, Finland (and part of Sweden). Called the Great Famine of Finland; wiped out almost one-third of the population.
1702–1704, India. Famine in Deccan; killed 2 million people.
1708-1711, East Prussia. Famine killed about 250,000 people or 41% of the population.
1709-1710, France. Food shortages.
1722, Arabia. Food shortages.

1727-1728, England. Famine struck in the English Midlands.
1738–1756, West Africa. About one-half the population of Timbuktu died of starvation.
1740-1741, Ireland. Calamity was called the Great Irish Famine.
1750-1756, Senegambia. Famine in the Senegambia region of West Africa.
1764, Italy. Famine centered around the city of Naples.
1769-1773, India and Bangladesh. Called the Great Bengal Famine of 1770; killed about 10 million people (one-third of the population).
1770-1771, Czech lands. Famine killed hundreds of thousands of people.
1771-1772, Germany. Famine in Saxony and southern Germany.
1773, Sweden. Food shortages.
1779, Morocco. The famine was centered in Rabat.
1780s, Japan. Called the Great Tenmei Famine; death toll estimates ranged from 20,000 to 920,000 people dead.
1783, Iceland. Famine caused by the Laki volcanic eruption; killed one-fifth of Iceland's population.
1783–1784, India. So-called Chalisa Famine killed around 11 million people.
1784, Egypt. Widespread famine throughout Egypt.
1784-1785, Tunisia. Famine killed up to one-fifth of all Tunisians.
1788, France. Famine stemmed from poor harvests and harsh winters, possibly caused by a strong El Niño cycle or by the 1783 Laki volcanic eruption in Iceland.
1789, Ethiopia. Famine afflicted the Amhara/Tigray north.
1789-1792, India. Called the Doji bara famine or Skull Famine; killed around 11 million people.
1810-1811, 1846, and 1849, China. Four famines ravaged the country, and about 45 million people died.
1811-1812, Spain. Famine devastated Madrid; 20,000 people died.
1815, Indonesia. After the eruption of Tambora Volcano, tens of thousands of people died in the subsequent famine.
1816-1817, Europe. In the "Year Without a Summer," around 65,000 people died of hunger.
1830-1833, Cape Verde. Famine killed some 30,000 people or 42% of the population.
1830s, Japan. The severe lack of food was called the Tenpo Famine.
1837-1838, India. In the so-called Agra Famine, about 1 million people died.
1845-1853, Ireland. Called the Great Famine, it killed more than 1.5 million people, with over 2 million others emigrating.

1845-1857, Scotland. The disaster was called the Highland Potato Famine.

1846, Portugal. The famine in northern Portugal led to the peasant revolt known as "Maria da Fonte".

1849-1850, Indonesia. The famine in Demak and Grobogan in Central Java was caused by four successive crop failures due to drought; some 83,000 people died.

1850-1873, China. As a result of the Taiping Rebellion, drought, and famine, the population of China dropped by more than 60 million – the number of those who died.

1860-1861, India. In what was known as the Upper Doab Famine, some 2 million people died.

1866, India. It was called the Orissa Famine, in which 1 million died.

1866-1868, Finland (and northern Sweden). In this Finnish famine, over 150,000 or 15% of the entire population perished.

1869, India. In the so-called Rajputana Famine, 1.5 million died.

1870-1871, Iran. Famine in Persia; around 2 million people died.

1873-1874, Turkey. The famine in Anatolia was caused by drought and floods.

1873-1874, India. The deadly event was called the Bihar Famine.

1876-1879, India, China, Brazil, North Africa (and other countries). The famine in northern China killed about 13 million; in India, around 5.25 million died in the Great Famine of 1876–1878; for a total of some 18.25 million in two countries alone. British policies were said to have been responsible for the deaths in India and China.

1878-1880, United States. Famine in St. Lawrence Island, Alaska.

1879, Ireland. The famine was caused by food shortages, but unlike in previous famines, the mortality was low.

1888-1889, India. Famine in Orissa, Ganjam, and northern Bihar.

1888-1892, Ethiopia. In the Ethiopian Great Famine, about one-third of the population died; conditions worsened with a major smallpox epidemic (1889-1890), cholera outbreaks (1889-1892), and a typhus epidemic.

1891-1892, Russia. Some 375,000-500,000 people died of hunger.

1896-1897, China. Famine in northern China led in part to the Boxer Rebellion.

1896-1902, India. Series of famines due to British policies killed some 6 million in the British Territories; mortality unknown in the Princely States.

1907, 1911; China. Famines in east-central China; 25 million+ died.

1914-1918, Lebanon. The Mount Lebanon Famine during World War I was caused by an Ottoman Turk blockade of food shipments; killed up to 450,000 Maronite Christians, about a third of the Lebanese population.

1916-1917, Germany. The famine was brought about by the British blockade of Germany in World War I.

1916-1917, Russia. Winter conditions caused the famine.

1917-1919, Iran. Famine in Persia; as much as one-fourth of the population living in the north of the country died.

1917-1921, Turkestan. A series of famines at the time of the Bolshevik Revolution killed about one-sixth of the population.

1918-1919, Rwanda and **Burundi.** The Rumanura Famine spurred large-scale migrations to the Congo.

1921, Russia. In this Russian famine, around 5 million people died.

1921-1922, Russia. Famine wrought havoc in Tatarstan.

1924-1925, Russia. Famine in the Volga German colonies; one-third of the entire population perished.

1928-1929, Rwanda and **Burundi.** The new famine set off large-scale migrations once more to the Congo.

1929-1930, China. Famine in northern China caused by heavy rains and flooding, resulting in over 2 million deaths.

1932-1933, Soviet Union and **the Ukraine.** The famine killed 7-10 million in the Ukraine, millions more in Russia.

1936, China. Around 5 million people died in the famine.

1940-1945, Poland. Famine in the Warsaw Ghetto, as well as in other ghettos and concentration camps (the result of deliberate denial of food to ghetto residents on the part of the Nazis).

1941-1944, Russia. Leningrad famine caused by a 900-day blockade by German troops; about one million residents starved, froze, or were bombed to death in the winter of 1941-1942, when supply routes to the city were cut off and the temperature dropped to -40°C.

1941-1944, Greece. Famine caused by the Axis occupation; some 300,000 people died.

1942-1943, China. The famine in Henan killed 3-5 million persons.

1943, India. The famine in Bengal wiped out 1.5-7 million people.

1943, Rwanda and **Burundi.** The famine again drove many local people to migrate to the Congo.

1943, Vietnam. During the Vietnamese Famine, 400,000–2 million people died.

1944, Netherlands. This Dutch famine during World War II took the lives of some 20,000-30,000 people.

1944, Rwanda. Food shortages.
1944-45, Indonesia. Famine in Java during World War II; around 2.4 million people died.
1947, Soviet Union. The Soviet Famine left 1-1.5 million dead.
1958, Ethiopia. Famine in Tigray; around 100,000 people died.
1958-1962, China. In the so-called Great Chinese Famine, an estimated 15–43 million individuals died.
1966-1967, Indonesia. Lombok Island famine caused by drought, exacerbated by restrictions on regional rice trade; about 50,000 died.
1967-1970, Biafra. Famine caused by the food blockade enforced by Nigerian government; about a million people died.
1968-1972, Mauritania, Mali, Chad, Niger, Burkina Faso. Sahel drought resulted in a famine that killed some 1 million people.
1972-1973, Ethiopia. Famine in Ethiopia caused by drought and poor governance; government failure to handle the crisis led to the fall of Emperor Haile Selassie and Derg rule; around 60,000 people died.
1974, Bangladesh. The famine due to floods killed some 1 million.
1975-1979, Cambodia. Under the Khmer Rouge, about 2 million people lost their lives to mass murder, forced labor and famine.
1980-1981, Uganda. Famine caused by drought and armed conflict; about 30,000 people died.
1984-1985, Ethiopia. Food shortages.
1991-1992, Somalia. Famine caused by drought and civil war; around 300,000 people died.
1994-1998, North Korea. Scholars estimate some 600,000 died of starvation (other estimates range from 200,000 to 3.5 million).
1998, Sudan. The famine was caused by war and drought; about 70,000 people died.
1998-2000, Ethiopia. The famine was made worse by the Eritrean-Ethiopian War.
1998–2004, Democratic Republic of the Congo. In the Second Congo War, about 3.8 million people died of starvation and disease.
2011-2012, Somalia. The famine was brought on by the 2011 East African drought.
2012; Senegal, Gambia, Niger, Mauritania, Mali, Burkina Faso. This widespread famine in West Africa was ushered in by the Sahel drought that year.
2017, South Sudan. Food shortages.
2017, Yemen. Food shortages.
2017, Somalia. Food shortages.
2017, Nigeria. Food shortages.

Appendix "D"

Strongest Storms (since early 20th century)

North Atlantic Ocean

"Cuba"	1924	270 km/h (165 mph)
"Bahamas"	1929	250 km/h (155 mph)
"Cuba"	1932	280 km/h (175 mph)
"Labor Day"	1935	295 km/h (185 mph)
Janet	1955	280 km/h (175 mph)
Hattie	1961	260 km/h (160 mph)
Camille	1969	280 km/h (175 mph)
David	1979	280 km/h (175 mph)
Allen	1980	305 km/h (190 mph)
Gloria	1985	230 km/h (145 mph)
Gilbert	1988	295 km/h (185 mph)
Hugo	1989	260 km/h (160 mph)
Andrew	1992	280 km/h (175 mph)
Opal	1995	240 km/h (150 mph)
Mitch	1998	285 km/h (180 mph)
Floyd	1999	250 km/h (155 mph)
Isabel	2003	270 km/h (165 mph)
Ivan	2004	270 km/h (165 mph)
Katrina	2005	280 km/h (175 mph)
Rita	2005	285 km/h (180 mph)
Wilma	2005	295 km/h (185 mph)
Dean	2007	280 km/h (175 mph)
Igor	2010	250 km/h (155 mph)
Irma	2017	295 km/h (185 mph)
Maria	2017	280 km/h (175 mph)

Eastern Pacific Ocean

Ava	1973	260 km/h (160 mph)
Gilma	1994	260 km/h (160 mph)
Guillermo	1997	260 km/h (160 mph)
Linda	1997	295 km/h (185 mph)
Elida	2002	260 km/h (160 mph)
Hernan	2002	260 km/h (160 mph)
Kenna	2002	270 km/h (165 mph)
Ioke	2006	260 km/h (160 mph)
Rick	2009	285 km/h (180 mph)

Celia	2010	260 km/h (160 mph)
Marie	2014	260 km/h (160 mph)
Odile	2014	220 km/h (140 mph)
Patricia	2015	345 km/h (215 mph)

North Western Pacific Ocean

Rita	1978	220 km/h (140 mph)
Hope	1979	205 km/h (125 mph)
Tip	1979	260 km/h (160 mph)
Wynne	1980	220 km/h (140 mph)
Elsie	1981	220 km/h (140 mph)
Bess	1982	230 km/h (145 mph)
Mac	1982	220 km/h (140 mph)
Abby	1983	220 km/h (140 mph)
Forrest	1983	205 km/h (125 mph)
Marge	1983	205 km/h (125 mph)
Vanessa	1984	220 km/h (140 mph)
Dot	1985	220 km/h (140 mph)
Peggy	1986	205 km/h (125 mph)
Betty	1987	205 km/h (125 mph)
Holly	1987	205 km/h (125 mph)
Flo	1990	220 km/h (140 mph)
Ruth	1991	215 km/h (130 mph)
Yuri	1991	220 km/h (140 mph)
Gay	1992	205 km/h (125 mph)
Zeb	1998	205 km/h (125 mph)
Megi	2010	230 km/h (145 mph)
Sanba	2012	205 km/h (125 mph)
Haiyan	2013	230 km/h (145 mph)
Vongfong	2014	215 km/h (130 mph)
Soudelor	2015	215 km/h (130 mph)
Nepartak	2016	205 km/h (125 mph)
Meranti	2016	220 km/h (140 mph)
Haima	2016	215 km/h (130 mph)

North Indian Ocean

Two	1963	195km/h (120 mph)
Three	1963	240 km/h (150 mph)
Andhra Pradesh	1977	205 km/h (125 mph)
Gay	1989	230 km/h (145 mph)
Andhra Pradesh	1990	230 km/h (145 mph)

Bangladesh	1991	240 km/h (150 mph)
BOB 02	1994	215 km/h (135 mph)
Pakistan	1999	195 km/h (120 mph)
"Paradip"	1999	260 km/h (160 mph)
India	2001	215 km/h (135 mph)
Gonu	2007	240 km/h (150 mph)
Sidr	2007	215 km/h (135 mph)
Giri	2010	195 km/h (120 mph)
Phailin	2013	215 km/h (130 mph)
Hudhud	2014	185 km/h (115 mph)
Nilofar	2014	205 km/h (125 mph)
Chapala	2015	215 km/h (130 mph)

South-West Indian Ocean

Chris-Damia	1981-82	210 km/h (130 mph)
Geralda	1993-94	200 km/h (125 mph)
Litanne	1993-94	190 km/h (120 mph)
Marlene	1994-95	180 km/h (110 mph)
Bonita	1995-96	180 km/h (110 mph)
Daniella	1996-97	190 km/h (120 mph)
Hudah	1999-2000	220 km/h (135 mph)
Dina	2001-02	215 km/h (135 mph)
Guillaume	2001-02	205 km/h (125 mph)
Hary	2001-02	220 km/h (135 mph)
Kalunde	2002-03	215 km/h (135 mph)
Gafilo	2003-04	230 km/h (145 mph)
Adeline-Juliet	2004-05	220 km/h (135 mph)
Bento	2004-05	215 km/h (135 mph)
Carina	2005-06	205 km/h (125 mph)
Hondo	2007-08	215 km/h (135 mph)
Edzani	2009-10	220 km/h (135 mph)
Bruce	2013-14	220 km/h (135 mph)
Hellen	2013-14	230 km/h (145 mph)
Bansi	2014-15	220 km/h (135 mph)
Eunice	2014-15	230 km/h (145 mph)
Fantala	2015-16	250 km/h (155 mph)

Australian Region

Mahina	1899	205 km/h (125 mph)
Joan	1975-76	230 km/h (145 mph)
Amy	1979-80	230 km/h (145 mph)

Orson	1988-89	250 km/h (155 mph)
Graham	1991-92	230 km/h (145 mph)
Theodore	1993-94	200 km/h (125 mph)
Vance	1998-99	215 km/h (135 mph)
Gwenda	1998-99	220 km/h (140 mph)
Inigo	2002-03	240 km/h (150 mph)
Fay	2003-04	215 km/h (130 mph)
Floyd	2005-06	195 km/h (120 mph)
Glenda	2005-06	205 km/h (125 mph)
Monica	2005-06	250 km/h (155 mph)
George	2006-07	205 km/h (125 mph)
Ita	2013-14	220 km/h (140 mph)
Ernie	2016-17	220 km/h (140 mph)

South Pacific Ocean

Oscar	1982-83	205 km/h (125 mph)
Hina	1984-85	220 km/h (135 mph)
Fran	1991-92	205 km/h (125 mph)
Ron	1997-98	230 km/h (145 mph)
Susan	1997-98	230 km/h (145 mph)
Beni	2002-03	205 km/h (125 mph)
Dovi	2002-03	205 km/h (125 mph)
Erica	2002-03	215 km/h (130 mph)
Zoe	2002-03	240 km/h (150 mph)
Heta	2003-04	215 km/h (130 mph)
Meena	2004-05	215 km/h (130 mph)
Olaf	2004-05	215 km/h (130 mph)
Percy	2004-05	230 km/h (145 mph)
Ului	2009-10	215 km/h (130 mph)
Pam	2014-15	250 km/h (155 mph)
Winston	2015-16	230 km/h (145 mph)

South Atlantic Ocean
(No cyclones above 100 km/h [65 mph] on record.)

Appendix "E"

Deadliest Floods on Record

Year	Location	Cause	Deaths
1099	Netherlands, England	High tides and storms	c. 100,000
1287	Netherlands	Storm broke a dike	50,000-80.000
1421	Netherlands	North Sea storm broke dikes	1,000-10,000
1642	Kaifeng, China	Army and peasant rebels diverted Yellow River	c. 300,000
1824	Neva River, Russia	Baltic Sea cyclone raised Neva River delta level	1,000-10,000
1887	Huang He River, China	Swollen river broke Yellow River dikes	900,000-2,000,000
1931	Huang He River, China	Series of floods from overflowing Yellow River	1,000,000-3,700,000
1931	Yangtze River, China	Heavy rains	c. 145,000
1938	Huang He River, China	Army dammed Yellow River to halt Japanese	500,000 - 900,000
1975	Ru River, China	Heavy rains, typhoon collapsed Banqiao Dam	90,000 - 230,000
2000	Mozambique	Heavy rains, cyclone	1,000s
2013	Uttarakhand, India	Heavy rainfall	5,700

Appendix "F"

Worst Landslides, Mudflows, Avalanches in History

Year	Location	Deaths	Notes
1248	Mont Granier, France	>1,000	landslide razed 5 villages
1618	Chiavenna Valley, Italy	2,240	rockslide from Monte Conto
1806	Goldau Valley, Switzerland	457	landslide caused tsunami in Lake Lauerz
1914	Neuquén and Mendoza, Argentina	190 -300	300-km debris flow ruined 2 towns in 60-km valley
1919	Kelud, East Java, Indonesia	5,110	185-km lahar flow destroyed 104 villages
1920	Haiyuan County, Ningxia, China	c.100,000	loess flows, landslides over 50,000 km^2 buried villages
1920	Rio Huitzilapan; Veracruz, Mexico	600-870	debris flows destroyed Barranca Grande
1921	Alma-Atinka River, Almaty, Kazakhstan	c. 500	40-km debris flow wrecked town of Alma-Ata
1933	Diexi, Mao County, Sichuan, China	c. 3,100	earthquake formed 255-m dam on Min River
1938	Kwansai, Hyogo Prefecture, Japan	c. 1,000	Mount Rokko landslides wrecked 130,000 homes
1941	Huaraz, Ancash, Peru	4,000-6,000	debris flow dammed Santa River, flooded valley
1948	Assam, India	c. 500	Guwahati landslide triggered by heavy rain
1949	Gharm Oblast, Tajikistan	c. 7,200	Khait and Yasman valley landslides; by earthquake
1953	Wakayama Prefecture, Japan	1,046	Arid-Kawa valley landslides due to typhoon
1953	Minamiyamashiro, Soraku, Kyoto, Japan	336	landslides destroyed 5,122 homes
1954	Salerno, Amalfi Coast, Italy	c. 300	landslides and debris flows; by 16-hour, 504-mm rain
1958	Shizuoka Prefecture, Japan	1,094	Kanogawa landslides destroyed 19,754 homes
1962	Ranrahirca, Peru	4,000 - 5,000	Nevado Huascaran debris avalanche of ice and rock
1963	Longarone, Italy	c. 2,000	Vajont landslide; by rains and drawdown of dam
1965	El Cobre, Chile	>200	landslide from 7.1 earthquake destroyed town

Year	Location	Deaths	Notes
1968	Darjeeling, India	1,000s	500-1,000-mm rain triggered many landslides
1970	Yungay, Peru	>22,000	Nevado Huascaran debris avalanche buried Yungay
1971	Chungar, Peru	400-600	avalanche and tsunami in Yanawayin Lake
1974	Junín Region, Peru	c. 450	Mayunmarca landslide dammed Río Mantaro.
1985	Armero, Tolima Department, Colombia	c. 23,000	Nevado del Ruiz eruption buried town of Armero
1999	Vargas, Venezuela	c. 30,000	landslide due to storm and 911 mm rain in a few days
2006	Southern Leyte, Philippines	1,126	rock-debris slide triggered by 10 days of heavy rain
2009	Xiaolin, Kaohsiung County, Taiwan	439-600	caused by Typhoon Morakot
2010	Bududa District, Uganda	100-300	due to heavy rains; landslide on Mt. Elgon slope
2010	Gansu, China	c. 1,700	mudslide due to heavy rains
2013	Kedarnath, Uttarakhand, India	5,700	landslides caused by monsoon rains
2014	Argo, Badakhshan Province, Afghanistan	350-2,700	mudslides buried around 300 houses

Appendix "G"

Deadliest* Tsunamis in History

Year	Location	Cause	Deaths
1293	Kamakura, Japan	7.1 earthquake	c. 23,000
1498	EnshunadaSea, Japan	8.3 earthquake	c. 31,000
1586	Ise Bay, Japan	8.2 earthquake	c. 8,000
1605	Nankai, Japan	8.1 earthquake	c. 5,000
1607	Bristol Channel, Great Britain	Earthquake off Irish coast?	>2,000
1707	Nankaido, Japan	8.4 earthquake	c. 30,000
1741	Oshima, Japan	Volcanic eruption	1,467
1755	Lisbon, Portugal	8.5 earthquake	c. 60,000
1771	Ryukyu, Japan	7.4 earthquake	c. 12,000
1783	Calabria, Italy	Earthquake	c. 1,500
1792	Kyushu, Japan	Volcanic eruption	c. 15,000
1854	Nankai, Tokai, and Kyushu, Japan	8.4 and 7.4 earthquakes	1,443
1855	Edo, Japan	Earthquake	>45,000
1868	Arica, Chile	8.5 earthquake	c. 70,000
1877	Iquique, Chile	8.5 earthquake	2,541
1883	Krakatau, Indonesia	KrakatauVolcano	c. 40,000
1896	Nankaido, Japan	8.4 earthquake	c. 30,000
1908	Messina, Italy	Earthquake	c. 123,000
1933	Sanriku, Japan	8.1 earthquake	3,068
1944	Tonankai, Japan	8.0 earthquake	1,223
1946	Nankai, Japan	8.4 earthquake	>1,400
1952	Kuril Islands, USSR	9.0 earthquake	2,336
1960	Chile-Peru coast	9.5 earthquake	c. 6,000
1963	Vajont Dam, Italy	Landslide	1,909
1976	Moro Gulf, Philippines	7.9 earthquake	c. 8,000
1998	Papua New Guinea	7.1 earthquake	>2,100
2004	Sumatra, Indonesia	9.1 earthquake	>230,000
2011	Pacific coast, Japan	9.0 earthquake	c. 18,550

*(Only those with 1,000 or more fatalities listed)

Appendix "H"

Major Volcanic Eruptions
(1st-19th centuries)

Year	Volcano	Location	Deaths
79 AD	Mt. Vesuvius	Italy	c. 18,000
1586	Mt. Kelut	Indonesia	c. 10,000
1600	Huaynaputina	Peru	>1,500
1630	Furnas	Portugal	192
1631	Mt. Vesuvius	Italy	c. 3,360
c.1700	Tseax Cone	Canada	c. 2,000
1783	Mt. Asama	Japan	1,151
1783	Laki (Grimsvotn)	Iceland	c. 9,350
1792	Mt. Unzen	Japan	c. 15,000
1814	Mayon Volcano	Philippines	c. 1,300
1815	Mt. Tambora	Indonesia	c. 102,000
1822	Mt. Galunggung	Indonesia	c. 4,000
1877	Cotopaxi	Ecuador	c. 1,000
1883	Krakatau	Indonesia	c. 36,000
1886	Mt. Tarawera	NewZealand	c. 150
1897	Mayon Volcano	Philippines	1,335

Major Volcanic Eruptions
(since early 20th century)

Year	Volcano	Location	Deaths
1902	Torishima	Japan	c. 150
1902	Soufriere	St. Vincent	. 1,680
1902	Santa Maria	Guatemala	c. 6,000
1902	Mt. Pelee	Martinique	c. 33,000
1911	Taal Volcano	Philippines	1,335
1919	Mt. Kelut	Indonesia	5,115
1930	Mt. Merapi	Indonesia	1,369
1951	Mt. Lamington	Papua New Guinea	2,942
1953	Mt. Ruapehu	NewZealand	152
1963	Mt. Agung	Indonesia	1,584
1968	Volcan Arenal	Costa Rica	87
1980	Mount St. Helens	USA	57
1982	El Chichon	Mexico	c. 3,500
1985	Nevado del Ruiz	Colombia	c. 23,000
1991	Mt. Unzen	Japan	43
1991	Mt. Pinatubo	Philippines	847
1993	Galeras	Colombia	9
1997	Soufriere Hills	Montserrat	19
2002	Nyiragongo	D.R. Congo	245
2010	Mt. Merapi	Indonesia	353
2011	Nabro Volcano	Eritrea	31
2014	Sinabung	Indonesia	15
2014	Mt. Ontake	Japan	57

Appendix "I"

Most Destructive Tornadoes

Date	Area	Country	Deaths
1551-09-23	Grand Harbour at Valletta	Malta	c. 600
1838-04-08	Calcutta	India	215
1840-05-06	Natchez, MS	USA	317
1851 Dec.	Sicily	Italy	c. 500
1896-05-27	St. Louis & East St. Louis	USA	255
1899-06-12	New Richmond, WI	USA	117
1902-05-18	Goliad, TX	USA	114
1908-04-24	Amite, LA, and Purvis, MS	USA	143
1908-04-24	Naria, Zajira, and Bhederganj	Bangladesh	141
1908-04-24	Dhaka	Bangladesh	118
1913-03-23	Omaha, NE	USA	103
1917-05-26	Mattoon and Charleston, IL	USA	101
1925-03-18	Tri-State (IL-IN-WI)	USA	695
1936-04-05	Tupelo, MS	USA	216
1936-04-06	Gainesville, GA	USA	203
1944-06-23	Shinnston, WV	USA	c. 100
1947-04-09	Higgins, TX & Woodward, OK	USA	181
1951-05-12	Faridpur District	Bangladesh	c. 200
1953-05-11	Waco, TX	USA	114
1953-06-08	Flint, MI	USA	116
1961-03-19	Faridpur and Dhaka	Bangladesh	210
1963-04-19	North of Cooch Behar and surrounding areas	India, Bangladesh	c. 300
1964-04-11	Magura and Narail	Bangladesh	c. 500
1969-4-14	Dhaka	Bangladesh	660
1969-4-14	Comilla	Bangladesh	263
1972-04-01	14 miles SW of Mymensingh	Bangladesh	c. 200
1972-04-29	Bhakua and Haripur unions	Bangladesh	c. 300
1973-04-12	Baliakandi	Bangladesh	c. 200

1973-04-17	Manikganj, Singair, Nawabganj	Bangladesh	681
1974-04-11	11 miles west of Bogra	Bangladesh	c. 100
1977-04-01	Madaripur and Shibchar	Bangladesh	c. 500
1977-04-02	MokshedpurBhanga,Tungipara	Bangladesh	111
1978-04-16	Jaipur and Keonjhar	India	173
1978-04-18	Karimpur	India	128
1981-04-12	Parshuram, Fulgazi, Somarpur	Bangladesh	c. 200
1981-04-17	Kapundi, Erandi, Dhanbeni	Bangladesh	c. 120
1984-06-09	Belyanitsky, Ivanovo, Balino	Russia	c. 400
1986-04-14	Borni	Bangladesh	c. 120
1989-04-26	Daultipur and Salturia	Bangladesh	c.1300
1993-04-09	Kandi	India	145
1998-03-24	Orissa and West Bengal	India	c. 250
2011-05-22	Joplin, MO	USA	162
2015-06-01	Yangtze River	China	442

Appendix "J"

Worst Terrorist Attacks Worldwide (since 1940)

1940 Nov 25: Haifa, Palestine. Ship carrying Jewish immigrants bombed and sunk; 267 deaths.
1968: **Rome-Algeria**. El Al airliner from Rome hijacked to Algeria by the Popular Front for the Liberation of Palestine.
1972: Munich Olympics, West Germany. Nine Israeli athletes kidnapped and murdered by members of Black September; 15 deaths.
1973 May 18: Chita, Siberia. Mid-air explosion of Aeroflot airliner over Siberia; 100 deaths.
1977 Dec 4: Malaysia. Hijacked Malaysian airliner crashed in Straits of Johore; 100 deaths.
1978 Aug 20: Abadan, Iran. Burning of theater; 477 deaths.
1979 Nov 20-Dec 5: Mecca, Saudi Arabia. Hostage taking at Grand Mosque; 240 deaths.
1983 Sep 23: United Arab Emirates. Mid-air explosion of Gulf Air flight; 112 deaths.
1983 Oct 23: Beirut, Lebanon. Truck bombings of U.S. Marines and French troops barracks; 301 deaths.
1985 May 14: Anuradhapura, Sri Lanka. Armed attack on crowds; 150 deaths.
1985 Jun 23: Ireland and Japan. Explosion of Air India flight near Cork, Ireland; second explosion in an Air India flight in Narita Airport, Japan 331 deaths.
1985 Nov 6: Bogota, Colombia. Fifty M-19 terrorists seized Palace of Justice; 100 deaths.
1987 Apr 18: Alut Oya, Sri Lanka. Tamil Tigers ambushed Sinhalese in five vehicles; 127 deaths.
1987 Apr 21: Colombo, Sri Lanka. Tamil Tigers bombed bus depot; 106 deaths.
1987 Nov 29: Burma. Mid-air explosion of Korean Air flight; 115 deaths.
1988 Dec 21: Lockerbie, Scotland. Mid-air explosion of Pan Am flight; 270 deaths.
1989 Sep 19: Bilma, Niger. Mid-air explosion of French UTA flight; 171 deaths.
1989 Nov 27: Bogota, Colombia. Mid-air explosion of Avianca flight; 110 deaths.
1990 Aug 3: Kathankudy, Sri Lanka. Armed attack on two mosques; 140 deaths.
1990 Aug 13: Eravur, Sri Lanka. Armed attack on mosque; 122 deaths.
1990 Oct 2: Guangzhou, China. Crash of hijacked PRC airliner; 132 deaths.

1993 Mar 12: Mumbai, India. Fifteen bombings throughout city; 317 deaths.
1993 Sep 22: Sukhumi, Georgia. Crash of airliner hit by missile; 106 deaths.
1995 Apr 19: Oklahoma City, USA. Truck bombing of Murrah Federal Building; 169 deaths.
1995 June 14-19: Budennovsk, Stavropol, Russia. Hostage-taking in hospital; 143 deaths.
1996 Nov 23: Moroni, Comoros. Crash of hijacked Ethiopian Air flight; 127 deaths.
1997 Aug 29: Algeria. Attacks on Sidi Moussa and Hais Rais; 238 deaths.
1997 Sep 22: Ben Talha, Algeria. Armed attack; 277 deaths.
1997 Dec 30: Ami Moussa, Algeria. Armed attack; 272 deaths.
1998 Jan 4: Algeria. Attacks on Had Chekala, Remka, and Ain Tarik; 182 deaths.
1998 Jan 11: Sidi Hamed, Algeria. Attack on movie theater and mosque; 103 deaths.
1998 Aug 7: Nairobi, Kenya, and Dar es Salaam, Tanzania. Truck bomb exploded outside US embassy in Kenya; second truck bomb outside US embassy in Tanzania; 303 deaths.
1998 Nov 3: Mitu, Colombia. FARC rebels attacked police barracks with rockets; 138 deaths.
1999 Sep 13: Moscow, Russia. Apartment building bombed; 130 deaths.
1999 Oct 31: Massachusetts, USA. Egypt Air flight intentionally crashed by co-pilot; 217 deaths.
2001 Aug 10: Luanda, Angola. Attack on a train; 152 deaths.
2001 Sep 11: New York City and Arlington, Virginia, USA. Two hijacked jetliners crashed into World Trade Center's twin towers; third jetliner plowed into the Pentagon; 2,993 deaths.
2002 May 2: Bojaya, Choco, Colombia. Armed attack on village and bombing of church; 119 deaths.
2002 Aug 19: Khankala, Chechnya, Russia. Helicopter carrying troops downed by missile; 127 deaths.
2002 Oct 12: Bali, Indonesia. Car bomb exploded outside nightclub; 202 deaths.
2002 Oct 23-26: Moscow, Russia. Hostage-taking and attempted rescue in theater; 170 deaths.
2003 Aug 29: Najaf, Iraq. Car bombing outside mosque; 125 deaths.
2004 Feb 1: Irbil, Iraq. Two suicide bombings of political party offices; 109 deaths.
2004 Feb 21: Uganda. Armed attack and arson in refugee camp; 239 deaths.
2004 Feb 27: Manila, Philippines. Bombing and fire on ship; 118 deaths.

2004 Mar 2: Karbala and Kadhimiya, Iraq. Suicide bombings of shrines; 188 deaths.
2004 Mar 11: Madrid, Spain. Bombing of four trains; 191deaths.
2004 Jun 24: Mosul, Baghdad, Ramadi, Baquba, Iraq. Bombings and armed attacks; 103 deaths.
2004 Sep 1-3: North Ossetia, Russia. Hostage-taking in school; 372 deaths.
2005 Feb 28: Hilla, Babil, Iraq. Car-bombing outside medical clinic; 135 deaths.
2005 Jul 16: Musayyib, Babil, Iraq. Suicide bombing in marketplace; 100 deaths.
2005 Sep 14: Baghdad, Iraq. Suicide bombings and shootings; 182 deaths.
2006 Jan 5: Karbala, Ramadi, and Baghdad, Iraq. Bombings; 124 deaths.
2006 Jul 11: Mumbai, India. Seven bombings of commuter trains; 209 deaths.
2006 Oct 16: Habarana, Sri Lanka. Suicide bombing of military convoy; 103 deaths.
2006 Nov 23: Sadr City, Baghdad, Iraq. Five car bombings and two mortar attacks; 202 deaths.
2007 Jan 22: Baghdad and Baquba, Iraq. Bombings; 101 deaths.
2007 Feb 3: Baghdad, Iraq. Truck bombing in marketplace; 137 deaths.
2007 Mar 6: Hilla, Babil, Iraq. Two suicide bombings; 137 deaths.
2007 Mar 27: Tal Afar, Ninewa, Iraq. Two truck bombings; 153 deaths.
2007 Mar 29: Baghdad, Khalis, and Mahmudiya, Iraq. Multiple bombings; 137 deaths.
2007 Apr 18: Baghdad, Iraq. Multiple bombings; 193 deaths.
2007 Jul 3-10: Islamabad, Pakistan. Hostage-taking and army troopers storming mosque; 102 deaths.
2007 Jul 7: Armili, Iraq. Multiple suicide truck bombings; 182 deaths.
2007 Aug 14: Al-Adnaniyah and Al-Qataniyah, Iraq. Multiple car bombings; 520 deaths.
2007 Oct 18: Karachi, Pakistan. Bombing of motorcade for former Prime Minister Benazir Bhutto; 141 deaths.
2008 Feb 17: Kandahar, Afghanistan. Suicide bombing at dog-fighting festival; 105 deaths.
2008 Oct 10: Orakzai, Pakistan. Truck bombing of anti-Taliban tribal meeting; 110 deaths.
2008 Nov 26-29: Mumbai, India. Shootings, grenade attacks, and hostage-taking; 174 deaths.
2008 Dec 24: Doroma, DR Congo. Armed attack on village; 189 deaths.
2009 Jul 26-30: Maiduguri, Borno, Nigeria. Armed attack on city by Boko Haram; 780 deaths.

2009 Aug 19: Baghdad, Iraq. Multiple bombings at government sites; 104 deaths.
2009 Oct 25: Baghdad, Iraq. Two vehicle bombings of government buildings; 155 deaths.
2009 Oct 28: Peshawar, Pakistan. Car bombing in marketplace; 119 deaths.
2009 Dec 8: Baghdad, Iraq. Five car bombings; 127 deaths.
2010 May 10: Hilla, Basra, al-Suwayra, Baghdad, Tarmiyah, Fallujah, Mosul, and Iskandariyah, Iraq. Multiple bombings and armed attacks; 111 deaths.
2010 May 28: Khemasuli, West Bengal, India. Sabotage derailed Jnaneswari express train, collided with another train; 148 deaths.
2010 Jul 10: Kakaghund, Pakistan. Two suicide bombings; 106 deaths.
2011 Nov 4: Damaturu, Yobe, Nigeria. Bombings and shootings in churches, police and government buildings, banks; 100 deaths.
2012 Jan 20: Kano, Nigeria. Multiple bombings and gun attacks; 178 deaths.
2012 Jul 23: Taji, Mosul, Baghdad, Dhuluiya, Baquba, and Diyala, Iraq. Multiple bombings; 116 deaths.
2012 Aug 16: Baghdad, Tal Afar, Kirkuk, Daquq, Garma, Kut, Husainiya, Tuz Khurmato, Mushahda, Falluja, Al-A'amiriya, and Baaj, Iraq. Bombings and armed attacks; 106 deaths.
2012 Sep 9: Baghdad, Amara, Kirkuk, Taji, Maysan, Tuz Khormato, Nasiriyah, Basra, Tal Afar, Hawija, and Ar Riyad, Iraq. Bombings and armed attack on Dujail army base; 106 deaths.
2013 Jan 10: Quetta and Mingora, Pakistan. Bombings at security checkpoint, billiard hall, nearby street, market, and mosque; 120 deaths.
2013 Apr 22: Baga, Nigeria. Boko Haram attack on village; 187 deaths.
2013 May 20: Baghdad, Hilla, Basra, Balad, Jisr Diyala, Samarra, Mosul, Baiji, Rutba, Baquba, Tuz Khormato, Haditha, Iraq. Bombings and armed attacks; 113 deaths.
2013 Sep 17: Benisheik, Nigeria. Ambush of civilian traffic on highway; 143 deaths.
2013 Sep 21: Baghdad, Beiji, and Mosul, Iraq. Bombings and shooting attacks; 100 deaths.
2014 Mar 16: Kaduna, Nigeria. Armed attacks on villages; 219 deaths.
2014 May 7: Gamboru Ngala, Nigeria. Armed attack on market, buildings burned; 310 deaths.
2014 May 20: Jos, Nigeria. Car bombings at market and bus station; 118 deaths.
2014 Nov 28: Kano, Nigeria. Bombing of mosque; 121 deaths.
2014 Dec 16: Peshawar, Pakistan. Shooting and bombing attack on school; 148 deaths.
2015 Jan 3-4: Baga and Doro Gowon, Nigeria. Boko Haram attacked and burned villages; 700 deaths.

2015 Jan 7: Paris, France. Two gunmen shot employees of satirical weekly newspaper *Charlie Hebdo* during lunchtime; 13 deaths.
2015 Mar 20: Sanaa, Yemen. Bombing of two mosques; 142 deaths.
2015 Apr 2: Garissa, Kenya. Attack on college campus by gunmen; 152 deaths.
2015 Jul 1: Kukawa, Nigeria. Attack of 50 gunmen on village; 118 deaths.
2015 Jul 17: Khan Bani Saad, Diyala, Iraq. Truck bombing in marketplace; 115 deaths.
2015 Sep 20: Maiduguri and Monguno, Borno, Nigeria. Bombing of a mosque, two markets, and football game; 108 deaths.
2015 Oct 10: Ankara, Turkey. Two suicide bombings at political rally; 102 deaths.
2015 Oct 31: Sinai, Egypt. Mid-air explosion of Russian Airbus airliner; 224 deaths.
2015 Nov 13: Paris, France. Suicide bombing at Stade de France stadium; bombings and shootings at bars, restaurants, and Bataclan concert hall; 130 deaths.
2016 Mar 22: Brussels, Belgium. Two suicide bombings at Brussels Airport and another at a Metro station; 32 deaths.
2016 May 23: Jableh and Tartus, Syria. Multiple bombings; 184 deaths.
2016 May 27: Baghdad, Iraq. Multiple bombings; 101 deaths.
2016 Jul 3: Baghdad, Iraq. Truck bombing of market and burning of shopping mall; 324 deaths.
2016 July 14: Nice, France. Terrorist in a truck mowed down revellers watching firework display on Bastille Day; 86 deaths.
2016 Nov: Hillah, Iraq. Suicide car bombing at a gas station; 125 deaths.
2016 Dec 19: Berlin, Germany. Truck driven by terrorist plowed into the crowd in a Christmas market; 12 deaths.
2017 March 8: Kabul, Afghanistan. Islamic State gunmen, some in hospital gowns, attacked Sardar Daud Khan Military Hospital; 100+ deaths.
2017 March 11,15: Damascus, Syria. Bombings by Tahrir al-Sham terrorists; at least 114 killed.
2017 April 7: Stockholm, Sweden. ISIS recruit drove truck into crowd shopping on busy Drottninggatanthen, then crashed into Åhlens Mall; 4 deaths.
2017 April 15: Aleppo, Syria. Car bombing by suspected Tahrir al-Sham militants; at least 126 deaths.
2017 April 21: Afghanistan. Suicide car bombing at northern Camp Shaheen military base by Taliban insurgents; 256 deaths.
2017 May 20: Libya. Shooting raid on Brak El-Shati airbase by suspected Misrata militants; 141 deaths.

2017 May 22: Manchester, England. Terrorist bombing of Manchester Arena during Ariana Grande concert; 22 deaths.

2017 May 23-October 23: Battle of Marawi, southern Philippines. Jihadists belonging to the ISIS-affiliated Maute and Abu Sayyaf Groups occupied several government buildings in the Islamic city of Marawi, sparking a five-month-long siege; 1,229 deaths.

2017 May 31: Kabul, Afghanistan. Car bombing by suspected Islamic Jihad Union members in diplomatic quarter; 150 deaths.

2017 June 3: London, United Kingdom. Three men mowed down pedestrians on London Bridge, then went on a stabbing spree at nearby pubs and restaurants; 8 deaths.

2017 August 17: Barcelona, Spain. A terrorist plowed a van into crowds in Las Ramblas; 13 killed.

2017 October 14: Mogadishu, Somalia. Suicide bombing by suspected Al-Shabaab terrorist; at least 320 deaths.

2017 October 31: New York, USA. ISIS-inspired Uzbek immigrant in a truck mowed down people in bike path in Manhattan; 8 deaths.

2017 November 4: Deir ez-Zor, Syria. Suicide car bombing by suspected Islamic State terrorist; at least 75 killed.

2017 November 24: North Sinai, Egypt. Mosque bombed in Bir al-Abed; worshippers trying to escape shot; over 300 deaths.

2018 January 24: Kabul, Afghanistan. Taliban suicide car bomber detonated explosives-filled ambulance near Sidarat Square, where several government offices are located; 103 deaths.

2018 February 16: Konduga, Nigeria. Three Boko Haram bombers struck local government area of Borno State; 21 killed.

2018 February 19: Farah, Afghanistan. Coordinated attacks by Taliban in Farah province; 24 policemen died.

2018 February 21: Al Anbar, Iraq. Islamic State militants staged an ambush on the Syrian side of the border with Iraq's western province Al Anbar; 20 truck drivers killed.

2018 February 23: Mogadishu, Somalia. Two car bombings and shootings by Al-Shabaab militants; 50 died, including 5 attackers.

2018 February 24: Aden, Yemen. Two suspected Islamic State suicide car bombers struck a military base and checkpoint near the Southern Transitional Council; 18 deaths.

Appendix "K"

Origin of the Names "Joshua" and "Jesus"

Notes	N. kingdom	S. kingdom	Europe	Notes
Heb. original: "God *(Yahu)* saves *(shua)*"		Yahushua		
'a' to 'e'; 'u' to 'o' – linguistic custom in Heb.		Yehoshua ——————	Iehosua	Transliteration in Latin, which had no "Y" or "sh"
			Jehoshua	17th c. spelling in English, "I" to "J"
Vowel *e* lost in 1st syllable		Y'hoshua		
		Yeh'shua		Vowel *o* lost in second syllable
'h' dropped	Ya'ushua			
a'u became diphthong *aw*	Yawshua			
aw became *o*, end 8th c. BC		Yoshua		
		Ye'shua		2nd syllable lost in 6th c. BC Babylon
		Yeshua		Popular form in Judea 1st c. AD
No 'a' ending in Rabbinical manuscripts		Yeshu ——————	Iesou	Transliteration in Greek, which had no "Y" or "sh".
			Iesous	"s" ending, Gk. sing. nominative, masculine case
"Y" to "I" in Latin, no "sh"		Iosua	Iesus	Transliteration in Latin, no "o"
Letter "I" became "J" -- 17th c. AD		Joshua	Jesus	Modern spelling: "I" became "J" -- 17th century AD

Appendix "L"

The Philippines in End-Time Prophecies?

Several times in Scriptures, God said He would take into His fold a nation other than His originally chosen people of Israel.

Another chosen people

Around 760 B.C., God said through the prophet Hosea: *"And I will sow her unto me in the earth; and I will have mercy upon her that had not obtained mercy; and I will say to them which were not my people, Thou art my people; and they shall say, Thou art my God."* (Hos 2:23). God put similar words on Isaiah's lips: *"I am sought of them that asked not for me; I am found of them that sought me not: I said, Behold me, behold me, unto a nation that was not called by my name."* (Isa 65:1). Seven centuries later, Christ told the Jews by way of a parable: *"Therefore say I unto you, The kingdom of God shall be taken from you, and given to a nation bringing forth the fruits thereof"* (Matt 21:43).

Who might this other nation be?

The Christian Church.

In 1 Peter 2:9-10, the apostle told the first Christians, *"But ye are a chosen generation, a royal priesthood, an holy nation, a peculiar people; that ye should shew forth the praises of him who hath called you out of darkness into his marvellous light: Which in time past were not a people, but are now the people of God: which had not obtained mercy, but now have obtained mercy."*

The people referred to were the members of the early Church, both Jews and Gentiles who accepted the Gospel of Christ. (All 12 tribes of Israel will nonetheless be saved in the end – Rom 11:25.)

A specific nation?

However, in both the OT Hebrew and NT Greek texts of the passages above, the use of the word "nation" (Hebrew *goy* – Gentile nation; Greek *ethnos* – foreign race) vis-a-vis the term "people" (Hebrew *am* – group of people; Greek *laos* – people in general) seems to suggest that the prophecies may also be pointing to a specific foreign ethnic nation.

Islands in prophecy?

Islands seem to have a special place in God's master plan. *"Keep silence before me, O islands; and let the people renew their strength: let them come near; then let them speak: let us come near together to judgment*" (Isa 41:1). *"Let them give glory unto the LORD, and declare his praise in the islands"* (Isa 42:12). The Philippines is an archipelago with some 7,500 islands.

95% Christian. Around 95% of over 113 million Filipinos are Christians. The only people in East Asia that is more than 50% Christian, they used to be called the only Christian nation in Asia.

More than 80% of the people are Roman Catholics, with many Protestants, members of the Philippine Church of Christ (Iglesia ni Cristo), Philippine Independent Church (Aglipayan), and various evangelical churches.

"New spiritual center of the world"

Several visionaries, not all of them Christians, saw the Philippines in an end-time context.

Guru. In July 1984, Maharishi Mahesh Yogi, Hindu founder of the Age of Enlightenment Movement promoting the Transcendental Meditation (TM) technique worldwide, said a number of times in a video message – "The Philippines is the new spiritual center of the world."[1]

Evangelist. On May 10-11, 2000, in his Mission to All the World: Asia-Pacific Prayer Conference held at Araneta Coliseum in Quezon City, Philippines, evangelist Dr. Morris Cerullo repeatedly declared – "The Philippines is the new spiritual center of the world."

His flyers and promotional materials bannered: "Philippines: Doorway to a Billion Souls! Destined to be a sign and a wonder to the nations, even unto the West, the Philippines is being raised up by God to be the Gospel Center for Asia and the world."[2]

"Prophetess". On October 27, 2001, seemingly Spirit-filled Cindy Jacobs, founder of the prayer network Generals of Intercession and called "prophet to the nations," prophesied at the "Catch the Fire" conference of Harvest International Ministries in California: "And the Lord says, Do not think I do not see you, Philippines, for I see you. You are the apple of my eye. You are a treasure unto me…"[3]

Note that the LORD had already said before that Israel was "the apple of his eye". *"For the LORD's portion is his people; Jacob is the lot of his inheritance. He found him in a desert land, and in the waste howling wilderness; he led him about, he instructed him, he kept him as the apple of his eye"* (Deut 32:9-10; cf. Zech 2:7-8).

Center of warfare? While some evangelists may think that "spiritual center" means gospel center, or a missionary-sending hub, the phrase can also mean "center of spiritual warfare" – where some of the most intense battles for the souls of men may be waged in these end-times! Let us read on and decide for ourselves.

Prophetic names

Many personages in Scriptures have prophetic names that are descriptive of their roles in God's scheme of things. Here are some of the most telling examples –

Methuselah (Noah's grandfather): His name is a combination of *muwth* ("death") and *shalach* ("send"), meaning "he dies (it is) sent." The Flood came a week after his death. **Noah** ("rest"): The Flood brought rest to the world from the wickedness of antediluvian men. **Ham** (Noah's second son): "hot". He settled in sunny places (Africa) and became the ancestor of dark-skinned peoples. **Abraham** ("father of a multitude") became the patriarch of the world's three great monotheistic religions: Judaism, Christianity, and Islam. **Yahushua** (Jesus) means "Yahu (God) saves (*shua*)". The Son of God came in the flesh to save His people from their sins.

In the same way, some modern-day, non-Biblical names appear to be prophetic as well.

The Philippines

Europeans first came to the islands in 1521 by way of a Spanish expedition led by explorer and navigator Ferdinand Magellan.

On a subsequent voyage in 1542 by Ruy Lopez de Villalobos from New Spain (today Mexico), Spanish sailor Bernardo de la Torre named the islands *Las Islas Felipinas* (Islands belonging to Felipe) in honor of Carlos I's son and heir Felipe, who later reigned as Philip II of Spain (1556-1598). *Felipinas* was corrupted in the vernacular and became *Filipinas,* irrevocably remaining as the name of archipelago.[4]

"Fond of horses." Etymologically, the name "Felipe" (Philip) is a combination of two Greek words: *phileo* ("to be a friend to or have affection for") and *hippos* ("horse"). In short, Felipe or Philip means "fond or lover of horses."

Man-horse monster. In local folklore, the Philippines is home to a supernatural part-man, part-horse monster inhabiting sparsely populated areas and forested places – the *tikbalang*. Unique in the world, the creature is pictured in popular literature as having the head and elongated kegs of a horse, the body and arms of a man, and the ability to leap over rooftops in a single bound; hence the root-word of its name –*balang* ("locust").

Bottomless pit beings. The *tikbalang* possesses the same three characteristics (though not in the same places) of beings from the bottomless pit – locust, horse, and man – all in one hideous chimeric creature! *"And there came out of the smoke locusts upon the earth: and unto them was given power, as the scorpions of the earth have power"*

(Rev 9:3-ff.). Like smoke, then locusts from afar, they really are more like flying horses ("*And the shapes of the locusts were like unto horses*"), with human heads ("*their faces were as the faces of men. And they had hair as the hair of women...*").

Divinity? Muslims in southern Philippines venerate a similar creature called "borak" – known in the Middle East as "Buraq." We read in *Encyclopaedia Britannica*: "Described as 'half-mule, half-donkey, with wings on its sides... in some traditions he became a steed with the head of a woman...'" In Islamic tradition, Buraq is said to have transported the Prophet Muhammad to heaven. The creature was first introduced in the story of Muhammad's night journey from Mecca to Jerusalem and back, thus explaining how the journey between the two cities was completed in a single night.[5]

In Revelation 9:1-2, we see how the swarm of Buraq look-alike creatures broke free – "*And the fifth angel sounded, and I saw a star fall from heaven unto the earth: and to him was given the key of the bottomless pit. And he opened the bottomless pit; and there arose a smoke out of the pit, as the smoke of a great furnace; and the sun and the air were darkened.*"

Prophetic preview? Mount Pinatubo, a central Philippine volcano that had been dormant for 600 years, suddenly erupted in June-July 1991. The eruptions spewed over 18 million metric tons of sulphur dioxide into the atmosphere, darkening the sun and raining thick ash on surrounding areas, including Metro Manila, 90 kilometers away. The ash and smoke thrown up were twice as much as those disgorged by El Chichón of Mexico in 1982, making Pinatubo the largest volcanic eruption of the 20th century. Much of the volcanic material spread around the globe in the upper atmosphere, later reported to have lowered the world temperature by at least one degree.

Rape-murder explosion. Curiously, swarms of locusts were reported in areas around Mt. Pinatubo in the months following the eruptions. In their wake came an explosion of rape-murder cases in the country, almost daily making the front pages of tabloids for many months, extending into years. One city in Metro Manila had the highest number of cases: "In the early 1990s, Marikina earned notoriety as the rape-and-murder capital of the country..."[6] When the crime persisted for years, in 1998 the Philippine Congress passed a law creating rape crisis centers nationwide.[7]

Were demons behind the rape-murder epidemic?

Hints of heaven?

Some words derived from the name "Philippines" seem to hint that many in the country will be heaven-ward bound.

Winged sons?

A Spanish adjective for *Filipinas* is *Filipina* (Philippine, f.). If we divide the word in two, we get a pair of Latin-sounding words: *"Fili"* and *"pina."* In Latin, *filii* means "sons," while *pinna or penna* means "feather or wing," Does this suggest "winged sons" – in other words, angels? Angels are the winged sons of God.

Keep in mind that those who will be saved spiritually and will enter into the kingdom of heaven will be like the angels. *"Neither can they die any more: for they are equal unto the angels; and are the children of God, being the children of the resurrection"* (Luke 20:36; cf. Matt 22:30; Mark 12:25).

Chosen and refined?

Early in the 20th century, though under American administration, nationalistic fervor grew rapidly in the Philippines. It included the development of a national language with many foreign words spelled in the vernacular. For instance, *Filipinas* became *Pilipinas*; *Filipino* was widely spelled as *Pilipino* (m.).

"Pilipino" may also be split to produce two different Tagalog words – *pili*, which means "chosen," and *pino*, which translates as "refined." Both terms have Biblical implications.

God will exalt His chosen people. *"For thou art an holy people unto the LORD thy God: the LORD thy God hath chosen thee to be a special people unto himself, above all people that are upon the face of the earth"* (Deut 7:6, etc.). As we have seen, God, perhaps in addition to Israel, will choose another nation.

To purify His chosen ones for spiritual salvation, God refines them through trials. *"Behold, I have refined thee, but not with silver; I have chosen thee in the furnace of affliction"* (Isa 48:10, etc.).

Archipelago de San Lazaro

Las Islas Felipinas was not the first and original name given by the Spaniards to the islands. Ferdinand Magellan, who came ahead of the others, reached the island of Homonhon (now part of Samar province) in the east-central part of the archipelago on the feast-day of Saint Lazarus of Bethany (March 16, 1521); and so he named the islands *"Archipelago de San Lazaro"*.

There appears to be a deeply hidden prophecy in that original name of the country. Let us scrutinize the four words for an in-depth examination.

Archipelago. This is a compound term from two words: Latin *archi* and Greek *pelagos*. According to the *Merriam-Webster's Dictionary and Thesaurus*, *archi* signifies "chief, principal," while *pelagos* simply means "sea". Hence, "archipelago" means "chief sea" or, perhaps better, "chiefly sea."[8]

"Sea," though, has a prophetic interpretation in the Bible. *"The waters which thou sawest, where the whore sitteth, are peoples, and multitudes, and nations, and tongues"* (Rev 17:15).

As we have touched on a few times earlier in this book, "waters" or "many waters" signifies "sea," which prophetically means a place with many peoples and languages. The Philippines is the world's 12th most populous country – with over 113 million inhabitants speaking more than 70 languages and dialects.

Racially, Filipinos descended from Malays and Indonesians, with a heavy infusion of migrant Chinese blood, as well as a sprinkling of Caucasian genes (Spanish, American, *et al.*), the country being a melting pot of cultures from the East and West.

De. "De" is a Spanish preposition denoting "of" or "from", as in, for example, "de España" ("of or from Spain").

San. "San" is abbreviation for *santo*, meaning "saint" or "holy" (used before masculine names, except those beginning with D or T).

Lazaro. The Spanish "Lazaro" came from the Latin "Lazarus," which is a corruption of the Hebrew "Eleazar," a variant of the original "Eliezer". Eliezer was the head servant in Abraham's household. *"But Abram said, "O Sovereign LORD, what can you give me since I remain childless and the one who will inherit my estate is Eliezer of Damascus?' And Abram said, 'You have given me no children; so a servant in my household will be my heir'"* (Gen 15:2-3, NIV).

Let us find out the meaning of "Eliezer," which consists of three parts: "El"-"i"-"ezer".

God's helper. "*El*" (OT:410), according to the *New Exhaustive Strong's Numbers and Concordance with Expanded Greek-Hebrew Dictionary*, as a noun, means "strength; as adjective, mighty; especially the Almighty (but used also of any deity)".[9] Hence, *El* is Hebrew for "God". ("*Elohim*", the plural form, is often used as a singular term of magnitude or respect.)

The second part, "*i*", means "of" or "belonging to"; as in "Israeli" ("of or belonging to Israel").

The third part, "*ezer*" (OT 5828), means "aid" or "help." Thus, Eliezer can mean "God of help"[10]; or "God is help"[11]; or "my God a help"[12]; or "God is helper"[13]. "Ezra," a variant of Ezer, according to *Fausset's Bible Dictionary,* means "the helper."[14] Thus, in the context of a prophecy of types, wherein Abram, the master, is a type for God, the name of the servant, Eliezer, can mean "God's helper", that is, an angel (or, in general, angels).

To summarize, the hidden prophecy in the name *Archipelago de San Lazaro* may be rendered as "chief (*archi*) people (*pelagos*) of (*de*) the holy (*San*) angels of God (*Lazaro*)". Will Filipinos, as well as other residents of the Philippine islands, live up to this supposed prophecy in the country's original name?

Luzon Island

The biggest and most populous island of the Philippines' some 7,500 islands is Luzon, where the national capital region, Metro Manila, is located. *Liu-sung* was the name used by the Chinese for the island – its shape resembling *lusong*, Tagalog word for a big wooden mortar used to separate the rice grains from the hull. When the Spanish colonizers made maps of the archipelago in the early 17th century, they called the island *Luçonia*, which was later respelled *Luzonia*, then simplified to Luzon.

Luz, in Spanish, means "light". In the Bible, "light" can mean "spiritual enlightenment" figuratively, as in Psalm 36:9b – "*...in thy light shall we see light*"; or John 1:4 – "*In him was life; and the life was the light of men.*" The suffix "*-on*" denotes bigness, *e.g.*, a big box (*caja*) is *cajon* (chest), a big spoon (*cuchara*) is *cucharon* (ladle), etc. Hence, "Luzon" can mean "big or great light", that is, "great spiritual enlightenment".

Epifanio de los Santos Avenue

The principal thoroughfare in the country's national capital region, passing through or along eight cities around the capial city of Manila, is the semi-circular, 23.8-km long EDSA (acronym for "Epifanio de los Santos Avenue"). It was named in 1959 after a little-known, but multi-talented scholar, scientist, artist, and patriot "regarded by some of his peers as the greatest Filipino genius after national hero Jose Rizal."[15]

Unnoticed by many, the name Epifanio de los Santos translates in English as "Epiphany of the Saints." As we know, "epiphany" means sudden appearance or manifestation, specially of a divine being. EDSA thus sounds like the prophesied transformation of the elect from mortals to immortals in the first resurrection of the dead and "rapture" of the living elect saints at the Second Coming of Christ (1 Cor 15:51-54)!

That the main transportation artery of the nation's capital is named EDSA is serendipitous – because Christ will also transport the elect to heaven on His return! Is this merely a coincidence or an end-time sign from God?

As if that were not enough, some streets intersecting EDSA seem to have prophetic names as well

Aurora Boulevard. On the eastern curve of EDSA, the Aurora Boulevard junction is the busiest point, besides the northern and southern ends of the highway. "*Aurora*" in Spanish means dawn or daybreak. Did we not see in Chapter 9 of this book that Christ will set foot on earth at daybreak? The boulevard was named after Aurora Quezon, wife of Manuel Quezon, president of the Philippine Commonwealth who opened the Philippines to Jewish refugees during the Holocaust. Just as Aurora was the wife of the president of the country, so will the Church be the Bride of Christ, the King of kings and Lord of lords!

Monte de Piedad Street. Just before Aurora Boulevard from the north is Monte de Piedad, a name meaning "pawnshop' in Spanish. Man "pawned" himself to Satan through Adam's sin of disobedience; but Christ, our Redeemer, gave His life as "*a ransom for many*" (Mark 10:45), so that we can have "*redemption through His blood*" (Eph 1:7; cf. 1 Peter 1:18-19). Moreover, behind the acquired meaning, *Monte* by itself means "mountain," while *piedad* means "piety" or "religious devotion"; hence, "mountain of piety," which means the same as "holy mountain." Jerusalem is God's holy mountain – "*thy city Jerusalem, thy holy mountain*" (Dan 9:16a; Isa 66:20; Joel 3:16-17; Zech 8:3). As the Bible tells us, Christ will return to Jerusalem on His Second Coming.

New York Street. The street before Monte de Piedad is named New York. The largest city in the United States, New York is often mistakenly deemed synonymous with Manhattan, its oldest and most important borough, which is also one of the world's leading commercial, financial, cultural, manufacturing, medical, and tourist centers. Manhattan Island has the city's tallest skyscrapers, some of the country's largest schools and colleges, and the world's most famous theatrical district.

In 1942, in the midst of World War II, the US government created the top secret "Manhattan Project" to create the first atomic bomb. The project scientists successfully exploded a prototype on July 16, 1945, near Alamogordo, New Mexico. On August 6, 1945, America dropped the first atomic bomb on the Japanese city of Hiroshima; followed by a second bomb three days later on the city of Nagasaki on August 9. Devastated, Japan agreed to the Allied forces' terms of surrender on August 14, 1945.

As New York Street is located before Aurora Boulevard, is it an omen that the long-feared atomic holocaust or nuclear war will take place shortly before the Second Coming of Christ?

"A nation of servants"

In March 2009, Chinese journalist Chip Tsao wrote a satirical article in *HK Online Magazine*, titled "The War At Home," about himself and his Filipina domestic helper in relation to the territorial dispute between China and the Philippines over the Spratly islands in the South China Sea. Tsao described the Philippines as a "nation of servants".

Filipinos insulted. Many Filipinos were incensed. Hundreds from around 130,000 Filipino domestic workers in Hong Kong marched through the region's financial district protesting Tsao's article.[16]

Senator Pia Cayetano said Filipinos "deserve no less than a formal public apology... HK Magazine and Tsao must apologize for insulting Filipinos." Congresswoman Risa Hontiveros-Baraquel also complained, "This disgusting, derogatory, and vile remark can only come from dim-witted and mediocre writing. The magazine should apologize straightaway."[17]

Synonym for servant. Were Filipinos rightfully upset by Tsao's article? In the early 20th century (1901-1946), when the Philippines was still a US territory, many Filipinos worked as domestic helpers in America, and "filipino" (with a lower case "f") was defined as a "servant" (e.g., gardener, cook, etc.) in at least one dictionary during that period. "In the 1990s, a dictionary in Greece defined the word 'Filipineza', the Greek word for Filipina, as 'domestic worker from the Philippines or a person who performs non-essential auxiliary tasks.'"[18] "In Tokyo, where there are some Filipinos working as babysitters, non-Japanese housewives would often refer to nannies as 'filipina'. One post at (a) foreign women in Japan blog asked, 'I need a filipina for my children.'"[19]

Principal trait. What makes Filipinos good servants? Paul gives us a good idea in Colossians 3:22 – *"Servants, obey in all things your masters according to the flesh; not with eyeservice, as menpleasers; but in singleness of heart, fearing God."*

In a word, the principal trait is obedience. Filipinos make good servants because, in general, they are by nature humble and obedient. One Bible commentator, Walter G. Clippinger, noted that Christ Himself is the one great illustration of obedience. He *'humbled himself, becoming obedient even unto death, yea, the death of the cross'* (Phil 2:8)... Obedience is the supreme test of faith in God and reverence for Him."[20]

A compliment? Was the epithet "nation of servants" an insult to Filipinos? We must remember that, as Eliezer was the servant of Abraham, likewise are the angels the servants of God (Ps 103:21). So, too, are the prophets and apostles (1 Cor 4:1-2), as well as the saints whom God will save (Rev 7:3). The foremost model of a servant is Christ Himself (Mark 10:45).

It may thus be a subtle compliment from God for Filipinos to be labelled a "nation of servants". We are in excellent company!

Endnotes

1. Are These the Last Days?
1. Eclipse, *World Book 2005 (Deluxe)*
2. Eclipse, *Encarta Encyclopedia 2004*
3. Eclipse, *Encyclopaedia Britannica 2009*
4. Prophecy of the popes, *Wikipedia*
5. *Ibid.*

2. The Beginning of Sorrows
1. False Christs, *Wikipedia*
2. Scott Ashley, "The Coming End to War," *The Good News*, July-August 2015, p. 5
3. Seismos NT 4578, *New Exhaustive Strong's Numbers and Concordance with Expanded Greek-Hebrew Dictionary*, 1994
4. Joseph Farah, "ISIS Rising – What It Portends," WND (formerly WorldNetDaily); June 23, 2014
5. Epidemic, *Encarta Encyclopedia 2004*
6. *Ibid.*
7. Anthrax, *World Book 2005 (Deluxe)*
8. "Pentagon sends anthrax to multiple labs", *The Philippine Star*, May 29, 2015; p. A-24

3. End-Time Kings and Beasts
1. Babylon, *Encarta Encyclopedia 2004*
2. Babylon, *World Book 2005 (Deluxe)*
3. Babylon, *Nelson's Illustrated Bible Dictionary,1986*
4. Dan 11:2, *Barnes' Notes*, 1997
5. Babylon, *Nelson's Illustrated Bible Dictionary,1986*
6. Iron Age, *World Book 2005 (Deluxe)*
7. Dan 7:7-8, *The Wycliffe Bible Commentary*, 1962
8. Stone, *Nelson's Illustrated Bible Dictionary*, 1986
9. Antigonid Dynasty, *World Book 2005 (Deluxe)*
10. Humphrey Prideaux, *The Old and New Testament Connected in the History of the Jews*, Vol. 1, p. 378; quoted by Uriah Smith, *Daniel and the Revelation*, Revised Edition, 1944, pp. 212-213
11. Sea, *International Standard Bible Encyclopaedia*, 1996
12. Dan 7:2, *The Wycliffe Bible Commentary*, 1962
13. Dan 7:4-6, *op. cit.*
14. Dan 7:1-8, *Matthew Henry's Commentary on the Whole Bible*, 1991
15. *Ibid.*
16. Dan 7:6, *The Wycliffe Bible Commentary*, 1962
17. Dan 7:1-8, *Matthew Henry's Commentary on the Whole Bible*, 1991
18. Prideaux, *loc. cit.*

19. Dan 7:1-8, *op. cit.*
20. Dan 7:7-8, *The Wycliffe Bible Commentary, 1962*
21. H. Grattan Guenness, *The Divine Program of the World History*, pp. 318-321; quoted in *Bible Readings for the Home*, MCMXLII, pp. 216-217; quoted by Jan Marcussen, *National Sunday Law*, 96th printing, 2007, Appendix 1, p. 73
22. Europe, *World Book 2005 (Deluxe)*
23. *The Western Watchmen*, St. Louis; quoted by Marcussen, *loc. cit.*
24. T.R. Birks, M.A., *The First Two Visions of Daniel*, London, 1845, pp. 258-259; quoted by Marcussen, *loc. cit.*
25. *Bible Readings for the Home*, 1942, p. 221; quoted by Marcussen, *loc. cit.*
26. *Concil Tolosanum*, Pope Gregory IX, Anno. Chr. 1229; ; quoted by Jan Marcussen, *op. cit.*, p. 79
27. Colleen Barry and Nicole Winfield, "Pope Francis to visit Sweden, apologizes for Catholic wrongs," The Associated Press, Monday, Jan. 25, 2016, 3:21 p.m. CST
28. Edward B. Elliott, *Hora Apocalypticae*, Vol. III, p. 130, Note 1); quoted by Smith, *op. cit.*, p. 113
29. *Ibid.*
30. Council of Toulouse, 1229; quoted by Marcussen, *loc. cit.*
31. D. Lortsch, *Histoire de la Bible en France*, 1910, p. 14; quoted by Marcussen, *loc. cit.*
32. Pope Pius IX, *Quanta Cura*, December 8, 1866; quoted by Jan Marcussen, *loc. cit.*
33. *Bible Readings for the Home*, 1942, p. 221; quoted by Marcussen, *op, cit.*, p. 82
34. *Ibid.*
35. *Decretal, de Translatic Episcop.*, quoted by Marcussen, *loc. cit.*
36. J. Mendham, *The Seventh General Council, the Second of Nicea*, Introduction, pp. iii-vi; quoted by Marcussen, *op. cit*, p. 81
37. Marcussen, *loc. cit.*
38. *Bible Readings for the Home*, *loc. cit.*
39. Edict of March 7, 321 A.D., *Corpus Juris Civilis Cod.*, lib. 3, tit. 12, Lex 3; quoted by Marcussen, *National Sunday Law*, 96th printing, 2007, p. 36
40. *The Convert's Catechism of Catholic Doctrine*, 3rd Edition, p. 50; quoted by Marcussen, *op. cit,*, p. 33
41. Stephen Keenan, *A Doctrinal Catechism*, p. 174; quoted by Marcussen, *loc. cit.*
42. Father Enright, C.S.S.R., Redemptoral College, Kansas City, Mo., *History of the Sabbath*, p. 802; quoted by Marcussen, *op. cit,*, p. 41
43. Rev 17:10. *Barnes' Notes*, Electronic Database, *1997*
44. Assyria, *Fausset's Bible Dictionary,1998*
45. Assyria, *The New Unger's Bible Dictionary, 1988*
46. Dan 7:6, *The Wycliffe Bible Commentary, 1962*
47. Egypt, *The New Unger's Bible Dictionary, 1988*

4. Two Women and Their Daughters
1. Moon, *Fausset's Bible Dictionary*, 1998
2. Hill, *The New Unger's Bible Dictionary*, 1988
3. Nick Squires, Rome, "Chief exorcist says Devil is in Vatican", 6:30AM GMT 11 Mar 2010; reprinted in *The Telegraph*, Thursday, 16 June 2016
4. "A History of Suffering," Chapter 3, *Can We Avoid the Next Holocaust?*, reprinted in *The Prophetic Word Magazine*, 9-1998, pp. 3-8
5. Eagle, *Fausset's Bible Dictionary*, 1998
6. United States (People), *Encarta Encyclopedia 2004*
7. Wallenberg, Raoul, *Encarta Encyclopedia 2004*
8. United States (People), *op. cit.*
9. Pearl Harbor attack, *Encyclopaedia Britannica 2009*
10. World War II, *Encarta Encyclopedia 2004*
11. Martin Hunter, tract, National Institute for Inventors (NIFI)
12. Judaism, *Encyclopaedia Britannica 2009*
13. J.N. Andrews and L. Conradi, *The History of the Sabbath*, 1912; quoted by Richard 'Aharon' Chaimberlin, "The New Covenant: Blueprint for a Messianic Lifestyle," *Petah Tikvah* (Door of Hope), Oct-Dec 2015, p. 15
14. Richard 'Aharon' Chaimberlin, "The Forgotten History of Messianic Judaism," *op. cit,*, p. 21
15. Chaimberlin, *op. cit.*, p. 20
16. Nazarenes, *Encarta Encyclopedia 2004*
17. Nazarene (sect), *Wikipedia*
18. J.N. Andrews and L. Conradi, *loc. cit.*
19. *Ibid.*
20. Chaimberlin, *op. cit.*, p. 22
21. Messianic Judaism, *Wikipedia*
22. Chaimberlin, *loc. cit.*
23. Messianic Judaism, *op. cit.*
24. Andrews, *loc. cit.*
25. Chaimberlin, "The New Covenant: Blueprint for a Messianic Lifestyle," *op. cit,*, p. 16
26. Chaimberlin, "The Forgotten History of Messianic Judaism," *op. cit.*, p. 20
27. Rev 17:1-12, *The Wycliffe Bible Commentary*, 1962
28. Rev 17:2, *Barnes' Notes*, 1997
29. Donation of Constantine, *Encarta Encyclopedia Deluxe 2004*
30. Donation of Constantine, *Encyclopaedia Britannica 2009*
31. Blasphemy, *The New Unger's Bible Dictionary,*.1988
32. Blasphemy, *Nelson's Illustrated Bible Dictionary*, 1986
33. Shell, *World Book 2005 (Deluxe)*
34. Peter de Rosa, *Vicars of Christ: The Dark Side of the Papacy*, 1988, pp. 99-100; quoted by Dave Hunt, *A Woman Rides the Beast*, 1994, p. 238
35. Nino Lo Bello, *The Vatican Empire*, 1968, p. 186 and jacket; quoted by Hunt, *loc. cit.*

36. Rev 17:1-6, *Matthew Henry's Commentary on the Whole Bible: New Modern Edition,* 1991
37. Rev 17:5, *Barnes' Notes, Electronic Database. 1997*
38. Phelan, *Western Watchman,* December 16, 1909
39. Chris Jackson, "Reports of Demonic Possession Increasing Since 'New Rite' of Exorcism," Fetzen Fliege newspaper blog, Monday, May 19, 2014
40. Raul Salvucci, *What to Do with These Demons?,* Ancora, p. 230; quoted in "Increase in Cases of Demonic Possession," A Zenit Daily Dispatch, Rome, 4 Aug 1999
41. *Ibid.*
42. Ralph Woodrow, *Babylon Mystery Religion,* 1981 Edition, pp. 68-69
43. Indulgences, *The Catholic Encyclopedia,* vol. 7, p. 783; quoted by Woodrow, *op. cit.,* pp. 65-66
44. Durant, *The Story of Civilization: The Age of Faith,* p. 753; quoted by Ralph Woodrow, *op. cit.,* p. 65
45. De Rosa, *loc. cit.*

5. The Beasts of the Apocalypse
1. Rev 13:1, *Barnes' Notes, Electronic Database 1997*
2. Rome, *Encarta Encyclopedia Deluxe 2004*
3. Pit, *Nelson's Illustrated Bible Dictionary,* 1986
4. Dan 7:4-6, *The Wycliffe Bible Commentary,* 1962
5. Democracy, *Encarta Encyclopedia Deluxe 2004*
6. Europe, *World Book 2005 (Deluxe)*
7. Dan 7:4-6, *The Wycliffe Bible Commentary, Electronic Database 1962*
8. Mithra, *Encyclopaedia Britannica 2009*
9. Mithra, *World Book 2005 (Deluxe)*
10. Mithra, *Encyclopaedia Britannica 2009*
11. Mithra, *Encarta Encyclopedia Deluxe 2004*
12. Mithra, *World Book 2005 (Deluxe)*
13. Mithra, *Encyclopaedia Britannica 2009*
14. *Ibid.*
15. Mithra, *Encarta Encyclopedia Deluxe 2004*
16. Roman religion, *Encyclopaedia Britannica 2009*
17. Jan Marcussen, *National Sunday Law,* 96th printing – 2007, p. 15
18. Dan 7:4-6, *loc. cit.*
19. Babylon, *World Book 2005 (Deluxe)*
20. Babylon, *Encarta Encyclopedia Deluxe 2004*
21. *Laissez faire, World Book 2005 (Deluxe)*
22. AFP, "US to cut 40,000 soldiers from Army," *The Philippine Star,* July 9, 2015, p. A-16
23. Mike Snyder, "Will Humanity Perish in a New Nuclear Age?," *The Good News,* July-August 2015, p. 10
24. United States, History of the; *World Book 2005 (Deluxe)*
25. Puritanism, *Encarta Encyclopedia Deluxe 2004*

26. NT:4352, *New Exhaustive Strong's Numbers and Concordance with Expanded Greek-Hebrew Dictionary, 1994*
27. Moon landing conspiracy theories, *Wikipedia*
28. Mary Bennett and David Percy, *Dark Moon: Apollo and the Whistle-Blowers* (video)
29. Moon landing conspiracy theories, *Wikipedia*
30. Democracy, *Encarta Encyclopedia Deluxe 2004*
31. Christianity, *Encyclopaedia Britannica 2009*
32. NT:615, *New Exhaustive Strong's Numbers and Concordance with Expanded Greek-Hebrew Dictionary, 1994*
33. Richard C. Longworth, "The New Global Economic Order," *Encarta Yearbook,* March 1999; Capitalism, Sidebar, *Encarta Encyclopedia,* 2003
34. Daryl Chen, "Profiles of Courage," *Reader's Digest*, January 2014, p. 68
35. Labor, Hours of: *Encarta Encyclopedia Deluxe 2004*
36. Federal Labor Standards Act, *op. cit.*
37. Labor, Hours of: *op. cit.*
38. Choon Leong-Seow, "The Ineffable Name of Israel's God," Glossary, *Bible Review*, December 1991, p. 49
39. Supermarket, *World Book 2005 (Deluxe)*

6. Adversaries and Antichrists

1. Uriah Smith, *Daniel and the Revelation,* Revised 1944, pp. 211-224
2. Antiochus III, *Encyclopaedia Britannica 2009*
3. Julius Caesar, *World Book 2005 (Deluxe)*
4. Isles, *Fausset's Bible Dictionary*
5. Augustus, *World Book 2005 (Deluxe)*
6. *Ibid.*
7. Augustus, *Encarta Encyclopedia Deluxe 2004*
8. Ancient Rome, *Encyclopaedia Britannica 2009*
9. Augustus, *op. cit.*
10. Idolatry, *Encarta Encyclopedia Deluxe 2004*
11. Augustus, *World Book 2005 (Deluxe)*
12. Ancient Rome, *op. cit.*
13. Idolatry, *loc. cit.*
14. Ancient Rome, *World Book 2005 (Deluxe)*
15. Roman Empire, *Encarta Encyclopedia Deluxe 2004*
16. Roman Empire, *Encyclopaedia Britannica Student and Home Edition 2009*
17. Peace, *World Book 2005 (Deluxe)*
18. Saddam Hussein, *op. cit.*
19. Iraq. *Funk & Wagnalls New Encylopedia*, MCMXCIII, Vol. 14, p. 209
20. *Nagiyd* OT:5057, *Biblesoft's New Exhaustive Strong's Numbers and Concordance with Expanded Greek-Hebrew Dictionary. 1994*
21. Saddam Hussein, *Encarta Encyclopedia Deluxe 2004*
22. *Ibid.*
23. Iraq, *op. cit.*

24. Iraq, *Encarta Encyclopedia Deluxe 2004*
25. *Ibid.*
26. Iraq, *Funk & Wagnalls New Encylopedia, loc. cit.*
27. *Ibid.*
28. Iran-Iraq War, *Encarta Encyclopedia Deluxe 2004*
29. *Ibid.*
30. Iraq, *World Book 2005 (Deluxe)*
31. Iran-Iraq War, *op. cit.*
32. *Ibid.*
33. *Ibid.*
34. Iran, *World Book 2005 (Deluxe)*
35. Iran-Iraq War, *op. cit.*
36. *Ibid.*
37. Iraq, *World Book 2005 (Deluxe)*
38. Kittim, *International Standard Bible Encyclopaedia, 1996*
39. Kittim, *The New Unger's Bible Dictionary. 1988*
40. Persian Gulf War of 1991, *World Book 2005 (Deluxe)*
41. Iraq, *op. cit.*
42. Iraq, *Funk & Wagnalls New Encylopedia, op. cit.*, p. 210
43. European Union, *Encarta Encyclopedia Deluxe 2004*
44. Clay, *International Standard Bible Encyclopaedia, 1996*
45. Brick, *Encarta Encyclopedia Deluxe 2004*
46. Arabs, *World Book 2005 (Deluxe)*
47. Saudi Arabia, *Encarta Encyclopedia Deluxe 2004*
48. Iraq, *World Book 2005 (Deluxe)*
49. Afghanistan, *op. cit.*
50. AFP, "Germany wants EU states to contribute to $3.2-B refugee fund," *The Philippine Star*, December 3, 2015, p. A-15
51. Paul Sperry, "Muslim Immigration Poses Serious National Security Threat," *Investors Business Daily*, http://news.Investors.com/ibd-editorials, quoted in *Petah Tikvah* (Door of Hope), April-June 2015, p. 39
52. Shira Sorko Ram, "A New and Different Europe," *Maoz Israel*, November 2015, pp. 2-3
53. Ram, "What Happens Next?", *op. cit.*, p. 7
54. "Islam Comes to Germany, *Maoz Israel*, November 2015, pp. 4-5
55. Ram, "A New and Different Europe," *loc. cit.*
56. "Islam Comes to Germany, *loc. cit.*
57. "Sweden Is Being Fundamentally Transformed," *Maoz Israel*, November 2015, p. 6
58. "Islam Comes to Germany, *loc. cit.*
59. Sperry, *loc. cit.*

7. The Road to Armageddon
1. Vial, *International Standard Bible Encyclopaedia*, 1996
2. Moshe ben Shaul, "The Nazarenes," *Petah Tikvah* (Door of Hope), July-Sept 2016, pp. 16-17
3. James Murdock, *Mosheim's Institutes of Ecclesiastical History*, 1861, p. 121; quoted by Dale Parkes, *The Proclaimer*, Vol. 8, No. 1, 2000
4. Temple Mount, *Wikipedia*
5. Military Affairs, *Encyclopaedia Britannica*, 2009
6. Weimorts, Albert Lee, Jr; *op. cit.*
7. Buraq, *op. cit.*
8. Abaddon, *Fausset's Bible Dictionary*, 1998

8. The Day of the LORD
1. Dan 11:45, *The Wycliffe Bible Commentary*, Electronic Database. 1962
2. Richard 'Aharon' Chaimberlin, "Gog & Magog: End-Time Battles Over Israel," *Petah Tikvah* (Door of Hope), July-Sept 2016, p. 3
3. Gog, *Fausset's Bible Dictionary*, 1998
4. Rosh, *op. cit.*
5. Rosh, *International Standard Bible Encyclopaedia*, 1996
6. Meshech, *Fausset's Bible Dictionary*,1998
7. Chaimberlin, *loc. cit.*
8. Gomer, *Nelson's Illustrated Bible Dictionary*, 1986
9. Gomer, *Fausset's Bible Dictionary*, 1998
10. Togarmah, *The New Unger's Bible Dictionary*, 1988
11. Togarmah, *Fausset's Bible Dictionary*, 1998
12. Chaimberlin, *op. cit.*, p. 4
13. Roger Walkwitz, "Good News About Israel's Future!", *Petah Tikvah* (Door of Hope), July-Sept 2014, p. 49
14. Dedan, *The New Unger's Bible Dictionary*, 1988
15. Tarshish, *Nelson's Illustrated Bible Dictionary*, 1986
16. Tarshish, *Fausset's Bible Dictionary*, 1998
17. Ex 10:21, *Barnes' Notes*, Electronic Database1997
18. Ex 10:21-23, *The Wycliffe Bible Commentary*, Electronic Database. 1962
19. Darkness, *Fausset's Bible Dictionary*,1998
20. Darkness, *The New Unger's Bible Dictionary*, 1988
21. Matt 27:33-49, *Matthew Henry's Commentary on the Whole Bible*, New Modern Edition, 1991
22. John and Mary Gribbin, The Guardian News Service, "97 Comet May Spread Chill to Planet Earth in 2000," *Manila Bulletin*, November 10, 1995
23. Ronald A. Schorn, "Comets: Mysterious Visitors from Outer Space," Sidebar, *Encarta Encyclopedia 2003*
24. *Ibid.*

25. John and Mary Gribbin, *loc. cit.*
26. *Ibid.*
27. David J. Eicher, "Here Comes Hale-Bopp," *Astronomy*, February 1996, p. 72
28. T.Y. Petrosky, "The cometary cloud in the solar system and the Résibois-Prigogine singular invariants of motion," *Journal of Statistical Physics*, September 1987, Volume 48, Issue 5, pp 1363-1372; Internet
29. James Ussher, Old Testament Chronology, *Treasury of Biblical Information*, p. 3, arranged by F.N. Peloubet, third part, *The Practical Bible Dictionary and Concordance*, Renewal 1952
30. Bob Schlenker, "The Noahic Flood Comet Sign," *The Open Scroll*, March/April 1997, p. 7
31. Ussher, *op. cit.*
32. Schlenker, *loc. cit.*
33. Schlenker, "The Orion Comet Sign," *loc. cit.*
34. Chiffre, "Earth could enter into dusty meteor shower from Comet ISON's tail," April 20, 2013; Internet
35. Karl Battams, "What happens to ISON's remains?", Wed, 12/18/2013 - 09:28, Internet
36. Schorn, *op. cit.*
37. Stephen P. Maran, "Celestial Trespassers: Asteroids, Comets, and Catastrophe," Solar System, Sidebar, *Encarta Encyclopedia 2003*
38. Gog, *The New Unger's Bible Dictionary*, 1988
39. Armageddon, *Nelson's Illustrated Bible Dictionary*, 1986
40. Armageddon, *The New Unger's Bible Dictionary*, 1988
41. Dan 11:45, *Barnes' Notes*, Electronic Database 1997
42. Chaimberlin, *op. cit.*, p. 5
43. Tophet, *Nelson's Illustrated Bible Dictionary*, 1986
44. Chaimberlin, *loc. cit.*
45. vates, *Collins Latin-English, English-Latin Dictionary*, 1957
46. overcomer 1, Fulfilled Prophecy.com, Sun Oct 28, 2007 10:50 pm, Internet
47. Number, *Nelson's Illustrated Bible Dictionary*, 1986
48. Number, *International Standard Bible Encyclopaedia*, 1996
49. Psalms 12:6, *Barnes' Notes*, Electronic Database 1997
50. Ps 119:164, *op. cit.*,
51. Schorn, *loc. cit.*
52. Maran, *loc. cit.*
53. *Ibid.*
54. Babylon, *The New Unger's Bible Dictionary*, 1988
55. Peter Lorie, The *Millennium Planner*, 1995, pp. 64
56. *Millennium Monitor*, Oct.-Dec. 1997/Expanded June 2002, p. 5
57. Barnabas 13:3-5; "The Epistle of Barnabus," *The Ante-Nicene Fathers*, 1987, Vol. 1, pp. 146-147
58. Talent, *Nelson's Illustrated Bible Dictionary*, 1986

9. The Time of the End
1. Ripley's Believe It Or Not
2. Jim Combs, "The Powerful Worldwide Impact of the Bible," *Mysteries of the Bible Now Revealed*, 1999, p. 163
3. Bible Societies, *Encarta Encyclopedia Deluxe 2004*
4. Ed. F. Vallowe, *Biblical Mathematics*, 1998, pp. 80, 83
5. Exodus 12:6-7, *The Wycliffe Bible Commentary, 1962*
6. Exodus 12:6, *Barnes' Notes, 1997*
7. Barnabas 13:3-5; "The Epistle of Barnabus," *The Ante-Nicene Fathers*, 1987, Vol. 1, pp. 146-147
8. Irenaeus, "Against Heresies," *op. cit.*, Vol. 1, p. 557
9. Lactantius, "The Divine Institutes," *op. cit.*; Vol. VII, p. 211
10. Rabbi Elias, quoted by Bishop Burnett, *The Sacred Theory of the Earth*, 1816, p. 408; cited by Grant Jeffrey, *Armageddon Appointment with Destiny*, Bantam rack edition, 1990, p. 179
11. James Ussher, Old Testament Chronology, *Treasury of Biblical Information*, p. 3, arranged by F.N. Peloubet, third part, *The Practical Bible Dictionary and Concordance*, Renewal 1952, p. 2
12. Beecher, *op. cit.*, p. 3
13. Ussher, *op. cit.*, p. 10
14. Grant Jeffrey, *loc. cit.*
15. M.M. Tauson, Ch. 6, "First Family Foibles," *The Deep Things of God*, 2012, pp. 171-175
16. Chronology, *Encarta Encyclopedia*, 1993-2003
17. *Loc. cit.*
18. Philistines, *World Book 2005 (Deluxe)*
19. J.R. Church, *Hidden Prophecies in the Psalms*, 1983, back cover
20. *Cheiro's Book of Numbers*, quoted by Church, *op. cit.*, p. 327
21. Feuer, *Tehillim*, p. 1406; cited by Church, *op. cit.*, p. 328
22. Church, *loc. cit.*, p. 327
23. USSR, *World Book 2005 (Deluxe)*

Appendix "L"
The Philippines in End-Time Prophecy?
1. Maharishi Mahesh Yogi, Age of Enlightenment video, July 1984
2. Mission to All the World 2000, Asia Pacific School of Ministry, flyer
3. Cindy Jacobs, "Prophecy for the Philippines," quoted by mystiqueowl, March 16, 2011, Internet
4. Name of the Philippines, *Wikipedia*
5. Buraq, *Encyclopaedia Britannica 2009*
6. Conrado de Quiros, "The Villain," There's the Rub @inquirerdotnet, *Philippine Daily Inquirer*, 09:17 PM January 01, 2013
7. Jess Diaz, "Rape crisis centers set up nationwide," *Philippine Star*, January

30, 1998
8. archipelago, *Merriam-Webster's Dictionary and Thesaurus*
9. El, *New Exhaustive Strong's Numbers and Concordance with Expanded Greek-Hebrew Dictionary.* 1994
10. Ezer, *The New Unger's Bible Dictionary, 1988*
11. Ezer, *International Standard Bible Encyclopaedia,* 1996
12. Ezer, *Fausset's Bible Dictionary, 1998*
13. Ezer, *Nelson's Illustrated Bible Dictionary, 1986*
14. Ezra, *Fausset's Bible Dictionary, 1998*
15. Art Villasanta, "Edsa: Greatest Filipino genius after Rizal," @inquirerdotnet, *Philippine Daily Inquirer* / 04:52 AM December 04, 2011
16. Nation of Servants, *New York Times,* April 9, 2009, 3:00 AM
17. e-souled, "Philippines: A Nation Of Servants," ABS-CBN, Chip Tsao, F. Sionil Jose, hong kong, news, OFW, Philippine Government, Philippines
18. salon, "Filipineza doesn't mean 'servant'", Internet
19. "Negative denotations of the word 'Filipina'," josecarilloforum.com, Internet
20. Obedience, *International Standard Bible Encyclopaedia,1996*

www.ingramcontent.com/pod-product-compliance
Lightning Source LLC
Chambersburg PA
CBHW061632040426
42446CB00010B/1384